On Shakespeare

to A. P. Rossiter who first hauled me aboard the
Ship of Fools, to Douglas Brown who set its course for
Utopia, and to my wife who keeps on baling

On Shakespeare

*Jesus, Shakespeare and
Karl Marx, and Other Essays*

Philip Brockbank

Basil Blackwell

Copyright © Philip Brockbank 1989

First published 1989

Basil Blackwell Ltd
108 Cowley Road, Oxford, OX4 1JF, UK

Basil Blackwell Inc.
3 Cambridge Center
Cambridge, Massachusetts 02142, USA

British Library Cataloguing in Publication Data

A CIP catalogue record for this book is
available from the British Library.

Library of Congress Cataloging in Publication Data

Brockbank, Philip.
    On Shakespeare : Jesus, Shakespeare, and Karl Marx, and other
essays / Philip Brockbank.
    Includes index.
    ISBN 0–631–15969–X
    1. Shakespeare, William, 1564–1616—Criticism and interpretation.
I. Title.
    PR2976.B67   1989   89–32417
    822.3'3—dc20   CIP

Typeset in 10 on 12 pt Imprint
by Photo·graphics, Honiton, Devon
Printed in Great Britain by Billings & Sons Ltd., Worcester

Contents

Acknowledgements

Thanks are due to the original publishers for permission to reprint seven chapters or papers. To Edward Arnold Ltd: 'The Frame of Disorder (*Henry VI*)', from *Early Shakespeare*, ed. J. R. Browne and B. A. Harris, 1961; 'The Tempest, Conventions of Art and Empire', from *Later Shakespeare*, ed. J. R. Browne and B. A. Harris, 1966. To Cambridge University Press: 'Shakespeare and the Fashion of these Times', *Shakespeare Survey*, 16, 1963; 'Hamlet the Bonesetter', *Survey*, 30, 1977; 'Blood and Wine: tragic ritual from Aeschylus to Soyinka', *Survey* 36, 1983; 'History and Histrionics in *Cymbeline*', *Survey* 11, 1958; '*Pericles* and the Dream of Immortality, *Survey* 24, 1971. For permission to include '*Richard II* and the Music of Men's Lives', I owe thanks to the editor of *Leeds Studies in English* new series vol. XIV (1983); for 'Myth and History in Shakespeare's Rome' to M. T. Jones-Davies, ed. *Mythe et Histoire*, Actes du Congrès 1983, Paris, Jean Touzot 1984; and to the British Academy for 'Upon Such Sacrifices . . .' from *The Proceedings of the British Academy*, vol. 62, 1976. A version of 'Shakespeare's Language of the Unconscious: the psychogenesis of terrorism' was first published in the *Journal of the Royal Society of Medicine* vol. 81, April 1988.

'Thought without affection,' said Blake 'makes no distinction between Love and Wisdom.' I owe a vital debt over the years to those colleagues and friends who have kept me in touch with Dante or the Golden Legend, and have taught me to mix theatre gossip with memories of Montaigne. More recently, in my less mobile but still privileged state, Susan Brock, the librarian of the Shakespeare Institute, has pursued and carried books and references through many bibliographical mazes; and Robert Smallwood has generously lent me his sharp eyes, quick ears and lively apprehension. Lionel Knights has read previously unpublished material, and his gracious encouragement has helped me to keep faith in the endeavour. My son Jonathan has often retrieved order from incipient chaos, and my wife, like Imogen the cave-keeper, has cooked my roots in characters.

I am grateful to colleagues in the University of Birmingham, the English Department and the Shakespeare Institute for enabling me to continue work on my publishing projects, including the present book, while too scant of breath to meet my obligations as a teacher. Claire Cochrane gave valuable assistance in preparing typescript and making the index, and I owe more than I care to confess to Caroline Bundy, the indefatigable and patient press-editor. The index and notes acknowledge other obligations but I fear that some names (like that of my old school-master A. E. Darke) may not be there because they taught in an oral tradition, and others (like Enid Welsford) because their spacious and fundamental work has been taken too much for granted. Any suspected residual debts should be charged to my account.

Preface

Of the seventeen papers in the present collection, six of the longest are printed for the first time, eight have previously appeared in Shakespearian periodicals or collections, and three elsewhere. Although written over a period of twenty-five years, they show few signs of advancing understanding and return obstinately to the same topics, large and small. Each has nevertheless been arrested while still in process of change. Papers prepared for one place and occasion have been re-fashioned, sometimes several times, for a different audience. 'Julius Caesar and the Catastrophes of History', for example, grew out of 1980 lectures on 'Shakespeare and the Catastrophes of History' (Birmingham) and 'The Theatre of Terror' given in Belfast, before mutations were offered at Aleppo (between armed guards) and in Weimar in the following year. Earlier versions of the paper on Othello were given in Ilorin, Nigeria (1979), in Aleppo, at the Shakespeare Institute and in Beijing (1985). Shorter versions of 'The Island of the Tempest' were given to the Royal Shakespeare Theatre Summer School in 1978, at the University of Tunis in 1982, and in Stockholm in 1985. 'Troilus and Cressida' is much expanded from '"A Kind of Self"; Creation of Character in Shakespeare', given in Madrid in 1985 and published in the conference proceedings. 'The Theatre of God's Judgement' grew from two contributions to seminars at the Shakespeare Institute, and its section on Measure for Measure retains some formulations from a review article (TLS, 26 November 1976).

I have meddled but little with the text of previously published pieces, but have reduced overlaps, supplied some cross-references, and corrected errors that have been brought to my attention. In both the earlier and later musings I have tried to look from a high altitude to far-away horizons and (fearing vacuity and abstraction) to alight upon demonstrative detail, supposing that the true theory, *theoria*, or figuring-forth is the demonstrative perception of the work itself, not any formal description or analysis of it. One perception can be displaced, or set in a changed perspective, only by another, more adequate perception, and one way of enjoying a play, by another, richer and fuller way.

I have arranged the contents in four groups, each including old and new contributions, and have been content to begin with, and to take my subtitle from, the one that bears the most intemperate and immodest title. But while the *Timon of Athens* essay alone invites direct attention to Jesus and Marx, all the pieces, including the last, show large related preoccupations with art, history and the ethical imagination. From the start I have been concerned to present Shakespeare as a great poet who did what he could to assume responsibility for the imaginative thought of the past, from the Old Testament prophets and the classical tragedians to what was 'still and contemplative in living art' in his own time.

Looking for a way of placing him in those movements of European civilized understanding we have come to call the Renaissance, the Reformation and the Counter-Reformation, I would like to call him a 'sceptical humanist'. He was 'sceptical', not because he kept a questioning distance between his intellect and his life-delight, but because, like Euripides, Erasmus and Montaigne, he was sensitive to the boundaries of what 'cool reason comprehends'. He was a 'humanist' because he did not come to rest in dogma or doctrine but used the arts of theatre to test all human claims, including those 'shaping fantasies' made about the gods and God, by human criteria, judgements and sympathies.

The first group, on Values and Perceptions, attends to three plays that most directly ask, 'What is aught but as 'tis valued?' in the market-place and the battlefield, in the ideologies of love and money, war and government. Shakespeare properly looked upon the six thousand years of the world's history as both a long time and a short. His plays from Homer and Plutarch keep the experience of the past at a distance while finding in it continuing and recurring processes and structures. The second group is about some Catastrophes of History in plays which owe their episodes and theatrical articulation to the theatre of events. The third group is concerned with Tragic Sacrifice, and shows that primordial festive tragic forms persist from pagan into urban modes of civilized consciousness. In the last group, Comedy Human and Divine, taking in some of the later comedies, there is reason to remember that Shakespeare as an actor and playwright was well placed to understand the constraints that both shape and frustrate the freedoms of the 'self'. As playwright he was responsible for a play's impersonal processes of history or providence, while as an actor he would be sensitive to the 'part played by' the individual's style, wit and affections.

The Globe Theatre was large enough for its audience to compose a diverse and representative community but small enough for performers to engage or alienate its sympathies through the intimate expression of personal character. The plays therefore (as I have a habit of saying) make us better communists and better idiots (or *ideotes*); they encourage us to cultivate a greater awareness of community and a fuller realization of the potentials of the 'self'.

Shakespeare's plots, characters and language can move easily and gracefully between the court and the populace, but they can also be exposed, like Renaissance civilization itself, to severe stresses and instabilities. A prince or nobleman may represent a love of order and perfection, or embody the cruel ascendancy of power and wealth over the decencies of our ordinary nature. I like to think that Shakespearian criticism can still be kept in touch with the arts of conversation, and that conversation can disengage from those Victorian confidences in progress that breed the jargons of scientism or the rhetorics of the market-place and of populism. It is a matter of sensitizing our subjective selves and our common sense (*sensus communis*) through quick thought and imaginative play. Rousseau, Adam Smith, Darwin and Marx were Titans – Giant Forms, as Blake would say – but as poets know, it is the fate of Titans to be deposed in order that life should make some sort of fresh start.

In the figure of Holofernes, Shakespeare found an early place for a pedant and scholar who was a far cry from a Titan; and whenever I 'over-glance the superscript' I am conscious of the vanity of the critic's art. We are talking to each other about plays and perhaps looking vainly for the compliment that Sir Nathaniel paid his fellow guest:

> Your reasons at dinner have been sharp and sententious: pleasant without scurrility, witty without affection, audacious without impudency, learned without opinion, and strange without heresy.

Shakespeare, tactfully, did not allow us to eavesdrop on that occasion.

J. P. Brockbank

Abbreviated References

References to Shakespeare's text are to the Riverside edition, edited by G. Blakemore Evans (Houghton Mifflin, Boston, 1974) to which the Harvard Concordance is keyed.

The following short forms of reference have been used for books and periodicals frequently referred to:

Bullough   Geoffrey Bullough (ed.), *Narrative and Dramatic Sources of Shakespeare*, 7 vols (i, 1956; ii, 1958; iii, 1960; iv, 1962; v, 1964; vi, 1966; vii, 1973; viii, 1975).

Hol.   Raphael Holinshed, *The firste [laste] volume of the chronicles of Englande, Scotlande and Irelande*. 3 vols, 1587; ed. H. Ellis, 6 vols, 1807–8. References to '*Holinshed*' in chapter 14 are to the 1587 edn (vol. i); elsewhere they are usually to the more available edn of 1807–8.

Montaigne   *The Essayes of Michael Lord of Montaigne, done into English by John Florio*, ed. Thomas Seccombe, 3 vols, 1908. References are to Book, chapter, and page.

STC   *A Short-Title Catalogue of Books Printed in England, Scotland, and Ireland, 1475–1640*, compiled by A. W. Pollard and G. R. Redgrave, 1950 [2nd edn, 1986]. References are to serial nos. in 1st edn.

Survey   *Shakespeare Survey*, published annually by Cambridge University Press (vol. i, 1948).

Part I

Values and Perceptions

1 Jesus, Shakespeare and Karl Marx – *Timon of Athens* and *The Merchant of Venice*: Parables for the City

Jesus, said William Blake, 'spoke in parables to the blind'. It is the way of all poets. 'At its simplest,' C. H. Dodd tells us, 'the parable is a metaphor or simile drawn from nature or common life, arresting the hearer by its vividness or strangeness and leaving the mind in sufficient doubt about its precise application to tease it into active thought.'[1] I propose to look at the story of the Unjust Steward (Luke 16) before letting Shakespeare's *Timon of Athens* and *Merchant of Venice* tease us again into active thought. The parable was probably known to Shakespeare in the Geneva version:

1 And he said also to his disciples, There was a certain rich man, which had a steward, and he was accused unto him, that he wasted his goods.

2 And he called him and said unto him, How is it that I hear this of thee? Give an account of thy stewardship: for thou maiest be no longer steward.

3 Then the steward said within himself, What shall I do: for my master will take away from me the stewardship? I cannot dig, and to beg I am ashamed.

---

[1] Quoted under 'Parables' in *A New Dictionary of Christian Theology*, ed. Alan Richardson and John Bowden (1983). 'Most of them,' says the article, 'are personal and relational, concerned with conventional versus radical ways of dealing with other people . . . Jesus's parables are also *disorienting* teaching devices, embodying the reversal of expectations which is at the heart of the gospel – the scandal of Jesus's identification in his table-fellowship as on the cross with outcasts and sinners.' See also C. H. Dodd, *The Parables of the Kingdom*, 3rd edn (1936), p. 30.

4 I know what I will do, that when I am put out of the stewardship they may receive me into their houses.

5 Then called he every one of his masters debtors, and said unto the first. How much owest thou unto my master? And he said, An hundreth measures of oil.

6 And he said unto him, Take thy writing, and sit down quickly, and write fifty.

7 Then said he to another, How much owest thou? And he said, an hundreth measures of wheat. Then he said to him, Take thy writing and write four score.

8 And the lord commended the unjust steward, because he had done wisely. Wherefore the children of this world are in their generation wiser than the children of light.

9 And I say unto you, Make you friends with the riches of iniquity, that when ye shall want, they may receive you into everlasting habitations.

10 He that is faithful in the least, he is also faithful in much; and he that is unjust in the least, is unjust also in much.

11 If then ye have not been faithful in the wicked riches, who will trust you in the true treasure?

12 And if you have not been faithful in another man's goods, who shall give you that which is yours?

13 No servant can serve two masters: for either he shall hate the one and love the other; or else he shall lean to the one and despise the other. Ye can not serve God and riches.

It is not easy to give a measured ethical account of either Jesus's parable or Shakespeare's, for each affords an elusive and paradoxical insight into the relationship between human values and what we have come to call market-values. Over the centuries commentaries on Luke 16 have offered an ironically revealing window into the attitudes of the commentators and of the city civilization which they, often inadvertently, represent. In Jesus's story the rich man commends the wisdom of the unjust steward because he knew how to look after his own interests, even at the expense of his master's. No translation or interpretation can sidestep the subversive strategy of the parable. Jesus invites us to take a leaf from the book of the money-makers, from the Mammon of unrighteousness, and some glosses are in consequence embarrassingly bland or evasive:

The chief lesson of this parable seems to be that we should do service to God by giving alms to the poor, while we have still time for it. The steward was prudent in making himself friends before the audit of his accounts, while he had still money to do it; so we must give alms while life still lasts. It is doubtful whether we are meant to interpret the parable more closely than this.[2]

It is clear that Ronald Knox was determined to keep his distance; for at a closer look the steward cheats the audit, and in his own interests disposes of property that does not belong to him. Another popular but disingenuous line of defence against the parable assures us that, 'Jesus commends the manager's astuteness, not his dishonesty. He knows how to make money work for him.'[3] The disconcerting truth about the parable is that the 'astuteness' (the word, incidentally, chosen in the *New English Bible*) is of a piece with the dishonesty. Some more sensitive accounts still try to iron out the difficulties and accommodate the meaning to the routines of monetary and ethical good sense. Thus G. B. Caird, under the headline 'The Use of Opportunities', finds that in the words of the lord (*kyrios* in v. 8) Jesus commends the unjust steward for what we now call good crisis management, 'his realism and determination in dealing with an emergency.'[4] 'Alternatively,' says Caird, 'we can say that the steward is called dishonest because of his previous mismanagement of the estate'; under Jewish law, it would seem, 'there was nothing fraudulent with his negotiations with his master's debtors.' Either of these sophistications destroys the vital tensions of the parable, for the phrase 'realism and determination' masks the flagrant chicanery that the parable exposes, while the point about the legality of the negotiations only reminds us of what a wheeler-dealer can get away with under the law.

Commentaries of Shakespeare's time are in comparison both lively and worried. The first marginal gloss of the Geneva version resembles Knox's on alms:

a) Christ teacheth hereby, that likewise that he who is in authority and hath riches, if he gets friends in his prosperity, may be relieved in his adversities: so our liberality towards our neighbour shall stand us in such stead at the day of judgement that God will accept it as done unto him.

Its second diverts attention to a precariously related topic – 'prodigality':

b) God, who doth here represent the master of the house, doth rather commend the prodigal waste of his goods, and the liberal giving of the same to the poor, than strait keeping and hoarding of them.

---

[2] See the Holy Bible, A translation [by R. A. Knox] from the Latin Vulgate (1945/ 1966), ad loc.

[3] D. and P. Alexander (eds), *The Lion Handbook to the Bible* (Berkhamsted, 1973).

[4] See G. B. Caird, *Saint Luke*, The Pelican Gospel Commentaries (1963), p. 185.

The remaining glosses take in a range of uncontrolled moral references and responses:

> c) That is, either wickedly gotten, or wickedly kept, or wickedly spent: and hereby we be warned to suspect riches which for the most part are an occasion to their possessors of great wickedness.

> d) They which can not well bestow worldly goods, will bestow evil spiritual treasures: and therefore they ought not to be committed unto them.

> e) As are riches and such like things, which God hath given not for yourselves only, but to be bestowed upon others. (Mat. 6: 14).

> f) Christ calleth the gifts, which he hath given unto us, riches.

William Perkins follows at greater leisure in the same discursive tracks, evading the parable with some subtle reconciliations of worldly and other-worldly insights.[5]

Shakespeare's story of Timon is no less stressful. Re-cast as a New Testament parable it might read:

> There was a certain rich lord who wasted his substance in prodigal living. When he had spent all and found himself in want he called his steward and said unto him, How is it that my lands are gone and my coffers are empty? Give an account of thy stewardship. And the steward answered and said, Master I have wept to see your gold squandered and your wine spilt, I have told you of your state and you have not listened. The lord comforted the steward saying, You are just and faithful. Go now to my friends to whom I have given gifts and money and tell them I have need of them. They too are just and will keep faith with me. And the steward went to the debtors and creditors and said as his lord spake. But they turned their backs upon the steward and would not help his master. When the lord heard of the ingratitude of his friends he called them to a feast and gave them water for wine and stones for

---

[5] See William Perkins, *The Whole Theatre of the Cases of Conscience*, bk 3, ch. 4 (*Works*, 2nd edn, Legatt, 1608, vol. 2), and *An Exposition of Christ's Sermon on the Mount* (*Works*, Legatt, 1608, vol. 3). A modern edition of the *Works* is edited by Thomas F. Merrill (The Hague, 1966). Perkins covers the topics of property and money comprehensively from a wide range of biblical texts and reaches 'temperate' conclusions that most sober well-to-do readers would find reassuring: 'For first, the law of Nature sets downe and prescribes distinctions of possessions, and propertie of lands and goods, and the Gospel doth not abolish the law of Nature' (1608, II, p. 128). Elsewhere, a covert appeal to natural law enables him to elude the disconcerting impact of the parable.

bread. He went forth from the city into the wilderness and filled his belly with the roots of the earth. He found gold in the earth but he cast it away, saying, I will die by the verge of the sea, having nothing but possessing all things. I say unto you that his lord was foolish in his life but wise in his death, for love is from God and can not be bought from the children of this world.

Both in Shakespeare's version and in its several precedents and analogues, the Timon fable has a disconcerting duplicity. When Jove in Lucian's *Dialogue of Timon* asks about the change that has overtaken 'that fine rich man surrounded by so many friends', Mercury answers: 'He was brought to this by his bounty, humanity and compassion towards all in want; or rather, to speak more correctly, by his ignorance, foolish habits, and small judgement of men, not realizing he was giving his property to ravens and wolves' (Bullough, VI, 265). Mercury's verdict on Timon can find no point of rest between the words 'compassion' and 'folly'. There is no point of balance in Jesus's story either; we must learn from Mammon to deal as prudently, self-interestedly and mendaciously with true riches as the children of this world do with false riches.

Both stories invite us to find a comprehensive, transcendent but perplexing truth in a particular moral anecdote. Like the parables of Jesus, Shakespeare's has a commanding but deceptive simplicity. Our reception of it will depend upon our own moral visions, traditions and inheritances; its effects in twentieth-century Poland will not be the same as those in nineteenth-century England; but they will always be upsetting. *Timon* has more than one way of teasing us into thought, some taking us into its pre-Shakespearian history and some into later times.

At the end of Boiarda's *Timone* (*c*.1487) we are told that Timon's gold will be given to his heir, Filicoro, who is in prison for debt, 'having fallen into need after lifting the burden of need from others'; once released he will be 'no longer prodigal but liberal, keeping expenses and his gifts in reason' (Bullough, VI, pp. 291, 293). He will have been schooled in an Aristotelian tradition. The leading principle of the *Nicomachean Ethics* finds a 'mean' (analogous to an arithmetic mean) between excess and defect in a range of ethical categories.[6] It requires, in respect to money and property, a proportionately measured virtue, vigilantly observed and fitted to each transaction. We should never be mean or stingy, and never extravagant or prodigal, but if we err a little in practice, it should be on the generous side. Our potential, however, varies with our resources. Even

---

[6] I have used J. A. K. Thomson's translation (1953; Penguin Books, 1955) together with H. H. Joachim's Commentary, ed. D. A. Rees (Oxford, 1951). See particularly *Ethics*, II. 6 and IV. 2.

a man of average means can afford to be liberal. Such is Flavius, Shakespeare's just steward, who would be outside Aristotle's social range, but seems to step into the *Ethics* from the Gospels (see IV. i.). The Lord Timon, however, has, in Aristotelian terms, a higher available range of virtues. As a man of great means he can be more than *liberal*, he can be *magnanimous*. But in supposing his finite resources inexhaustible, Timon fails to keep his accounts, fails to be goldenly mean 'For bounty, that makes the gods, do still mar men' (IV. ii. 410). Through the habitual practice of virtue Aristotle expects its calculations to become spontaneous. But Timon mistakes the acquired spontaneities of prodigality for those of munificence and magnanimity. His generous and magnificently noble image of himself collapses suddenly and catastrophically, at the height of his confidence, and he declines into the figure of another wastrel with an empty belly. The Poet who enjoys prodigal patronage provides the fable that shapes the play:

> When Fortune in her shift and change of mood
> Spurns down her late beloved, all his dependants
> Which labour'd after him to the mountain's top
> even on their knees and hands, let him slip down,
> Not one accompanying his declining foot.
>
> (I. i. 84–8)

Patrician Athenian Aristotelians, like Lucullus, wise child of the world and Mammon, sensibly shrug their shoulders and sneak away, along with a high proportion of Shakespeare's critics. Flavius alone is moved by compassion to follow Timon (and his creator) into the wilderness and into a different moral universe.

That scholars and critics have found Timon repellent is not surprising. Montaigne,[7] writing *Of Democritus and Heraclitus*, glances aside to find even the most celebrated of Cynics more congenial and entertaining than Timon:

> Even so Diogenes, who did nothing but trifle, toy, and dally with himselfe in rumbling and rowling of his tub, and flurting at *Alexander*, accompting us but flies and bladders puft with winde, was a more sharp, a more bitter, and a more stinging judge, and by consequence more fitting my humor, than *Timon*, surnamed the hater of all mankinde.
>
> (I. 50. 418)

There is such a Diogenes, known to Shakespeare, in Lyly's *Campaspe* (Bullough, VI, pp. 339–45). Cynicism is hardly a systematic philosophy,

---

[7] References are to the reprint of the 1603 edition of Florio's Montaigne with introduction by Thomas Seccombe (3 vols. 1908).

but an aggregation of anecdotes, austere life-style and reductive wit. A complete account of it would have to find a central place for Timon's encounters with Apemantus, made from some promptings in North's *Life of Marcus Antonius*:

> What wouldst thou do with the world. Apemantus, if it lay in thy power?
>
> Give it o'er to beasts to be rid of the men.
>
> Woulds't thou have thyself fall in the confusion of men, and remain a beast with the beasts?
>
> Ay, Timon.

That tradition of Cynic thought which opposes the money-corrupted life of the city to the candid instinctual life of animals has a complex imaginative history which (to different effects) takes in, for example, Book 4 of *Gulliver's Travels*, Conrad's *Under Western Eyes*, and Ionesco's *Rhinoceros*. The play actively assimilates this aspect of the Cynic vision but refuses to endorse it. Timon quits Athens for the woods in the optimistic Cynic expectation that 'he shall find / Th' unkindest beast more kinder than mankind', but once he has himself assumed the unaccommodated animal state he finds it of a piece with the commonwealth of Athens:

> wert thou a bear thou shoulds't be killed by the horse; wert thou a horse, thou wouldst be seized by the leopard; wert thou a leopard thou wert germane to the lion, and the spots of thy kindred were jurors on thy life; all thy safety were remotion and thy defence absence. What beast couldst thou be, that were not subject to a beast? And what a beast art thou already, that seest not thy loss in transformation?
>
> (IV. iii. 338–345)

Exposed to the elemental and instinctual condition of the 'two legged forked thing' in *King Lear*, both the king and the courtier in his role of bedlam beggar see their 'loss in transformation' when 'man's life's as cheap as beast's'. Apemantus, although a 'lord', appears in comparison like Montaigne's Diogenes, a licensed fool in a slave-state, both scorning and fitting the humour of his masters in return for maintenance and ethical status. Outside the city he is one of several focal points for a tragic rage that takes in city, forest, earth and cosmos.

In an anthology of comprehensive diatribes Shakespeare's Timon would find a conspicuous place between (say) the Old Testament prophets and those nineteenth-century seers who confronted (or turned aside from) a new Babylon. Here is Tennyson, outside the great hall, in 1855:

I keep but a man and a maid, ever ready to slander and steal.
I know it, and smile a hard-set smile, like a stoic, or like
A wiser epicurean, and let the world have its way:
For nature is one with rapine, a harm no preacher can heal.
The mayfly is torn by the swallow, the sparrow spear'd by the
    shrike,
And the whole little wood where I sit is a world of plunder and
    prey.

(Maud, ii. iv)

Tennyson's 'stoic or wiser epicurean' indulges a passive response to the competitive ferocity of the commercial world, covertly vindicated by a reading of Darwin ('A monstrous eft was of old the Lord and Master of Earth)'. It could be said of his rhetoric, as of Timon's, that it leads nowhere and is not designed to have an effect on a world whose 'harm no preacher can heal'.

Timon's indictments of the social and natural orders are not addressed to an Athens (or a London) capable of reforming itself or to a 'great creative nature' capable of change. It may be claimed, however, that they found their best public (if not theatre audience) in Victorian times; for by way of Karl Marx the effect of Timon's wrath upon the world has been immeasurable. Marx's reflections on the play occur in the *Economic and Philosophical Manuscripts* of 1844 and they have been fully presented and discussed by Kenneth Muir and others.[8] Marx offers a full and precise account of the play's most central and searching insights into the nature of money and property in what we may call the capital city, whose life and prosperity depend upon credit and rates of interest. Taking his first cue from Goethe's Mephistopheles, who entertains us with the thought that the man who buys a stallion believes himself to possess its attributes, he recalls Timon's soliloquies from iv. iii., focusing sharply on his first address to gold (26–43) and on the words that attend the retreat of Apemantus:

O thou sweet king-killer, and dear divorce
'Twixt natural son and sire! thou bright defiler
Of Hymen's purest bed! thou valiant Mars!
Thou ever young, fresh, lov'd and delicate wooer,

---

[8] See Kenneth Muir, 'Timon of Athens and the Cash Nexus', *Modern Quarterly Miscellany*, reprinted in Muir, *The Singularity of Shakespeare and Other Essays* (Liverpool, 1977). Marx's remarks on *Timon*, from the Economic and Philosophic Manuscripts of 1844, are in the *Collected Works* (1975), iii, pp. 322–6. Muir also draws attention to a footnote on *Timon* in *Capital*. See also Johanna Rudolph, 'Karl Marx und Shakespeare', *Shakespeare Jahrbuch* (Weimar), 105 (1969), pp. 25–53.

For a general survey of critical opinion on the play see Francelia Butler, *The Strange Critical Fortunes of Shakespeare's 'Timon of Athens'* (Iowa, 1966).

Whose blush doth thaw the consecrated snow
That lies on Dian's lap! Thou visible god,
That sold'rest close impossibilities,
And makes them kiss! That speak'st with every tongue
To every purpose! O thou touch of hearts,
Think thy slave man rebels, and by thy virtue
Set them into confounding odds, that beasts
May have the world in empire!

(IV. iii. 381–92)

'Shakespeare,' says Marx, 'stresses especially two properties of money':

1 It is the visible divinity – the transformation of all human and natural properties into their contraries, the universal confounding and distorting of things: impossibilities are soldered together by it.
2 It is the common whore, the common procurer of people and nations . . . Money, then, appears as this *distorting* power both against the individual and against the bonds of society, etc., which claim to be *entities* in themselves. It transforms fidelity into infidelity, love into hate, hate into love, virtue into vice, vice into virtue, servant into master, master into servant, idiocy into intelligence and intelligence into idiocy.

Since money, as the existing and active concept of value, confounds and confuses all things, it is the general *confounding* and *confusing* of all things – the world upside down – the confusing and confounding of all natural and human qualities.

(Karl Marx, *Works*, III, pp. 324–6)

The tensions of the play express the destructive contrarieties of value in a sophisticated moneyed society, and the economic analysis to which Marx's thought relates them is, in a longer perspective, consistent both with the attitudes of Diogenes and with Bible stories of divine values in the 'golden city' (Isaiah 14) perverted by 'gods of gold' (see Exodus 32), 'golden images' (Daniel 5) and harlotry (Isaiah 1).

Marx's précis does not in itself, however, exhaust the significance of Timon's tragic vision, which has a place in the history of Shakespeare's theatre as well as in moral fable, economic history and prophecy. The play changes its effects upon us as we come upon it from different directions. Turning from the Tudor Interludes, for example, it looks like one of a sequence of didactic dramas about prodigality, including *Liberality and Prodigality* (performed at court in 1601) which draw both on the parables and on classical ethics.[9] Alighting upon it after readings or performances

[9] See M. C. Bradbrook, 'Blackfriars: The Pageant of Timon of Athens', in *Shakespeare the Craftsman* (1969), pp. 144–67; and '*The Comedy of Timon*: A

M. C. Bradbrook, is a 'role' rather than a character.[10] That role is tragic, moving us through the imaginative design and flux of the play, and giving shape to our understanding of money and city life.

Shakespeare's comedic art had been this way before. 'A most incomparable man,' says the Athenian Merchant about Timon, 'breath'd, as it were, / To an untirable and continuate goodness; / He passes' (I. i. 10–12). 'Antonio,' says Shylock, 'is a good man . . . my meaning in saying he is a good man is to have you understand me that he is sufficient' (*The Merchant of Venice*, I. iii. 15–17). Events will prove the one good man to be bad at conserving his resources and the other bad at assessing the risks to which he exposes himself on behalf of another. The two plays are intimately interrelated in what again can be seen as a biblical tradition. For the prophet Isaiah (ch. 23) Tyre was 'the crowning city, whose merchants are princes, whose traffickers are the honourable of the earth'; the same city sings 'as an harlot', 'makes sweet melody' and commits 'fornication with all the kingdoms of the world'. In a creative vision the merchandise of the city is 'holiness to the Lord' not 'treasured nor laid up', but distributed, enabling good men 'to eat sufficiently' and wear 'durable clothing'. A catastrophic vision, however, tells of wars and disasters that make the earth empty, 'maketh it waste, and turneth it upside down':

> And it shall be, as with the people, so with the priest; as with the servant, so with his master; as with the maid, so with her mistress; as with the buyer, so with the seller; as with the lender, so with the borrower; as with the taker of usury, so with the giver of usury to him.
> The land shall be utterly emptied and utterly spoiled.
>
> (Isaiah, 24: 2–3)

Venice was for the imagination of Renaissance writers what Tyre was for Isaiah, but the figure of the prodigal *misanthropos* offers Shakespeare the opportunity to represent Athens as the merchant city which breaks the 'everlasting covenant' between man and man and therefore between man and God. The bonds are broken too in *The Merchant of Venice*, but restored (however precariously) in a fabulous world of comic romance which is still recognizable as the Venice and London of Shakespeare's time.

Timon's poet enthrones Fortune upon 'a high and pleasant hill'. When Bassanio makes his 'secret pilgrimage' to Belmont, he goes like Jason to seek his fortune, hoping to find it in a lady 'richly left', 'fair' and 'fairer than that word, / Of wondrous virtues'. But the play is so designed that he can win the gold only by repudiating it in favour of lead. As I have

---

[10] Bradbrook, *Shakespeare the Craftsman*, p. 154.

argued elsewhere,[11] enlightened capital in the shape of Portia's father has set a trial to ensure that the fortune-hunter who wins his daughter knows how and when to pay tribute to values very different from those that energize the market-place. The casket plot is the comedy's way of expressing the poise that at its best Renaissance civilization could find between the mercantile motives of its prosperity, and the aspirations of biblical and classical tradition. In *Timon* Shakespeare directly stages the relationship between painters and poets and their patrons. Although the arts are in the hands of servile and venal practitioners, they have critical revelations to make about those on whom they depend. Through patronage, courtiers, merchants and bankers of the Renaissance found ways of transmuting worldly goods into spiritual treasures – a Donatello *Magdalene*, a Titian *Pietà*, a Palestrina Mass, a Shakespeare *Lear*. Patronage at its best calls for the exercise of creative hypocrisy – 'Assume a virtue if you have it not', as Hamlet says to his mother. In the Van Eyck's masterpiece, *The Adoration of the Lamb*, the burghers of Antwerp who had made money enough from butchery and wool to pay for a place in the picture assemble outside a transfigured version of their golden city, in an exuberant countryside, to worship the sacrificial lamb of God (clearly a good market beast). 'Christ,' says the Geneva commentator on Luke 16, 'calleth the gifts, which he hath given unto us, riches.' Shakespeare's *Merchant of Venice* is a more specifically urban mystery of the Renaissance, transforming money-grubbing greed and murderous aggression into the pursuit of perfection in a golden world. It offers apt occasion for the Geneva commentator's ambiguous observation that 'They which can not well bestow worldly goods, will bestow evil spiritual treasures: and therefore they ought not to be committed unto them.'

'I stand for sacrifice,' says Portia at the central point of the play (III. II. 58), while Bassanio, in the course of his 'pilgrimage', begins to learn how to bestow worldly goods and spiritual treasures. Were it not for his taste for gold he would never have come to Belmont, and the play makes Portia herself a golden commodity ('Her sunny locks / Hang on her temples like a golden fleece'). While therefore he has wit and style enough to make the right choice of casket, it is an entertaining irony that he does not rail against gold as money but as an instrument of hypocrisy and false appearances, against what we now call public relations (salesmanship, image-making and advertising) which mask and gild the simple truth:

> Look on beauty,
> And you shall see 'tis purchas'd by the weight,
> Which therein works a miracle to nature,

[11] 'Our Ducats & Our Daughters', *Times Higher Education Supplement*, 19 February 1988, pp. 15–17.

Making them lightest that wear most of it.
So are those crisped snaky golden locks,
Which make such wanton gambols with the wind
Upon supposed fairness, often known
To be the dowry of a second head,
The skull that bred them in the sepulchre.

(III. ii. 88–96)

Shakespeare himself is making light of weighty matters. He, like the painter
of Portia's portrait, weaves 'A golden mesh t' entrap the hearts of men',
subtly engaging and alienating our sympathies and admiration. But the
ironies are not pressed home. Portia's golden hair (making 'wanton gambols
with the wind'?) and golden disposition are at one with the gold that she
inherits and to which the city aspires. She is, like Isaiah's Harlot of the
merchant city, a maker of 'sweet melody'. Her love is to be won at a price
which Bassanio knows how to pay, for, under the spell of Portia and
Belmont, he is sufficiently well-read in courtier literature to find the words
the occasion requires and grace his courtship with a touch of ethical
imagination.

Among the books Bassanio brought to Shakespeare's English Belmont we
are free to speculate on a copy of William Jones's translation of *Nennio, or
a Treatise of Nobility* by Giovanni Battista Nenna (1595).[12] In it he would
find an eloquent plea from Possidonio, speaking in contention for the ring
of a certain Lady Virginia, for the necessary union of riches, breeding,
beauty and virtue:

> Riches do drive all sorrow and sadness from the mind: they expel
> all melancholie thoughtes from the imagination: they keep the body
> from wearisome labour: they increase sweete friendship: they cause
> in man waighters of honor and renowne, and finally they are the
> occasion of all high fame and glorie. Who is then so void of reason,
> who hearing thse things so conformable unto trueth, doth not judge
> riches, not onely to be an ornament of Nobilitie, but an inseparable
> part thereof? (p. 24)

But from Fabricio (who in due course wins the prize) he would find 'the
retort courteous':

> For auncient authors have left us in writing, that riches (whosoever
> first had the sight thereof) is a thing most deformed, wearing on
> the naturall visage thereof, a masque of most fine gold, denoting
> thereby, that it is fair in apparence, but foule within: wherefore

[12] I have used the Renaissance Library Facsimile Edition, with an Introduction
by Alice Shalvi.

they who travell so many Countries, and tak such paines to seeke
it, are enamoured with the outward shewe, which blindeth the eyes
of the understanding: so that they can hardly discerne how hurtfull
the inward deformitie thereof is. Which maketh man who is
forgetfull of himselfe, to addict his minde thereto.

Bassanio might have noticed, however, that the 'pleasant and merry talk'
is conducted in the fair and delightful gardens of the Grange, some seven
miles out of town – a Belmont one must be able to afford. He speaks,
therefore, in mortgaged finery, as an image-maker, and wins the lady in
terms that she moves playfully between the affections and the Rialto:

> I would be trebled twenty times myself,
> A thousand times more fair, ten thousand times more rich,
> That only to stand high in your account,
> I might in virtues, beauties, livings, friends,
> Exceed account. But the full sum of me
> Is sum of something; which, to term in gross,
> Is an unlesson'd girl, unschool'd, unpractis'd,
> Happy in this, she is not yet so old
> But she may learn; happier than this,
> She is not bred so dull but she can learn;
> Happiest of all, is that her gentle spirit
> Commits herself to yours to be directed,
> As from her lord, her governor, her king.
> Myself, and what is mine, to you and yours
> Is now converted.
>
> (III. ii. 153–67)

Looked at one way, part of the play's innocence is what has been aptly
called the 'usury of love',[13] is to be taken disarmingly in the same spirit as
Bassanio's confession of his debt to Antonio, whose investment is designed
to breed 'virtues, beauties' and 'friends' as well as 'livings' (more material
assets). Looked at another way, however, when Portia offers a ring as token
for her bond, Shakespeare charges Portia's affections with a little of her
father's prudential sophistication; the moment must be so played that we
recall it when Bassanio draws back his hand in the fourth act (IV. i. 428).

As Bassanio is more than a simple lover of truth in a naughty world, so
Portia is more than the 'unlesson'd girl' that she charmingly affects to be.
Nor is she passively Bassanio's 'to be directed'; she will in due course teach
him to refine his accomplishment in the management of his fortune. Belmont
is a place where rich and beautiful ladies can afford to cultivate 'wondrous

---

[13] See ch. 3 below, p. 71 and note 12.

virtues' and a spirit attentive to the music of the spheres. It takes its place in a line of country houses in fact and fiction from Horace's Sabine farm to Sidney's Penshurst, Mansfield Park, the Hall of Tennyson's *Maud* and Yeats's Coole Park. Ideally, each (like the villas on the Brenta outside Venice) offers the prospect of a protected life reconciling plenitude, exuberance, simplicity and order:

> Surely among a rich man's flowering lawns
> Amid the rustle of his planted hills
> Life overflows without ambitious pains;
> And rains down life until the basin spills.
> (Yeats, 'Ancestral Houses')

The great houses have usually been built from trade and war; 'Bitter and violent men,' says Yeats, 'Called architect and artist in', to 'rear in stone the sweetness that all longed for night and day.'[14]

While not a hermitage or ivory tower, Belmont is a retreat. Portia is no recluse, but is quick to find a role in Venice, mediating between the sustaining truths of Belmont and the obsessive and fantastic 'reality' of the Rialto, where Shylock dreams of money-bags in his indispensable but virulent role of money-lender. As Aristotle understood, the exchange rates dislodge our ethical values; from the prophet Isaiah to the poet Pound the practice of 'usury', of making money out of money, has been seen to work against the true festive life of the city. Shylock's cry when he hears that Jessica had swapped a turquoise ring for a monkey poignantly expresses the absurdity of the terms of trade when measured by the affections, 'I had it of Leah when I was a bachelor. I would not have given it for a wilderness of monkeys.' The more humane aspects of his nature – his Jewishness and devotion to his family – turn sour under stress of persecution, itself the venomous Christian response to his wealth and power as a financier. An obsession with money destroys his household and threatens the city's mercantile stability.

Shylock's uncreative hypocrisy consists in the play-making wit by which he turns a 'merry sport' into a death trap, and when Portia comes in disguise to the court she finds that he can use the contractual laws of Venice to assist him in an act of murder. She is not only honouring her personal bridal loyalty and healing a bond of friendship, therefore, she is also seeking momentarily to restore the laws of Venetian community to their equitable condition. She is at once the divine voice of law and its artful practitioner, and her exquisitely hypocritical performance has been called 'a consummate

---

[14]'Meditations in Time of Civil War: Ancestral Houses'; it is apt also to adduce Ben Jonson's 'Penshurst', and to recall Pope's treatment of Timon and his villa in the 'Epistle to Burlington'.

piece of Jew-baiting'.[15] It is designed, however, to test the money-lender and his murderous attachment to his bond. Shylock himself invokes his Jewishness by demanding the unqualified rigour of the law ('a Daniel come to judgement'), and gives an opening for the vindictive baiter Gratiano. Portia nicely demonstrates the operation of 'wondrous virtue' in the compromised chaos of the world. As Florio's Montaigne puts it, 'a scholasticall and novice vertue' is 'very unapt and dangerous' in the 'service of Publike affaires'; virtue must be up to all the tricks:

> He that goeth in a presse or throng of people, must sometimes step aside, hold in his elbowes, cross the way, advance himselfe, start backe, and forsake the right way, according as it falls out: Live he not so much as he would himselfe, but as others will, not according to what he proposeth to himselfe, but to that which is proposed to him: according to times, to men and to affaires, and as the skilfull Mariner, saile with the winde.
>
> (III. 9. 297: 'Of Vanitie')

Montaigne is here rather more compromised and accommodating than Shakespeare's Portia needs to be, the poet-playwright's solution being more exquisite than that of the philosophic essayist. She is very much The Witty Lawyer (as the Chinese sometimes call the play) and her intervention is neither sentimental nor pragmatic. She is one of a number of Shakespeare's creative manipulators who like Vincentio apply 'craft against vice' (Prospero, 'in liberal arts without a parallel', is another); and her lawyer's wit finds the spirit of the law in precise attention to its letter.[16] In the comedy's last phase her bridal wit plays out the ring-game begun in the casket-scene and establishes her affectionate ascendancy over Bassanio, who still has much to learn. Marriage too is a state of harmony, but in a changing and unstable world it needs wit to keep it live. Thus the comedy finds a satisfyingly positive rhythm between retreat and engagement, the contemplative understanding and the urban savageries.

'Nature's world is brazen, the poets only deliver a golden'; under Sidney's spell, it might be said, Venice is brazen and Belmont golden. Like Penshurst, Belmont is a fit homecoming for poets, music-makers and contemplatives. But it is also well endowed with 'brazen' Venetian ducats. 'Gold' and 'money' are converging and diverging words. For Shakespeare's Timon it is not specifically money that is the 'common whore', but the earth itself through its 'most operant poison', gold. Marlowe was also sensitive to the sameness and the difference; money is a degraded version of gold. Power in Tamburlaine is secured by the sword, in Dr Faustus by knowledge, and

---

[15] See ch. 3 below, pp. 72 and 74.
[16] See ch. 3 below, pp. 73–4.

in *The Jew of Malta* by money. It is epitomized in *Tamburlaine* by 'a crown enchased with pearl and gold / Whose virtues carry with it life and death', in *Faustus* by 'a world of profit and delight', and in *The Jew*, initially by a 'costly stone' to 'ransome great kings from captivity' but, after 'policy' has done its worst, by money-bags ('Three hundred crowns, and then five hundred crowns') that 'shag-rag knaves' steal from one another. At Belmont the 'gold' that symbolizes a rich life and the 'money' that affords a vain one are perplexingly intermeshed. The Prince of Morocco muses upon an English 'coin that bears the figure of an angel / Stamp'd in gold' and thinks of Portia's image in the casket as 'an angel in a golden bed'. His is 'a golden mind' that stoops not to shows of dross', and Shakespeare casts him in the mould of Tamburlaine (II. i. 24–31).[17] While Morocco is proud of his breeding, Arragon is vain about his deserts and makes the meritocrat's choice of silver (II. ix. 36–51). Bassanio, because he chooses the lead, hears the usury of love translated back into the usury of the Rialto ('Double six thousand and then treble that') but still in the service of the affections.

Portia in the play's last acts shows that magnanimity and munificence, managed with hypocritical skill (disguise and court-tactics) can salvage lives and relationships in a city trapped by its own adventurous rapacity. Shakespeare has confidence enough in his city civilization to keep up his assured delight in romantic comedy. The play, like Jesus's story, provokes bewildered reactions from performers and audiences who don't know how to divide their ethical sympathies, but both relate to a familiar condition of life which both do much to clarify. We cannot serve God and Mammon but we are under a dual obligation to come to terms with contending modes of value. Like Portia and Bassanio we must learn to play the cards of virtue.

When we reach it from *The Merchant of Venice*, *Timon of Athens* looks like the play that waits for us when comic resources fail or when Portia runs out of money. There is no villa outside Athens and its forest is quite without the pastoral solace that Arden offers the exiled Duke and the railler Jacques in *As You Like It*. If there were a comic solution to the plight of the city – a happy ending – Shakespeare would have had to find it either in the Senators' embassage to Timon or in Alcibiades' coup. As it is, Athens survives on terms that are expedient and historically probable enough but do not meet either our comic or our tragic expectations.

There are, however, other ways of looking at it as we turn towards *Timon* from other tragedies and tragic heroes. After *King Lear* we may be very conscious of the connections established in both plays between rage and love and property, and the exposure of pomp to what wretches feel. Yet many have seen Timon's rage not as a *saeva indignatio* bred from what

[17]See ch. 11 below, p. 202.

Lucian's Mercury calls his 'bounty, humanity and compassion', but as a further manifestation of his 'foolish habits and small judgement of men'. In his rejection of a corrupt and usurious society, says L. C. Knights, 'There is something excessive in the *terms* . . . something strange, even tedious.'[18] Where Coleridge sees the play as 'an after-vibration of *King Lear*', Knights supposes it earlier; its hero (who 'hath ever but slenderly known himself') is 'deeply flawed' and 'there is nothing in his mind that corresponds to Lear's gropings towards self-knowledge.'

Timon's invectives by this account expose us to his 'primitive rage at the destruction of an ego-ideal'. But (as the quotation from Regan may remind us) Shakespeare's tragedies, including others derived like *Timon* from Plutarch, are highly equivocal in their treatment of prudential courses, shadowing Blake's infernal proverb – 'The road of excess leads to the palace of wisdom', and 'if the fool would persist in his folly he would become wise.' Those of us who find Hamlet, Lear, Antony, Coriolanus and Timon foolish or *fol*, may well find maturity in Claudius, prudence in Goneril and Regan, poise and sanity in Octavius Caesar, wisdom in Menenius and discretion in Timon's indebted creditors. Shakespeare's theatre courts such responses; but we are not meant to make them comfortably, but rather to be surprised into discovering our own duplicities in those of character and language.

While it offers 'the most Aristotelian of Shakespeare's plots' and compels us to endorse Apemantus's observation,[19] 'The middle of humanity thou never knewest, but the extremity of both ends,' the play reaches beyond its scope as parable, moral fable, masque or satire, and works through the art of the poet towards the kind of tragic *catastrophe* that demands extreme responses from its hero. The poet's art may be seen at its most distinctive in what Kermode calls the 'strangely perverted anacreontics' of Timon's address to the thieves:

> I'll example you with thievery:
> The sun's a thief, and with his great attraction
> Robs the vast sea; the moon's an arrant thief,
> And her pale fire she snatches from the sun;
> The sea's a thief, whose liquid surge
> Resolves the moon into salt tears; the earth's a thief

---

[18] L. C. Knights, 'Timon of Athens', in *The Morality of Art: Essays Presented to G. Wilson Knight by his Colleagues and Friends*, ed. D. W. Jefferson (1969), p. 8.

[19] M. C. Bradbrook observes that the name Apemantus means 'feeling no pain' (*Shakespeare the Craftsman*, p. 157). Whether Shakespeare exploits the name or not, he sees to it that the cynical Apemantus enjoys the minimal comforts – he puts his shirt on warm.

That feeds and breeds from a composture stol'n
From gen'ral excrement; each thing's a thief.
(IV. iii. 435–42)

'Shakespeare,' says L. C. Knights, 'expected his audience to recognize a
bad argument when they heard one . . . Timon, in becoming nastier, has
become sillier.' But while we may protest, in defence of a more reassuring
version of the natural order, the poet makes searching demands on our
attention as he creates a metaphoric interface between Timon's ideological
condition and his changed perception of the cosmos. Much of the awed
delight he once felt is reinvoked: 'great attraction . . . vast sea . . . pale
fire . . . whose liquid surge resolves the moon into salt tears', but it is
broken in upon by 'thief', 'robs', 'arrant' and 'snatches' – each word poised
to do maximum damage. The narcissistic rage is transposed into that 'spirit
of music' from which, Nietzsche tells us, tragedy is born. 'How came the
noble Timon to this change?' Alcibiades asks, and Timon answers with a
candid version of the same lunar figure:

As the moon does, by wanting light to give:
But then renew I could not, like the moon;
There were no suns to borrow of.
(IV. III. 68–70)

The metaphor is first activated by the poet watching the flowing tide of
Timon's attendants in the first scene:

You see this confluence, this great flood of visitors.
I have in this rough work, shap'd out a man
Whom this beneath world doth embrace and hug
With amplest entertainment. My free drift
Halts not particularly but moves itself
In a wide sea of wax.
(I. i. 42–7)

The cadences of the fallen state of the sublunar 'beneath world' are already
sounding. Moving in its wide sea of wax Shakespeare's free drift prepares
an harmonic ground for the fallen Timon's dual indictment of the solar
universe and the City of Athens:

O blessed breeding sun, draw from the earth
Rotten humidity; below thy sister's orb
Infect the air! Twinn'd brothers of one womb,
Whose procreation, residence and birth
Scarce is dividant, touch them with several fortunes,
The greater scorns the lesser. Not nature
(To whom all sores lay siege) can bear great fortune

But by contempt of nature.
Raise me this beggar, and deny't that lord,
The senator shall bear contempt hereditary,
The beggar native honour.
It is the pasture lards the brother's sides,
The want that makes him lean.

(IV. iii. 1–13)

Again, verbal outrages are inflicted upon visionary principles; here by 'Rotten' and 'Infect' upon plenitude and fecundity. But they are not merely verbal. The rebound of 'rotten' from 'humidity' to 'breeding' has reverberations in Shakespeare's plays as a whole, in his larger harmonies of 'great creating nature' (*Winter's Tale*, IV. iv. 88); compare Hamlet's 'if the sun breed maggots in a dead dog' (II. ii. 181), for example, or Lucio's 'teeming foison' (*Measure for Measure*, I. iv. 43). Timon's rage, like Lear's ('dry up in her the organs of increase'), recoils upon the genesis of life itself, but his argument as it passes to the breeding of children and the distribution of inherited wealth finds its vindication in the 'natural' state of the world – of the *polis*, of the solar order in general and (here) of the agricultural economy in particular.[20] In a natural world vulnerable to all diseases (we may remember 'the fatness of these pursy times' (*Hamlet*, III. iv. 153) human nature can't carry the privileges of fortune and great wealth without contempt for others. Timon is telling us in the plainest terms why it is only natural for the lords of Athens (and of any moneyed city) to behave so unnaturally. But Shakespeare discreetly insists on giving the routine offences a biblical analogue; the damage done to communal values is expressed (as in *Macbeth*) by the desecration of the communal and communion feast. The feast for Timon is a festive and symbolic occasion for him to display his hubristic munificence. His ego-ideal aspires to be self-transcending and self-effacing ('Near? why then another time I'll hear thee', I. ii. 178), but Shakespeare's ironical theatre exposes its vanity, its failure to observe human limitations. In the initial readiness of Ventidius to honour his obligations and repay the talents that freed him from prison we glimpse the possibility of humane and equitable exchange of wealth and courtesy, but corrupted by Timon's rich faults (I. ii. 10–14), when he is touched he is found to be 'base metal' (III. iii. 6). The feast is parasitic and not an act of fellowship. 'They shall not drink wine with a song,' says Isaiah as he watches the collapse of the 'joyous city' (23: 7) into the 'city of confusion' (24: 10). Apemantus, the seer at Timon's board, does what

---

[20] The Folio reading 'brother' (IV. iii. 12) conceals the 'rother' which Singer and other editors have preferred; some follow Warburton's 'wether' (compare *As You Like It* (III. ii. 26), 'good pasture makes fat sheep.' The Folio covertly conjoins fat brother and fat beast.

he can to spoil the party, and while not specifically alluding to the last supper, he makes its treachery commonplace in the hospitalities of the society:

> O you gods! what a number of men eats Timon, and he sees 'em
> not! It grieves me to see so many dip their meat in one man's
> blood, and all the madness is, he cheers them up too. I wonder
> men dare trust themselves with men.
> Methinks they should invite them without knives:
> Good for their meat and safer for their lives.
> There's much example for it: the fellow that sits next him, now
> parts bread with him, pledges the breath of him in a divided draft,
> is the readiest man to kill him; 't' as been prov'd. If I were a huge
> man, I should fear to drink at meals.
>
> (I. ii. 38–50)

When the 'huge man' Timon is 'shrunk' and Servilius is asked to redeem his credit, Shakespeare uses the First Stranger to recall us again to the Betrayal ('Who can call him / His friend that dips in the same dish?' III. ii. 65–6). 'The treacherous dealers,' as Isaiah (24: 16) says, 'have dealt treacherously.'

In the comedy of the play men of high credit can hold their liquor in a one-way consumption of life-resource:

> Let it flow this way, my good lord.
> *Apemantus* Flow this way? A brave fellow! he keeps his tides well.
>
> (I. ii. 54–6)

But the tide of wine and blood contributes to the more covert and tragic metaphor of a tide of life flowing, ebbing away, and again returning in grief and compassion. The sources all tell of Timon's choice of death by the sea's edge, in a final repudiation of humanity, and Shakespeare contrives from the report a cleansing tide that leaves all traces of life erased.

Flavius, who as steward has grieved at Timon's 'flow of riot' and found the wine left running from 'a wasteful cock' that set his 'eyes at flow' (II. ii. 163), keeps a reckoning of confluent wine, blood, tears and money:

> when I have
> Prompted you in the ebb of your estate
> And your great flow of debts.
> (II. ii. 140–2)

'Their blood is cak'd,' says Timon of the ageing lords,' 'tis cold, it seldom flows' (III. i. 213–15), and, when talents are demanded, he asks that they 'Tell out my blood' (III. iv. 93–4).

Attending in one way to the play's verbal structure, these words hark back to the Poet's allusion to those who deify Timon and 'Rain sacrificial whisperings in his ear' (I. i. 81). The actor who plays Timon must carry both the human comedy (the good-natured spendthrift who makes a fool of himself) and the tragedy, demanding a sacrificial figure to atone for the society's moral distress. He is stretched between his manifest inadequacy and his formidable insight, his silliness and his prophetic fury. Yet he must remain at the centre of the Golden City's masquerade of folly, hypocrisy and flattery.[21]

Playing a 'character' the actor (including perhaps the actor Shakespeare) looks for an intimate and personal continuity in his role. Since the play does not provide one there is a temptation to supply it by postulating a covert trauma. Timon's sexual nausea ('Maid to thy master's bed, / Thy mistress is in the brothel', IV. i. 12–13) is given no history resembling those in *Othello* or *Hamlet*. But the play demonstrates Timon's complicity in the polite harlotry of Athens when for three talents he buys for his servant the 'love' of a richly endowed bride; 'His honesty rewards him in itself,' says the Old Athenian, 'It must not bear my daughter' (I. i. 130–1). Feast and masque are ceremonies of Athenian love:

> [*The Lords rise from table, with much adoring of Timon, and, to show their loves, each single out an Amazon, and all dance, men with women, a lofty strain or two to the hoboys, and cease.*]
>
> (I. ii. 145, stage directions)

Timon outside the city walls would see the event with Apemantus's eyes ('the worst is filthy and would not hold taking'), and there is no need for a specific, as distinct from a representative, occasion for his revulsion. But the wounded ego visibly aspires to an impersonal wrath whose truth cannot be evaded by diagnosis of a narcissistic wound. Shakespeare, by retrospectively finding biblical co-ordinates for Timon's rhetoric, leaves it active in his own time, and proleptically alive in a tradition of thought promoted by (among others) that nineteenth-century prophet Marx.

In the Brecht and Weigel adaptation of *Coriolanus* Volumnia leads a people's army to meet the threat to the city. A similar Brechtian version of *Timon* might have the hero return to Athens with Alcibiades to liberate the populace from their oppressors. But Shakespeare's play shows no confidence in that prospect. The military *coup d'état* will not in fact change the Athens that Timon has lived through and seen through. Both the soldiery and their general are compromised by the city's values as well as being victims of its hypocrisies. Alcibiades himself has need of Timon's gold and man cannot escape from the corrupting values he himself creates. The play, however,

---

[21] For the central place of hypocrisy and flattery in the theatre of city life, see Erasmus, *In Praise of Folly*, ch. 4.

finds other ways of coming to terms with money and property.

Through the continuing flux of the metaphors Timon's death prefigures the last plays – not the pastoral dying-into-life of *The Winter's Tale* but the marine dissolutions of *The Tempest*, first expressed by Flavius upon the wreck of the household:

> And we, poor mates, stand on the dying deck,
> Hearing the surges threat; we must all part
> Into this sea of air.
>
> (IV. ii. 20–2)

The image, strangely transmuting death by drowning into aerial liberation, allows the community of servants a human validity ('Rich in sorrow, parting poor') denied to the city of their masters where the exemplar of the highest virtue, 'undone by goodness', is 'blest to be most accurs't'. In the wide perspective of Shakespeare's art this way of putting it recalls the *Henry VI* plays in which the ambiguous and culpable innocence of 'Holy Harry' has disastrous consequences for the commonwealth while retaining a kind of moral ascendancy over the hypocrites who know how to flourish in it. Just as the Christian virtues cannot be practised in uncompromising form in the England of Cardinal Beaufort, Queen Margaret and the Duke of Gloucester, so the Aristotelian ones cannot be practised in their purity in a city whose hierarchy of values is totally dependent on money. Working as seer or *vates*, the poet of *Timon* dislodges the serenely ascending structure of authority and musical order that was transiently and conditionally offered to the lords of Ulysses' Greece (and Shakespeare's London) in the celebrated 'degree speech':

> Piety, and fear,
> Religion to the gods, peace, justice, truth,
> Domestic awe, night rest and neighbourhood,
> Instruction, manners, mysteries and trades,
> Degrees, observances, customs and laws,
> Decline to your confounding contraries;
> And yet confusion live!
>
> (IV. i. 15–21)

The rhetors of hierarchical ideology are themselves bought by their moneyed superiors:

> for every grize of fortune
> Is smooth'd by that below. The learned pate
> Ducks to the golden fool.
>
> (IV. iii. 16–18)

'Money is the highest good,' says Marx, still listening to Timon, and assimilating his words into his own mode of thought:

> It raises me above the trouble of being dishonourable, for I seem
> to be honourable. I may be unintelligent; but since money is the
> real mind of things, how should its owner be unintelligent? And,
> besides, he can buy intelligent people; and is not he who has power
> over the intelligent more intelligent than they?[22]

These are perhaps open secrets for Bassanio, but truths that can be limited
in his Venice are felt to be overwhelming in Timon's Athens. Again, as
Marx puts it, 'Since money does not disclose what has been transformed
into it, everything, whether a commodity or not, is convertible into gold.'
Marx, however, grows excited at a discovery and apocalyptic prospect that
the play does not unequivocally offer:

> In place of all physical and intellectual senses there has been
> substituted the self-alienation of all of them – the sense of possession.
> Man's essence had to be reduced to this, its absolute poverty, so
> that it could be allowed to bring forth its inner wealth. The
> abolition of private property is therefore necessary to the freeing
> of all the senses and attributes of man.[23]

Seen from this direction the play yields another extravagant paradox.
Timon's absolute dedication to the virtue that Aristotle predicates about
great wealth is sustained by egalitarian and communist sentiment: 'O, what
a precious comfort 'tis to have so many like brothers commanding one
another's fortunes!' (I. ii. 103–4) where the 'many', as in the case of
Lucilius, appears to extend from masters to servants. Isaiah's wish that the
god-fearing men of Tyre should 'eat sufficiently' finds an ironical analogue
in Timon's grace, 'Lend to each man enough, that one need not lend to
another; for were your godheads to borrow of men, men would forsake the
gods' (III. vi. 73–5).

While the tragic playwright characteristically takes into account the
continuing life of the society, however, he focuses it on the mortality of
the tragic hero. The sources bring the story to an end where it often begins,
in a choice of epitaphs that offer only the misanthrope's resolution. In the
play a poignant symbol is found not so much in the gravestone's inscription
as in its location:

> Then, Timon, presently prepare thy grave;
> Lie where the light foam of the sea may beat
> Thy grave-stone daily.
>
> (IV. iii. 377–9)

---

[22] Muir, *The Singularity of Shakespeare and Other Essays*, p. 71.
[23] Ibid., p. 74.

The cynical and misanthropic repudiations ('Destruction fang mankind!', 'Consumptions sow / In hollow bones of man'), are transcended by a nihilistic affirmation which enables Shakespeare to prepare Timon's grave in a tradition very different from that represented by the historical Diogenes and the theatre's Apemantus:

> My long sickness
> Of health and living now begins to mend.
> And nothing brings me all things.
> (v. i. 186–8)

The arduous voyages and incarcerations of St Paul are several times recalled in Shakespeare's plays, from the shipwreck of Egeus on the shores of Ephesus in *The Comedy of Errors* to the protracted ordeals of Pericles. In 2 Corinthians 6, Paul brings to a climax the paradoxes by which he would ultimately choose to live and die:

> 9 As unknowen, and yet *knowen*: as dying, and beholde, we live: as chastened, and yet not killed:
> 10 As sorowing, & yet always reioycing: as poore, and yet make manie riche: as having nothing, and yet possessing all things.
> (Geneva version)

Paul may be remembering a version of Jesus's parable of the rich man in Luke 12 ('man's life consisteth not in the abundance of the things which he possesseth'), but Paul's teaching is less accommodating than Jesus's appears to be; and more hospitable to accept those final renunciations of property and life that Timon expresses at the sea's verge.

Jesus's teasingly comic parable of the unjust steward leaves us a way of keeping going in the world. But Paul would have the man of the world 'become a fool, that he may be wise' (1 Corinthians 3: 18) and his Manichean imagery leaves no scope for the children of light to learn from the children of darkness:

> 14 Be not unequally yoked with the infideles: for what felowship hathe righteousnes with unrighteousness? and what communion hath light with darkenes?
> 15 And what concorde hath Christ with Belial? . . .
> 16 And what agreement hathe the Temple of God with idoles? . . .
> 17 Wherefore come out from among them, and separate your selves, saith the Lord: and touch none uncleane thing, & I will receive you.

In the fifth act the play is suspended between the tragic solution focused in the commitment of Timon's separated self to death, the purge proposed by Alcibiades to Timon and the pragmatic solution finally agreed between Alcibiades and the senators. 'If the senators are clearly untrustworthy,' says L. C. Knights, 'Alcibiades does not represent an acceptable norm.' The makeshift hypocrisies, moral stances and compromises of the leaders of Athens, however, are all part of the city comedy and represent the precarious terms on which the city survives. Timon himself plays the game convincingly when in a celebrated rhetorical *hirmus* or 'suspender' he invites the senators to join him at his tree and hang themselves (v. i. 207–12).

> Come not to me again, but say to Athens,
> Timon hath made his everlasting mansion
> Upon the beached verge of the salt flood,
> Who once a day with his embossed froth
> The turbulent surge shall cover; thither come,
> And let my grave-stone by your oracle.
> Lips let four words go by and language end!
>
> (v. i. 214–20)

Alcibiades reads the sea-riddle admirably, not because Shakespeare is treating him as an 'acceptable norm' but because his is the dominant available voice:

> These well express in thee thy latter spirits;
> Though thou abhorr'dst in us our human griefs,
> Scorn'dst our brains' flow, and those our droplets which
> From niggard nature fall, yet rich conceit
> Taught thee to make vast Neptune weep for aye
> On thy low grave, on faults forgiven.
>
> (v. iv. 74–9)

The displacement of hatred by compassion is a mutation understood by Montaigne and Bruegel. 'For looke,' says Montaigne, pursuing his comparison with Diogenes, 'what a man hateth the same thing he takes to hart. *Timon* wisht all evil might light on us; He was passionate in desiring our ruine . . . Whereas the other so little regarded us, that wee could neither trouble nor alter him by our contagion' (I. 50. 418). Bruegel's *Misanthropos* shows a figure hooded in black having his purse snatched by an impudent pick-pocket representing the globe; a Flemish inscription reads, 'I am in mourning for the ingratitude of the world.' Biblical prophecy has its misanthropic analogues too: 'The spiritual man is made, for the multitude of thine iniquity, and the great hatred,' says Hosea, about an Israel whose festivals of bread and wine have been polluted (9: 7). 'Give them a miscarrying womb and dry breasts.' (9: 14).

The death of Timon, sometimes thought inexplicable and therefore a sign of the copy's unfinished state, is perfectly consistent with the design and movement of the play. Schopenhauer might have said of it what he says less aptly of other tragic deaths: the hero surrenders the will to live.[24] Having seen through the state of Athens and of 'the world as will and idea', he lets them go. Playing the part in Ron Daniels's Royal Shakespeare Company production in 1980, Richard Pasco, while speaking his last 'four words', pulled a fishing net across his body and face, becoming indistinguishable from the jetsam at the sea's edge, and giving an unintended further point to the Senator's comment, 'His discontents are unremoveably / Coupled to nature' (v. i. 224–5).

Timon in the last two acts is no longer looking for a way to live, only for a way to die. But the experience of the spectator is more comprehensive, and his understanding more objective, than that of the tragic hero. Shakespeare knew that at the end of the play few would be left dead in their seats; the rest would return to Athens, that is to say, to the cash nexus of London, and to a world which continues to respond to Alcibiades' final pragmatic proclamation:

> Make war breed peace, make peace stint war, make each
> Prescribe to other, as each other's leech.

Within the distinctly unfestive boundaries of Alcibiades' state, the children of light and the 'learned pates', children of Holofernes, must, it seems, do what they can to learn from the children of this world, and keep a place at their tables. Those, like William Perkins, who defended their privileges from Luke 16 with an appeal to 'natural law', are free to make a similar appeal outside the play; but within the mood of the theatre, readers of Erasmus's *In Praise of Folly* will, like Alcibiades, recognize that the show must go on.

---

[24] See ch. 3 below, p. 66. A complete Schopenhauerian analysis of the topic would try to establish the connections between death and other modes of transcendence of 'the world as will' by 'the world as idea [*Vorstellung*]'; Belmont and Coole Park ('Dreams! mere dreams!') could be represented as such modes, but 'Fortune's hill' is not a sustaining idea of value to Timon in the last act.

2   Troilus and Cressida: Character and Value 1200 BC to AD 1985

'The poor world is almost six thousand years old, and in all this time there was not any man died in his own person, *videlicet*, in a love-cause. Troilus had his brains dashed out with a Grecian club, yet he did what he could to die before, and he is one of the patterns of love' (*As You Like It*, IV. i. 94–9). Rosalind would have been less startled by the play *Troilus and Cressida* than Lorenzo in *The Merchant of Venice*, who has a lyrical memory of the lovers:

> In such a night
> Troilus methinks mounted the Troyan walls,
> And sighed his soul toward the Grecian tents,
> Where Cressid lay that night.
>
> (v. i. 4–7)

Shakespeare's mature art may be said to have it both ways. In writing *Troilus and Cressida* Shakespeare was not only re-creating the love story with some sighing for the soul but, like Sir Walter Ralegh, attending to the six thousand-year history of the world, which tells of much dashing out of brains.

In the current cant-phrase, the play is 'culture-specific'. Shakespeare was addressing himself urgently to audiences of his time including, it seems

This is a much expanded version of ' "A Kind of Self": Creation of Character in Shakespeare', *En Torno a Shakespeare III*, Fundación Instituto Shakespeare, Madrid, 1987.

probable on one festive occasion, an audience at the Inns of Court.[1] We have reason to remember that it was made under a monarchy that often depended on its advisers in council, and continued to be exposed to threats from overseas and from recalcitrants at home. We may recall too (though the play does not prompt us) that chronicle tradition represented London as Troynavaunt in a Britain revealed to Aeneas in a dream.[2] Spectators to *Henry V* at the Globe, some three seasons earlier, might well have left the theatre moved by the pathos of battle but excited by ideas of heroic leadership and in a mood to accept the Chorus's invitation to welcome the return of Essex from Ireland. The audience of *Troilus and Cressida* would be much more likely to keep its distance, and indeed to treat sceptically all human pretensions to more than ordinary powers and perceptions, including those that make kings and heroes.

But what is culture-specific is not necessarily culture-circumscribed. Shakespeare makes an immense imaginative effort to re-enact the experience and understanding of the remote past, and to bring it live into the present. It is an endeavour of art that we repeat whenever we read or perform the play, and it contributes to our own capacity for freeing ourselves, however provisionally, from those routines of thought and value to which our social co-ordinates would confine us.

'What is aught but as 'tis valued?' *Troilus and Cressida* engages directly with a question that haunts other plays (and other lives), only to leave it suspended upon a distressing and de-stabilizing paradox:

> O madness of discourse,
> That cause sets up with and against itself!
> Bifold authority, where reason can revolt
> Without perdition, and loss assume all reason
> Without revolt! This is, and is not, Cressid.
> (v. ii. 142–6)

The words mark a critical moment in Shakespeare's theatre of courtship, relating to the bonds and allegiances men and women create about, or impose upon, one another. But versions of the paradox ('Bifold authority') are equally active in the play's theatres of government and war, and in the course of making connections between its three kinds of theatre it works

---

[1] See W. R. Elton, 'Textual Transmission and Genre of Shakespeare's *Troilus*', in *Literatur als Kritik des Lebens: Festschrift sum 65. Geburtstag von Ludwig Borinski*, ed. Ruldoph Haas, Heinz-Joachim Müllenbrock and Claus Uhlig (Heidelberg). I am also indebted to W. R. Elton, 'Shakespeare's Ulysses and the Problem of Value', *Shakespeare Studies II*, 1966. See also Kenneth Muir's edition, Oxford Shakespeare (1982), pp. 8–9, and Kenneth Palmer's edition, Arden Shakespeare (1982), pp. 307–10.

[2] See discussion of Aeneas's dream in ch. 14.

on our puzzled intellects and confused sympathies, exposing human values and perceptions to searching analysis:

> O let not virtue seek
> Remuneration for the thing it was
> (III. iii. 169–70)

'Remuneration', says Costard, looking at the tip which quantifies the value of his wit and services in Shakespeare's Navarre, is 'the Latin word for three farthings.' The Trojan war story has often provoked reflections on its cause and its cost. In the complex puns of the *Agamemnon* of Aeschylus, for instance, traders on the quayside weigh against coffers of gold dust the urned dust of the returning dead.[3] In the same tradition, Shakespeare's Diomedes weighs Helen's worth:

> For every false drop in her bawdy veins,
> A Grecian's life hath sunk; for every scruple
> Of her contaminated carrion weight,
> A Troyan hath been slain.
> (IV. i. 70–3)

The relationship between market-values and human values, communal and personal, may be grossly and grotesquely disproportionate or tantalizingly close enough to invite delicate calculation and provision. Thus the Clown in Shakespeare's Bohemia can take a more auspicious measure of the cost of festival:

> I cannot do't without compters. Let me see: what am I to buy for our sheep-shearing feast? Three pound of sugar, five pounds of currants, rice – what will this sister of mine do with rice? But my father hath made her mistress of the feast, and she lays it on. She hath made me four and twenty nosegays for the shearers . . .
> (*Winter's Tale*, IV. iii. 36–41)

In *Troilus and Cressida*, however, we can do without counters. The 'remuneration' of which Ulysses speaks to Achilles has nothing to do with money. Shakespeare will treat of gold, usury, credit and honour in *Timon of Athens*, where the warrior leader Alcibiades challenges the corrupt men of the city, but the focus in the earlier play is on the reputation and acclaim of its several heroes.

'Value,' says Shakespeare's Hector, 'dwells not in particular will, / It holds his estimate and dignity / As well wherein 'tis precious of itself / As in the prizer' (II. ii. 53–6). The play is much concerned with the 'particular will' as the 'prizer' or 'appraiser'. In the current, popular sense it is about

---

[3] See below, p. 188.

'characters' and their contending values. But Shakespeare never used the word 'character' to signify the individuated self, and it is a tricky word to use about a play which opens so many questions about the nature of the 'self'. It is a persistent mystery and paradox, sometimes delightful and sometimes tormenting, that our differences from others make us both individuals and eccentrics; alienation from community breeds idiocy. Civilized conformities require us to satisfy the same citizen paradigms and cultivate the same virtues. But if we do only that we fail in responsibility to our individuated self. The old character-writers know that 'characteristics' detach us from society and expose us to its critical gaze; which is true, but not true enough, for our very characteristics are owed to our peculiar social roles (as cooks, schoolmasters, kings or concubines).

We know that community paradigms are not indivisible; they are multiple, and they are interrelated in constantly changing ways. Characters are not merely distinguished by their functions but by the contribution they make to the plenitude and variety of the human world. Nor are they merely self-created; they are responses to the pressures of expectation that society puts upon them, and these expectations are themselves cultivated and clarified by those in the civilization who assume responsibility for inventing, delineating and rendering 'characters'; playwrights, poets, essayists, novelists and actors. The joy of creation and the delight in plenitude are at odds with the more austere demands of our communal selves, requiring civil, political, social and ethical conformities. Thus it happens that, whatever focus they may provide for our reflective moral indignation, Falstaff, Sir Epicure Mammon, Thersites and Achilles are primarily celebrations of our shared human condition.

To a greater extent than any other Shakespearian play, *Troilus and Cressida* scrutinizes the ideological, philosophical and metaphysical fields from which characters and their values are generated, and it invites fresh thought about the relationship between our private and public selves. The etymological sense of 'scrutiny', says the *OED*, sceptically, is 'to search even to rags'. But 'character' and 'values' are interdependent, our perceptions depend on what we are, and the play not only excites and challenges our abilities to look and search, it makes us more than usually conscious of how treacherous they can be. What we make of the play (and what it makes of us) depends upon our age, on our own characters, and on the play's performance. Our age can be measured as our distance from Homer, from Chaucer or from Shakespeare and the court of King James; or it can find a place on the scale of mortal years between Troilus and Nestor. Our 'characters' (which, the play reminds us, are not co-extensive with our individuality) owe something to our social function, our age, knowledge and disposition, and to our ideological conceit of ourselves.

Any one performance of the play is likely both to illuminate it and to put it in the dark. The job of the critic is to clarify our perceptions, the job of the scholar, to inform them; both need to engage with the performed play and with the unperformed plays left behind, or only glimpsed as latent in the text. The recognition of confluences and displacements of perception remains one of the responsibilities of the academic Shakespearian, but he too is a character and can be assigned his characteristic lineaments. John Earle, writing a dozen years after Shakespeare's death about the Downright Scholar, finds him solipsistic and down-at-heel: one whose 'fault is only this, that his mind is somewhat too much taken up with his mind', and one who 'has been used to a dark room and dark clothes', whose 'eyes dazzle at a satin suit'.[4] Other character-writers of Shakespeare's time are harder on academics if not on Shakespearians. Overbury's Pedant, for example, 'never had meaning in his life, for he travelled onely for words'; 'He values phrases, and elects them by the sound.'[5] Perhaps he is by disposition vulnerable to nominalism and therefore likely to enjoy a play in which values retreat into mere words. Earle's Critic too is on his way to being an active academic Shakespearian: 'a troublesome vexer of the dead' and 'one that makes all books sell dearer, while he swells them into folios with his comments.'

It is in my character of troublesome vexer of the dead that I look back at a court company (of players) performing the work of an actor/playwright before an audience (of individuals), probably on a festive occasion at one of the Inns of Court. As vexer of the living, I shall look at some of the play's distinguished re-creators in the 1985 Stratford season: the play's director, Howard Davies, and a cast that included Peter Jeffrey as Ulysses, Alun Armstrong as Thersites and Juliet Stevenson as Cressida. 'The best of this kind are but shadows', and we are becoming increasingly aware of the transience of the art of theatre and of its dependence upon the occasion. In offering to keep track of the play across a span of more than three thousand years I hope to engage with it in much the spirit of Agamemnon's welcome to Hector, moving between 'oblivion' and 'this extant moment'. The first phase of my account has to do with Shakespeare's prefatory treatment of war, love, time and value as they reach him in the stories told by Homer and Chaucer, and with the setting-up of Ulysses' plot or play. The second phase follows the art and tactics of Juliet Stevenson's performance of Cressida through what I take to be the tragic movement of the play, and it represents Cressida's mutability as one expression among others of the mutability of the world. The third treats Thersites and his vision in relation to Alun Armstrong's acting of the part.

---

[4] John Earle, *Micro-cosmographie*. I quote from the edition of 1633 (1904). Passages can be found under the name of the character.

[5] Thomas Overbury, *Characters*, ed. W. J. Taylor (Oxford, 1936).

Thersites' perception of the play's events is the most coherent. It might be called the satiric, comic, cynic, demotic or material view; and distinguished from the lyric, tragic, urbane, courtly or idealist views projected in the play. But that is emergent blackboard thought, what Blake called 'confident insolence springing from systematic reasoning'; it is not poetic and theatrical thought, which is the kind needed to keep in touch with the playwright's art.

Since 1985 I have visited theatres in East Berlin and in China, and new images swim into the mind's eye – of an actual production by the Berliner Ensemble in Brecht's old theatre, and of an imaginary performance at the Peking Empress's Summer Palace in the early seventeenth century: the one demotic, the other courtly. The Wekwerth/Tentschert production at the Berliner Ensemble did indeed 'search even to rags'.[6] There were some who saw it as an anti-war production, and perhaps that was intended by some of its promoters. But, as in the *Caucasian Chalk Circle* and *Mother Courage*, war seemed like an inescapable condition of life – like mortality itself. We were made more conscious of the dust of war than of its blood. The Greek commanders looked like monumental ancient vultures on whom centuries of volcanic ash had settled; their virtue was an almost-exhausted residual power of endurance, and their rhetoric expressed as much commitment to 'the hell of pain and world of charge' as attachment to 'insisture, course, proportion, season, form'. The war had no beginning and no prospect of ending, its warriors had aged to the point where Nestor had to be given a mask to make his antiquity a part of the spectacle. Achilles and Hector might have been in their late fifties, but they were skilled in the routine tricks of combat. When Hector does battle with a startlingly young Ajax who charges down on him with an affectation of heroic frenzy, he trips him as Kent does Oswald (the base football-player) in *King Lear*, and Achilles' slaughter of Hector seems grimly of a piece with what has gone before. There was no sense of betrayal of an heroic and chivalrous tradition, for of that there were no glimpses. Greeks and Trojans are caught in the same trap. Just as the Greeks steel themselves for the prospect of each thing meeting in mere oppugnancy, so the Trojans, stopped in their tracks by Cassandra's apocalyptic vision of total destruction, pull themselves together to carry on as before. Troilus and Cressida themselves, however, were of a different generation and committed to a different style; they were capable of lyrical language and might have been (had the wardrobe afforded it) graceful and accomplished courtiers. It was clear that as actors too they were comparative newcomers to Brecht's theatre; they engaged our sympathies, awakened some sense of lost human potentials. But the dominant

---

[6] Berliner Ensemble, 1985; directed by Manfred Wekwerth and Joachim Tenschert; German trans. by Wekwerth.

figure of the performance was Thersites, looking very much a survivor from Caucasian wars, and fit to stand up against Agamemnon and Ulysses as an intellectual and moral force, and indeed (if you put him to it) probably as a warrior. It was not that he lacked strength, but that he disdained to use it. As an actor he had the richest voice, the most commanding movements, and the readiest rapport with the audience.

But what, we may ask when all that dust has settled, became of the Angels? Aeneas's Trojans – 'Courtiers as free, as debonair, unarmed, as bending angels', and Troilus' 'Grecian youths', 'full of quality' and 'composed with gifts of nature'? They were not to be found in Howard Davies's production, or even in the distinctly more courtly Peter Hall and John Barton version at Stratford in 1960.

I would like to believe, merely from the evidence of the text, that the first performances belonged at once to the courtly and popular traditions of theatre, very rich in ceremony and style, but never ceasing to be in touch with common human feelings and dispositions. In my imagined production, glimpsed in recent but archaic Shakespeare productions in China,[7] the audience would enjoy a prospect of brutes and of angels, and the theatrical excitement would flourish in the dual traditions of festival. For festivals are both celebrations of life and acquiescences in death; they are simultaneously committed to everything that sustains life and to everything that carries it away.

Not that *Troilus and Cressida* is conspicuously festive in the commonly accepted sense. Shakespeare uses the Prologue to mediate between the epic source material and 'what might be digested in a play'. But it does not announce itself as an epic play, celebrating the community's feats of war. The voice of the Prologue Armed, unlike the Chorus to *Henry V*, is not the herald of an heroic theatre seeking in any sense to transport its audience. It is at once timeless, articulating the annals of the society, and time-afflicted, expressing the moods of a soldier caught up in 'broils' that seem to have no beginning, no end, and very little point. It oscillates between commemorative, resonant speech ('To Tenedos they come'), and sardonic bathos ('the ravished Helen sleeps', 'And that's the quarrel'), exposing the past to the critical wit of sophisticated onlookers. The epic narrator's time, moreover, differs from the playwright's, and the warrior's time from the lover's. Shakespeare displays and explores the differences in the scenes that follow. The first opens out into the lovers' time and Chaucer's, requiring leisure enough to 'tarry the grinding' at the pace of Pandar's conversation. But both modes of time are vehicles of tedium and frustration; the plight of the lover expresses the exhaustion of the values and causes that sustain

---

[7] I give some account of the Shakespeare Festival of China in *Shakespeare Quarterly*, Summer 1988.

the war.

In the desolate opening prospects of the comedy the possibility that the service of Venus can re-dedicate Troilus to the service of Mars is sceptically treated. Both Howard Davies and the Berliner Ensemble found material for a reductive presentation of elite warrior groups in a futile imperial conflict. A Renaissance ideal of human value finds pat expression in Pandarus's questions, teased away by Cressida: 'Do you know what a man is? Is not birth, beauty, good shape, discourse, manhood, learning, gentleness, virtue, youth, liberality, and such like, the spice and salt that season a man?' The war provides a sporting theatre for those who climb the eastern tower to see more of the game. But Shakespeare endows both the participant Troilus and the spectator Cressida with a resisting sophistication that looks for a response from the theatre audience.

> Fools on both sides: Helen must needs be fair,
> When with your blood you daily paint her thus.
> I cannot fight upon this argument:
> It is too starved a subject for my sword.
> (I. i. 90–3)

Cressida is only marginally more stirred by military vanity and panache than Beatrice was in *Much Ado* when Signior Montanto returned from the wars, and far less moved by Trojan chivalry than Desdemona will be by tales of Othello's prowess. There is scope nevertheless for the flowering of affections already dedicated to Troilus ('my heart's content firm love doth bear' (I. ii. 280). Troilus expresses a soldier's exasperation and a lover's importunity, Cressida, a lover's elusiveness (playing hard to get). But their divided selves are generated in a profoundly divided world whose action and acting will breed split versions also of Ulysses, Hector and Achilles. In its theatres of war, government and courtship the play offers high and exquisite human values together with their gross desecration; and its modes of language span the most intimate to the most abstract and remote.

In the debating scene (I. iii) Shakespeare engages with Homer, but continues to disappoint expectations awakened by the Prologue of hazards undertaken by skittish spirits. He puts immense pressure on the language in order to create what might be called the impersonal characters of the Greek leaders:

> The ample proposition that hope makes
> In all designs begun on earth below
> Fails in the promised largeness. Checks and disasters
> Grow in the vein of actions highest reared,
> As knots, by the conflux of meeting sap,

Infects the sound pine and diverts his grain,
Tortive and errant, from his course of growth.
                                              (I. iii. 2–8)

The tortive and errant laws of history and nature seem to be at work in
Agamemnon's vocabulary and syntax, making it difficult to express any
values other than those of a pessimistic stoicism that finds virtue only in
the 'persistive constancy' of men. The pessimism owes its keenness, however,
to the deflection or frustration of high designs for which he is responsible:

Sith every action that hath gone before,
Whereof we have record, trial did draw
Bias and athwart, not answering the aim,
And that unbodied figure of the thought
That gave't surmisèd shape.
                                              (I. iii. 13–17)

Like the other Greek leaders, Agamemnon stands on a dignity which seeks
to embody the 'unbodied figure of the thought'. In the comedy of the play
the effect is absurd (as Aeneas reminds us when he tries to distinguish
Agamemnon from other mortals), but in the heroical history it has its
poignancy and is of a piece with effects of disappointed aspiration in the
play's love story.

The scene is so designed that it articulates the 'ample proposition' and
initiates yet another stage in the process of its betrayal – the failure of the
'promised largeness'. In Nestor's version of Stoic virtue, 'In the reproof of
chance lies the true proof of men', Shakespeare gives ethical, historical and
dramatic weight to the Prologue's dismissive and casual ''Tis but the chance
of war.' Higher possibilities are entertained in Ulysses' celebrated degree
speech, but Shakespeare seems to have been very active as poet and
playwright when he insinuated into the Folio version of the text the lines
with which Agamemnon introduces it:

Speak, Prince of Ithaca; and be't of less expect
That matter needless, or of importless burden,
Divide thy lips than we are confident,
When rank Thersites opes his mastic jaws,
We shall hear music, wit, and oracle.
                                              (I. iii. 69–74)

The playwright is active in creating both the dignity and the absurdity of
the high rhetorical occasion, in demanding special attention to what follows,
and in giving the actor an opportunity to play the game of class solidarity
and mutual self-glorification. Poet and playwright work together in drawing
attention to and ironically raising expectations about another voice – that
of the absent Thersites.

The distinction between the visions of Ulysses and Thersites can be expressed in either political or theatrical terms, and it concerns the kind of 'gathering' to which the actor of each role addresses himself, both on the stage and in the theatre audience – gatherings in which we catch each other's eyes and know what we are all feeling. The Greek council scene creates the one gathering and prepares us for the other. 'Thy godlike seat', 'great commander, nerve and bone of Greece' – hyperbolic decorum of address and rhetoric bring the scene close to the styles of the Elizabethan parliament and to the tenor of the *Homilies against Wilful Rebellion*. Powerful demands are made on the answering sympathies of the theatre audience.

These are the 'high designs' (all affording matter to lawyers):

> communities,
> Degrees in schools, and brotherhoods in cities,
> Peaceful commerce form dividable shores,
> The primogenity and due of birth,
> Prerogative of age, crowns, sceptres, laurels.
> (I. iii. 103–7)

And they are the values, depending upon the 'speciality of rule' (which might now be called 'the right to manage') which many hope to find vindicated in the play. But 'the enterprise is sick' and the history of the sickness can be traced not only through the past of the Trojan wars and through the play's acts to come, but also through Shakespeare's earlier and later plays. The failure of earthly designs confronted by Agamemnon will be repeated in the unfolding history of Ulysses' manipulative plots, and both answer to Troilus' account of the lover's experience: 'The will is infinite, the execution confined, / The desire boundless, the act a slave to limit.' The mind renews but the blood decays. Ulysses speaks from a renewing mind to a privileged audience on stage and off, with prerogatives of age, sceptres and laurels, and he proclaims principles of obedience to law which at their highest require the planets to observe their laws of motion and at their most routine require the Greeks to do as they are told. Given the chance, the apt audiences continue to respond.

But, moving from the cosmic to the comic truths, Shakespeare has Ulysses tell of another performance before a smaller audience:

> The great Achilles, whom opinion crowns
> The sinew and the forehand of our host,
> Having his ear full of his airy fame,
> Grows dainty of his worth, and in his tent
> Lies mocking our designs. With him Patroclus
> Upon a lazy bed the livelong day
> Breaks scurril jests,

And with ridiculous and awkward action,
Which, slanderer, he imitation calls,
He pageants us.

(I. iii. 142–51)

We do not see Patroclus's histrionic performances and it may be that
Shakespeare changed his mind when, in III. iii, for example, he made
Thersites and not Patroclus the skilled mimic and therefore the more
probable target for Ulysses' rage against the players:

> like a strutting player, whose conceit
> Lies in his hamstring, and doth think it rich
> To hear the wooden dialogue and sound
> 'Twixt his stretch'd footing and the scaffolage.

(I. iii. 153–6)

Shakespeare is playing a meta-theatrical game, as we all know that the
Ulysses before our eyes is himself a strutting player, and that he is himself
the re-creator of Agamemnon's 'topless deputation' as well as its travesty.
Suspended between these rival audience responses, we are engaged by
poised and contrary truths, demanding different kinds of attention and yet
converging at the end of the play in a unity of impression and experience
that is not readily translated into systematic thought. We are not invited,
for example, to look for the mediating way of good sense which Hector's
'young men, whom Aristotle thought unfit to hear moral philosophy' were
incapable of finding, and which Bullough and Muir (perhaps true to their
characters as scholars) resolutely seek. Muir himself recognizes a crucial
difficulty at the centre of the degree speech,[8] when he pauses on the lines:

> Force should be right; or rather, right and wrong,
> Between whose endless jar justice recides
> Should lose their names, and so should justice too.

(I. iii. 116–18)

He follows Dobrée in retaining the Q and F spelling *recides* and explains
it as a coinage from the Latin *recadere*, to fall down. Otherwise justice
'resides' paradoxically between right and wrong. Young men who have read
Aristotle, however, will know from the *Nicomachean Ethics* that we must
cultivate a middle state between excess and defect, while erring on the right
side, and will pick up similar signals when Troilus in the last acts reads
Hector's 'fair play' as 'fool's play'. Lawyers too, as Kenneth Palmer remarks,
would be accustomed to arbitrating between contending parties. The laws
and values of chivalry are also valid for both sides, and therefore 'reside'
between right and wrong. Those acquainted with Platonic and Augustinian

[8] In his 1982 edition, ad loc.

traditions will pick up the musical sense of 'jar' (compare *1 Henry VI*, IV.
i. 188, *2 Henry VI*, II i. 55, *As You Like It*, II. vii. 5) and recognize that
the harmonies of the cosmic and moral orders are composed of discords as
well as concords. Shakespeare is again putting the language under enormous
pressure in his scrutiny – searching to the rags – of a mystery. That pressure
is rather more than Ulysses as a character and performer before his fellow
commanders needs. His main motive is to win agreement on the need to
teach Achilles a disciplinary lesson; he gets his accord, and that strain of
the comedy gets under way.

Where the Greek council is concerned with the conduct of the war, the
Trojan one is concerned with its causes – those that occasioned it and those
that sustain it. The narrative link between the two is not, as one might
have expected, the Greek ultimatum demanding Helen's return, but the
'roistering challenge' that Hector at the end of the scene confesses to issuing,
covertly pre-empting the debate. Where the Greek scene finds cosmic
precedents for harmony and order in a disciplined hierarchical society, the
Trojan one makes and breaks relationships between 'the law of nations and
of nature' and the allegiances and commitments attaching to 'honour'. As
the Greek scene prepares the audience for a searching inquisition of the
Ajax/Achilles/Hector episodes, the Trojan one opens sceptical eyes upon
the love of Helen and Paris and the courtship of Troilus and Cressida:

> but modest doubt is called
> The beacon of the wise, the tent that searches
> To th' bottom of the worst.
>
> (II. ii. 15–17)

Hector's sceptical analysis distinguishes between intrinsic and attributed
value:

> 'Tis mad [F: made] idolatry
> To make the service greater than the god:
> And the will dotes that is attributive [F: inclineable]
> To what infectiously itself affects,
> Without some image of th' affected merit.
>
> (II. ii. 56–60)

And it offers what appears to be a definitive account of the war's occasion
and momentum:

> What nearer debt in all humanity
> Than wife is to the husband? If this law
> Of nature be corrupted through affection,
> And that great minds, of partial indulgence
> To their benumbed wills, resist the same,
> There is a law in each well-ordered nation

> To curb those raging appetites that are
> Most disobedient and refractory.
>
> (II. ii. 175–82)

Troilus' flagrantly irrational responses try throughout the scene to transcend the corrupt affections by pursuing the idea of constancy, starting, oblivious to the irony, from the notion of constancy in marriage ('I take today a wife') but growing confident as it touches what for most of us is the Marlovian Faustus's image of Helen's value ('a pearl / Whose price hath launched above a thousand ships.') It is apt that at this point Cassandra enters 'raving, with her hair about her ears'. When Hector in spritely temper sets aside his 'opinion by way of truth', the catastrophes of the play and the history seem irreversible. Hector, without yielding to Troilus' arguments, nevertheless voices (and has already enacted) Troilus' apparently deepest convictions ('Why there you touch'd the life of our design'). In Lacan's terms 'the unconscious is the discourse of the other.'[9] Yet it is possible to trace in Troilus convictions about Helen's worthlessness (I. ii. 90–3) and the validity of marriage (II. ii. 62–8), underlying attitudes closer to Hector's 'truth'. As in other Shakespearian scenes in which persuasive pressures win a response, a self-betraying self seems to prevail over the rational and sceptical self; to borrow Ulysses' phrase, 'thoughts in their dumb cradles' – pre-articulate thoughts – disable the 'free determination betwixt right and wrong'. But the intimate course of the catastrophes that attend Hector's peripeteia is still to be traced in Troilus' and Cressida's pursuit of 'fame in time to come'.

The same giant stride that carried the play from pre-Homeric Troy to Chaucer's England and Shakespeare's carries it into our own time. Cressida lives still; her condition can be proved upon the pulses, while 'the bitter disposition of the time' remains familiar to our political experience and observation. Like the Bastard of *King John* and like Thersites, 'bastard in mind, bastard in valour, in everything illegitimate', Cressida is required 'from the inward motion to deliver / Sweet, sweet, poison for the age's tooth.' 'Like', and yet also quite unlike. A great artist does not repeat himself. Shakespeare used the theatre to explore the troubled mind, the 'mystery in the soul of state', and to make discoveries about the creative and destructive ways in which we shape and express the individual and peculiar self.

Over the past few years female critics (and their friends among the men) have shown us that Shakespeare's treatment of women is not of a piece with the orthodoxies of his time, or indeed of ours. But to my knowledge

---

[9] Here, and elsewhere, I am grateful to Faith Miles for prompting me on Lacan. See also ch. 7.

it is the actress Juliet Stevenson who has tried most sensitively to realize the significance of Cressida's experience, seeing it as the focus of the play's tragedy. It is a truth that may come to be universally acknowledged that harmony and design are often to be perceived in plays that in festival tradition mix everyday circumstance with comprehensive historical, metaphysical and even arcane concerns. It may therefore be no accident that Cressida's diagnosis of her divided state is found at the centre of the play:

> I have a kind of self resides with you;
> But an unkind self, that itself will leave
> To be another's fool.
> (III. ii. 148–50)

In the theatre there is as much time still to pass as we have already passed. In the language of characterization we are about to hear, as Overbury, speaking of the Excellent Actor, teaches us to say, the 'quick and softe touch of many strings, all shutting up in one musical close', 'wit's descant on the plainsong'. In the narrative and in the theatre of courtship we reach a precarious climax, at this point attended by the character's, and the playwright's, proleptic perception, for an audience that knows the play may connect the words with one of its last moments:

> Troilus, farewell! one eye yet looks on thee,
> But with my heart the other eye doth see.
> (v. ii. 107–8)

And if it is metaphysically inclined it may link them too with Troilus' cry: 'If there be rule in unity itself, / This was not she' (v. ii. 141–2). The words are located too between Helen's history and Cressida's, between the dying love of the previous scene and the nascent love of this one, and between the playwright's satiric and lyric art. Pandarus has just mimicked the quick pants that Helen and Paris make in one another's arms in a song that 'tickles still the sore' (III. i. 120).

Troilus, when he first hears of Cressida's 'unkind self', will allow nothing to daunt his infinite desire and refuses to confront the perception he affects to admire. He persists in his role as romantic wooer and is hypocritically determined to act the part:

> Well know they what they speak that speak so wisely!
> (III. ii. 152)

Cressida speaks a disabling truth, but he flies above it and loses sight of it, because Cressida's apprehension of her own inconstancy cannot be assimilated into his sustaining illusions. His illusions are self-created and self-creating and there is in Cressida a kind of self, a kindred self, that would assist in their creation.

Juliet Stevenson played Cressida with great intelligence and dedication. Her dedication of professional skills was sustained by her convictions about the way women are treated in a man's world, and her intelligence was exercised both upon the support the play afforded her and on the obstructions it put in her way. As a character and as a player she must respond in the courtship scene to the theatrical occasion stage-managed by Pandarus, and to the pressures of expectation that Troilus, the other performer, puts upon her. Hence that precarious self-conscious suspension between spontaneity and calculation: 'Perchance, my Lord, I show more craft than love, / And fell so roundly to a large confession, / To angle for your thoughts' (III. ii. 153–5).

Encompassing the occasion, however, there is a great reach of imaginative space and a stretch of time looking before and after. The 'will is infinite and the execution confin'd', 'the desire is boundless and the act a slave to limit' (II. ii. 82–3).' In the sustained exchange of lovers' vows and aspirations there is much occasion for the 'quick and soft touch of many strings'. Shakespeare gives to Troilus lines that express most fully what Kierkegaard called 'the presumption of eternity in romantic love':

> O that I thought it could be in a woman –
> As if it can, I shall presume in you –
> To feed for aye her lamp and flames of love,
> To keep her constancy in plight and youth,
> Outliving beauties outward with a mind
> That doth renew swifter than blood decays!
>
> (III. ii. 158–63)

Marvellously said; at once impersonal and personal, out of the ordinary boundaries of talk yet still within them. Juliet Stevenson, at those moments at least when Anton Lesser abstained from reducing the lines to everyday chatter and let them sing out, responded both sympathetically and sceptically. A 'kind of self' looked for the mind that renews swifter than blood decays, but the 'unkind self' kept a certain distance, expressed by a poise between coming closer and going away (made more difficult by the fact that both were performing on the stairs to bed). At once impersonal and personal; the point must be made again about the 'iterations' that follow:

> As true as steel, as plantage to the moon . . .
> As iron to adamant, as earth to th' centre,
> Yet after all comparisons of truth
> (As truth's authentic author to be cited)
> 'As true as Troilus' shall crown up the verse
> And sanctify the numbers.
>
> (III. ii. 177–83)

Howard Davies and Anton Lesser allowed the plain song to be only a little orchestrated, yet the actor playing the part has no choice but to make music, if only, in this instance, of a conventional and compliant kind. He speaks a flourish of recollections from proverbial and poetic tradition; yet we cannot, the play being what it is, fail to notice that its uncritical assumption of a transcendently innocent role – 'As true as Troilus' – is very much in character. In the same way, his speculations about woman's constancy are specifically about woman, not about man. These are points that Juliet Stevenson of course picked up, and the help she gets from the playwright is substantial.

Cressida's responding lines required in the writing a much fuller exercise of the Shakespearian imagination:

> Prophet may you be!
> If I be false, or swerve a hair from truth,
> When time is old and hath forgot itself
> When water-drops have worn the stones of Troy,
> And blind oblivion swallowed cities up,
> And mighty states characterless are grated
> To dusty nothing, yet let memory,
> From false to false among false maids in love,
> Upbraid my falsehood!
>
> (III. ii. 183–91)

The insight that Cressida displays into her own nature is here extended to the operation of those impersonal processes of time and mutability that appear to correlate with human inconstancy. Her understanding of what Shakespeare elsewhere in the play calls 'the husks and formless ruins of oblivion' (IV. v. 166–7), the 'instant way' (III. iii. 153) and 'alms for oblivion' (III. iii. 146) is authentically self-transcendent. Is it therefore 'out of character'?

It is not within the expectations of character that Thersites accommodates in his reductive notion of 'the commodious drab', though the lightness of woman is a common theme of the character-writers (all, of course, men). Through Overbury's windows we can peep at A Whore and A very Whore; A Whore is 'a hie way to the Divell' and he who enjoys her 'is at his journey's end'.[10] But neither their rhetoric, nor Webster's in The White Devil,[11] can touch Shakespeare's Cressida. For full articulation of the bonds between the inconstancy of woman and those of the mutable world we must look to Donne's 'Defence of Womens Inconstancy' in Paradoxes and Problems:

---

[10] Overbury, Characters, pp. 28, 29.

[11] See Monticelso's exposition of 'their perfect character' in response to Vittoria's question, 'whore! what's that?' (White Devil, III. i. 83–107); Fortune is described as 'a right whore' in the play's opening lines where the gods of Democritus are said to 'govern the whole world'.

> That Women are *Inconstant*, I with any man confess, but that
> *Inconstancy* is a bad quality, I against any man will maintain: For
> every thing as it is one better than another, so is it fuller of *change*;
> The *Heavens* themselves continually turn, the *Stars move*, the
> *Moon* changeth; *Fire* whirleth, *Aire flyeth*, *Water ebbs* and flows,
> the face of the *Earth* altereth her looks, *time* stays not.[12]

Shakespeare's Timon exhorts the bandits to realize their cosmic profession:
'the moon's an arrant thief, / And her pale fire she snatches from the sun
(*Timon of Athens*, IV. iii. 437–8)', but his persuasions charm them from it.
Cressida's words, 'as false / As air, as water, wind, or sandy earth', are
spoken cosmically too, but again, neither playwright nor character loses
sight of the human occasion and motive. Nor does Donne:

> so in Men, they that have the most reason are the most alterable
> in their designes, and the darkest or most ignorant, do seldomest
> change; therefore Women, changing more than Men, have also
> more *Reason*. They cannot be immutable like stocks, like stones,
> like the Earths dull Center . . . then why should that which is the
> perfection of other things, be imputed to Women as greatest
> imperfection? Because they deceive men.

Donne's answer returns us to the play's human comedy, which we reach
in Pandarus's bit of stage-business: 'Go to, a bargain made, seal it, seal it'
(III. ii. 197).

Cressida is returned from poetic, story-telling and elemental space and
time to the exigencies of pretty encounters and Pandar's gear. She is about
to be carried away – as it is, carried away, first to bed and then from one
camp to another in a war-stricken world; and it is this area of the play that
offered Juliet Stevenson both her best opportunities and her frustrations.
Time passes in the theatre to give us opportunity to reflect with Ulysses
that:

> beauty, wit,
> High birth, vigour of bone, desert in service,
> Love, friendship, charity, are subjects all
> To envious and calumniating Time;
> (III. iii. 171–4)

that 'The present eye praises the present object' (III. iii. 180), and that
some 'creep in skittish Fortune's hall, / While others play the idiots in her
eyes!' (III. iii. 134–5); and in that same interlude of envious Time, skittish
Fortune herself (operating through Calchas's tactics to recover his daughter)

[12]John Donne, *Complete Poetry and Selected Prose*, ed. John Hayward (1947),
p. 335.

requires that Cressida be borne from Troy.

Touches of lyrical love ('infants empty of all thought') grace the importunity of Pandarus's comedy in Act IV, scene ii ('how go maidenheads?') but when she and Troilus are forced to part Cressida is catastrophically destabilized, first by a 'fine, full and perfect grief', and then, more destructively, by Troilus' repeated demand that she 'be true'. 'O heavens!' – she is shocked and hurt – ' "Be true" again?' Troilus' urbane commendation of the Greeks ('Their loving well compos'd with gifts of nature') cultivated from a courtly sophistication far removed from 'the infancy of truth', is attended by what in self-regard he calls 'a kind of godly jealousy'; and Juliet Stevenson's Cressida reacted accordingly. His destructiveness is a tardy response to her early insight into the duality of the self:

> And sometimes we are devils to ourselves.
> When we will tempt the frailty of our powers
> Presuming on their changeful potency.
> (IV. iv. 95–7)

For he himself gives voice to the 'dumb-discoursive devil / That tempts most cunningly.' 'My lord,' – Juliet Stevenson spoke in panic the last words that she is allowed to address directly to Troilus – 'will *you* be true?' And again, in transcendent vanity, he tells her that with 'great truth' he catches 'mere simplicity'. Howard Davies intervened on behalf of Juliet Stevenson's Cressida by telescoping and re-ordering the scenes to have her carried off to the Greek camp in her nightdress, a conspicuously vulnerable sexual victim.

From another point of view, however, she is a victim of 'skittish Fortune', as well as being a bit of luck for the Greeks. Shakespeare had several ironic assignations in his art with the Strumpet Fortune. Helena, exercising the strumpet's arts, determines Bertram's fortune in *All's Well*;[13] and it is not surprising that in this play one 'daughter of the game' should foster another. Cressida must assume her own fortune. When in 1985 she came to the Greek camp, it was both as Cressida and as Juliet Stevenson. The actress could not bring herself to play the role that Ulysses (and – there's the rub – perhaps Shakespeare) would thrust upon her. The Greeks failed to live up to Troilus' account – 'full of quality', and 'Their loving well compos'd' (IV. iv. 76–7). In 1985 Cressida was brutally manhandled and had to look to her protector Diomedes, carefully provided by Shakespeare, to rescue her. She protested as best she could, managed to recover her wit in time to put down Menelaus, but then found herself confronted by Shakespeare's Ulysses. Shakespeare finishes the episode by assigning to Ulysses the formal characterization of Cressida that begins, 'There's language in her eye, her

---

[13] See the fuller discussion of Helena's role in ch. 13.

cheek, her lip', and ends, 'Set them down / For sluttish spoils of opportunity, / And daughters of the game' (IV. v. 55–63). In the text we find the stage direction 'Flourish' and the cry goes up 'The Troyans' trumpet', a perhaps fortuitous pun from which Davies's production, out of mercy for Cressida, disengaged. The real difficulty for Cressida, however, is in the playing of the lines immediately preceding, in which Ulysses most often appears to beg a kiss from Cressida and to refuse it when it is conceded. This went very much against the grain of Juliet Stevenson's Cressida; but a very effective theatrical solution was found that, as far as I know, was a performance innovation. The lines go:

> May I, sweet lady, beg a kiss of you?
> *Cressida* You may.
> *Ulysses* I do desire it
> *Cressida* Why, beg then.
> *Ulysses* Why then, for Venus' sake, give me a kiss
> When Helen is a maid again and his.
> *Cressida* I am your debtor, claim it when 'tis due.
> *Ulysses* Never's my day, and then a kiss of you.
>
> (IV. v. 47–52)

Peter Jeffrey, playing Ulysses, reports that after many unsuccessful attempts to play the scene the usual way to this Cressida's satisfaction, Juliet Stevenson found in a late rehearsal the gesture to redeem, as it were, the dignity of the sex. On the words 'Why, beg then' she pointed Ulysses to his knees; he refused to comply, of course, turned away humiliated and self-disgusted, and spoke his characterizing lines out of pique.

Unfortunately a comparably deft solution is not available in the scene in which we next see Cressida, and for the last time, where, to return to that disabling perception, we find her 'unkind self'. There is much in the betrayal episode to recall us to earlier Cressida scenes and indeed to others apparently distant from Cressida: 'Men prize the thing ungained more than it is' (I. ii. 289); 'The present eye praises the present object' (III. iii. 180); 'The error of our eyes directs our minds' (v. ii. 110). It proved impossible to sustain Cressida's integrity in the form that Juliet Stevenson was seeking. The play would not allow it, in spite of the measures the director took to support her. Cressida was emphatically trapped in a world in which, as Nietzsche's Zarathustra puts it, woman is born for the sport and amusement of warrior man, and has no choice but to become a daughter of that game.

Yet the effect was to make it impossible for her to play either her 'kind' or her 'unkind self', Troilus' or Diomedes' Cressida, or indeed their co-active presence, with conviction. Davies again intervened. Ulysses' words about Diomedes' bearing, 'He rises on his toe. That spirit of his / In aspiration lifts him from the earth' (IV. v. 14–15), were cut, and Bruce

Alexander, who played the part, was stuck very fast to the earth, perhaps to assist Juliet Stevenson's Cressida to accommodate herself to brutal realities. But it is a clue to the unperformed, as distinct from the 1985 performed, play, that grace and courtliness, and indeed 'aspiration' can co-exist with the 'clapper-clawing' and 'abominable varletry'. In the then unperformed play there is continuity between the sophisticated, knowing flirtatiousness that characterizes Cressida before the division of the play and that which persists to the end, an effect we can pick up by returning from 'Come hither once again' and 'visit me no more' in her play with Diomedes (v. ii. 48, 74), to 'I might have still held off, / And then you would have tarried' (IV. ii. 17–18), in her play with Troilus. The plays are poised either side of a loss of innocence which is not the same thing as loss of maidenhead; Shakespeare appears almost to have forgotten that the Cressida of the sources was a widow, although he allows her a touch of experience in 'You men will never tarry' (IV. ii. 16). The loss of innocence is itself a story to be told in different ways. To tell it in the shape of a morality play, at either side of the play's ethical watershed there is a flowing-back towards the unspoilt, eternalized states of love, honour and allegiance, and a tumble forward in a travesty of the same states towards orgasmic death ('ha, ha, he!') a generation of vipers, and the damnation of hell (see III. i. 133). To tell it as a war story, Cressida is carried off to another camp and to survive must practise her wiles upon her guardian; that was how Juliet Stevenson played it, but with reluctant, factitious wiles, not falling under Diomedes' erotic spell, perhaps for the good reason that there was no spell.

Tell the story yet again, in search of the unperformed play, and it is a parable about the exposure of adolescent romanticism to reductive scrutiny. Yet no matter how we tell it, we are returned at some point to eyes, perception, time, will, judgement, value and the divided self. Chaucer's narrator tells us that before Troilus looked on Criseyde he:

> Was ful unwar that Love hadde his dwellinge
> With-inne the subtile stremes of hir yën.
>   (I. 44)

Only a busy idler would count eyes in Shakespeare's plays (and poems), or equally value each eye-word in this one, from 'all eyes and no sight' (I. ii. 30), through:

> My will enkindled by mine eyes and ears,
> Two traded pilots twixt the dangerous shores
> Of will and judgement;
>   (II. ii. 63–5)

to:

> The error of our eyes directs our mind.
> What error leads must err; O then conclude,
> Minds sway'd by eyes are full of turpitude.
>
> (v. ii. 110–12)

The theatre-goer looking for one kind of ideological solace will be content to listen to Cressida's appropriation of the doting eye and the doting will to 'poor our sex' (v. ii. 109): women are like that, they don't know a good man when they see one, and they are always letting us down. The 'character' of Cressida herself at this point encourages him. But the structure of the play will not let him rest. Troilus' will, like Cressida's, is swayed by eyes, the 'present eye' in Ulysses' experience 'praises the present object', and the eye that looks on Troilus and that which looks on Diomedes recall the two selves with which Cressida (whose 'fears have eyes') confronted Troilus in the courtship scene. The 'unkind self that itself will leave to be another's fool' finds fuller definition in her equivocal commitment to Diomedes; she more knowingly becomes his dupe and instrument (his 'fool') than she was Troilus', but she does not therefore escape the desolation of her own perceptions. The word 'characterless' that she uses to express the failure of 'persistive constancy' in the very history of Troy can be played back upon her own condition.

In casting the play, and looking for ways in which Cressida's Diomedes-self might be convincingly played, one might with advantage choose for Diomedes an actor who had played a debonair Troilus some ten years earlier, and for whom wilful innocence in love and war could no longer come naturally. In another story Diomedes' character might have been for Troilus the next station on the line: urbane pathologist of the war, hunter to the death, seizer of sexual opportunities. As it is, it appears to be Troilus' virtue that he achieves no comparable integrity:

> Within my soul there doth conduce a fight
> Of this strange nature, that a thing inseparate
> Divides more wider than the sky and earth,
> And yet the spacious breadth of this division
> Admits no orifex for a point as subtle
> As Ariachne's broken woof to enter.
>
> (v. ii. 147–52)

Troilus is responding to what he has witnessed, yet there is a 'credence' in his heart, a belief in Cressida's truth (the creation of his will, affections, or renewing mind) 'That doth invert th' attest of eyes and ears' (v. ii. 119). Cressida has a similarly impotent understanding of the 'thing inseparate' which 'Divides more wider than the earth and sky', knowing that she is the thing itself. But the play allows a glimpse of the values of romantic integrity, now evaporated into verbal speculations:

If beauty have a soul, this is not she;
If souls guide vows, if vows be sanctimonies,
If sanctimony be the gods' delight,
If there be rule in unity itself.

(v. ii. 138–41)

Within a few stage-minutes we look on with Thersites at the abominable varlet and the foolish knave clapper-clawing one another. As far as the play is concerned, they are still at it. What, to borrow Conrad's phrase, does that intimacy of antagonism signify? It tells us that unresolvable conflict between Diomedes' commitment to what he sees as 'a hell of pain and world of charge' (IV. ii. 58) and Troilus' to 'the venom'd vengeance' that now rides upon Trojan swords (v. iii. 47), sustains all wars long after their causes are spent. The play's creative and reductive perceptions in the territories of love, war and government sensitize our judgement and make it possible for us to be our age.

Thersites, Kenneth Muir tells us in the Oxford edition, generalizing at some distance from the play, 'is the most despicable character in the *Iliad*' and his portrayal 'belongs to an unbroken tradition'.[14] Because he is a Fool, he is 'licensed to be scathing about everyone and everything'. The suggestion, which is common, is that we can enjoy the raillery and shrug it off, with some acknowledgement that as Muir and Bullough say, 'some of the mud he throws is bound to stick.' The clichés are potent and they have their validity. But both Homeric tradition and the role of Fool are richer than the common view allows, and Shakespeare left neither as he found them. The 'bifold authority' of the play is so designed that what we make of its most aspiring and creative rhetoric must keep pace with our responses when 'rank Thersites opes his mastic jaws'.

Henry James, writing on Honoré Daumier, describes pessimism as 'the expression of the spirit for which humanity is definable primarily by its weakness'. Thersites, from the time of Homer, is both the anatomist of weakness and its embodiment. When in Book 2 of the *Iliad* he rails at Agamemnon for taking gold to his tents and Trojan girls to his bed as his private property, Odysseus, in Rieu's demotic translation, retorts without answering: 'This may be eloquence, but we have had enough of it. You drivelling fool, how dare you stand up to kings?' The point is not that Thersites' charges are false (Odysseus admits them in blander form) but that he dares to make them against his betters. Odysseus beats him until 'a bloody weal, raised by the golden studs on the rod swelled up and stood out on the man's back.' ' "Good work!" cried one man, catching his neighbour's eye and saying what they were all feeling. "There's many a fine

---

[14] pp. 22–3.

thing to Odysseus's credit . . . But he has never done us a better turn than when he stopped the mouth of this windy ranter." ' 'Such was the verdict of the gathering,' says Homer; it is a gathering that has learned to respect not only the golden words of Odysseus but also the golden studs on his rod of office. Thersites is not a fool (he is an informed advocate of Achilles' cause) and he is certainly not licensed.

But Homer's own art invites some ironic responses: 'And now Odysseus, sacker of cities, rose to speak with the staff in hand.' In the Homeric confrontation between Odysseus and Thersites, brute force prevails over weakness, strength is lord of imbecility, and Homer does not pretend otherwise. Chapman's amplifications are in a piously Elizabethan strain, 'Prophane not kings then with thy lips', and work less ambiguously to sustain the popular anti-democratic ideology that he found in his source: 'The rule of many is absurd,' says Chapman's version, 'one Lord must lead the ring / Of far-resounding government.' We are close in the narrative here to the occasion of the 'degree speech', but Shakespeare contrives a much ampler rhetorical and moral perspective. Homer admits Thersites to the counsels of state; Shakespeare excludes him, but also promotes him to a fuller significance in the story. 'Strength will be lord of imbecility', not conspicuously at the play's outset, but in a course of events which Ulysses' own policy does much to determine. Ulysses and Thersites do not confront each other in the play but Shakespeare uses them to assist in creating the radical polarities of its language. Each offers his own perspective, at his own distance, upon the spectacle of the play's events, and the lines of sight converge only late in the action, when Ulysses and Thersites are simultaneous spectators of Cressida's duplicity and Troilus' distress.

Like the scholar and the pedant, the Player, in the seventeenth-century sense of the word, has his 'character', both representative and personal. Here is Overbury, speaking again about An Excellent Actor:

> By his action he fortifies morall precepts with example; for what we see him personate, we think truely done before us.

Keeping Overbury's language, we may say that in the player of Ulysses (Peter Jeffrey in 1985) 'a man of deep thought might apprehend the Ghost of an ancient hero walks again.' Peter Jeffrey tells how in rehearsal he was content to talk his part neutrally, instructed by Howard Davies not to worry about the poetry, but increasingly in performance he felt bound to do what he could to honour the rhetoric, the high-flying language of government and the subtler arts of political suasion. 'All men have been of the actor's occupation,' says Overbury, 'and indeed what he doth fainedly that do others essentially.' Ulysses in the council-scene and in his encounter with Achilles is putting on a performance; he is an actively engaged creative hypocrite, working on behalf of the community upon the perverse person of Achilles, trying to discipline the idiot self, the self that has ceased to relate to the society. Shakespeare nowhere makes direct use of the root sense of the word 'hypocrisy' but his plays are rich in occasions when we might be startled into recalling it. Poins, for example, calls Hal 'a most princely hypocrite' in a play that keeps us step by step in touch with the Prince's acting skills. While Hamlet exhorts Gertrude to assume a virtue if she has it not, Hal would have us believe that he assumes vices when he has them not. In *Troilus and Cressida* the interest in hypocrisy and in acting persists, but to very different effect. Ulysses' manipulative plot is designed to recover from 'privacy' an Achilles whose impersonal significance as the lapsed and disaffected hero of a disorientated community is immense, but whose motives are obscure even to himself ('My mind is troubled, like a fountain stirred, / And I myself see not the bottom of it', iii. iii. 308–9). Ulysses' diagnosis and therapy entails another probing of the nature of time ('a wallet at his back', 'a fashionable host', 'the instant way', together with searching glances at Achilles' affections and his dealings with Priam's daughter. Shakespeare's language again surprises us with its indirection:

Achilles   Of this my privacy
  I have strong reasons
Ulysses   But 'gainst your privacy
  The reasons are more potent and heroical.
  'Tis known, Achilles, that you are in love
  With one of Priam's daughters.
Achilles   Ha! Known?
Ulysses   Is that a wonder?
  The providence that's in a watchful state
  Knows almost every grain of Pluto's gold.
  Finds bottom in th' uncomprehensive deeps,
  Keeps pace with thought and almost like the gods
  Do thoughts unveil in their dumb cradles.
                                        (iii. iii. 190–200)

Ulysses' governing intelligence looks for complete (totalitarian) knowledge of the subject's most intimate self, and he speaks as if his own analytical powers are supported by something resembling Orwell's Thought Police:

  There is a mystery, with whom relation
  Durst never meddle, in the soul of state,
  Which hath an operation more divine
  Than breath or pen can give expressure to.

All the commerce you have had with Troy
As perfectly is ours as yours, my Lord.
(III. iii. 201–6)

Shakespeare's contemporaries would readily pick up the allusions to secret intelligence in a divinely ordained state troubled by wayward heroes;[15] but the play is also probing the inter-inanimations of sexual passion and warrior virtue, loving and slaughtering. Achilles' precarious emotional state is exposed to pressures (and performances) from both Ulysses and Thersites.

Ulysses is seeking to recover the intimate, individual, *ideotic* self to the service of the community. But the play compels fresh thought about our private and our public selves. The 'self' that both Achilles and the Greek army hold in high regard is 'The sinew and the forehand of our host', 'Whose glorious deeds . . . made emulous missions 'mongst the gods themselves, / And drave great Mars to faction.' The 'self' that is active in Ulysses is a governor talking to a hero and a social equal. There is prompt response, even accord, as the hero meets from 'the other' some of his own dormant convictions. When Achilles interrupts Ulysses at his reading he is reminded that

> man, how dearly ever parted,
> How much in having, or without or in,
> Cannot make boast to have that which he hath,
> Nor feels not what he owes, but by reflection;
> As when his virtues, shining upon others,
> Heat them and they retort that heat again
> To the first giver.
(III. iii. 96–102)

'This is not strange,' says Achilles; as in the *Sonnets* (written at much the same time), reflection is a process through which the self perceives the self. But it is a long way to the bottom and stirred fountain of Achilles' troubled mind (III. iii. 306–7). The recovery of the hero to the governing vision of Ulysses will be among the 'actions highest reared' that prove 'tortive and errant' in the course of growth. Shakespeare's Ulysses ironically will take courage from an Achilles that, roused by the death of Patroclus, with his 'mangled myrmidons' redeems himself with desecrating violence and 'lust' (v. vi. 30–42); the ladder of his high design carries the war and its chivalry

---

[15] Alice Walker (ad loc., New Shakespeare, 1957) reads 'mystery' in the theological sense; Kenneth Palmer takes it as 'matter unexplained or inexplicable' and, like others before him (see New Variorum, 1953, ad loc.), sees it as a reference to the Greek intelligence service. Shakespeare is ready elsewhere to associate Providence with spying, and to pursue the ironic implications of 'power divine' that looks upon our 'passes' (see the discussion in ch. 12 of 'God's spies' in *King Lear*.

into the 'chaos which follows the choking' when 'degree is suffocate'.

The Actor in Overbury's account is not only able to make moral discoveries, to re-create ancient heroes, and to pretend to do what others actually do, he also

> . . . addes grace to the Poets labours: for what in the poet is but ditty, in him is both ditty and musicke. He entertaines us in the best leasure of our life, that is betweene meales, the most unfit time either for study or bodily exercise.

The actor entertains us in the festive interludes of our lives. But looked at this way, the player of Ulysses or Prince Hal is the politic actor, the player of Thersites or Falstaff the festive one. And it happens that the skills allowed to Thersites, which he practises as an entertainer, as a creator of character, are analogous to those of the character-writers, as well as to those of James's master caricaturist Daumier, the re-creator of Don Quixote and Sancho Panza. 'If I must speak the Schoole-masters language,' says Overbury, 'I will confess that Character comes of this infinitive moode χαράδδειν which signifieth to ingrave, or make a deep impression.' Then he glances at ways of intensifying an impression. 'To square out a character by our English levell, it is a picture (reall or personall) quaintlie drawne in various colours, all of them heightned by one shadowing.' The play makes Thersites a master of caricature, and his mimicries cast 'derision medicinable' upon the pretensions of the heroic society.

Thersites first opens his jaws on the English stage in an Interlude dating from 1537.[16] In the first episode, carrying his club, he procures a sallet (helmet, or *headibus*) and a sword from Mulciber; in later episodes he bullies his mother, does battle with a snail, hides from a soldier behind his mother's skirts, receives from Ulysses a letter congratulating him on slaying a monster and prevails on his mother to cast a spell on Telemachus to cure him of worms; he is finally routed by the soldier who invites us to pray for the queen (Jane Seymour) and rejoice in the birth of a royal prince (afterwards Edward VI).

There is no reason to believe that Shakespeare knew the play, but it is apparently the first English popular play to make a kind of vice from a Homeric character and indirectly to enlist him into the service of the monarchy. On the one hand it offers us the cowardly braggart, and on the other the resolute *miles*; the braggart entertains us and the soldier calls us to order. Two generations later, in Shakespeare's plays of *Henry IV*, the braggart Falstaff confronts the *miles* Hotspur. After two or three theatre-seasons, Shakespeare offers us another Thersites – not a braggart but still

---

[16] Available in *Three Tudor Classical Interludes*, ed. Marie Axton and D. S. Brewer (Cambridge, 1982).

a coward, and quite other *milites*.

After four centuries Howard Davies approached the play with certain preconceptions, and my own apprehensive preconceptions about his production owed much to my experience of his 1983 version of *Macbeth*. Davies is an admirer of Brecht, and he did all he could to turn *Macbeth* into a social spectacle, denying its phantasmagoric, hallucinatory ethos and its 'supernatural soliciting'. The approach had its politics, even its unconscious politics. It denied autonomy to the actor's assumed private self and to our co-related private selves, and looked for a consolidated audience response.

Troilus and Cressida proved much more hospitable than *Macbeth* to a Brechtian approach, but I shall be less concerned with the approach than with the arrival. For in this instance the complex movement from calculation to spontaneity and improvization that always attends the transition from the play's text to rehearsal and performance was broken in upon by accident. Touchstone fell off his motor bike. It was once intended that the part of Thersites should be played by Nicky Henson; but he was hurt in a road accident and recovered to the point where he could continue in *As You Like It* but not take on an exacting new role. At a fortnight's notice Alun Armstrong joined the company and the effect, it is said, was instantly electrifying. Thersites is at the centre of the play's virulent comedy with all its unsettling ideological potency. Armstrong saw him as in himself an idiosyncratic character, a player of characters, and as analyst of character in the afflicted commonwealth, and when he spoke his most comprehensive indictment of that warring world he elicited from the audience a warm and sympathetic laugh:

> I would fain see them meet, that that same young Troyan ass, that loves the whore there, might send that Greekish whoremasterly villain with the sleeve back to the dissembling luxurious drab, of a sleeveless errand. A' th' t' other side, the policy of those crafty swearing rascals, that stale old mouse-eaten dry cheese, Nestor, and that same dog-fox Ulysses, is not prov'd worth a blackberry. They set me up, in policy, that mongrel cur, Ajax, against that dog of as bad a kind, Achilles, and now is the cur Ajax prouder than the cur Achilles, and will not arm today; whereupon the Grecians begin to proclaim barbarism, and policy grows into an ill opinion.
>
> (v. iv. 5–17)

There may have been an element of type-casting in the choice of Armstrong; his Petruchio in Shakespeare's Padua and in Justice Shallow's Stratford in 1983 was very much the outsider. He played Thersites in the 'Geordie' accent of the North-East, opening up regional and class differences of values and outlook that might have found an even more sympathetic response had the production visited Newcastle-on-Tyne (as most do at the end of the Stratford season).[17] Because Davies's production made more discoveries about soldiers (from Troy to the Crimea) than it did about Renaissance and antique courtiers, it was possible to give him what he usually lacks – specific functions in the military set-up. He served as batman to Achilles and as a kind of steward in the officers' mess. True to the description given in Chapman's Homer, Armstrong gave himself goggle-eyes, round shoulders and a compacted head with huge teeth. His lines were, I believe, very little cut, and were brought home to a modern audience with great conviction, allowing the actor to win a vehement and exuberant ascendancy of insight. With only a fortnight to rehearse it would not have been surprising had the character seemed imported into the play, but in fact it appeared to grow very convincingly out of it. It was a powerfully impersonal as well as a strongly individual performance. His long, railing soliloquy in Act II, sc. iii (on the thunder-darter of Olympus and the Neapolitan bone-ache) was delivered as he set about his chores. But he was in a double sense, like Ulysses, bringing order to the mess. He knocked over chairs, swept dust under the carpet, drained the bottles and then smashed them. His most expressive gesture was with the ash-tray of the Stratford season (it was purloined by Falstaff in a production of *The Merry Wives*). Having cleared the table by pushing everything on to the floor, he condescended to return the ash-tray, walked away, and then came back to put it exactly in the centre. The play was true to military vanity and folly when it showed the officers on both sides trying to keep up appearances of order within the shattered walls of a disintegrating state. The Trojans brought out the silver; the Greeks had their ash-tray.

In festive and comic spirit (what better entertainment between meals?) the reductive view of events and human values prevails, and Thersites becomes a source of ideological solace to those whose scepticism about the pretensions of the governing class allows them to enjoy a punk Homer. It is possible to find Thersites' responses true and just, but still to ask, in the intricate perspective of a play which finds other vanishing points in Ulysses, Cressida, Hector, Pandarus, Troilus, are they true and just enough?

In the tragic and comic festivities of the theatre our powers of discriminating good and evil are not suspended. On the contrary, it is in the theatre that they are capable of being most keenly stimulated, sensitized and challenged. The theatre, more than any other art-form, puts our precepts and our abstract insights to the tests of transient life and instant humanity. In the Chester Pageant of the Deluge, for example, Mrs Noah

---

[17]The assumption that the play is unpopular (vindicated by the following season at London's Barbican) therefore prevented what might have proved a popular performance from making its impact.

has to be dragged kicking and protesting away from her fellow 'gossips' to join her husband in the ark; the structure of the play makes it clear that her gossips are in the audience, and it is the audience that is left to drown. It will serve to remind us that the player of a character must look to himself, to other players and to the audience. He is caught up, moment by moment, in that puzzling and constantly changing relationship between the private and domestic self, the community, and those apparently impersonal processes that encompass both – the will of God or the movement of history. Mrs Noah may well have improvised herself into the text that has come down to us. Her moral vision may be inadequate but so, in the play and in the story, is Noah's and so indeed is God's, both in the story the Bible tells and in the play that the scribe and the people in the street make of it. Where is the 'adequate moral vision'? The play's contribution to it is in the total festive experience that it offers and not in any one of its moral voices.

In Shakespeare's play the structure of response is more complex but its elements are recognizably the same. And like the old play it does offer a choice of perspectives. In the Chester pageant we are aware of the 'here and now' and of the 'eternal verities'; the need to drink and gossip and the need to sustain a transcendent order. In *Troilus and Cressida* the values of love, war and government are blighted by the formidably destructive processes of time, but flourish ephemerally in what Agamemnon, in a line cut from the German production, calls the 'extant moment'. 'The end crowns all,' says Hector of the continuing war, and then, shifting the word 'end' from 'aim' to 'bring to a stop', 'And that old common arbitrator time will one day end it.' Odysseus in Homer's version supposes it will end at the whim of the father of Zeus, the Titan Cronos, 'he of the crooked ways'. By a whim of time that Cronos was in the Renaissance mixed up with chronology and the inexorable movement of time: the blind oblivion of Cressida's imagining that 'swallows cities up'. Agamemnon, in an interlude in the war, assumes his own prerogatives of 'music, wit and oracle' in his welcome to Hector:

> Understand more clear,
> What's past and what's to come is strew'd with husks
> And formless ruin of oblivion;
> But in this extant moment, faith and troth.
> Strain'd purely from all hollow bias-drawing,
> Bids thee, with most divine integrity,
> Great Hector welcome.
>
> (IV. v. 165–71)

In my imagined Chinese play Hector and Ajax would momentarily appear with the panache and splendour of medieval and Renaissance chivalry, before the action declines into the kind of comedy we can laugh at as we loll upon our beds. The creating mind would be allowed – momentarily – in war, as in love and government, to disengage from the destructive flux of time.

The play moves from one such disengagement to another, with flurries of action in between (Cressida bought and sold) until the several heroic histories converge in the final battle scenes of 'mad and fantastic execution'. They are in more than one sense 'characterless'; nothing remains of the Hector who debated with his brothers and spared Ajax, or of the reflective Achilles who eyed and scorned the enemy he entertained. 'Each thing melts', to revert to the language of Ulysses in the Greek council, 'In mere oppugnancy.' Thersites and Pandarus alone may be said to keep their shapes, and in the Quarto Epilogue Pandarus slips out of what Shakespeare elsewhere calls 'cormorant devouring time' into the 'present' of the Elizabethan Inns of Court.

Shakespeare does not in this play call on the tradition, best represented by Henryson, in which Cressida's betrayal of Troilus is punished by disease,[18] but nothing survives from the love, heroism and justice of that remote war in which all constancies were contracted to an 'extant moment' of gratification, but the hold-door trade and Winchester goose, the venereal affliction of the London property of the Bishop of Winchester.

Is this, then, Shakespeare's ultimate account of time and human values? No. There are others, past and to come. But it is the one that appears to have most validity in an arbitrarily divided world, 'dedicate to war', in which Thersites' account is as true as those of Ulysses and Troilus. Love's infinity, heroic glory and universal harmonies of state have only a transient, visionary and verbal validity in a world that has lost touch with the values by which it pretends to live. Again, it is a matter of being one's age; the age, among others, of Yeats's Ireland and Europe. Thinking of Troilus, 'We fed the heart on fantasies / The heart's grown brutal from the fare / More substance in our enmities than in our love'; and thinking of Ulysses, 'We sought to bring the world under a rule / Who are but weasles fighting in a hole' (like Thersites' fitchews, or his polecats). But Yeats's state of the world still finds its poet's voice, like Shakespeare's state of Elizabethan Troy, and the two can now be heard together.

[18] Shakespeare's Pistol apparently recalls Henryson in *Henry V* (ii. i. 76), 'a lazar kite of Cressid's kind'.

3 Shakespeare and the Fashion of These Times

In the course of a very useful review of Elizabethan theatre studies over the past sixty years, Arthur Brown tells us that 'we are still in a period of stock-taking' and that we must 'continue to apply ourselves to fundamental material, to minutiae if necessary, until we are perfectly certain that the foundations for broader and more general studies are secure'.[1] Some will feel that this is the scientific spirit manifesting itself as the heroic caution of modern scholarship (as Brown says of the reception given to Hotson's views of the round theatre, 'Most scholars are prepared to be non-committal'). But others may recognize in our own period some of the signs of imaginative exhaustion. It is like the end of *Uncle Vanya*, where a routine of work is to keep us going somehow, so that future generations will profit and may even be grateful: 'First, Uncle Vanya, let us write up the accounts. They are in a dreadful state. Come, begin. You take one and I will take the other.'

Our continuing eagerness to come to rest in objectively secured positions is a sign that our age is of a piece with that which, under the distant presidency of Auguste Comte, inaugurated the New Variorum Shakespeare. But the New Variorum, particularly in its earlier volumes,[2] has been concerned less with fundamental material than with the ample and comprehensive recording of opinion; and it may be thought to have done less to consolidate objectively valid knowledge and understanding than to exemplify and testify to the fascinating relativity of critical judgement. It reminds us that understanding is a complex of knowledge and insight, and

---

[1] *Shakespeare Survey*, 14 (1961), 14.

[2] *Romeo and Juliet* (1873) carried the general preface to the series. It is Positivist in temper, but the principal debt acknowledged in that volume is to Mommsen's edition of *Romeo and Juliet*.

that each generation has (for all the swelling of windpipes) contrived to add something to the stock of relevant facts and to the current of relevant perceptions.

Each age – it would seem in retrospect – enjoys a privilege of available insights; but where the insights seem to us to be valid we are apt to believe them timeless, and it is only when we can watch them retreating into the more exclusively mannered shades of a period that we can recognize their essentially historical character. The point might be demonstrated by glancing at some of the comments made (and for the most part recorded in the 1907 New Variorum) on Cleopatra's suicide speech opening Act v, sc. ii:

> My desolation does begin to make
> A better life: Tis paltry to be Caesar:
> Not being Fortune, hee's but Fortunes knaue,
> A minister of her will: and it is great
> To do that thing that ends all other deeds,
> Which shackles accedents, and bolts up change;
> Which sleepes, and neuer pallates more the dung,
> The beggers Nurse, and *Caesars*.

Johnson offers a brisk paraphrase of 'Fortunes knaue' – 'the servant of fortune'. But it is Johnson's strength that he expects a word to do only one job at a time. It was left to the twentieth century to speculate on a pun.[3] Caesar may be the nave of Fortune's wheel too, with Antony and Cleopatra at its periphery. The notion would lend precision to the braking metaphors, 'shackles accedents' and 'bolts up change'; but it also diffuses the sense and invites us to enjoy a grotesquely suggestive eloquence rather than a telling clarity of statement. Were we to pursue the point we should be promptly committed to a discussion of the history of poetry, and of Johnson's as well as Shakespeare's place in it. And we could not for long defer discussion of the poetry that has shaped our own kind of awareness in our own time.

A more direct demonstration of the connection between criticism and current poetic taste, however, is afforded by Warburton's meddlings with the second half of the passage. To restore 'sense and propriety' he postulates the loss of a line after 'change', and an emendation of 'dung': '[Lulls wearied nature to a sound repose] Which sleeps and never palates more the dugg: The beggar's nurse and Caesar's.' The insinuated line declares the age of Young's *Night Thoughts*. Warburton's paraphrase has Cleopatra die a victim of Augustan melancholia: 'It is great to do that which frees us from all the accidents of humanity, lulls our over-wearied nature to repose (which now

---

[3] Helge Kökeritz, *Shakespeare's Pronunciation* (1953). In discussing the sounding of 'k' in 'knave' he touches the possibility of a pun very lightly.

sleeps and has no more appetite for worldly enjoyments), and is equally the nurse of Caesar and the beggar.'

Seward, in the same period, offers an excellent vindication of the Folio reading which sharply challenges Cleopatra's claims to transcendent vision:

> When we speak in contempt of anything, we generally resolve it into its first principles: Thus, man is dust and ashes, and the food we eat, the dung, by which first our vegetable, and from thence our animal, food is nourished. Thus Cleopatra finds she can no longer riot in the pleasures of life, with the usual workings of a disappointed pride, pretends a disgust to them and speaks in praise of suicide . . . Nothing can be clearer than this passage, 'both the beggar and Caesar are fed and nursed by the dung of the earth'. Of this sense there is a demonstration in 'Our dungie earth alike feeds beast and man'.

The Augustan Roman refuses to be taken in.

Dr Johnson, as we might expect, is yet more revealing – about the play, about himself and about his age:

> The difficulty of the passage, if any difficulty there be, arises only from this, that the act of suicide, and the state which is the effect of suicide, are confounded. Voluntary death, says she, is an act *which bolts up change*; it produces a state, 'Which sleeps and never palates more the dung, the Beggar's nurse and Caesar's'. Which has no longer need of the gross and terrene sustenance, in the use of which Caesar and the Beggar are on a level. The speech is abrupt, but perturbation in such a state is surely natural.

It is a nice insight into the syntax that discovers the elliptical transition from the act of suicide to the state which is its effect. But Johnson finds virtue in the ellipsis only by explaining it as an appeal to decorum of manners. He shows the same resource when confronted by Hotspur's similarly romantic nihilism ('pluck bright honour from the pale-fac'd moon'), which can be soberly and rationally vindicated' as 'the hasty motion of turbulent desire' and 'the dark expression of indetermined thoughts'. It is a humane and civilized placing of extravagant rhetoric (compare Worcester on Hotspur and Dolabella on Cleopatra). Nevertheless, we have only to notice the decorous tautology 'gross and terrene sustenance' which mediates between Johnson's endorsement of the sentiment and his reluctance to let it strike his senses, to be returned to the eighteenth century and to the boundaries of its values. Within those boundaries, too, Johnson's own Irene meets death in a state of perturbation which licenses abrupt syntax and extravagant sentiment:

O, name not death! Distraction and amazement,
Horrour and agony are in that sound!

A complete account would clearly require us to dwell on Augustan attitudes to death, and on the representative quality of Johnson's private fears.

The nineteenth-century editors divide their allegiances fairly equally between 'dug' and 'dung'. Boswell and Knight take the 'nurse' to be 'death', not 'dung', but they retain 'dung' in the text. Collier and Dyce appeal to palaeography and bibliography with an alleged compositor's misreading of MS 'dugge', but the argument is merely permissive and it settled nothing. It would be premature to generalize about the changing tenor of critical judgements through the nineteenth century (although the New Variorum gives many unhappy instances of its individualism); but it is noticeable that several commentators in the period concur in recognizing a wilful contempt in Cleopatra's words where the Augustans had found moral weakness, exhaustion or distress. In 1860 the American R. G. White says, 'As I am unable to discern what is the dug which is 'the beggar's nurse and Caesar's', and as the word in the text is expressive of the speaker's bitter disgust of life, I make no change.' Hudson, writing in about 1880, puts the point in the accents of his time: 'Cleopatra is speaking contemptuously of this life, as if anything which depends upon such coarse, vulgar feeding were not worth keeping'; and F. A. Marshall finds 'dung' to be 'simply a periphrasis for the fruits of the fertilizing earth, used, certainly, in a spirit of bitter mockery and supreme contempt'. It is apt enough that Dowden and Swinburne have in the meantime assimilated Shakespeare's Cleopatra into their mythologies of fatal women, and Furnivall has recalled us to Shakespeare's own fickle and serpentine mistress, the Dark Lady.

Thiselton, writing at the turn of the century, may be taken to illustrate one of the ultimate fantasies of character criticism. Noting the poetry's glance back to Antony's words about the dungy earth, he finds in it one of several reminiscences that 'suggest the integrity of Cleopatra's attachment to Antony'; by this subtlety of technique 'Shakespeare meant us to leave Cleopatra, notwithstanding her failings, with feelings of sympathy and admiration, and that our last thoughts should be of "the glory of her womanhood".'

Furness allows himself the privilege of a last word, commending 'dung' for its 'elemental vigour . . . wholly lacking in Warburton's substitution'. The controversy was revived in the *Times Literary Supplement* of 1926, but the correspondence was eclectic – hardly any of its proposals had not been made before, including the conjectures 'tongue' and 'wrong'. But to exemplify the insight of our own age at its most commanding, it may be possible to single out, for some future Variorum, Wilson Knight's remarks on the passage in *The Imperial Theme*:[4]

> So far we have noted death's effect from the side of life: now we
> pass to its own essential sovereignty. First, it is like sleep; second,
> it tastes no longer that 'dungy earth' which is unworthy of its child;
> finally, it is nurse alike to Caesar in his glory and the beggar in
> his penury – a kindly presence, dear nurse to life, eternity calling
> back the child of time to its bosom. Thus we pass from noting its
> aesthetic appeal to a quick and tight analysis of its apparent effects,
> and finally contemplate its more personal, moral attitude to man:
> that of a nurse to a child. Is this 'death'? What is the 'death' of
> *Antony and Cleopatra*? Not that the word itself is elsewhere absent:
> but it is continually welcomed as something of positive worth and
> sweet nourishing delight, like love:

> > Where art thou, death?
> > Come hither, come! come, come, and take a queen
> > Worth many babes and beggars!
> >
> > (v. ii. 47–9)

Knight's appeal is to the secret organization of the metaphor, which he
mimics in the course of his description (contriving to suggest 'dug' even as
he takes the reading 'dung'). Images of breeding and death are quietly
assimilated into each other until the two kinds are almost identical: from
Antony's teasing of Lepidus:

> > as it ebbes, the Seedsman
> > Upon the slime and ooze scatters his graine
> > And shortly comes to Harvest
> >
> > (ii. vii. 21–3)

to the closing scene when the asp is a baby that sucks the nurse asleep.
When the play is read with this kind of responsiveness it is easy to see how
the squabble about 'dug' and 'dung' arose; had the Folio read 'dugge' some
watchful editor would have emended to 'dung', and his successors may all
have changed their mounts.

Is Wilson Knight among the first to recognize this tragic equation between
death and nourishment in *Antony and Cleopatra*? Is he representative of a
generation better placed to understand this aspect of the play, or have
others in other times enjoyed the same insights but abstained from flaunting
them? Both the stage history and the critical history suggest that Knight is
healing a long sustained insensibility. Although it is just possible that the

---

[4] *The Imperial Theme* (1931, 1951), p. 312. For Knight's earlier view, preferring
'dug' and citing *2 Henry VI*, iii. ii. 392, see *The Sovereign Flower* (1962; article
reprinted from *The New Adelphi*, September 1927).

play was given at Blackfriars before 1642, the Theatre Royal under the Restoration seems not to have exercised performance rights, and it may be that an authentic version was first mounted by Phelps at Sadler's Wells in 1849. The stage had in the interim been dominated by *All for Love* and by a number of Shakespeare Dryden travesties; and it is characteristic of them that they etiolate the Shakespearian metaphors. Dryden, perhaps mimicking the soothingly erotic 'languishingly sweet' manner of Fletcher in *The False One*, was to win Scott's applause for his Cydnus speech because it was 'flowery without diffuseness and rapturous without hyperbole'. Judging from descriptions of late nineteenth-century performances, even the rediscovered Shakespearian version was not allowed too close a contact with Nilus slime.

Large critical comment on the play (as distinct from glosses on detail) again testifies to a prolonged failure to receive its elemental insights. Johnson is particularly ungracious about the poetry (in spite of his skill at disentangling it). He enjoys the tumult of events and the moral fable, but that endeavour of art by which visionary hyperbole seeks to foil death is alien to him: conceit, hyperbole and wit have no place in his Augustan charnel house.

Coleridge was the first Englishman to approach the play primarily through its 'happy valiancy of style' which he called 'but the representative and result of all the material excellencies so expressed'. Yet his resolutely general tribute is defective in insight where it might have been triumphant. Cleopatra's passion, he says, 'is supported and reinforced by voluntary stimulus and sought-for associations, instead of blossoming out of spontaneous emotions'. Like many a witness from Johnson to L. C. Knights, Coleridge is echoing Dolabella's cool, sympathetic, civilized disclaimer, 'Gentle madam, no.' But Coleridge not only disowns the extravagance, he detects the culpable moral energies that promote it – sensation seeking and self-dramatization. And yet he can marvel at the 'angelic strength' and 'fiery force' of the language. Does he believe that Shakespeare collaborated with the sensational appetites of his heroes in order simply to 'astonish us'?

Oddly enough, modern criticism has been sensitized by Coleridge at precisely the point where Cleopatra answers Dolabella:

> yet t'imagine
> An Antony were Natures peece 'gainst Fancie,
> Condemning shadowes quite.
>
> (v. ii. 98–100)

Shakespeare's distinction between fancy and imagination requires that the Antony of Cleopatra's final vision should be made neither by nature alone nor by fantasy alone, but by an eternalizing imaginative transfiguration of nature – a feat of the poet's art and the lover's. The vision is hard-won by both Cleopatra and by Shakespeare (and by the audience) from a full experience of the play.

Antony and Cleopatra offers to vindicate the imagination in a fashion that the Romantics should have found highly congenial ('The gates of the senses open upon eternity'). But it had to wait for a new romanticism before it could be fittingly acclaimed by hyperbole; a romanticism whose critical postulates owe much to Nietzsche's *The Birth of Tragedy from the Spirit of Music*.[5]

Modern romanticism (a fugitive and provisional category scarcely fit for so confident a label) knows the value of extreme commitments and seeks to excite ranges of thought and feeling hostile to decorous moral and intellectual conformities. It is an intensifying rather than a directing temper of mind, and it has energized many rival and irreconcilable kinds of art and criticism (Yeats, Lawrence, Pound, Joyce). T. E. Hulme exemplified it even as he undertook to denounce it; Wyndham Lewis presented Shakespeare to readers of *Blast*; and Frank Harris, who saw himself as the prophet of a long overdue emancipation from puritanism, betrays the lines of continuity that might be traced between Nietzsche and the novelette.[6]

We have now, perhaps, reached a last phase with the work of Samuel Beckett which, with its trick of sanctifying boredom, recalls Schopenhauer rather than Nietzsche. *End Game*, for example, is a Schopenhauerian parable, and it may be read as one sign among many of a romantic nihilism infecting (or reinfecting) an area of contemporary sensibility. Ionesco's *Rhinoceros* is in comparison a cynic parable, inviting social man (an absurd creature and unhappy) to revert to the condition of a beast (still absurd but less unhappy). It is likely that these moods too will bring their privileges of insight, and it may be that the time is ripe for a study of Shakespeare's pessimism, for some enquiry into what lies behind that disturbing cluster of paradoxes in *Timon of Athens*:

[5] A full account of the English assimilation of Nietzsche would probably begin with Pater, who showed a similar awareness of the significance of the Dionysiac strain in ancient literature and modern thought. See 'A Study of Dionysus' [1876], 'The Bacchanals [1878], in *Greek Studies* (1895): 'Denys L'Auxerrois', *Imaginary Portraits* (1887); 'Apollo in Picardy' [1893], in *Miscellaneous Studies* (1904). Arthur Symons wrote about Nietzsche and Tragedy in 1903 (*Plays, Acting and Music*, 1907) in a critical rhetoric much fitter for *Antony and Cleopatra* than that which he used in his early essay on the play (reprinted in *Studies in the Elizabethan Drama*, 1920). Wilson Knight discusses his own immediate obligations to Bradley, Murry, Colin Still and others in his preface to the 1951 edition of *The Imperial Theme*.

[6] 'When we English have finally left that dark prison of Puritanism and lived for some time in the sunlight where the wayside crosses are hidden under climbing roses, we shall probably couple "Antony and Cleopatra" with "Hamlet" in our love as Shakespeare's supremest works' (*The Man: Shakespeare*, 1909).

> My long sicknesse
> Of Health, and Liuing, now begins to mend
> And nothing brings me all things . . .
>
> (v. i. 186–8)

and behind the radical renunciations of rhetoric and life in 'Lippes, let foure words go by and Language end' (*Timon*, v. i. 220). Renaissance pessimism might well serve to qualify and refine our own, with Shakespeare supplying the most instant points of contact; some pessimisms are more vital than others.

We would take a false impression, however, from a history of critical sensibility which confined itself to responsiveness to the *poetry* of Shakespeare's plays. The expressiveness of a play it more than the language alone affords; it is won from the playwright's deployment of a complex range of theatre conventions – the treaties controlling our interpretation of speech, character, action and spectacle. It is in this area, perhaps, that we may most immediately recognize an opportunity to sharpen our reactions to the subtleties and indeed the simplicities of Renaissance drama. The ironic self-consciousness of modern playwrights from Chekhov and Pirandello, together with their readiness to play upon the nerves of the audience by dislocating the established conventional relationships, should (quite properly) make us more watchful for this kind of thing in the past.

The convention particularly affected is the soliloquy. What we make of the soliloquy convention depends largely upon what we assume and believe about 'the self', about human identity. One reason why nineteenth-century criticism differs so strikingly from our own is that it could use words like 'character', 'individual' and 'soul' much more confidently than we can (see, for example, Carlyle on The Hero as Poet, talking of Shakespeare). We are more apt to brood upon the question first pursued in a characteristically modern way by David Hume; what do we mean by human identity, what is it that makes a man unique? Or, to focus the question on stage situations, what is it that sets a man apart? M. C. Bradbrook some years ago remarked that 'the graduation between the frank appeal *ad spectatores* and the subtlest nuances of Shakespearian dramaturgy make the dead level of modern dialogue seem a very primitive affair'.[7] It is in this respect (in the plays of Beckett at least) less primitive than it was; but the range of possibilities in Renaissance drama remains insufficiently recognized. In talking of soliloquy and aside in Shakespeare we need to keep in mind the multiple kinds of 'apartness' that 'characters' are made to cultivate or suffer. The Elizabethans did their best thinking (I believe) in the theatre, and by and through the conventions of theatre. Appeals to 'the soliloquy convention' can be

---

[7] *Themes and Conventions of Elizabethan Tragedy* (1935, 1952), p. 112.

premature and ingenuous without an awareness of the swift and intricate changes that occur minute by minute, or line by line, in the course of its more sophisticated developments.[8]

One such development may be traced in the second scene of *The Winter's Tale*, taking as starting-point Leontes' aside:

> I am angling now,
> Though you perceive not how I give line.
>
> (I. ii. 180)

This may not be technically soliloquy since at least two other characters are on the stage, and the last words 'How now boy?', if not the whole speech, are addressed to Mamillius. Within the context, however, the technical question is an idle one. Leontes has not long uttered that notoriously obscure speech with the apostrophe: 'Affection! Thy intention stabs the centre.' He is supposed to be talking at the time to Mamillius, but the boy can be taken to make no more of it than Polixenes who 'overhears' and then asks of Hermione, 'what means Sicilia?'; she, nonplussed (like most of the commentators) can only say, 'He something seems unsettled'; and a moment later we learn from the dialogue that Leontes 'held a brow of distraction' – a precise direction for the playing of the episode. The obscurity is a calculated effect. We are made witnesses to the recession of Leontes' character into private, obsessed monologue, addressed to himself. It would not do for the words 'Affection! Thy intention stabs the centre' to be instantly lucid; for them to be a means of direct communication with other people; the obscurity collaborates with the 'aside' to quicken the drift into isolation. But the words are not inconsequential raving either. They are haunted by several possible meanings which have to be teased out in the light of what we recognize of Leontes' obsession. We might paraphrase: 'Love indeed! Your disloyalty is manifest to me and it cuts to the heart'; but the point is that the language at this moment is not public – it is pre-articulate, imperfectly formed, like most *private* thought.

So it happens that when we reach the soliloquy 'I am angling now' we are sufficiently aware of its perversely private nature. Having accepted the intricate terms of our treaty with the playwright we feel that we are listening to self-communing mutterings. Whether Camillo and Mamillius are also listening is a minor question asking 'are they, like us, witnesses to this betrayal of a private obsession?' There is a disturbing discord in this scene between the social and the private self; at a high moment of hospitable ceremony the ego turns in upon its own fragmented being. And this effect is attained in spite of the more routine soliloquy convention which allows

---

[8]The second scene of *King Lear* is a rich example.

a man to appear to talk to himself without seeming mad. Leontes, in brief, 'talks to himself' in a more naturalistic as well as in a theatrical sense. Our reaction is not, 'we must by convention allow these words to disclose the facts about Leontes' state of mind.' It is rather, 'he's talking to himself, he must be off his head.' The interjection, 'Go, play, boy, play' is addressed to a Mamillius who is encroaching on his father's vocal self-torturings, trying to treat them as if they were what the earlier 'distracted' speeches half struggled to be – conversation, straight dialogue. We watch the breakdown of communications; the severing of a human bond.

So far the Leontes soliloquy is a piece of quasi-naturalism; this figure soliloquizes on the stage because he is representing a character talking to himself in court. But there is a momentous peripeteia to come. The obsessive nature of the speech has made it intimate to the point of exclusiveness and the audience is sufficiently insulated from Leontes to treat him as a maniacal self-styled cuckold, totally out of touch with normal values. But Shakespeare does not allow the audience to keep its watchful Olympian security for long:

> Thy Mother playes, and I
> Play too; but so disgrac'd a part, whose issue
> Will hiss me to my Grave. Contempt and Clamor
> Will be my Knell.
>
> (I. ii. 187–90)

The pun on 'plays' announces an astonishing excursion into the soliloquy of direct address. Leontes ceases to appear to be the King of Sicilia, playing cuckold to a playful wife, and reverts to being an actor playing the part of Leontes before an audience which brings to the theatre its own anxieties about adultery:

> There have been
> (Or I am much deceiv'd) Cuckolds ere now,
> And many a man there is (even at this present,
> Now while I speake this) holds his wife by th' Arme
> That little thinkes she has been sluyc'd in's absence,
> And his Pond fish'd by his next Neighbor (by
> Sir Smile, his Neighbour).
>
> (I. ii. 190–6)

It may be that a pause after 'by his next Neighbor' can catch the audience grinning and turn the next words 'Sir Smile, his Neighbor' into an allusion to 'the man next to you in the theatre'. Gielgud once played the speech this way, Sprague tells us, with electrifying effect.

The obsession which, a moment before, was by use of one soliloquy convention attached exclusively to the self-deluded cuckold figure on the stage, is now, by the use of another convention, excited communally. But the terms of the treaty are daring and hazard the very play convention itself – yet deftly so, and almost unobtrusively.

These enterprising uses of convention have grown out of, or been adapted from, a number of more commonplace, more conventional, conventions. And conventional conventions are used often enough in *The Winter's Tale*; the second scene, for example, ends with a disarmingly transparent use of soliloquy when Camillo explains to the audience his intention to quit the court. The association of soliloquy with 'talking to oneself', with madness, paranoia or obsession, haunts a number of plays in the Elizabethan repertory, starting perhaps with Kyd's *Spanish Tragedy*. A history of the convention might begin with Seneca, *Hercules Furens* and *Hercules Oetaeus*, and reach a climax with *King Lear* and *Macbeth*. Lear's storm and heath speeches are not strictly soliloquies but they are utterances of the isolated self, and the presence of other figures on the stage intensifies the isolation. But the simplest precedent to the Leontes speech is the cuckold soliloquy. The isolation of the paranoiac cuckold is a clear opportunity for soliloquy; there is no one he can trust, and no one in whom he can confide without shame. Kitely talks to himself in *Every Man in his Humour* and fears that he has been overheard. Shakespeare's Ford is a soliloquizing cuckold and there is a hint of the convention operating (among other more complex soliloquy conventions) in *Othello*.[9] The convention permitting the actor *as actor* to address the audience directly is usually confined to prologues and epilogues, and it is hard to find a close parallel to Leontes on adultery.

Probings into convention conducted in this spirit – at the instigation, as it were, of the modern playmaker – would reveal a highly accomplished resourcefulness in the control of the distance between the players and their auditors. Each kind of play tends to use soliloquy to express its own characteristic modes of isolation; in the comedies they are often the isolations of the unrequited or the jealous lover, in the histories the isolations of power or of weakness, and in the tragedies the isolations of malice, madness and suffering. But one would not wish to promote categories of this kind. It is enough that we keep our eyes open to the possibilities. To trace, for example, the nuances of self-observation, self-dramatization and self-analysis through *Hamlet* would reveal an astonishing suppleness of changing relationships between soliloquizer and audience. Soliloquy in this play is closely expressive of sense of guilt – the king is most guilty but the prince has (diminishingly) the keener consciousness of guilt; hence the impression

---

[9] *Othello* enjoys the isolation of the Tamburlaine-like hero (alone fit to voice his own virtue) and suffers the isolation of the Jonsonian cuckold; he is trapped by the deployment of the soliloquy convention which isolates Iago, Morality-fashion, as devil and intriguer. Like Edmund, Iago is made a self-consciously theatrical figure.

of Hamlet taking into his consciousness the sins of the realm, and fitting himself (in the eyes of the audience) for a tragic death. Most of the *Hamlet* soliloquies, including the tardy prayer of Claudius, are by their impulsive syntax and complex shifts of thought designed to be *over*heard. The possible exceptions are, "'Tis now the very witching hour of night', and 'Now might I do it pat.' But these have the histrionic quality which we associate with Hamlet the good actor – he is playing the part of revenge killer, imitating the Lucianus of the mouse-trap play; and it is a part that neither his sensibility nor circumstance allow him to play for long.[10]

As these last remarks are intended to hint, there is much more to be said about the dialogue between our own preoccupations and those of the Renaissance. It could touch all that Sir James Frazer might have found particularly interesting in English Seneca, *Titus Andronicus* and *King Lear*.[11] Or it could pursue, in an idiom that Pirandello and Yeats would have found congenial, the Renaissance fascination with masks, assumed parts and the playing of roles.

It would be misleading, however, to leave the impression that modern sensitivities and insensitivities to Shakespeare must be exclusively controlled by our experience of modern literature and thought. The plays keep alive many modes of understanding and delight that are alien to current life and belief, and the miracle is that the art can stay quick when our understanding of it is virtually dead. In such cases it is better to consult more thoroughly the fashion of Shakespeare's times and let our own go momentarily unregarded.

I take, for an instance, the trial-scene of *The Merchant of Venice*. In the course of one of his sensitive accounts of the play J. R. Brown draws attention to a pervasive difference of opinion between those who have written on the trial scene in recent years; some, like Coghill, idealize and allegorize, seeing Portia against Shylock as Mercy opposed to Justice, the Old Law and the New; and there are those who find it 'most ingenious satire'.[12]

I think it characteristic of the play that from the beginning we watch it with, as it were, one auspicious and one dropping eye or, changing the implication slightly, an innocent eye and a sceptical. With an effacing tact

[10] I owe this point to Roy Walker, *The Time is out of Joint* (1948).

[11] See Robert Hapgood, 'Shakespeare and the Ritualists', *Shakespeare Survey*, 15 (1962), for a review of criticism pursued under the shadow of Frazer. John Holloway, *The Story of the Night* (1961), writes in the Gilbert Murray tradition, and has a chapter dealing with the Idea of Human Sacrifice. *Titus Andronicus* takes a human sacrifice as a starting-point, and its imagery often reminds us that blood must be shed to fertilize the earth.

[12] H. Sinsheimer, quoted in J. R. Brown (ed.), *The Merchant of Venice* (1955), p. li.

Shakespeare reminds us that Belmont is doubly golden – vibrant with rare harmonies and richly endowed with money. And Venice offers both an image of youthful inconsequence and an image of the acquisitive society. In the same way the legal masquerade of Act IV can appear in two lights. To the more sceptical eye it appears a magnificent exercise in lawcourt virtuosity. Shylock is most skilfully outplayed, for this is another game, another 'merry sport' turned to earnest. Even the famous mercy speech is an adroit piece of tactics, for it disables Shylock from a mercy plea and nevertheless puts him at the mercy of Antonio and the Duke's court. Sceptically received, the episode is what Gratiano takes it to be in his wrestling image, 'Now, infidel, I have you on the hip'; it is a consummate piece of Jew-baiting. But if we take it only sceptically we find ourselves sentimentalizing Shylock and brutalizing Portia.

There is an equal and opposite response which greatly enriches the play's allegory. Portia comes to the Venetian court from Belmont and brings with her a sum of money, her wit, and a principle. The money is refused, and the wit succeeds only because it serves the principle. And to illuminate that principle we must consult, not the *Gesta Romanorum* or the Record Office, but the Renaissance philosophers of law. If we ask why the play is memorable alike for the music of Belmont and the trial scene, we find an answer in (for example) Hooker's *Laws of Ecclesiastical Polity* and Bodin's *The Six Bookes of a Commonweale*. Music both symbolized and effected those higher harmonies that contingent laws tried to promote in civil societies.

Before insisting on the analogues, however, we do well to remember that the play keeps constantly in touch with its comedy traditions of romance and intrigue. Belmont transforms hard-up courtiers and scheming runaway couples into dedicated lovers by the agency of music:

> Since nought so stockish, hard and full of rage,
> But music for the time doth change his nature.
> (v. i. 81–2)

'For the time' is a realistic, if not a sceptical touch, just as it is realistic if not sceptical to place those memorable evocations of the music of the spheres in a space of idyllic leisure enjoyed by young lovers. The pythagorean vision:

> Such harmony is in immortal souls,
> But whilst this muddy vesture of decay
> Doth grossly close it in, we cannot hear it
> (v. i. 63–5)

owes as much to one of the rarer moods of courtship as to Lorenzo's education at Padua.

It is nevertheless relevant to glance at Hooker's handling of the same range of ideas:[13]

> Touching musical harmony whether by instrument or by voice, it being but of high and low in sounds a due proportionable disposition, such notwithstanding is the force thereof, and so pleasing effects it hath in that very part of man which is most divine, that some have been thereby induced to think that the soul itself by nature is or hath in it harmony.
>
> In harmony the very image and character even of virtue and vice is perceived, the mind delighted with their resemblances, and brought by having them often iterated into a love of the things themselves. For which cause there is nothing more contagious and pestilent than some kinds of harmony; than some nothing more strong and potent unto good.
>
> They must have hearts very dry and tough, from whom the melody of the psalms doth not sometime draw that wherein a mind religiously affected delighteth.
>
> (II. 5.38.1)

Ideally, by Hooker's account, the harmonies that are intimated in music ought to pervade the total hierarchical structure of laws from the Divine, through the Natural to the Civil. But the more contingent laws – touching directly the fallen and mutable world – cannot be relied on to operate harmoniously. Hence it sometimes happens that Equity must redress the false balance of the Law:

> We see in contracts and other dealings which daily pass between man and man, that, to the utter undoing of some, many things by strictness of law may be done, which equity and honest meaning forbiddeth. Not that the law is unjust, but unperfect; nor equity against, but above, the law, binding men's consciences in things which law cannot reach unto.
>
> (II. 5.9.3)

Hooker establishes for us some of the proper perspectives for the play. The situation in Venice is the sort that he postulates: by contract and by strictness of law, something is about to be done 'which equity and honest meaning forbiddeth'.

It might loosely be said that Portia brings from Belmont the principle of Equity 'above the law' but not against it. But this of course understates the wit of the intervention – Equity is vindicated in Venice by an attention to the letter of the law which is yet more strict than Shylock's. Hooker

[13] *Laws of Ecclesiastical Polity*, ed. J. Keble, 3 vols (1874).

recognized that the 'literal practice' of law might sometimes prejudice equity, and Shylock would seem to prove his point; but Shylock, in refusing the mercy plea, refuses to allow Equity its most humane opening; the words of the bond are squeezed harder, and an ultimate loyalty to the letter of the law is found, after all, to vindicate its spirit. Lawcourt virtuosity is therefore indispensable to render the letter of the law equitable and so keep it consonant with the high intimations of divine harmony touched so lightly and finely in the music of Belmont.

But what of the ring trickery that ends the play? It is a hint that comedy of intrigue and romance might go in other directions too; that a clever plot can sound a discord and contrive a concord in the harmonies of marriage. Bodin's translator, Richard Knolles, offers us these marginalia: 'Harmonicall Justice of all others the best'; 'Harmonicall proportion good to be in marriage observed, and so likewise in the government of a whole Commonweale'; 'The judge bound unto the verie words of the law, is not yet therby embarred to use the equitie of the law or yet the reasonable exposition therof.'[14] All come within a page or two of each other, as guides to a sustained and highly technical discussion of music, marriage, and the duty of the magistrate on certain occasions to admit equity into law. It is unlikely that Bodin was among the volumes that Shakespeare imagined Nerissa carrying from Belmont; but we can be confident that had Richard Knolles seen the play he would not have supposed that 'Shakespeare planned a *Merchant of Venice* to let the Jew dog have it, and thereby to gratify his own patriotic pride of race.'[15]

The Merchant of Venice is not a profound play. It touches profound issues but with a becoming lightness, within the decorum of comedy. Portia is made sufficiently human; her rare gifts remain this side the magical and divine. And Shylock is sufficiently stereotyped; the sources of his obsessions are distinctly traced to the flaws in Venetian society, a broken family and a wounded psyche, but they are not tragically explored. And Shakespeare, like Spenser, carries on tip-toe his burden of Renaissance thought.

There is a Japanese test for colour-blindness, by which defective vision recognizes one configuration in a pattern of coloured dots and true vision recognizes another. So it is, perhaps, with changing phases of judgement and sensibility. The metaphor need not deter us from 'the common pursuit

---

[14] Jean Bodin, *The Six Bookes of the Commonweale*, R. Knolles, 1606 (*STC*, 3193), bk. 6, ch. 6. Bodin also writes: 'And this is it for which the auntient Greekes aptly fained, Love to have bene begotten of *Porus and Penia*, that is to say, of *Plentie* and *Povertie*, love growing betwixt them two; so as in song the Meane betwixt the Base and the Treble, maketh a sweet and melodious consent and harmonie.'

[15] H. B. Charlton, *Shakespearian Comedy* (1938), p. 127.

of true judgement' but it might make us more wary. For it may even happen that where true vision finds mere medley the colour-blind discover a most dainty design.

Part II

Catastrophes of History

4   The Frame of Disorder –
Henry VI

Three of the four plays about the Wars of the Roses were staged fully and in sequence, probably for the first time, in 1953.[1] The experience was arresting and moving, testifying to the continuity of our own preoccupations with those of Tudor England; here, it seemed, was yet another historical instance of anarchy owed to innocence and order won by atrocity. The three parts of *Henry VI* express the plight of individuals caught up in a cataclysmic movement of events for which responsibility is communal and historical, not personal and immediate, and they reveal the genesis out of prolonged violence of two figures representing the ultimate predicament of man as a political animal – Henry and Richard, martyr and machiavel. But one would not wish to over-stress whatever analogues there may be between the fifteenth century and the twentieth, since these might be proved quite as striking for ages other than our own. If we are now more sympathetically disposed towards Shakespeare's history plays than were the readers and audiences of seventy years ago, it is largely because we have more flexible ideas about the many possible forms that history might take. We are less dominated by the Positivist view that the truth is co-extensive with, and not merely consistent with, the facts. Contemporaries of Boswell-Stone were reluctant to take seriously a vision of the past that made free with the data for purposes they took to be simply dramatic. Following the lead of Richard Simpson, critics began to read Shakespeare's histories as documents of Tudor England, addressed primarily to contemporary problems and not fundamentally curious about the pastness of the past.[2] Now we are better

[1] For Sir Barry Jackson's own account see 'On producing *Henry VI*', *Survey*, 6 (1953), pp. 147–55.
[2] Richard Simpson, 'The Politics of Shakespeare's History Plays', in *Trans. New Sh. Soc.* (1874). A similar approach is made by L. B. Campbell.

placed to see them from the point of view represented, for instance, by R. G. Collingwood's *The Idea of History* and Herbert Butterfield's *Christianity and History*, putting a less exclusive stress on facts, and looking harder at the myths and hypotheses used to interpret them – at ideas of providence, historical process, personal responsibility and the role of the hero. These are precisely the ideas that the playwright is fitted to explore and clarify, and Shakespeare's treatment of them is the most searching our literature has to offer. For Shakespeare was peculiarly sensitive to the subtle analogues between the world and the stage, between the shape of events and the shape of a play, between the relationship of historical process to individuals and that of the playwright to his characters. He tried from the beginning to meet the urgent and practical problem of finding dramatic forms and conventions that would express whatever coherence and order could be found in the 'plots' of chronicle history. Where narrative and play are incompatible, it may be the record and it may be the art that is defective as an image of human life, and in the plays framed from English and Roman history it is possible to trace subtle modulations of spectacle, structure and dialogue as they seek to express and elucidate the full potential of the source material. A full account would take in *The Tempest*, which is the last of Shakespeare's plays to be made out of historical documents and which has much to do with the rule of providence over the political activities of man. But from these early plays alone there is much to be learned about the vision and technique of historical drama, and these are the plays that are submitted most rigorously to the test of allegiance to historical record.

Part 1: The Pageantry of Dissension

We might begin by taking a famous passage of Nashe as the earliest surviving critical comment on *Part 1*:

> How would it have joyed brave *Talbot* (the terror of the French) to think that after he had lyne two hundred yeares in his Tombe, hee should triumphe againe on the Stage, and have his bones new embalmed with the teares of ten thousand spectators at least, (at severall times) who, in the Tragedian that represents his person, imagine they behold him fresh bleeding.[3]

This, primarily, is the ritual experience Shakespeare sought and won. He transposed the past of the tombs, the 'rusty brass' and the 'worm-eaten books' into living spectacle. Whatever else must be said about all three

---

[3] Quoted in E. K. Chambers, *Shakespeare* (1930), II, p. 188.

plays, they keep this quality of epic mime and with it an elementary power to move large audiences. There is, too, something in Nashe's glance at those early performances that chimes with Coleridge's observation that 'in order that a drama may be properly historical, it is necessary that it should be the history of the people to whom it is addressed.'[4] Shakespeare's early histories are addressed primarily to the audience's heroic sense of community, to its readiness to belong to an England represented by its court and its army, to its eagerness to enjoy a public show celebrating the continuing history of its prestige and power. This does not mean, however, that we must surrender these early plays to Joyce's remark that Shakespeare's 'pageants, the histories, sail full-bellied on a tide of Mafeking enthusiasm.' In the more mature plays of *Henry IV* the heroic sense of community will be challenged by the unheroic – by that range of allegiances which binds us less to authority and the King than to each other and to Falstaff; and the death of Hotspur is a more complicated theatrical experience than that of Talbot in Nashe's description. But the early histories too express stresses and ironies, complexities and intricate perspectives beyond the reach of the condescensions usually allowed them.

Even *Part 1* has its share. If this is a play more moving to watch than to read it is because it makes the historical facts eloquent through the language of pageantry. In a way that Nashe does not sufficiently suggest, Shakespeare exploits the poignant contrast between the past nostalgically apprehended through its monuments, and the past keenly re-enacted in the present – between the pasts 'entombed' and 'fresh-bleeding'. The effect which testifies to the continuity of stage techniques with those of the Tournament and the civic pageant, is felt immediately in the first scene (where the mood of a cathedral entombment is mocked by the energies of the brawl), in the scene of Bedford's death (III. ii), and, most distinctly, in the death of Talbot (IV. vii). These are among the several episodes of *Henry VI* that are presented both as 'events' – as if they actually happened, the figures caught up in them alive and free, and as 'occasions' – happenings that have some symbolic significance, or are (in retrospect) 'inevitable' turning-points in the history. Thus the scene of Talbot's and Lisle's death would, if perfectly executed, present the chronicled event with convincing documentary detail, in a style befitting the occasion – the fire of English chivalry glowing brightest before it expires. The context ensures that Talbot stands at his death for the martial glory of England, and Bordeaux for the dominion of France. When the English and French nobles meet over his corpse (IV. vii), the retrospective, reflective mood and the instant, practical mood are sustained side by side; the first calling to mind the image of a

---

[4] T. M. Raysor (ed.), *Coleridge's Shakespeare Criticism* (1930) I, p. 138.

memorial tomb seen in the remote perspective of a later time, and the second recalling us to the hard realities of the battlefield. Talbot is discovered dead with his son 'enhearsed in his arms' (IV. vii. 45), resembling a figure on a monument. Lucy's long intonement of Talbot's titles was taken at first or second hand from the inscription on Talbot's actual tomb at Rouen, and it retains its lapidary formality.[5] Joan's lines,

> Him that thou magnifiest with all these titles
> Stinking and fly-blown lies here at our feet.
>
> (IV. vii. 75)

have been mocked for their documentary impropriety (fly-blown in two minutes!) but they serve to accent the recollection in the spectacle of a Tudor tomb. Beneath the effigy of the complete man in, as it were, painted marble finery, lies the image of the rotten corpse. Joan's jeer mediates between the mutability threnody and the return to the exigencies of battle; the action gets under way again – there is a body to dispose of.

While there are other opportunities to arrest the flux of events, they are not all of this kind. The changes in pace and shifts of perspective owe as much to the chronicle as to the techniques of pageantry. The essential events and the processes and energies that shape and direct them are transmitted into the spectacle with a high sense of responsibility to the chronicle vision.

The three parts of *Henry VI* coincide with three distinct phases of the history and show that Shakespeare did what he could to tease a form for each of the plays out of the given material. The first phase of Holinshed's version reports about four hundred incidents in the French campaign, some perfunctorily and some with full solemnity.[6] The siege of Orleans is the most conspicuous in both chronicle and play. Holinshed finds occasion to deploy his epic clichés, with the 'Englishmen' behaving themselves 'right valiantlie under the conduct of their couragious capteine' to keep and enlarge 'that which Henrie the fift had by his magnanimite & puissance atchived' (*Hol.* (1808), p. 161). But the accent changes to sombre historical prophecy, marking the ineluctable, impersonal historical law:

---

[5] See J. Pearce, 'An Earlier Talbot Epitaph', *Modern Language Notes* (1944), p. 327.

[6] Pp. 585–625 in vol. III of the 1587 edn used by Shakespeare. These are the 'first phase', as they supply almost all the material of *Part 1*. *Part 2* uses pp. 622–43, and *Part 3* pp. 643–93. For convenience references in the text are to the 1808 reprint of vol. III (referred to as *Hol.*). Holinshed's *Chronicle* is a compilation from many sources and the use of his name does not imply authorship. Extracts are provided, with annotations, by W. G. Boswell-Stone, *Shakespeare's Holinshed* (1896), here referred to as *Boswell-Stone*, and in Bullough, III.

But all helped not. For who can hold that which will awaie: In so much that some cities by fraudulent practises, othersome by martial prowesse were recovered by the French, to the great discouragement of the English and the appalling of their spirits; whose hope was now dashed partlie by their great losses and discomfitures (as after you shall heare) but cheeflie by the death of the late deceassed Henrie their victorious king.

These opening pages license a chauvinistic battle-play framing an historical morality about the evil consequences of civil dissension. Here is Holinshed on the loss of a group of towns in 1451:

Everie daie was looking for aid, but none came. And whie? Even bicause the divelish division that reigned in England, so incombred the heads of the noble men there, that the honor of the realme was cleerelie forgotten. (*Hol.* (1808), p. 228)

The chronicled sources of disaster are more nakedly sprung in the play: the loss of the puissant and magnanimous Henry V, the hostile stars, the hard fortunes of war, the perverse skill of the French, the steady eclipse of English chivalry with the deaths of its ageing heroes, and the corrosive quarrels and dynastic rivalries of the nobles at home. All this is manifest in the mere pantomime of *Part 1* – its force would be felt by the stone-deaf, and the routine of the play's rhetoric does much to accent and little to qualify, explore or challenge the basic simplicities of the history.

The originality of Shakespeare's accomplishment is in the shedding of all literary artifice except that which serves to express the temper and structure of the history. The first scene, for instance, establishes at once that double perspective which controls the mood of the chronicle – the sense of being close to the event together with a sense of knowing its consequences. The messenger's long review of the calamities of thirty future years, spoken in the memorial presence of the dead Henry V, is a precise dramatic expression of the narrative's parenthesis, 'as after you shall heare', of which many repetitions catch the effect of a remorseless historical law expounded by an omniscient commentator.

The symmetrical sallies and counter-sallies of the next hour of the pantomime express the fickle movement of Mars, so often moralized by Holinshed: 'thus did things waver in doubtful balance betwixt the two nations English and French'; 'thus oftentimes varied the chance of doubtful war'; 'thus flowed the victory, sometimes on the one party, and sometimes on the other' (*Hol.* (1808), pp. 172, 180, 192). So speaks the dramatic Dauphin:

Mars his true moving, even as in the heavens
So in the earth, to this day is not known:
Late did he shine upon the English side;
Now we are victors; upon us he smiles.

(I. ii. 1)

The literary commonplace carries the chronicle moral in a naïve rhetoric transparent enough to let the raw facts tell.

It is French cunning that most often conspires with Mars to confound the English. The sniping of Salisbury at Orleans exemplifies it in an arresting stage effect ready-made in Holinshed for upper stage (tarras) performance. But as Holinshed's material is otherwise scanty and undramatic, Shakespeare amplifies it by making the French instead of the English employ 'counterfeit husbandmen' to capture Rouen (*Boswell-Stone*, pp. 205–7). He betrays the chronicle detail in order to enforce one of its generalizations, for while on one occasion defending the use of fraud in lawful war, Holinshed habitually prefers honest violence – an impression strengthened in the play by the rival characterizations of Joan and Talbot. Talbot's stratagem at Auvergne (II. ii) is not subtle-witted but represents the triumph of soldierly resourcefulness over French and female craft.

While 'martiall feates, and daily skirmishes' continue in France, the play returns in four scenes to England and conveys the essential Holinshed by keeping the civil causes coincident with the military effects. Thus the dramatic concurrence of the siege of Orleans and the brawl outside the Tower of London (I. iii) directly expresses the chronicle point, 'Through dissention at home, all lost abroad' (*Hol.* (1808), p. 228). The Gloucester–Winchester feud is elaborately chronicled and patience and some skill go into Shakespeare's abbreviation of it. More important than his management of the intricate detail, however, is the strategic liberty taken with the facts in order to reduce the formal reconciliation elaborately mounted in the chronicle to a repetition of the earlier squabble, but this time concluded with a reluctant, casual handshake; the Mayor, the muttered asides, and the servants off to the surgeon's and the tavern, demote the dignity of the event (*Hol.* (1808), p. 146).[7] That quarrel thus becomes representative of those which Holinshed ascribes to 'privie malice and inward grudge', while the dynastic rivalry assumes by contrast a status appropriate to its remoter origin and more terrible consequence.

It is in his presentation of the struggle between Lancaster and York that Shakespeare does most to transcend the temper and enrich the data of the chronicle. For in the early pages of Holinshed the struggle is nowhere

---

[7] Here it is Bedford who formally rebukes the quarrelsome lords; the play's homely figure of the mayor is borrowed from Fabyan.

clearly epitomized. There are only allusions to things that will 'hereafter more manifestlie appeare'; Henry, for instance, creates Plantagenet Duke of York, 'not foreseeing that this preferment should be his destruction, nor that his seed should of his generation be the extreame end and finall conclusion' (*Hol.* (1808), p. 155; *Boswell-Stone*, p. 223). Hence Shakespeare's invention of four scenes which, through the heraldic formality of their language, reveal the hidden keenness and permanence of the dynastic conflict. The only distinguished one – the Temple scene – is much in the manner of *Richard II*; there is the same tension between ceremony and spleen:

> And that I'll prove on better men than Somerset,
> Were growing time once ripen'd to my will.
>
> (II. iv. 98)

But the note is caught again in the scene of Mortimer's death:

> Here dies the dusky torch of Mortimer,
> Choked with ambition of the meaner sort.
>
> (II. v. 123)

The two scenes between Vernon and Basset (III, iv and IV, i) extend the Roses dispute from the masters to the 'servants'; but unlike those other servants who 'enter with bloody pates' (III. i. 85, stage directions) in pursuit of Winchester's and Gloucester's causes, these conduct their quarrel according to 'the law of arms'. Ceremony and savagery are equally characteristic of chronicle taste, and in *Part 1* a full range of types of dissention is displayed by the mutations of the spectacle.

The laboured and repetitious data of the chronicle are clarified without undue simplification, with the audience required to dwell at leisure on episodes of momentous and lasting significance to the course of history. The rhythm between pattern and process is maintained; the play like the history must be both reflected upon and lived through, its moral shape apprehended but its clamour and hurly-burly racking the nerves. But not all the chronicle material is adroitly and happily assimilated. Shakespeare's embarrassment as heir to the facts and judgements of Holinshed is disconcertingly evident in his treatment of Joan. Holinshed presents two versions; a 'French' one, stated at length but unsympathetically, 'that this Jone (forsooth) was a damsell divine' (*Hol.* (1808), p. 171; *Boswell-Stone*, pp. 210–12); and an 'English' one, owed to Monstrelet, that she was 'a damnable sorcerer suborned by Satan' (*Hol.* (1808), p. 172). Shakespeare pursues the chronicle by making her a manifestly evil angel of light, and as the trick of turning devil into seeming angel was a Morality Play commonplace, a technique of presentation lay to hand.[8] But the figure was much easier to accept under the old allegoric conventions of the Morality Play that Shakespeare has all but discarded than under the new historical documentary ones he was forging. In the early scenes the nice and nasty views about Joan are credibly distributed between the French and English,[9] but after allowing her to voice an authentic French patriotism (winning Burgundy back to her cause) Shakespeare capitulates and throws his French Daniel to the English lions, 'Done like a Frenchman: turne and turne againe' (III. iii. 85). Shakespeare – as an examination of the detail would show – does nothing to mask and much to stress the tension between the rival images of 'Puzel' and 'Pussel', the 'high-minded strumpet' and 'the holy prophetess'. Late in the play she is made to speak a searching indictment of English hypocrisy (v. iv. 36ff) whose barbs are not removed by the spectacle of her converse with evil spirits.

The play ends with the patching of a false peace which holds no promise of a renewed civil order, and whose terms, born out of a silly flirtation, prefigure the final loss of France. None of the many reconciliations have any quality of goodwill, Shakespeare taking his tone again from the *Chronicle*'s general comment on the French Wars:

> But what cause soever hindered their accord and unitie . . . certeine it is, that the onelie and principal cause was, for that the God of peace and love was not among them, without whom no discord is quenched, no knot of concord fastened, no bond of peace confirmed, no distracted minds reconciled, no true freendship mainteined. (*Hol.* (1808), p. 183)

Suffolk's courtship of Margaret (v. iii) prefaces a false peace with a false love. To parody the absurdities of political romance Shakespeare allows Suffolk the style of a professional philanderer (one thinks of de Simier's wooing of Elizabeth for Alençon) and compiles for him 'A volume of enticing lines' more felicitous than Lacy's in *Friar Bacon and Friar Bungay*; but in Greene's play the courtship is an engaging frolic merely, while here the treacheries exercised in the politics of flirtation are as sinister as they are amusing – the betrayal of trust must have evil consequences in the harsh chronicle setting.

Holinshed grieves that 'the God of peace and love' was not among the jarring nobles; but in a sense he was – in the unfortunate person of King Henry – and Shakespeare is well aware of the irony. Henry is 'too virtuous

---

[8] e.g. John Bale, *The Temptation of our Lord* (see *Works*, ed. Farmer, p. 155), and *The Conflict of Conscience* (see Hazlitt-Dodsley, VI, p. 35).

[9] The only mocking lines spoken of Joan by the French are Alençon's at I. ii. 119; the English messenger calls her 'holy prophetess' at I. iv. 102.

to rule the realm of England', like Elidure, the comically naïve King in the early chronicle-morality *Nobody and Somebody*,[10] but Shakespeare makes the point unsmilingly. In the *Henry VI* plays, virtue, through varying degrees of culpable innocence, connives in its own destruction. Had they been performed in the reign of Henry VII, when the canonization of 'Holy Harry' was still a point of debate and his martyrdom a theme for civic spectacle, those who thought the King an innocent might have appealed to the first two plays, and those who took him for a saint, to the last. For as the plays advance, the paradoxical plight of moral man under the rule of historical and political processes grows more disturbing until it reaches something like a tragic solution.

Part 2: The Sacrifice of Gloucester and the Dissolution of Law

There is much in *Part 2* to remind us that we are witnessing the education of a tragic playwright. Shakespeare assimilates and puts to the test theological, political and moral outlooks which, however ugly and pitiless, seem to meet with unsentimental honesty the recorded facts of human experience. *Part 1* could not end in the manner of an heroic tragedy, for the history confronted Shakespeare with the fact that society somehow survives the deaths of its heroes and the conditions for its survival must go on being renewed – a point that tells again in *Julius Caesar*. *Part 1* concludes by establishing the minimal and provisional terms of survival – the death of Joan and the marriage bargain, but the historical facts allow no revival in *Part 2* of the austere, soldierly virtues that supply the moral positives of the first part – Talbot will be displaced by Gloucester.

From one point of view the second and third plays share the same structural frame, supplied by Holinshed in passages such as this:

> But most of all it would seeme, that God was displeased with this marriage: for after the confirmation thereof, the kings freends fell from him, both in England and in France, the lords of his realme fell at division, and the commons rebelled in such sort, that finallie after manie fields foughten, and manie thousands of men slaine, the king at length was deposed, and his sonne killed, and this queene sent home again, with as much miserie and sorrow as she was received with pompe and triumphe: such is the instabilitie of

---

[10]This play (edited by Richard Simpson for the Shakespeare Society) treats the ups and downs of Elidure's reign with challenging irreverence. The extant edition is of 1606, but the original may antedate *Henry VI*.

worldlie felicitie, and so wavering is false flattering fortune. Which
mutation and change of the better for the worse could not but
nettle and sting hir with pensiveness, yea and any other person
whatsoever, that having beene in good estate, falleth into the
contrarie. (*Hol.* (1808), p. 208)

In their unabashed drift from God's displeasure to the waverings of fortune
Holinshed's pieties are characteristic of chronicle theology. The subtler
medieval distinctions between the will of God and the waywardness of
Fortune are lost, but the dominant ideas remain, and they are crucial to
an understanding of Shakespeare's tetralogy, and more particularly, of the
role of Queen Margaret. The chronicle is enlisting Old Testament theology
to rationalize the processes of history: when the land is sinful, God's
judgement recoils upon it, and evil must be atoned by blood sacrifice.
Shakespeare makes fullest use of Margaret to exemplify this moral order;
through the span of the plays she is in turn its agent, victim and oracle. It
is in *Richard III* that Shakespeare's ironic questioning of the chronicle
providence is most telling, when Margaret, disengaged from the action but
brought to the court in the teeth of historical fact, is made the malignant
prophetess of God's displeasure, and Clarence is allowed to protest with
humane eloquence against the theology of his murderers (I. iv. 171–265).
In the *Henry VI* plays the chronicle theology is exposed to a different kind
of test – that of the chronicle's own political ideology.

The chronicles were more ready to accept the tragic-religious solution of
social disorder as a past and finished process than as an omnipresent law.
They wrote in a tradition which had quietly assimilated the mundane,
realistic attitudes for which Machiavelli was to become the most persuasive
apologist; and whenever they write with an eye on the prospect of Tudor
security, they show themselves sympathetic to the 'machiavellian' solution
– stability imposed by strong authority. Hence their strictures on the
'overmuch mildness' of a Henry found 'too soft for governor of a kingdom',
and hence the coolness with which they recognize the peace and prosperity
of the later part of Edward IV's reign,[11] which owed more to the King's
military ability and popularity (however limited) with nobility and commons
than to his integrity as Rightful King and Servant of God. Shakespeare's
most decisive criticism of the chronicle is his virtual suppression of the
temporary recovery under Edward, thus making his moral of peace at the
end of *Richard III* distinctly less 'machiavellian' than it appears in Holinshed
– peace returns by God's ordinance only when the forces of evil are quite

[11] See Edward Halle, *Union of the two noble and illustrate [illustre] famelies of
Lancastre and York*, 1548; ed. H. Ellis, (1809; 1965), Hall's chapter titles pass
from the 'troublesome season' of Henry VI to the 'prosperous reign' of Edward IV.
Shakespeare's judgement of Edward is harsher than that of any of the chroniclers.

expended. The kind of dramatic thinking about history that makes Shakespeare's plays does not prove hospitable to the kind of uncritical good sense that allows the chroniclers to shift from one scale of values to another. In *Henry VI* the sacrificial idea, which makes catastrophe a consequence of sin, is sharply challenged by the 'machiavellian' idea that makes it a consequence of weakness.

While this range of problems is entertained in *Part 2* about the plight of the King himself, the unique form of the play is yielded by the martyrdom of Gloucester. The play climbs to one crisis – a central point in Act III where the killing of Gloucester calls out the strongest statement of the moral-political positives; and it falls to a second – where the battle of St Albans occasions the most powerful poetry of negation.

It opens with a 'Flourish of Trumpets: Then Hoboyes' announcing Margaret with chronicled 'pompe and triumph', but almost at once, as he lets the paper fall and addresses his 'peroration with such circumstance' to the assembled peers, it is Gloucester who dominates the theatre, assuming his representative and symbolic role. Like Gaunt in *Richard II*, he recollects the chivalry of the past and epitomizes a political wisdom alienated in the dramatic 'present'. But there is none of the spiritual and physical malaise that complicates the figure of Gaunt, no sterility or decay. Gaunt's prophecy is the 'ague's privilege' – his approaching death calls out his honesty; but Gloucester is vigorous and defiant, and his honesty brings about his death. If the Gaunt study is the more penetrating exploration of the relation of moral strength to political impotence, this version of Gloucester is the shrewder study of heroic virtue.

Holinshed says that Gloucester's praise should be undertaken by writers of 'large discourse', and notes (as he takes over the Tudor legend) the 'ornaments of his mind', his 'feats of chivalry', 'gravity in counsell' and 'soundness of policy' (*Hol.* (1808), p. 211; *Boswell-Stone*, pp. 250, 265). Together with his magnanimity Holinshed finds a love of the commons and a devotion to the public good. With so strong a lead from the chronicle Shakespeare makes Gloucester's qualities both personal and symbolic. In the first two acts he comes to stand for the rule of law and for the integrity of nobility and commons – the conditions of social order that cease to prevail the moment he is murdered. Holinshed is outspoken about the destruction of the rule of law: 'while the one partie sought to destroie the other, all care of the common-wealth was set aside, and justice and equitie clearelie exiled (*Hol.* (1808), p. 237). But his moral is untied to any single incident, and Shakespeare gives it greater dramatic force by linking it specifically with the destiny of Gloucester. The chronicle supplied hint enough:

Suerlie the duke, verie well learned in the law civill, detesting
malefactors, and punishing offenses in severitie of justice, gat him
hatred of such as feared condigne reward for their wicked dooings.
And although the duke sufficientlie answered to all things against
him objected; yet, because his death was determined, his wisedome
and innocencie nothing availed. (*Hol.* (1808), p. 211; *Boswell-
Stone*, pp. 250, 265)

In the chronicle Gloucester's learning in civil law takes the form of a
wearisome passion for litigation. In the play he is first the severe executor
of Justice and then its patient, vicarious victim.

As Protector he prescribes the judicial combat between Horner and his
prentice, and replaces York by Somerset in France: 'This is the Law, and
this Duke Humfreyes doom' (I. iii. 210). When Eleanor is banished he
again speaks the formal language of his office: 'the Law thou seest hath
judged thee, I cannot justifie whom the Law condemnes' (II. iii. 16). Too
much in this manner would have been wearing, but Shakespeare traces in
Gloucester the humane impulses from which and for which the Law should
speak. His practical genius for improvising justice is exemplified in the
mock-miracle of St Albans (II. i); it delights the dramatic townsmen as
much as the theatre audience, making Humphrey the shrewd, popular hero
respected and 'beloved of the commons'. The King's piety gives place to
laughter, displaying his curiously mixed qualities of ingenuousness and
insight; and the scene concludes with an elegant exchange of sarcasms, a
timely reminder that Suffolk and Beaufort are jealous of Gloucester's public
virtues.

Shakespeare makes less use in *Part 2* of the heraldic and pageant devices
which accent the pattern of *Part 1*, and fuller use of the specifically dramatic
techniques of the Morality Play and English Seneca. Borrowing as much
of the chronicle language as he can, he illuminates the historical event by
casting it into a Morality perspective:

Ah, gracious lord, these days are dangerous:
Virtue is choked with foul ambition
And charity chased hence by rancour's hand;
Foul subornation is predominant
And equity exiled your highness' land.
(III. i. 142)

'Justice and equitie clearelie exiled,' says Holinshed (p. 237). But the
Morality abstractions are in their turn tempered by the immediate interest
in people that Shakespeare learned from his attempts to make historical
facts dramatically convincing.

The private man is never for long masked by the public figure. Gloucester speaks of his condemned Duchess in tones admirably poised between personal feeling and the decorum of his office (II. i. 185), and he speaks from his office unequivocally when she is led from the court (II. iii. 16). But as soon as she is gone, his eyes 'full of teares', he asks the King's permission to leave, and for the first time we learn that Shakespeare's Gloucester (not the chroniclers') is an old man; the personal pathos is heightened and we are reminded that honour is the prerogative of a fading generation. When he next appears, as looker-on at Eleanor's penance, the scene enlarges into a mutability threnody, including the conventional *Mirror for Magistrates* image of summer giving place to barren winter, and the chronicle sentiment about the irony of personal misfortune – 'To think upon my pomp, shall be my hell' (II. iv. 41). But it remains an event in the London streets. The picture of Eleanor's humiliation (however deserved) confesses the cruelty of

> The abject people gazing on thy face,
> With envious looks, laughing at thy shame.
>
> (II. iv. 11)

The intensely passive philosophy of Gloucester meeting the frustrated malice of his Duchess foreshadows the second scene of *Richard II*, but Gaunt puts jaded faith in the principle of non-resistance to an anointed king, while Gloucester's more naïve faith is in the integrity of the law: 'I must offend, before I be attainted' (II. iv. 59). His trial-scene (III. i) takes on a symbolic quality. Henry's reaction to it, undescribed in the chronicles, is used in the play to disclose the natural sympathy between the King's impotent saintliness and Gloucester's political and personal integrity:

> Ah, uncle Humphrey! in thy face I see
> The map of honour, truth, and loyalty . . .
> And as the butcher takes away the calf,
> And binds the wretch and beats it when it strays,
> Bearing it to the bloody slaughter-house;
> Even so remorseless have they borne him hence.
>
> (III. i. 202)

Gloucester's murder is a piece of politic butchery at the centre of the 'plotted tragedy' of the conspirators who are credited with a perverse skill in making an unnatural offence taste of expediency and practical wisdom: 'But yet we want a Colour for his death', and ''Tis meet he be condemned by course of Law' (III. i. 234).

We are not made witnesses to the actual murder, but Gloucester's strangled body is exhibited in a sort of verbal close-up, a remarkable passage, which throws an unusual stress on physical horror (III. ii. 160ff). By this device a frightening spectacular force is given to the dominant historical and tragic idea of the play. By a staged metaphor now, 'Virtue is choked with foul ambition', and the play's mime displays the historical cause and effect by which the murder of Gloucester issues in the Cade rebellion. The strangled body lies on the stage while the commons 'like an angry hive of bees' beat upon the doors.

His death, as Gloucester says himself, is but the prologue to the plotted tragedy. Shakespeare is exposing a period of English history when atrocities became part of the routine of public life and stayed so for some twenty years. Hence his knowledge, if not experience, of the arts of English Seneca becomes relevant to his own art as dramatic historian. It is perhaps no accident that at this point of the narrative Holinshed refers us to 'maister Foxe's book of acts and monuments' (*Hol.* (1808), p. 212). No reader of Foxe could be easily startled by the *Thyestes*, the *Troades*, or *Titus Andronicus*. And in the central acts of *Part 2* we can observe the confluence of the Senecal dramatic tradition, with its ruthless retributive morality, and the Christian (or Hebraic) cult of *Vindicta Dei*. These acts present not only what Foxe calls 'the cruel death or martyrdom of the Good Duke of Glocester' but also 'the judgement of God upon them which persecuted the Duke' (*Foxe* (1583), p. 706). But Shakespeare is not uncritical of the myth behind the grim theocratic drama that features the deaths of Suffolk and Winchester. Although he allows some of his characters to enjoy a complacent relish in witnessing or executing the interventions of the wrath of God, the audience is not allowed to share it. All the acts of retribution in this play and the next are invested in an atmosphere of evil – the images sickening and grotesque:

> And thou that smiledst at good Duke Humphrey's death
> Against the senseless winds shall grin in vain.
>
> (IV. i. 76)

Suffolk's death is an act of lynch law, and one of several similar happenings which is at once a satisfying act of retribution, and therefore a recognition of the chronicle 'Providence'; and 'a barbarous and bloody spectacle' (IV. i. 144), and therefore a moral and aesthetic challenge to the validity of that Providence. In his presentation of the Cardinal's death (III. iii), however, and in his insinuations of the causal chain of prophecy, omen, curse, imprecation and dream, Shakespeare does stage the pitiless pageant of Holinshed and Foxe – *Vindicta Dei* works through revenge figures, through the worm of conscience (as plastic as a tapeworm) and through 'chance' contingencies. But so much (were it not for the tightness of the organization) might have been within the range of Peele or Greene. Shakespeare's play is distinguished by its understanding of the tragic rhythm of political history.

At first glance it might seem that Shakespeare's treatment of the Cade rebels is less sympathetic than Holinshed's. The chronicle Cade is 'of goodlie stature and right pregnant wit'; his 'fair promises of reformation' and his 'Complaint of the Commons of Kent' are responsible and sensible (*Hol.* (1808), p. 222); and his tactics at the start are admirably humane. Why then the comic but bloody spectacle of Act IV of *Part 2*? Brents Stirling[12] suggests that Shakespeare was aligning himself with those who most severely judged the rioting Brownists and Anabaptists of his own day, and claims a specific parallel between the dramatic Cade and Hacket, a riot leader convicted in 1591. But Hacket was a far grosser fanatic than the Cade of the play (out of spiritual zeal he bit off a man's nose and swallowed it), and in any case there is evidence that Shakespeare deliberately avoided giving any religious savour to the rebellion; it might have been quite otherwise had he delayed the Cardinal's death for a scene or two. It has been said too that Shakespeare coarsened his stage mobs from personal antipathy, and no doubt he had an eye for outrages in the London streets, a nose for the sour breath of the plebeians and an ear for riotous choplogic; but at no point in any play do they pervert Shakespeare's objectivity of judgement or his rich human sympathies.

To understand the Cade scenes we must recognize that Shakespeare distorts Holinshed's account of the rebellion itself merely in order to emphasize its place in a larger and more significant movement of historical cause and effect. The rebellion is offered as an evil consequence of misrule, specifically of the misrule of Suffolk. The fuse is touched early, when Suffolk tears the petitions of the innocent, conscientious citizens (I. iii. 37). But the petitioniers, voicing their bewildered, nervous protests, the apprentices of the Peter Thump scenes, and the crowd at St Albans, while they make up the 'populace' are not yet the 'mob'. The mob emerges at the moment of Gloucester's death, when the people are compelled, through lack of a law-giver, through the total breakdown of the constitutional rule of order, to take the law into their own hands. The 'populace' with a just grievance is by the exercise of violence transformed into the 'mob', executors of lynch law. At first they are free from a 'stubborn opposite intent' (III. ii. 251), but finally, 'thirsting after prey' (IV. iv. 51), they are capable of a full range of atrocities.

The violence is not merely self-generated; all that York stands for in the way of destructive political purpose is right behind the reprisals of Smithfield. Nor are the reprisals quite arbitrary. Since Gloucester is the dramatic symbol of regular administration of the law, and unquestioning faith in its authority, it is no accident that Shakespeare focused the iconoclasm of the rioters upon the agents and monuments of the civil law.

[12] *The Populace in Shakespeare* (1949), pp. 101ff.

To do so he turned back in the chronicle to the Tyler rebellion in the reign of *Richard II* and borrowed just those touches which furthered his purpose – the killing of the lawyers, the destruction of the Savoy and the Inns of Court, and the burning of the records of the realm.[13] It is significant too that Lord Say, the 'treasurer of England' in 1450, is merged with the Lord Chief Justice beheaded by Tyler in 1381; his stage martyrdom (IV. vii) is that of a humane judge – thus obliquely repeating the point about Gloucester.

Holinshed tells how the rising was subdued by Canterbury and Winchester bringing to Southwark a pardon from the King (*Hol.* (1808), p. 226; *Boswell-Stone*, p. 280). In the play the bishops figure only momentarily, in a soft-hearted plan of Henry's (IV. iv. 9), and Shakespeare abstains from giving to Lord Say the role he allows Sir Thomas in comparable circumstances in *Sir Thomas More*, quietening the people by authoritative eloquence (II. iv. 62–177). Although Lord Say has a comparable dignity,

> The trust I have is in mine innocence,
> And therefore am I bold and resolute,
>
> (IV. iv. 59)

he shares the vulnerability of Gloucester as well as his integrity, and his head soon dances on a pole. Stafford tries abuse (IV. ii. 122), but that fails too, and it is left to Buckingham and Clifford to restore their version of 'order' (IV. viii). In place of the leisured approach of two prelates, gathering exhausted citizens about them, Shakespeare offers the murderous rabblement, their full cry silenced by a trumpet and by the appearance of two leading soldiers with their bodyguards. The pardon, garbled by Buckingham (IV. viii. 8), is not made a factor in the peace. Clifford steps in with a sharply different appeal, invoking, as Shakespeare puts it elsewhere, the ghost of Henry V. Cade brutally reminds the people that they have still to recover their 'ancient freedom', but his brand of demagoguery is surpassed by the fine irrelevance of Clifford's patriotic exhortation – as from soldier to soldiers, from one Englishman to another. The oratory is not endorsed by the situation in the play (no French invasion threatens) but its effect is to canalize destructive energy along a track less threatening to the nobles of England – profitable indeed, and as Shakespeare shows in *Henry V*, even glorious in its own way. But *Henry V* touches the heroic through its setting of a tiny group of English against terrible odds; here the mob yell of 'A Clifford! A Clifford! We'll follow the King and Clifford' (IV. viii. 53), is ironically close in spirit to the 'Kill and knock down' of the scene's opening. The true interpretation of these events is voiced by the only figure on the stage who is not implicated any longer, in

---

[13] See *Boswell-Stone*, pp. 271, 277–8, for the relevant chronicle passages.

Cade's: 'Was ever feather so lightly blown to and fro, as this multitude? The name of Henry the Fifth hales them to an hundred mischiefs and makes them leave me desolate' (IV. viii. 54). Cade is seen for what he is, but when he is chased off stage by his followers, there is a strong impression that he is victimized. The blood-lust of the mob has been diverted but not sublimated.

In accents reminiscent of his apostrophe on Horner's death (II. iii. 99), Henry acknowledges the gruesome gift of Cade's head: 'The head of *Cade*? Great God, how just art thou?' (v. i. 68). There is this recognition that God's spirit showed itself in the dispersal of the rebels, not in the tide of rebellion; in the killing of Cade, not in his subornation. But Henry's outlook is of a piece with his isolation and impotence. Cade's death is not much more than a marginal note (IV. x); it occurs when he is alone and starving and cannot have the central significance that Henry's piety attributes to it. Iden, the yeoman in the garden and Cade's killer, is (as E. M. W. Tillyard puts it) a 'symbol of degree', one who 'seeks not to wax great by others' waning'; but he is a formal symbol, mechanically put together out of the chronicle, and can only appear as a 'representative figure' to King Henry himself in a scene which Shakespeare is careful not to put last. As it is, the silence of the stage garden is not allowed to still the audience's memory of the clamour of Southwark; the internecine violence of the rebellion is carried through, across the recessed interludes, to the battlefield of St Albans, where Clifford himself speaks the most terrible of Shakespeare's pronouncements about war (v. ii. 31ff).

Thus the moral of the last part of the play is not the simple-minded one of the *Mirror for Magistrates* which tells 'How Jack Cade traitorously rebelling against his King, was for his treasons and cruel doings worthily punished'.[14] It is assimilated into a firm, comprehensive structure, a version of political and historical tragedy that will serve later as the ground of *Julius Caesar* – another play which moves through the plotting and execution of an assassinatoin , through the generation of lynch law in the streets, to the deflection of that violence into civil war.

Part 3: The Shape of Anarchy

The tragic alignments of *Part 3* are declared on the St Albans battlefield. Henry prefigures the sacrificial victim, suspended between action and inaction – he will, 'nor fight nor fly' (v. ii. 74). Richard of York is the agent of that political realism that is born in *Part 2* to flourish in the later plays; he is the calculating joker and the killer who despises the law of

---

[14]*Mirror*, ed. L. B. Campbell (1938), p. 171.

arms, rejoicing in the superstitious prophecy by which he slaughters
Somerset underneath 'an ale-house' paltry sign', and he states the harsh
moral assumption that makes for anarchy in *Part 3*

> Sword, hold thy temper; heart, be wrathful still:
> Priests pray for enemies, but princes kill.

(v. ii. 71)

Clifford, Richard's antagonist in fact and symbol, is not a 'machiavel' but
a nihilist, recognizing the virtues of chivalry and order but dedicated to the
defilement of both. Some disturbances of the text and inconsistency of fact
suggest that his key speech (v. ii. 31–65), provoked by York's killing of the
elder Clifford, was written during or immediately after the composition of
Part 3, and set back into *Part 2* to offer intimations of the violence to
come.[15] Its opening lines are powerfully symbolic:

> Shame and confusion! all is on the rout;
> Fear frames disorder, and disorder wounds
> Where it should guard.

(v. ii. 31)

They refer literally to the sort of confusion sometimes reported in the
chronicles, where men are led to kill their friends instead of their enemies.
But Shakespeare abstains from specifying the kind of disorder; by not
limiting the connotation of 'disorder', 'frame' and 'confusion' he keeps the
abstract force of the words and makes the image immense and the idea
metaphysically reverberant. In the next lines war is both the son of hell
and the minister of heaven, ideas from Holinshed transmuted into a
searching and disturbing rhetoric:

> O war, thou son of hell,
> Whom angry heavens do make their minister,
> Throw in the frozen bosoms of our part
> Hot coals of vengeance!

But while the speech epitomizes scattered groups of chronicle ideas, it keeps
the urgency of the battlefield and it charges its destructive generalizations
about war with heroic resolution. The simple idea that the true soldier does
not nurse his life is transformed with measured, emphatic finality, into an
absolute acceptance of an ideal of nihilistic self-sacrifice. The words glance
with magnificent assurance from the image of the last judgement to the

---

[15] In 3HVI I.i.9, the elder Clifford is said by York, his stage killer, to have been
slain by common soldiers. Since *2 Henry VI*, v. ii and *3 Henry VI*, I. ii. are both
indebted to a passage in Hall (see *Boswell-Stone*, p. 297) it is possible that
Shakespeare revised the earlier scene to motivate Clifford's killing of Rutland.

dead figure of old Clifford, to age and wisdom in time of peace. There is a suddenly gathering intimacy, and then, out of the personal pathos, a regeneration of the mood of total war:

> Even at this sight
> My heart is turn'd to stone: and while 'tis mine,
> It shall be stony.
>
> (*Pt 2*, v. ii. 49–51)

The rare accomplishment of Clifford's speech should not blind us to its organic function in the plays. It is simply the most lucid and telling expression of one range of anarchic impulses at large in the tetralogy. The other range, which does as much or more to precipitate anarchy, is represented in the emergence of the Richards of York and Gloucester. In the play as history, Richard of York is isolated from the rival barons by his greater political know-how. But, equally important, in the play as theatrical entertainment he is isolated by his privileged relationship with the audience. The politician is from the chronicle; the soliloquizer is from the dramatic conventions of the Morality Play, and the key to Shakespeare's success is the intimate connection that he found between the two. The main fact about the chronicle York is that he takes his opportunities skilfully because, unlike the unreflective opportunists among his peers, he anticipates, calculates, and prepares the ground. His 'attempt,' says Holinshed, 'was politicly handled', 'secretly kept' and his purpose 'ready' before it was 'openly published' (*Hol.* (1808), p. 212; *Boswell-Stone*, p. 255). If all that York stands for in history is to be properly conveyed in the play, his emergence when 'mischief breaks out' must take his enemies by surprise. But it must not take the audience by surprise; hence Shakespeare introduces short conspiratorial scenes to put fellow Yorkists partly 'in the know' (the colloquialism fits the mood), and adds a number of soliloquies to put the audience wholly in the know. The soliloquy given to York at *Part 2* (i. i. 209) becomes the first experiment in the form to be turned to such advantage in *Richard III*; it enlists the audience's sympathy against the 'others', exploits its readiness to take a low view of human nature and be brutally realistic about politics. In this first soliloquy York voices the muscular chronicle judgement that critics have sometimes taken for Shakespeare's definitive verdict on Henry:

> And force perforce I'll make him yield the crown.
> Whose bookish rule hath pull'd fair England down.
>
> (*Pt 2*, i. i. 253)

But the rough verbal shoulder-shrugging of York is precisely expressive of the factious energy which does most to pull down fair England. A second soliloquy, in the same manner, sets York, 'the labouring spider', behind the inception of the Cade rebellion (Pt 2, v. i. 1).

In a passage of reflection on 'the tragicall state of this land under the rent regiment of King Henrie', Holinshed speaks of the 'sundrie practices' which 'imbecilled' the 'prerogative' of the King, and wonders at the pitched battles, which he divides into two groups, that were fought over and about him (*Hol.* (1808), pp. 273-3). Shakespeare keeps the outline and emphasizes the distinction between the military and political sources of catastrophe. The first two acts deal with the battles of 1460-1, when Henry had that 'naked name of king'; the third and fourth acts are dominantly political, and about the chicanery of the nobles with their rival kings; and the last presents the campaigns of 1471, in which politics and war are indistinguishable. Once again one is struck in performance by the expressive force of the mere dumb-show and noise (witness the stage directions); kings and crowns are treated as stage properties to enforce the chronicle moral about contempt for sovereignty, and Warwick is made quite literally the setter-up and plucker-down of kings (e.g. IV. iii). The pantomime is as skilful in the political scenes. The scene in the French court (III. iii), for instance, where Margaret has won the support of King Lewis, only to lose it to Warwick who comes as ambassador from Edward, becomes a superb exercise in the acrobatics of diplomacy, when letters are at last brought from Edward about the Bona marriage.

For the greater part of the third play Shakespeare is content to follow Holinshed in making his characters public masks, without intimately felt life, and therefore hardly seeming responsible for what they do. He tightens the sequence of atrocities, telescopes time, and eliminates all rituals of government, until the stage action and reaction appear yet more savagely mechanical than in the chronicle. So long as the characterization is neutral the first tetralogy displays a barbarous providence ruling murderous automatons whose reactions are predictable in terms of certain quasi-Hobbesian assumptions about human nature: when argument fails men resort to force; when an oath is inconvenient they break it; their power challenged, they retort with violence; their power subdued they resort to lies, murder or suicide; their honour impugned, they look for revenge; their enemies at their mercy, they torture and kill them; and if a clash of loyalties occurs they resolve it in the interest of their own survival. Such might be the vision of the play's pantomime, but its dimensions are not confined to its pantomime and to its shallower rhetoric. The anarchic, egocentric impulses are not presented as the inescapable laws of human nature; they are at most manifestations of forces that automatically take over when the constraints of government are withheld. Law and order cease to prevail when men cease to believe in them, and the process by which this comes about is explored in the play's dominant characters.

The figures of Clifford and York who, in *Part 2*, personalize two kinds of anarchic scepticism – the soldier's nihilism and the politician's realism – are displaced in *Part 3* by the more significant contrast between Richard of Gloucester and King Henry. With obvious propriety these are chosen to characterize the moral tensions which give meaning to the deep chaos of the last phase of the reign. But the crimes of the Roses Wars are so multiple, and their agents so numerous, that Shakespeare could not attempt, even if at this early date it were within his power, the comprehensively intimate exploration of evil he undertakes in *Macbeth*, and he allows himself only that measure of intimate soliloquy and address which will accord with the conventions of historical pageant.

In the first two plays the chronicle myth of a king absurdly and irrelevantly virtuous can just about pass muster, and in the first scene of *Part 3*, Henry's virtue is still associated with impotence; his war of 'frowns, words, and threats' is disarmed by his readiness to concede the Yorkist claims, by the wry defection of Exeter (unwarranted by the history), and by the Robin Hood trickery of Warwick; his conscience-stricken asides carry as little conviction as his military posturing, and one feels the *gaucherie* is the playwright's as well as the character's. In the next phase, however, Shakespeare's tragic art wins distinction from the ferocity of the material and Henry assumes a stature outside the chronicle compass.

Both the finer qualities of Henry's virtue and the intensity of Richard of Gloucester's virulence spring from Shakespeare's treatment of the Battle of Wakefield. Conventional heroic ideals cannot survive the battle, which turns on two blasphemies of chivalry – the killing of the prince and the degradation of the mock-king. Clifford's slaughter of Rutland (i. iii), in calculated contempt of the Priest and the law of arms, is a repudiation of the myth that expects from every 'gentleman' in battle the virtues of the lion. The values apt to an heroic battle play are displaced by those prevailing in parts of English Seneca; in Heywood's *Thyestes*, for example, where 'ire thinks nought unlawful to be done', 'Babes be murdered ill' and 'bloodshed lies the land about' (i. i. 79–89). Shakespeare gives the revenge motive a great political significance by relating it to the dynastic feud for which Clifford is not alone responsible.

Anarchism, Shakespeare had learned from the Cade scenes, is more dramatic when it is iconoclastic, and the next Wakefield outrage, the paper crowning (i. iv), mutilates the idols of Knighthood, Kingship, Womanhood and Fatherhood. In making a ritual of the atrocity Shakespeare imitates the history – the scene is a formal set-piece because it was so staged by its historical performers. Holinshed tells how the Lancastrians made obeisance and cried, 'Haile, king without rule' – 'as the Jewes did unto Christ' (*Hol.* (1808), p. 269; *Boswell-Stone*, p. 299). Although Shakespeare suppresses the open blasphemy, he keeps the crucifixion parallel with the line, 'Now looks he like a King' (i. iv. 96), and, more significantly, by combining the mockery reported in one of a choice of chronicle accounts with the paper-coronation in another (*Hol.* (1808), p. 268; *Boswell-Stone*, p. 299). He takes little liberty with the chronicle, moreover, when he makes the stage-managed historical ceremony into an ordered, antiphonal combat of words, with Northumberland presiding, as it were, in the rhetorical lists. In spite of the controlling formality the language moves on several planes between gnomic generalization, "Tis government that makes them seem divine, / The want thereof makes thee abominable' (I. iv. 132–3); stylized feeling, 'Oh tiger's heart wrapt in a woman's hide! / How could'st thou drain the life-blood of the child' (I. iv. 137); plain, personal pathos, 'This cloth thou dip'dst in blood of my sweet boy' (I. iv. 157); and colloquial venom, 'And where's that valiant crook-back prodigy, / Dicky, your boy, that with his grumbling voice / Was wont to cheer his dad in mutinies?' In the blinding scene of *King Lear* the same changes will be rung in a richer peal, but there is enough in the Wakefield scene's counterpoint of reflection and feeling to tax the resources of its actors.

Henry is not made witness to the event. He is allowed the dignity of total isolation, and when he comes to the stage molehill at Towton (II. v), it is to speak the most moving of Shakespeare's comments on the civil wars. Shakespeare is less fully engaged when he writes about the objectives of the battle as seen by the participants than by its futility as it appears to a suffering observer. Hall in 1548 had felt a similar need to withdraw into reflection:

> This conflict was in maner unnaturall, for in it the sonne fought agaynst the father, the brother agaynst the brother, the Nephew agaynst the Uncle, and the tenaunt agaynst hys Lorde, which slaughter did sore and much weaken the puyssance of this realme. (1809, p. 256)

In *Gorboduc* and in Daniel's *Civil Wars* the commonplace is retailed with a complacent omniscience damaging to living language.[16] But by attributing it to the King in the course of battle Shakespeare is able to quicken it with personal feeling; beneath the ceremonious surface we again sense the pulse and surge of events.

The hint for the opening lines is one of Hall's 'ebb and flow of battle' clichés (*Boswell-Stone*, p. 306), but Shakespeare insinuates rarer images of the peaceful, symmetrical rhythms of nature – 'the morning's war' and 'the shepheard blowing of his nails', and after touching the conflicts inherent in nature, arrests the movement of battle in that of the sea – 'the equal poise of this fell war'. A glance at the humour and pathos of Henry's isolation (Margaret and Clifford have chid him from the battle), with a touch of

[16]The peroration of *Gorboduc* and the first stanza of *The Civil Wars*.

wry exhaustion ('Would I were dead, if God's good will were so'), offers assurance of Shakespeare's gift for 're-living the past', and the sequent lines of exquisite pastoral seem to re-create the convention out of the kind of human experience which underlies it. An alarum returns us to the battle and to a glimpse of its victims in another statuesque mirror-scene in which blood and pallor are made heraldic (II. v. 97ff). Once again the feeling for the past is the cathedral-pavement sort, not the chronicle sort; it is at once a refreshing and a potentially devitalizing mood, and after 120 lines Shakespeare pulls us out of it and lets the pantomime get under way again.

The authority of Henry's commentary on Towton is sufficiently memorable to help vindicate the innocence of the speech he makes before the keepers arrest him: 'My pity hath been balm to heal their wounds. / My mildness hath allay'd their swelling griefs, / My mercy dry'd their water-flowing tears' (IV. viii. 41–3). From this and a few other passages in the plays it would be possible to present Henry as the centre of a moral parable whose lineaments are traced in Thomas Elyot's *The Governour*. The King, says Elyot, must be merciful, but too much *Clementia* is a sickness of mind; as soon as any offend him the King should 'immediately strike him with his most terrible dart of vengeance'. But the occasions when Henry seems guilty of an excess of virtue are rare, and he is at his most impressive when he is martyred in his last scene of *Part 3*, not when he tries to throw his weight about in *Part 1*. The Wakefield battle once fought, moreover, 'the terrible dart of vengeance' is lost to the armoury of virtue. Henry's bemused and disappointed faith in the political efficacy of mercy, pity, peace and love does not deserve the editorial mockery it has received – 'characteristically effeminate' and 'smug complacency'.[17] Henry's virtue may be defective but Shakespeare commands from his audience a full reverence for it when, at the moment of his extermination, the King confronts his ultimate antagonist, Richard of Gloucester.

Richard is introduced as York's heroic soldier son, but in his first characteristic speech of length (II. i. 79ff) he becomes the bitter, unchivalrous avenger – a reaction to the Messenger's report of Wakefield which seems instinctive and inevitable. But Richard not only reacts to events (all the barons do that), he also becomes the conscious embodiment of all the drives – moral, intellectual and physical – that elsewhere show themselves only in the puppetry. Translating into theatrical terms, we might say that when he takes the stage for his first exercise of the soliloquy-prerogative he inherits from York (at the end of III. ii), his language shows him capable of playing the parts of York, Clifford, Edward, Margaret or Warwick. All their energies are made articulate: the doggedness of York 'that reaches at the moon' and

[17] See notes to IV. viii. 38–50 in Wilson's New Shakespeare editions.

the same eye for the glitter of the Marlovian crown; the dedication to evil which characterizes Clifford; the prurience of Edward; the decorated and ruthless rhetoric of Margaret; and Warwick's gifts of king-maker, resolute 'to command, to check, to overbear'. Shakespeare has him use the fantastic lore about his birth to admirable effect: it strengthens the impression of blasphemy against love and fertility, makes deformity license depravity and, most important, allegorizes the birth of a political monster in the present by recalling that of a physical monster in the past, 'like to a chaos or an unlick'd bear-whelp'. But it is not all specifically birth-imagery – about Richard having teeth and the dogs howling. The sense of violent struggle, of unnatural energies breaking free, is best caught in lines that are not explicitly about birth at all:

> And I – like one lost in a thorny wood,
> That rends the thorns and is rent with the thorns,
> Seeking a way and straying from the way;
> Not knowing how to find the open air,
> But toiling desperately to find it out –
> Torment myself to catch the English crown:
> And from that torment I will free myself,
> Or hew my way out with a bloody axe.
>
> (III. ii. 174)

It is from the kennel of England's womb that this hell-hound is to bite itself free. At the end of the soliloquy Richard promises the audience a performance more entertaining than any heroic fantasy or medieval Trojan legend; he will outplay all politic dissemblers, 'add colours to the camelion', 'change shapes with Proteus' and 'set the *murtherous* Machevil to school'. The ground is prepared for *Richard III*, where for three acts the comic idiom will dominate the tragic, with politics a kings' game best played by cunning actors.

But the continuity with the mood of *Richard III* is deliberately fractured and the tragic mode made to dominate the comic in the scene of Henry's death. The King opposes Richard's tongue and sword with a moral force that Shakespeare makes all but transcendent and the 'scene of death' that 'Roscius' – the actor and devil Richard – performs at last, comes near to a tragic consummation. Yet the qualifications 'all but' and 'comes near' are, after all, necessary. The brute facts of history will not allow a satisfying tragic outcome; Shakespeare cannot pretend that the martyrdom of an innocent king appeased the appetite of providence or exhausted the sophisticated savagery that Richard stands for.

Nor can Hall's dynastic myth be enlisted to reassure us that all will be well when the White Rose is wedded to the Red – that will only be possible at the end of *Richard III* when, in a kind of postscript to the complete tetralogy, Richmond will step into the Elizabethan present and address an audience sufficiently remote from Henry's reign. As it is, the plays of *Henry VI* are not, as it were, haunted by the ghost of Richard II, and the catastrophes of the civil wars are not laid to Bolingbroke's charge; the catastrophic virtue of Henry and the catastrophic evil of Richard are not an inescapable inheritance from the distant past but are generated by the happenings we are made to witness.

The questioning of the ways of God and the roles of good and evil in English history will be re-opened in *Richard III*, but in the interim *Part 3* ends, as tragedies remotely derived from fertility rites of course should, with some elaborate imagery of autumn reaping. It is fitting that Richard should be standing by to blast the harvest and to boast himself a Judas.

5 *Richard II* and the Music of Men's Lives

When Richard II, in Shakespeare's play, is approaching the end of his life, he has reason to reflect that the concord of his state and time is shattered:

How sour sweet music is
When time is broke, and no proportion kept!
So is it in the music of men's lives.

(v. v. 41–3)

We are watching an historical and personal catastrophe, but since we are also approaching the end of one of the most lyrical tragedies of Shakespeare's early maturity, we are attending to the climax of the poet's harmonious art. Shakespeare, reading the old histories of the disastrous reign of King Richard (perhaps as many as seven of them) and turning them into theatre for our delight, has been making music of men's lives.

An adequate account of the play must attend to the subtle interrelationships that Shakespeare creates, or re-creates, between the styles of theatrical poetry and historical events, and between the larger processes of human community and the more poignantly focused, personal processes of the individual life. That the art of the Renaissance should invite this kind of critical attention is a sign of its continuity with the art and thought of the Middle Ages. For Shakespeare, like Boethius, Dante and Chaucer before him, continued to be interested in the ways in which human confusions could be contained within a divine order and an ultimate harmony. The poet, in Chaucer's time and in Shakespeare's (even in our own), is under traditional pressure to satisfy our ethical imaginations, to make art and design out of its representation of muddled passages of life. Thus Dante at the end of the *Purgatorio* is wryly aware that he is obeying both the laws of his poem and the laws of a divine moral dispensation. The *Consolations* of Boethius enable Chaucer to change the perspective of *Troilus and*

Criseyde in order that the lovers' human tragedy should be transfigured to divine (and human) comedy.

In her deft analysis of 'The Knight's Tale' Elizabeth Salter warns us 'not to confuse rhetorical ordering with imaginative';[1] but clear distinctions in this territory are not easy to come by. Theseus (from his reading of Boethius) tries to transcend the lovers' undignified history:

Thanne may men by this ordre wel discerne
That thilke Moevere stable is and eterne;
Wel may men knowe, but it be a fool,
That every part dirryveth from his hool.
(Chaucer, 'Knight's Tale', 3003–6)

But, as Elizabeth Salter observes, 'Our difficulty does not lie in reconciling the death of Arcite with a divinely ordained plan, but in reconciling the noble account of this plan with the ugly manifestation of divine motives and activities which Chaucer has allowed his poem to give.'[2] The perplexities faced by all theodiceans, from classical times, through the Enlightenment of Leibnitz, to the most recent endeavours to vindicate the ways of God to man, recur and persist in insoluble forms, and Shakespeare's *Richard II* is a crucial document in a long tradition. If Chaucer did indeed read his Troilus story to Richard, the king would have had reason to reflect upon his own prospects of looking down from 'the holughnesse of the eighthe spere' to contemplate 'with ful avysement, / The erratik sterres herkenyng armonye, / With sownes ful of hevenyssh melodie.'[3] Bushy in the play speaks of 'perspectives which rightly gazed upon / Show nothing but confusion; ey'd awry / Distinguish form' (II. ii. 18–20). Richard's own story very much needs to be viewed awry to distinguish form.

The play's historicity can, in certain perspectives, be seen to be of a piece with its harmony, inviting us to glance backwards in Shakespeare's art to the fair conjunction of the white rose and the red at the end of *Richard III*, which is itself a glance forward in history to the final end of the 'great discord and division' proclaimed by Edward Hall as 'the union of the two noble and illustre families of Lancaster and York'. Hall's resonant phrases offer a musical resolution of the discords of the reign which has given solace to many since it was first offered to the Tudor public – most recently to those whose responses to Shakespeare's histories have been orchestrated by the late E. M. W. Tillyard. But I wish to look in other directions – towards certain principles at work in the structure of the play, and towards Jean Bodin's ample and complex theories of law, sovereignty

[1] Chaucer: *The Knight's Tale and The Clerks Tale* (1962).
[2] Ibid., p. 31.
[3] Chaucer, *Troilus and Criseyde*, v. 1809–12.

and (to return to a phrase from the play) the concord of state and time.

I cannot confidently claim that Shakespeare had read Bodin's *Six Books of the Commonweal* before they were translated from the French by Richard Knolles in 1606, although I think it perfectly possible that he had, but I am concerned with certain convergences and divergences of thought and insight between Bodin's contemplative thought and Shakespeare's theatrical thought. Shakespeare is the poet and playwright of commonwealth, and nowhere more so than in two musically alert plays of the middle period – *The Merchant of Venice* and *Richard II*.

The Tudor myth of Polydore Vergil's and of Hall's devising is notoriously an instrument of propaganda. In outline it is intended to reassure the subject state of the divine authority of the sovereign figure; Providence has worked to such good purpose that the conflicts of the past are assuaged, the moral and political wounds of the state healed, and under the high and prudent dominion of Henry VIII, the indubitable flower and very heir of the contending lineages, all will be well.

Bodin's awarenesses are philosophically more spacious, affording an apparently more direct access to the ideology of Renaissance monarchism. 'Of the three lawfull Commonweales, that is, a popular estate, an Aristocraticall, and a royall,' says Bodin, 'a royall monarchie is the best.'[4] The royal monarchy satisfies the elegant principle that a body should have only one head, together with some more intricate principles of geometric proportion which are meant to harmonize the multiple inequalities of society.

With the encouragement of the more conservative scholars of the past fifty years, including Theodore Spencer, Lily B. Campbell and Hardin Craig, we would have little difficulty in reconciling Hall's outline of a stabilizing Providential process with Bodin's account of a poised and harmonious society. Shakespeare's histories might then be received on much the same terms as the homilies against wilful rebellion. A nostalgic Tudor recollection of Edward III, or even of Hotspur's Richard ('that sweet lovely rose'), might create the illusion that an old divine dispensation had been recovered and restored.

I prefer to allow the imaginative art its own momentum and autonomy, but I wish at the same time to see it engaging with and dislodging the historical myth and the political wisdom from which it derives some of its effects.

Shakespeare's *Richard II* was not the only play of the period to deal with the reign. At least one (reported by Simon Forman) has been lost. But each of the two survivors has its style and modest structure. *Jack Straw*

---

[4] Jean Bodin, *The Six Bookes of the Commonweale*, R. Knolles, London, 1606 (*STC*, 3193), p. 700.

is made to express the grievances of the populace, exploited by usurers in the market-place and saved by the solicitude of an innocent king. *Woodstock* is made of a verse answering to the plain-living and plain-speaking virtues that the playwright attributes to his hero. In the sense of the terms that *Richard II* invites, however, they are not lyrical plays; they have no music.

Marlowe's *Edward II*, which has also occasioned comparison with *Richard II*, does have its music – a music that modulates as the poet diverts the flow of our sympathies from the king's victims to the victim-king:–

And there in mire and puddle have I stood
This ten days space; and least that I should sleep
One plays continually upon a drum.
They give me bread and water, being a king.
                              (v. v. 58–61)

The words are spoken to that drum-beat. The music is in the indefatigable pulse of life holding on, and it is made out of the historical event, not contemplatively but re-creatively.

Shakespeare's play is about many of the same things as Marlowe's – political assassination, misgovernment, nostalgia for an old chivalric dispensation, royal minions and royal martyrdom – but it does not repeat Marlowe's effects. It offers a fuller manifestation of the nature of historical process and a greater awareness of the significance of style, personal and ideological, in the commonwealth. That historical process, both in the time of Shakespeare and in the time of Richard, was dispossessing the myths of divine kingship even before they could properly establish themselves. The symmetries of Shakespeare's play are related to the fidelity with which he traces this process in the realm and in the consciousness of the king.

In *Richard II* Shakespeare at once re-creates, celebrates, anatomizes and repudiates the idea and figure of the divine sovereign. The play realizes the pressures of the past upon the present and of the play's present upon England's future. Shakespeare had already written about the Wars of the Roses and in *Richard II* he is aware of their not-too-distant coming on. In *Woodstock* and *Edward II* we may be persuaded that the mess of the realm is the immediate responsibility of those who make it, within the boundaries of the play. In *Richard II*, obscure unstabilizing damage has already been done within the reign but out of reach of the play, the validity of the institution of royal monarchy itself is called in question, and we are made to feel that there can be no going back.

The feat of historical analysis is also a feat of style. For although the style of the play resembles that of others of the same phase (*Romeo and Juliet, A Midsummer Night's Dream*), it is here used upon historical material to historical advantage. Shakespeare's plays of fifteenth-century English history are about the paradoxes attending the exercise of power. In the aesthetically and ethically satisfying speculations of Bodin, power is the ceremonious exercise of high moral authority, in the service of divine and natural justice. In the world that falls under Montaigne's sceptical scrutiny in the *Apology for Raymond Sebonde*, a Pacific island is ruled by a dog – recalled in *Lear* as 'The great image of authority – a dog's obeyed in office' (IV. vi. 156–7).

Style of a highly formal kind, enlisting many rhetorical devices and refining the symmetries of the language, is particularly apt in *Richard II* because the play is primarily about the relationship between power and ceremony. It is so constructed that the ceremony which makes 'high majesty look like itself' fails as a vehicle of government, an instrument of harmony in the commonwealth, but proves to be a source of solace for the abdicating king. It is politically sterile but personally efficacious.

Prompted by Hall,[5] Shakespeare chose to start his play at the moment when the chronicles tell of Henry, duke of Hereford, presenting a supplication to the king 'wherein he appealed the duke of Norfolke in field of battle, for a traitor, false and disloyall to the king, and enemy unto the realm'. A 'great scaffold' is erected in the castle at Windsor, and the king sits in his 'seat of justice' in order to 'minister justice to all men that would demand the same, as appertained to his royal majesty'. The king commands the constable and marshal of the realm formally to call on appellant and defendant to 'shew his reason' or else make peace without delay. Shakespeare's stage is therefore already set in the ceremonious theatre of history. But in what Hall himself calls the 'sumpteous theatre' of the lists at Coventry, the ceremony is arrested, the presiding king abjures it.

Responding to the chronicle material, *Richard II* was probably first played before a stage version of that traditional pageant property, the tournament façade. Evidence of a circumstantial kind might be found in analogues with medieval settings for play and tournament, in more distant analogues from the Netherlands, but – most convincingly – in the play itself: in its deployment of heraldry and of tournament settings, its stylizations of language and its mounting of certain key episodes. In the play's first phase the façade is background for a throne, a display of the rituals of government and of tournament justice, and for the last words of Gaunt, composing a memorial to England's equitable and chivalrous past. The façade may well have carried the devices of Edward's seven sons, the 'seven vials of his sacred blood' counted by the duchess in the second scene, devices still to be found (if incompletely) over the main gateway of Trinity in Cambridge. As the play advances, however, the relationship of the action to the façade changes. The splendours and symmetries of public show give place to more

---

[5] The chronicle material for *Richard II* is selectively reprinted in Bullough, III.

intimate episodes of power exercised, mourned, frustrated or abdicated. The play may therefore be said to become less medieval as it advances or, more precisely, less like a Tudor tournament with its inheritance of medieval paraphernalia. In Bodin's terms, it becomes less geometric and harmonical.

Mark Rose (in *Shakespearean Design*, 1972) has shown that the play responds well to chiastic analysis, and it happens that his little pictures of the play's structure offer the same kind of dainty reassurance as Bodin's. But *Richard II*, like all of Shakespeare's plays, is not only a pattern to look back upon, it is also a process to be lived through. And I turn now to the way in which that process is regulated.

In order to perceive the consonance in the play between the movement of events and the changing significance of theatrical ceremony and of the attendant verbal music, we may compare the three occasions on which appeals are heard before authority: the first and third scenes; the first scene of Act IV (when Fitzwater and Aumerle appear before Bolingbroke); and the third of Act V (when Aumerle and the Duchess plead for pardon). The appeals are widely spaced but significantly interrelated in the momentum and design of the play and the history.

In the first scene authority in the person of Richard presides from the throne in full decorum, and all who play the game obey its rules. The conventions of tournament are themselves the principal sources of theatrical art. The chronicles offer Shakespeare the appellant styles of speech that he can amplify and refine:

> Right dear and sovereign lord, here is Thomas Mowbray duke of Norfolk who answereth and saith, and I for him, that all which Henry of Lancaster hath said and declared (saving the reverence due to the king and his council) is a lie; and the said Henry of Lancaster hath falsely and wickedly lied as a false and disloyal knight, and both hath been, and is a traitor against you, your crown, royal majesty and realm.
>
> (Bullough, III, 390)

Shakespeare's rhetorical amplifications are more spacious than Holinshed's and more hospitable to technical analysis. Puttenham, for example, might have found *merismus* or 'the distributer' in Richard's address to Mowbray – 'the distribution of every part for amplification sake':

> Mowbray, impartial are our eyes and ears.
> Were he my brother, nay, my kingdom's heir,
> As he is but my father's brother's son,
> Now by my sceptre's awe I make a vow,
> Such neighbour nearness to our sacred blood
> Should nothing privilege him nor partialize

> The unstooping firmness of my upright soul.
> He is our subject, Mowbray, so art thou:
> Free speech and fearless I to thee allow.
>   (I. i. 115–23)

But it is not mere *merismus*; the amplifications are creating a music of divine authority, a language of command. The music-of-state is in tune with the vocal poise and symmetry, and with the play's structure. The spectacle of this particular scene owes its symmetry to the ascendancy of the throne between contending parties, poised in equal scales. But in a wider span of the play the first scene is itself poised on one side of a point of balance located in the second scene – on a principle that, if Rose is right, operates elegantly throughout the play; Rose decorates his page with patterns (see figure 1).

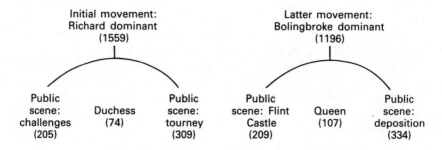

Figure 1 *Symmetry figure from Mark Rose*

Mark Rose takes more comfort from Pythagoras than I instinctively can; but not, I think, more than Bodin. Bodin's analysis of the harmonies of state comes to rest in analogous diagrams, but only after reflecting upon the dominion of his 'wise prince', governing according to the laws of equity and equal poise:

> The wise prince shall set his subjects in a most sweet quiet, bound together with an indissoluble bond one of them unto another, together with himselfe, and the Commonweale. As is in the foure first numbers to be seene: which God hath in Harmonicall proportion disposed to show unto us, that the Royal estate is Harmonicall, and also to be Harmonically governed. For two to three maketh a fift; three to foure, a fourth; two to foure, an eight; one to three, a twelft, holding the fift and the eight; and one to foure, a double eight, or *Diapason*: which containeth the whole ground and compasse of all tunes and concords of musicke, beyond

which he that will passe unto five, shall in so doing marre the harmonie, and make an intollerable discord.[6]

In the margin at this point Bodin sets a simple diagram, meant to demonstrate the plain aesthetic satisfactions to be derived from royal monarchy:

> Now the sovereigne prince is exalted above all his subjects, and exempt out of the ranke of them: whose maiestie suffereth no more division than doth the unitie it selfe, which is not set nor accounted among the numbers, howbeit that they all from it take both their force and power.

The numerals 2, 3 and 4 in Bodin (see figure 2) are the three estates: 'Ecclesiasticall . . . Martiall . . . and the common people of all sorts . . . as schollers, marchants and labourers.'

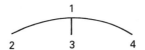

Figure 2   *Bodin's diagram*

The tournament, as trial-by combat, expresses in spectacle and language an undivided aspiration and allegiance to God, the sovereign, and the martial self. The freedoms that are allowed and taken are contained within the space of the lists. In this play, as in *Romeo and Juliet* and *Love's Labour's Lost*, Shakespeare encourages his audience to be acutely conscious of the arts of language: 'The boisterous late appeal', 'the accuser and the accused freely speak', 'with a foul traitor's name stuff I thy throat', 'what my tongue speaks my right-drawn sword shall prove', 'giving reins and spurs to my free speech'. But the rhetorical ornament takes on a political and historical significance by exploiting the pace and purpose of trial by tourney – it makes a cavorting temper of language, spurred, curbed or wheeling, to charge or to keep within bounds, as occasion requires. Neither in the chronicle at this point nor in the play is it of any use to probe beneath the bright armour of the style for the circumspect souls of Bolingbroke and Mowbray, for they are contestants in verbal lists, and ride the language as they ride their horses. We can judge their skills more readily than their causes, and honour seems more at stake than justice.

Had this trial by combat taken place it might have been the last in Europe's history. As it is, Richard arrests it because he cannot rest secure

[6]Bodin, *Six Bookes*, p. 790.

in the myth of his divinely derived authority, for reasons made plain both in the murmurings about Woodstock and in his sudden appropriation of Gaunt's property. Richard himself does violence to those harmonies of state which the tournament ritual is designed to honour. 'A royal Monarch or king,' says Bodin, 'is he which placed in soveraignty yeeldeth himself as obedient unto the lawes of nature as he desireth his subjects to be towards himself, leaving unto every man his naturall liberty, and the propriety of his own goods.' That concern with 'natural liberty' and private property might be the cue for a Marxist historian to remark that Bodin had bourgeois motives for proclaiming a royal monarchy, but in the play Richard's offence is against the proper expectations of the dynastic nobility. He takes 'from Time / His charters and his customary rights' and dislocates 'fair sequence and succession'.

The second appeal-scene of the play, which virtually opens Bolingbroke's reign in Westminster (IV. i) finds the old harmony marred, and making an intolerable discord. Shakespeare contrives for it an embarrassing decline in the old rhetorical skill. Bolingbroke is no longer playing that game and makes no attempt to compete. His first words are designed by Shakespeare to recall and to dismiss Richard's equivalent words. From the nine lines beginning, 'Mowbray, impartial are our eyes and ears' (I. i. 115–23), we come to: 'Call forth Bagot; / Now Bagot, freely speak thy mind' (IV. i. 1–2). But Shakespeare makes appellant and defendant persist in the old mode – of first-scene speech – even if they have lost the old mastery.

To measure the distance between harmonies of justice in the first and fourth acts, we may compare two feats of expectoration. This is Bolingbroke, offering to spit in the first scene:

> Ere my tongue
> Shall wound my honour with such feeble wrong
> Or sound so base a parle, my teeth shall tear
> The slavish motive of recanting fear,
> And spit it bleeding in his high disgrace,
> Where shame doth harbour, even in Mowbray's face.
> (I. i. 190–5)

And here is Fitzwater, spitting in Act IV:

> I dare meet Surrey in a wilderness,
> And spit upon him whilst I say he lies,
> And lies, and lies. There is my bond of faith,
> To tie thee to my strong correction.
> As I intend to thrive in this new world,
> Aumerle is guilty of my strong appeal.
> (IV. i. 74–9)

Puttenham would have found much to deplore in Fitzwater's poverty of invention, and would surely have counted 'I say he lies, and lies and lies' among the vices of speech. But we can't from this evidence accuse Fitzwater of having nodded through the rhetoric lectures of the trivium, we can say only that Shakespeare has relaxed his control of ceremonious hyperbole in order to make the squabble uglier and its energies more arbitrary and dangerous, and to make Bolingbroke's laconic interventions more decisive than Richard's elaborate ones could have been. The play's structure has changed its music. We are no longer being invited to enjoy appellant rhetoric in a fan-vaulted monarchy: we are being invited to keep our ears tuned for the new language which makes Bolingbroke 'thrive in this new world'. His brevities cut like sword-thrusts through the embroidered, tarnished, fabric of the old speech, while gauntlets shower absurdly about his feet.

The effect won from the words is won again by the spectacle. Richard in the first scene presided from the throne, Bolingbroke in this dominates from the stage platform; he dominates without presiding, and it is only when he has done what he wants to do that he moves, casually, 'in God's name' to 'ascend the regal throne'. Power has been exercised but ceremony slighted. Carlisle's impressive protest (the Ecclesiastical estate still speaks the old language) is against the exercise of power without the ritual authority to endorse it:

What subject can give sentence on his king?
And who sits here that is not Richard's subject?
(IV. i. 121–2)

The rest is a familiar re-statement of what are sometimes, mistakenly, supposed to be the unchallenged dominant Elizabethan assumptions about the nature of monarchy:

Shall the figure of God's majesty,
His captain, steward, deputy elect,
Anointed, crowned, planted many years,
Be judg'd by subject and inferior breath,
And he himself not present?
(IV. i. 125–9)

– to which the unmusical answer is, 'Yes'. The figure of God's majesty is a cypher; power now belongs to the platform, not to the throne and the façade. When Richard is called in, it is not in response to Carlisle's eloquence, but to serve Bolingbroke's laconically expressed purpose, 'So we shall proceed without suspicion.'

The third appeal, Aumerle's before Bolingbroke in Act v, sc. iii, has often been cut from performance. In this scene authority becomes casually peremptory and all ceremony turns to farce. The king is musing upon his prodigal son who prefers the stews in London to the triumphs in Oxford, when he is broken in upon by the stage direction, '*Enter Aumerle amazed*', and responds, 'What means our cousin that he stares and looks so wildly?' Bolingbroke dismisses the court but Aumerle still won't talk until the door is locked. 'Have thy desire,' says the king – another shoulder-shrugging brevity, humouring his mad cousin, and speaking the distance between Henry's possession of power and Richard's. Then York hammers on the door.

Any attempt to make the next exchanges tense and solemn is liable to miscarry. York shouts a breathless warning through the door, 'Thou hast a traitor in thy presence there', and Bolingbroke, according to Dr Johnson's stage directions, draws his sword as he cries, 'Villain, I'll make thee safe.' Then York, 'Open the door or I will break it open', and Bolingbroke lets him in. 'What is the matter, uncle? Speak, recover breath; tell us how near is danger / That we may arm us to encounter it.' The effect of the king trying to keep his crazy relatives under domestic control is inescapable. I doubt if Bolingbroke is even carrying a sword (he speaks to York as if he is unarmed) and to draw it over Aumerle who, the dialogue tells us, is on his knees in abject terror, cannot but be gratuitously comic. Bolingbroke keeps his new-style dignity well enough, but the scene is also a valediction to the old style. York treats the new king as he did the old, and the new King for a moment plays the old part

> Thou sheer, immaculate, and silver fountain
> From whence this stream through muddy passages
> Hath held his current and defil'd himself
>
> (v. iii. 61–3)

but not for long. There is more banging on the door, and another frantic voice: 'What ho, my liege, for God's sake let me in!' and Bolingbroke: 'What shrill-voiced suppliant makes this eager cry?' answered: 'A Woman, and thine aunt, great King; 'tis I!' At this point we hardly need Bolingbroke to tell us that 'Our scene is altered from a serious thing / And now changed to 'the Beggar and the King'. 'My dangerous cousin,' he says to Aumerle (who may be still on his knees), 'let your mother in.' And mother comes, recovering breath enough to re-enact, for the last time, the antique proprieties in the rhetorical music of Richard's reign. 'A God on earth thou art,' she says at last. That extravagant claim about monarchy is given an appropriate but distinctly absurd human context; the king can spare her son ('such is the breath of kings') and therefore deserves these orisons. But they count for nothing; Aumerle was spared before his mother arrived, and his father's persistence in the old rigour grows fatuous ('Speak it in French, King, say "pardonne moy"'). The God on Earth has to silence the Duchess's intricate antithetical eloquence – 'Good Aunt, stand up,' he says, twice, as he turns aside to cope with his 'trusty brother-in-law' and the rebel abbot. It is an extraordinary episode, but, as the last of the appeal-scenes, its function in the play's structure is clear if not crucial.

To compare these three scenes is to attend to one of the large extra-personal movements of the play. Ceremonies of government, with their attendant verbal music, however decorous and impressive at the start, are shown to be impotent and farcical at the end. The increasingly manifest political impotence of Richard's elaborate machinery and style of government entails a continuing but almost unseen gravitation of power and allegiance to Bolingbroke. I call this movement unseen and impersonal because Richard's abdication of the throne and Bolingbroke's abdication of ceremony are not explicitly motivated; they are responses to an historical inheritance. The play is obscure about Bolingbroke's ambition. He enlists the support of the people and returns from Ireland not 'for England' but 'for Lancaster'. We are not allowed to see the gathering armies of the rebels; there are no battles, no riots, no street-scenes. There is just the sense of a dissolving false order, which grows with the discovery that Richard's authority is merely a show, a pageant, like the stage-setting, like the language, and indeed like the play itself.

Take, for example, another of the play's more modest scenes – where Bolingbroke confronts York at Berkeley Castle. The question which we might think of urgent importance – did Bolingbroke come for Lancaster or England? – is hardly asked and the play supplies too few data for an answer. 'The noble Duke hath sworn his coming is but for his own' (II. iii. 148–9), says Northumberland, and York disdains to reply. It is enough that Bolingbroke has the power – power that has gravitated towards him since Richard sought to dispossess him of his property; and power cannot for long be dissociated from 'authority', that is, from acknowledged power.

'Well, well,' says York, 'I see the issue of these arms. / I cannot mend it, I must needs confess.' York's impotence is not merely a manifestation of his personal 'character' – although it is that – but also a comment on his public predicament – one that is made representative of this particular moment of English history. York, like Gaunt, epitomizes age, weakness, and a nostalgia for an England in which, to return to an earlier formulation, government would be the ceremonious exercise of high moral authority. First the weakness: 'Because my power is weak and all ill left'; then the nostalgic, ceremonious assertiveness, authority looking for divine sanction but lacking military power:

> But if I could, by Him that gave me life,
> I would attach you all and make you stoop
> Unto the sovereign mercy of the King.
>
> (II. iii. 155–7)

and finally, a collapse to unceremonious simplicity, directly meeting the human situation:

> But since I cannot, be it known unto you
> I do remain as neuter. So, fare you well;
> Unless you please to enter in the castle,
> And there repose you for this night.
>
> (II. iii. 158–61)

York's plight is in part a moral one; he seeks Richard's injustice ('I have had feelings of my cousin's wrongs'); but it can find no moral solution. Once the new king is crowned he will try, comically and eccentrically, to make high majesty look like itself. Government, therefore, finds less and less use for harmonies of speech and ceremony as the play advances. But it does not follow that Shakespeare finds less and less use for them. On the contrary, through Gaunt and through Richard, through York, the Duchess of Gloucester, and the Queen, and even through the gardeners and the groom, he diverts them to a different end. Ceremony, the play reveals, may be politically spent at this historical moment, but it remains a vehicle of emotional solace.

In the geometry of Rose's *Richard II* certain scenes are called 'private', and this in itself might suggest a line across his roving arcs, below which hides the intimate as distinct from the public self. But, alas for diagrammatic thought, the intimate motives of the self are often active in public scenes, while private scenes yield public truths of comprehensive consequence. Like Philomel in *Lucrece* (1121–41) the Gaunt of the play's second – private – scene, still finds 'frets upon an instrument' to 'tune our heart-strings to true languishment' when his 'deep groans the diapason hear' for the state of England, in the scene of his death. The banishments of Bolingbroke and Mowbray occasion much consolatory eloquence, with Mowbray evoking the vocal music whose solace exile will deny him:

> The language I have learnt these forty years
> My native English, now I must forgo
> And now my tongue's use is to me no more
> Than an unstringed viol or a harp,
> Or like a cunning instrument cas'd up
> Or being open, put into his hands
> That knows no touch to tune the harmony.
>
> (I. iii. 159–65)

Gaunt and the Duchess still know how to tune the harmony. In the scene played between them we glimpse the hidden significance of the spirited exchanges that make the first scene. The Duchess hopes that justice will be done in the ceremonious trial of strength in Coventry: 'Be Mowbray's sins so heavy in his bosom, / That they may break his foaming courser's back.' But that kind of moral gravity is an indulgence of feeling; there is no real hope in it; nor any reassurance in the quiescent pieties of Gaunt:

> God's is the quarrel; for God's substitute
> His deputy annointed in His sight,
> Hath caused his death; the which, if wrongfully
> Let Heaven revenge; for I may never lift
> An angry arm against His minister.
>
> (I. ii. 37–41)

These are not, as they occur, the unequivocal moral and political positives of the play; although they have a representative quality and remind us of clusters of medieval and early Tudor beliefs about the sanctity of the throne and the efficacy of the lists as providential justice. They are not only in the play, they are also in character. And the character of Gaunt in this scene, and through to his last, is made up of a sequence of speeches about old age, impotence, quiescence, disease, guilt and decay. This 'character' is used by Shakespeare to structural purpose, disclosing the moral exhaustion masked by the pageant rhetoric of the first scene. The scene works as the play works, moving from an authoritative to a consolatory ceremonious music of speech. Compare the Duchess's first speech with her last:

> Finds brotherhood in thee no sharper spur?
> Hath love in thy old blood no living fire?
>
> (I. ii. 9–10)

with

> Yet one word more – grief boundeth where it falls
> Not with an empty hollowness, but weight.
>
> (I. ii. 58–9)

The spent spirit plays itself out in subtle verbal quibbles. The rhetorical figure that puns upon 'empty hollowness' and 'weight' was known as *Atanaclasis*, or in Puttenham's English, 'The Rebound', 'alluding to the tennis ball which being smitten with the racket rebounds back again'. Thus the figure plays upon itself, and is still rebounding in the last lines where 'hollowness' is still a dominant effect in the cadence of the verse and in the 'empty lodgings and unfurnished walls / Unpeopled offices, and untrodden stones' of Plashy.

The play's second act, largely about the dying Gaunt, opens with an eloquence which is about eloquence: 'O, but they say the tongues of dying men / Enforce attention like deep harmony.' Gaunt's prophecy culminates effects built up in the first act. Shakespeare insinuates into it the chroniclers' and the *Woodstock* author's indictments of the reign – the 'farming' of the realm, the blank charters, and other marks of Richard's ineptitude and importunity. But it is also, and equally, an heroic exhortation recalling England's fading greatness. Those felicities about the 'demi-paradise' and the 'silver sea' belonged then, as now, to an age other than the dramatic present, and to a rarer dimension than the solid geometry of political history. What is solid and actual is the nostalgia itself. For Edward III's reign was remembered by the chroniclers and by the anonymous playwright as the heyday of English chivalry. The deep harmonies of language about which and through which Gaunt speaks are related to the harmonies of state which were thought to be a reality in the time of Edward but ceased to be so in the time of Richard. A chivalrous age and the harmonies of its language are, we are made to feel, dying together – betrayed, violated, leased out.

But Gaunt's eloquence has a personal as well as a political function. It is not only condemnatory of the living, it is also consolatory to the dying:

> The setting sun, and music at the close,
> As the last taste of sweets is sweetest last,
> Writ in remembrance of things long past.
> (II. i. 12–14)

'More are men's ends mark'd than their lives before,' says Gaunt. We allow the claim for him as we must later allow it for Richard himself. He makes a self-consciously good end: 'Will the king come, that I may breathe my last?' He is made to fulfil the role that one tradition requires of a dying statesman – he makes music at the close.

What is true of the secondary figures of the play is more commandingly true of Richard. He too, but in a different range of senses, is an impotent figure; incapacitated not by guilt, age and disease, but by culpable innocence, fecklessness and vanity. York redeems himself by acting the perfect subject, to either king; the Duchess by acting out her threnody of grief; Gaunt by playing the part of dying prophet. Richard redeems himself, in his own eyes, and before his court and theatre audiences, by fulfilling the kingly roles that circumstance requires him to play.

First he plays the king in office – the megaphonic voice of authority, the president of the lists. Off the throne he plays the impulsive, reckless sophisticate, the man of 'wicked and naughty demeanour' described in the chronicles, who bungles the Irish business, grabs money and jeers at Gaunt. The spoiled-patrician-child posturings of the 'natural' Richard are themselves theatrical. This is the second role that mars the harmony of the first and makes intolerable discord.

When Richard returns from Ireland, however, the boyish petulance is shed. Little by little, through the superb self-dramatizations of the third and fourth acts, he comes to dominate our imaginations in his role as abdicating king. We discover that, whatever the political vanity of 'thrice gorgeous ceremony' it opens immense perspectives of solace. His language entertains the great medieval themes – the wheel of fortune, *contemptus mundi*, the dance of death and the sanctity of sovereignty – whose resonances make it paltry to be Bolingbroke. Richard's glorious angels cannot contend against Bolingbroke's 'hard bright steel' but his voice and bearing still command the theatre. 'Yet looks he like a king!' York cries when Richard appears on the walls of Flint Castle, and throughout the scene Shakespeare turns spectacle into word to vindicate him. The sun-king is unmoved (as we all are) by Northumberland's politic reassurances ('His glittering arms he will commend to rust') but lets the sun-metaphor itself proclaim the truth – 'Down, down, I come, like glist'ring Phaëton, / Wanting the manage of unruly jades.' Bolingbroke refuses to hear; he is deaf to the king's music. 'What says his majesty?' 'He speaks fondly,' says Northumberland, 'like a frantic man, Yet he is come.' *Richard II*, the play and the king, open up that space between political truth and imaginative truth which continues to interest Shakespeare in *Antony and Cleopatra*. But when the great king-metaphors have served their turn as aesthetic and imaginative solace to the man Richard, there is nothing more they can do. They cannot salvage his power or stop him from sharing other men's vulnerabilities. Like Gaunt's vision of England, Richard's magical sovereignty is nostalgic and cannot be effective.

His public self-dramatization reaches its climax when he compares himself to Christ: 'Did they not sometimes cry "All hail" to me? So Judas did to Christ.' These are the words that prompted Dover Wilson to speak of 'Shakespeare's miracle play'. But the miracle play is not Shakespeare's precisely, but Richard's. Shakespeare probably got the idea from Holinshed's comments on the King's flatterers. Bushy, he says, 'invented unused terms, and such strange names as were rather agreeable to the divine majesty of God, than to any earthly potentate.' Yet the miracle-play pose is moving because as an abdicating king Richard still speaks for and from his office, and because the claims he makes for his sacred status are consciously ironic, made in the course of discovering his own weakness. Richard remembers the coronation ceremony and, as it were, plays the film backwards:

I give this heavy weight from off my head,
And this unwieldy sceptre from my hand.
(IV. i. 204–5)

Through another rhetorical figure – this time anaphora – poet and king together unweave the spell that the ritual had once cast:

> With mine own tears I wash away my balm
> With mine own hands I give away my crown,
>
> (IV. i. 207–8)

returning the king to his humanity. The king, said Tudor law, with one of its voices, had two bodies.[7] The doctrine was a convenient one for lawyers and court advisers, but in the perspectives of Shakespeare's play it is allowed no final validity. The political body is the community; the human body is not sword-proof; and the divine body is an illusion, however powerful its spell upon the imagination.

Richard's final role is, like Gaunt's, to make a good end. In the abdication scene Richard plays what he calls a 'woeful pageant' to a court audience – much as his own story might have been played in fact before Henry VIII. But at Pomfret he is without an audience. He plays to himself, in private, become mere man. His isolation is established before we see it, when he bids goodbye to the Queen:

> I am sworn brother, sweet,
> To grim necessity; and he and I
> Will keep a league till death.
>
> (v. i. 20–1)

That heroic commitment to the inevitable sounds a stoical note in Richard's closing music. Chaucer's Theseus too had found it wisdom 'To maken vertu of necessitee' ('Knight's Tale', 3042) but did not charge his thought with such chivalric irony. The Queen's response recalls Gaunt on 'men's ends' ('The lion dying thrusteth forth his paw / And wounds the earth, if nothing else, with rage / To be o'erpower'd.') And there shortly follows York's talk of the procession through London, using a theatre image to express the contempt the public feel for one whose role in public spectacle has been usurped; but Richard remains the 'well-graced actor' and his last soliloquies are histrionic still.

The Pomfret speeches are rich in an extreme mode of self-dramatization:

> My brain I'll prove the female to my soul,
> My soul the father, and these two beget
> A generation of still-breeding thoughts.
>
> (v. v. 6–8)

The king's mind mimics the playwright's and the players':

---

[7] See Ernst Kantarowicz, *The King's Two Bodies* (Princeton, 1977). Kantarowicz found one of his starting-points in Dover Wilson's New Shakespeare edition of *Richard II*.

> Thus play I in one person many people,
> And none contented;
>
> (v. v. 31–2)

and while the ironies are sardonic and self-directed, they are also bringing Richard's consciousness right into the centre of our final experience of Shakespeare's play. The virtuosity of Richard's thought is both his solace and ours:

> How sour sweet music is
> When time is broke, and no proportion kept!
> So is it in the music of men's lives.
> And here have I the daintiness of ear
> To check time broke in a disordered string;
> But for the concord of my state and time
> Had not an ear to hear my true time broke.
> I wasted time and now doth time waste me.
>
> (v. v. 42–9)

The solace is in the symmetry, in the equal poise of that last line. But it is also in the imaginative art which puts political disorder into a satisfying verbal order. Shakespeare, to return to my beginning, making his plays out of Hall and Holinshed, is making music of men's lives.

Yet Shakespeare's music bids farewell to Hall's and Bodin's; there is no prospect of geometrical harmonies of state being restored on the old terms. To adapt Elizabeth Salter's words on Chaucer's Theseus, neither Hall's nor Bodin's accounts of the divine plan can be reconciled with its ugly manifestations in the history of Richard's reign. Out of an episode of bad government Shakespeare has nevertheless made a good play, and history has provisionally been made to yield an aesthetic form. The plays to come in Shakespeare's theatre will make fresh but equally transient treaties between authority, soldiery and the populace in the common weal. And plays to come will attend afresh to the tragic processes shadowed by the Bishop of Carlisle: 'Disorder, horror, fear and mutiny / Shall here inhabit, and this land be called / The field of Golgotha and dead men's skulls.' The catastrophe courses of history are another story, but after the play of *Richard II* we can say that the ritual allegiance that Carlisle is asking for cannot in itself avert them.

6 Julius Caesar and the Catastrophes of History

Shakespeare in all his English and Roman histories (excepting perhaps *Henry VIII*) shows that the peace and stability of society are vulnerable to the operation of certain catastrophic processes. They can be described either in the language of theatre-criticism or in the language of political history. There is a theatre of events, and there are multiple ways in which we dramatize ourselves and others in order to play a more satisfying role in history. Every human event is likely to yield something to theatrical analysis: a riot, a strike, a battle, a committee meeting, a quarrel at the breakfast table, an assassination.

'Catastrophe' in Shakespeare's time meant 'the latter end of a comedy'. 'Pat he comes,' says Edmund of Edgar, half way through the first act of *King Lear*, 'like the catastrophe of an old comedy'; and he comes again at the end, as if fully to honour Shakespeare's meta-theatrical joke, and resolve one set of the play's tensions. But when Falstaff's page cries, 'I'll tickle your catastrophe', he is only offering to tan Mistress Quickly's backside: 'the latter end of anything', says the *OED*. Over the past twenty years the word has acquired a more sophisticated significance in the elaborations of catastrophe theory in pure and applied mathematics. The French mathematician R. Thom demonstrated that there are seven topologically distinct kinds of predictable discontinuity that can occur in the dynamical systems of the physical world — that is, those composed of four variables (three in space and one in time). There have been many enterprising attempts to apply the general theory to the biological and human sciences,[1]

Versions of this paper were given at Birmingham in 1980, at Aleppo in 1981 and at Weimar in 1982.
[1] A useful introduction for the non-specialist reader is to be found in Denis Postle, *Catastrophe Theory* (Glasgow, 1980).

but I am not setting out to apply it systematically to theatre. I adduce it only in the hope of a little diminishing the conceptual innocence we usually bring to bear when we are discussing 'catastrophe', either in the ordinary force of the word – ruin, ending, disaster – or in its technical sense, as the last phase of a play. The plotting, in three dimensions, of Thom's seven equations yields seven beautifully ordered forms that a modern oracle of literary mysteries might delight in: the fold, the cusp, the swallow-tail, the butterfly, the hyperbolic umbilic, the elliptic umbilic and the parabolic umbilic. But those forms belong strictly to mathematics, and it would not be wise to look for a swallow-tail or elliptic umbilic in the large structure of *Julius Caesar*. The symmetries of dramatic art ask for a different account and mode of perception.

Sympathetically considered, catastrophe theory may remind us that in the human world, as in the physical world, incremental changes can have more than incremental effects; they can bring human consciousness and society into zones of critical instability from which there is no little-by-little recovery: the wave breaks, the milk boils over, the patient dies, the civilization disintegrates. The mathematician Christopher Zeeman, writing in the *Times Literary Supplement* (10 December 1971, p. 1556) introduces us to a dog from the kennel of Konrad Lorenz. The dog is cornered and is under the rival pressures of rage and fear; we approach it: if it is neither frightened nor enraged it is neutral; if it is merely frightened it runs away; and if it is merely enraged it bites us. But when it is both frightened and enraged, our approach gradually brings the dog towards that point of maximum tension in which it is least likely to be neutral. Its responses as we approach can be represented in the form of a cusp. A marginal change in the dog's reactions as their track carries them towards the cusp will have a major effect upon its later behaviour – a phenomenon that mathematicians call the divergence effect.

The cusp is a mathematical form. Theatrical forms were discussed in different but overlapping terms by Renaissance writers, who found the comedies of Terence shaped into three movements – *protasis, epitasis*, and *catastrophe*; Baldwin's study of *Shakspere's Five-Act Structure* traces many refinements.[2] Shakespeare's comedic structures respond modestly to this kind of analysis, but it becomes more than merely technical when we recognize that theatrical resolutions of a play's complexities are expressions of human, or quasi-divine, resolutions of human perplexities. *Catastrophe* comes to mean the way things fall out, and in the theatre it often entails surprising discoveries and metamorphoses. It may be that *Julius Caesar* is in some perspective answering to the laws of comedy. North's Plutarch is

[2]T. W. Baldwin, *Shakspere's Five Act Structure* (Urbana, 1947).

looking for an over-arching creative design in the history of events when he attributes first to 'ill fortune' and then to 'God' the confusion and ignorance that led to Brutus's defeat at Philippi; and in the play we have a strong sense of the history of Rome taking a new direction (for good or ill) as the personal tragedies recede into the past.

Shakespeare started his career as a history-play writer, if not as a playwright, by conjoining tragedy and historical disaster in *1 Henry VI*, which opens with black draperies across the canopy of the theatre, comets in the sky, and the spectacular funeral of Henry V. These are sombre excitements, and the public, as we know from Thomas Nashe's report, was moved and delighted.[3] For the audience of the time, therefore, a satisfying theatrical experience was shaped from a catastrophic episode in the English past. That experience, however, was not co-extensive with the life and death of Talbot; it was response to the play's celebration of the continuing life of the English community, and the history-play therefore has its affinities with comedy. The catastrophe of a comedy may signify that all's well that ends well; that of a tragedy, that we fall and cease; that of a history-play, that the community comes through, changing its values and its direction.

Of Shakespeare's mature Roman plays it might be said that each is about a critical moment in the history of Rome:[4] in *Coriolanus*, a crisis in the growth of the city-state (the virtue it breeds almost destroys it); in *Antony and Cleopatra*, a crisis of empire (imperial power seeking to resolve conflicts of outlook it has itself created; and in *Julius Caesar*, a crisis in the republic, re-enacted in obedience to laws that are at once political and theatrical. Discursive modes of political and historical thought have often addressed the question, how is a 'Caesar' made and unmade? and judging from the ubiquitous and persisting interest taken in the play, Shakespeare's contribution to the answer is of some moment. Antonio Gramsci, victim of a latter-day Caesar, wonders in his prison notebooks about the 'catalogue of the historical events which have culminated in a great "heroic" personality.' It is a Shakespearian speculation, but it does not find in Gramsci's thought a Shakespearian response. His understanding of historical catastrophe is in the wake of Marx and Hegel:

> Caesarism can be said to express a situation in which the forces in conflict balance each other in such a way that a continuation of the conflict can only terminate in their reciprocal destructon . . . But Caesarism – although it always expresses the particular solution in which a great personality is entrusted with the task of 'arbitration' over a historico-political situation characterised by an equilibrium

[3] E. K. Chambers, *Shakespeare* (1930), II, p. 188. See also p. 80 above.
[4] This point is developed in a different perspective in ch. 7 below.

of forces heading towards catastrophe – does not in all cases have the same historical significance. There can be both progressive and reactionary forms of Caesarism; the exact significance of each form can, in the last analysis, be reconstructed through concrete history, and not by means of any sociological rule of thumb.[5]

The reconstruction of catastrophe in *Julius Caesar* is a theatrical realization, but in-theatre audience responses are urgently and significantly related to the dynamics of the community, English and Roman, in the larger world, outside the theatre. Shakespeare's Caesar is not 'entrusted with the task of "arbitration" over a historico-political situation characterised by an equilibrium of forces heading towards catastrophe'. Unlike his historical counterpart he is not appointed dictator, and initially he is himself the precipitant, if not the agent of one of the contending forces. The play begins with a festival in the streets and ends with a defeat and a victory on the battlefield. Its last act is meant to meet imaginative and emotional expectations awakened in the first four acts – expectations characteristically satisfied in tragedy by death and disaster. The play, however, refuses to assume a tragic form. Its very active tragic patterns are subsumed in the catastrophic processes of Roman history.

It is a distinctive feature of the play that it offers a wide choice of centres of instability and divergence effects, moments when events or our consciousness of them could go either way. The meeting in the forum where Caesar refuses the crown to the acclaim of the populace; the seduction of Brutus to Cassius' cause; the decision to spare Antony; Calpurnia's attempt to persuade Caesar to stay at home; the orations in the forum after Caesar's death; the murder of Cinna the poet; the quarrel between Brutus and Cassius; and finally, the battle of Philippi itself. All these episodes are catastrophically displayed before they are resolved, and all may be said to satisfy converging laws of theatre and history, of tragedy and terror.

'Der Schrecken ist ein Ausfluß der Tugend, er ist nicht anders als die schnelle, strenge und unbeugsame Gerechtigkeit': 'Terror is an outflowing of virtue; it is no more than swift, rigorous and inexorable justice.' That is not, as we may imagine, the voice of Bade Meinhof, but of Robespierre, in Georg Büchner's *Dantons Tod*.[6] Büchner was writing in a Shakespearian tradition, making his own connections between tragic sacrifice and political violence, knowing that in the history of communities, terror, butchery and atrocity are often pursued, in a dedicated way, from motives that aspire to the highest moral purity. Men kill to redeem, to atone, to purge, to purify.

---

[5] Antonio Gramsci, *Selections from the Prison Notebooks*, ed. and trans. Quintin Hoare and Geoffrey Nowell Smith (1971/1976), p. 219.
[6] Georg Büchner, *Werke und Briefe* (Munich, 1976). *The Plays of Georg Büchner*, trans. Victor Price (1971/1977); the quotation is from Act I, sc. iii.

Robespierre himself, both in the play and in historical fact, died a victim to the destructive forces he helped to release; for his own doctrine of terror was overreached by the ironically named Saint Just, fraternal member of the Committee of Public Safety. Here he is, speaking in vindication of the Terror at the end of the play's second act:

> Moses led his people through the Red Sea and into the wilderness till the old corrupt generation was exterminated, before he found his new state. Legislators! We have no Red Sea and no wilderness, but we have war and the guillotine. The revolution is like the daughters of Pelias; she dismembers mankind to make it young. Humanity will emerge from the cauldron of blood like the earth from the flood waters, with limbs primordially strong, as though from a second creation.

Sustained applause, says the stage direction, *Some DEPUTIES stand up in their enthusiasm*:

> We call upon all the secret enemies of tyranny, throughout Europe and the whole world, who carry the dagger of Brutus under their cloaks, to share with us this sublime moment!

The spectators and deputies strike up the 'Marseillaise'. They are ready to participate in the sublime moment of killing and dying into life – a sublimity that both Shakespeare and Büchner teach us to distrust. Yet the dagger of Brutus known to Büchner had been beaten into shape in the quick forge and working-house of Shakespeare's imagination. It had become the symbol for liberation by violence – liberation from terror by terror. Shakespeare makes us well aware of the disabling pain of the paradox and of the related experience; and Büchner makes us all live through it again, in another phase of Europe's history. The French Revolution tried to model its styles and its convictions quite self-consciously on Rome, and Büchner sees the catastrophic history of Caesar's Rome repeating itself in what looks like the acting-out of a remorseless historical process and law. Death and destruction are felt to be essential to the renewal of life, and the conviction is held with religious intensity: 'We must bury the great corpse with dignity,' says Saint Just, speaking of the bulky Danton (still alive at the time), 'like priests, not like murderers.' Büchner is remembering Brutus's noble admonition, 'Let's be sacrificers but not butchers, Caius . . . Let's carve him as a dish fit for the gods.' A little later in Büchner's play Robespierre also casts himself in a high religious role:

Yes, a bloody Messiah who sacrifices and is not sacrificed. He
redeemed men with His blood, and I redeem them with their own.
He invented sin, and I take it upon myself. He had the joys of
suffering and I have the pangs of the executioner.

Both *Julius Caesar* and *Dantons Tod* work in those areas of consciousness
where religious, moral and political impulses become indistinguishable from
murderous impulses, as the one flips to the other. Sacrificial rite is a central
terrain of tragedy, and Shakespeare and Büchner recognize it both as a
preoccupation of the psyche and as a province of history.

Neither in *Dantons Tod* nor in *Julius Caesar* is that elevated ecstasy of
violence allowed to dominate unchallenged. Both Büchner and Shakespeare
expose it to an intimate, ironical scrutiny which for Shakespeare is part of
a continuing process. In his first Roman play, *Titus Andronicus*, he had
explored both the meretricious attractiveness (for theatre-goers) of the
revenge-and-sacrifice complex of ideas and metaphors, and their destructive
manifestations in society.[7] The play opens with a proclamation in what,
with Brutus in mind, we could call the high Roman fashion:

> Suffer not dishonour to approach
> The imperial seat, to virtue consecrate,
> To justice, continence and nobility;
> But let desert in pure election shine;
> And, Romans, fight for freedom in your choice.

But irrational, primordial movements subvert the civilization. Events are
ordered to disastrous ends by jealousies and factions, ranging from the most
intimately sadistic to the most public, and from family squabbles to issues
of imperial succession, but also by archaic religious rites, solemnly
performed. Sacrifice in this play is a form of propitiation of the 'shadows
that are gone' and is attended by the prospect of interminable acts of
revenge. Shakespeare makes the revenge cycle in that remote Roman society
seem inescapable, like a physical or biological law built into the human
world. But however natural and inevitable the mutilations and murders are
made to seem, Shakespeare also makes it clear that the catastrophic processes
that overtake the Roman tribe have human causes. No gods are to blame;
only men, but men who are the victims still of their own primitive codes
and compulsions. The collective propensities of the Romans and the Goths
operate like gods. Historically speaking, Titus lived long after Julius Caesar,
but Shakespeare seems to recognize that at a late date Rome declined into
a barbarity close to that of the once despised Goths – as England indeed
did in the fifteenth century.

[7] See below, pp. 190, 146.

In *Julius Caesar*, the insights of the earlier plays, into the nature of civil war, of political process and sacrificial rite, have been thoroughly assimilated and are now re-created in a stage-world that has been brought closer to the familiar world both of Shakespeare's time and ours. *Julius Caesar*, moreover, is one of those plays (*Hamlet* is another) in which we are made very aware of the fitness of the Elizabethan stage for dramatizing both public and private life. Shakespeare's newly opened Globe Theatre was large and formal enough to convince an audience it was watching events in the Forum at Rome, and small enough to make it feel close to Brutus and the boy Lucius in the tent on the eve of battle. Thus the play is remembered both for its commemoration of a great political and historical event, and for its intimate exploration of personal relationships.

The play's movement between the *polis*, or community, and the *ideote* – the private man – intensifies our sense of the stresses and turbulences of the Roman world that breed its catastrophic and tragic processes. What we make of the ironies, conflicts and contrary truths will, within limits, depend upon our own predispositions of response, but certain Shakespearian strategies are visible and demonstrable. The play's anatomy of Rome's instability differs significantly from Plutarch's, as it does from Gramsci's account of Caesarism. Plutarch's Caesar, for example, has already been chosen 'perpetual Dictator', because the Romans hoped that to be ruled 'by one man alone' would be 'a good means for them to take breath a little' after the miseries of the civil wars. It is a view that Plutarch himself endorses and for which indeed he claims divine sanction (see Bullough, v. p. 127), but it is unexpressed in the play, which is much more equivocal and ambivalent than its source, making us aware of the presence in the society of rival values that are treacherously difficult to distinguish, and of the co-presence in personal consciousness of conflicting responses to the same experience; the stresses are within characters as well as between them.

Some hints in Plutarch's *Life of Brutus* invited Shakespeare to see in the intimacy of Brutus and Cassius a paradox about the nature of revolution. Character and ideology reciprocally interrelate. Cassius is the activist, Brutus the idealist and ideologue. The revolution needs both kinds and they must work together. Brutus was an enemy of tyranny, says North's Plutarch, but 'Cassius hated the tyrant'; Cassius 'felt his friends and did stir them up against Caesar', but it was necessary for the conspirators 'to have a man of such estimation as Brutus, to make every man boldly think, that by his only presence the deed were holy and just' (Bullough, v, p. 95). If we keep a certain distance from the play such an account of it can be made to work, and it is the basis for much routine interpretation.

While holiness and justice are very much Brutus's preoccupations, however, they are not, as events prove, under his command or at his disposal. Marcus Brutus is prompted by Cassius to see himself as the spiritual heir of the Brutus who slew Tarquin. He is a self-consciously noble patrician, standing for the liberal traditions of the Republic. In Cassius, liberal tradition takes a pragmatic and reductive form, a levelling reluctance to allow any to grow beyond his own stature. The play is at once about how leaders are created and destroyed by the community, and about how the community is created and destroyed by its leaders. In the subtle, rapid and rhythmic movement between the public and private realms of experience, the theatre of the market-place and the theatre of the isolated consciousness, holiness and justice are ambiguous and even contending aspirations.

The play's first movement conjoins public festival with private colloquy, and its first scene expresses with great naturalness and precision the easy-going relationship between the swarming plebeians and their Caesar. 'Why dost thou lead these men about the streets?' A cobbler answers, 'Truly sir, to wear out their shoes to get myself more work. But indeed, sir, we make a holiday to see Caesar, and to rejoice in his triumph.' Street festivals delight in heroes and are apt to create them even out of unpromising material. Flavius and Murellus, plebeian leaders but not heroes, try to stem the festive tide:

> Wherefore rejoice? What conquests brings he home?
> What tributaries follow him to Rome,
> To grace in captive bonds his chariot wheels?
> You blocks, you stones, you worse than senseless things!
> O you hard hearts, you cruel men of Rome,
> Knew you not Pompey?
>
> (I. i. 32–7)

In their holiday mood the populace have forgotten Pompey; they need their hero for the day. But they are not – not yet – 'cruel men of Rome'.

The Tribunes, trying to recall the people to their old allegiance to Pompey, speak with an imperial and ample voice. The language of *Julius Caesar* is Roman in quite another way from that of *Titus Andronicus*; in the earlier play Shakespeare had learned from Seneca and from Ovid a lyrical dialect that plays with exquisite grace upon exquisite pain. Here the language creates vast presences before collapsing again to ordinariness:

> Have you not made an universal shout,
> That Tiber trembled underneath her banks
> To hear the replication of your sounds
> Made in her concave shores?
>
> (I. i. 44–7)

That 'universal shout' comes back to us as a vast, hollow echo, anticipating distant shouts to be heard from the Capitol in the next scene; but before our imaginations are allowed too much space they are recalled to everyday domesticities: 'And do you now put on your best attire? / And do you now cull out a holiday?' What exasperates the tribunes is that Caesar's homecoming is just another chance for a day off. But on such days, the tribunes perceive and the play reminds us, kings and emperors may be proclaimed and dictators licensed.

Shakespeare is careful to keep his Romans sufficiently English, and human nature and society are sufficiently unchanged for the play's central perceptions to stay alive. But the ability to make giant forms of men is made to seem specifically Roman. In its large design and in its detail, the play makes men big, then cuts them down to size. The poetry compels us to collaborate in this process of creative treachery:

> These growing feathers pluck'd from Caesar's wing

says Flavius, as he pulls down the flowers and ceremonies from the public monuments,

> Will make him fly an ordinary pitch,
> Who else will soar above the view of men
> And keep us all in servile fearfulness.
>
> (I. i. 73–5)

When Cassius speaks confidingly to Brutus we are taught how the tired Caesar is 'now become a God', but a god likely to be struck down by fits:

> I did mark
> How he did shake – 'tis true, this god did shake;
> His coward lips did from their colour fly,
> And that same eye whose bend doth awe the world
> Did lose his lustre.
>
> (I. ii. 120–4)

The process of making gods of men is made a manifestation of the imperial spirit; the ability to cut them down to human size again is made to seem characteristically republican. The tribunes try to teach the people the republican skill. Cassius teaches it to Brutus, and Shakespeare compels his audience to acquire it. This way of putting it emphasizes the value that the play puts upon human solidarity – we are all mortal, flesh-and-blood, ordinary men, belonging to the same community, Roman or English. But we may also recognize in republican and imperial aspirations the Shakespearian counterpart of Gramsci's conflicting historical forces.

Cutting down to size is not the only skill we acquire. The giant forms, including the titanic Caesar, are created as well as reduced. That propensity to create heroes and leaders, to make the community heroic and to see it embodied in great men, is not without honour in the history, thought and theatre of the Renaissance. The will to be god-like, to transcend the ordinary boundaries of our human growth, can be creative as well as malignant. The Caesar of the play is created by many processes, in the theatre of the Roman Capitol and in the theatre of the mind.

For while Cassius forges in his mind, in Brutus's, and in ours, the great image of Caesar:

> Why man, he doth bestride the narrow world
> Like a Colossus, and we petty men
> Walk under his huge legs, and peep about
> To find ourselves dishonourable graves.
>
> (I. ii. 135–8)

the universal shouts are proclaiming Caesar in the Capitol. Casca describes Caesar's acting and the crowd's response:

> If the tag-rag people did not clap him and hiss him, according as he pleas'd and displeas'd them, as they use to do the players in the theatre, I am no true man.
>
> (I. ii. 258–61)

Shakespeare had been this way before, for Caesar's performance as he refuses the crown, in the sight of the people, had already had its imitator in the English history of Shakespeare's theatre, where Richard of Gloucester three times refuses the crown at Baynard's Castle. The people on that occasion, says the chronicler Hall, 'much merveiled at this maner of dealing' and said 'these matters be kings' games, as it were stage plays . . . in which poor men be but lookers-on.'[8] But the Roman audience in *Julius Caesar*, unlike the London audience of *Richard III* is not composed of sceptical onlookers but of festive participants, eager to be moved by, and taken in by, the theatre of the occasion. As in Plutarch, Shakespeare's populace cheers Caesar when he declines the crown, not when he is offered it. But where Plutarch represents the people as resisting the show that Caesar and Antony are staging between them, Shakespeare has them delighting in the show even while they frustrate the political design it has upon them. They grow more and more ambiguously excited as the performance is repeated. The 'general shout', heard offstage and ominously interpreted by Brutus's predisposition, encroaches incrementally upon the theatre audience's awareness before Casca re-creates it; 'he put it by once . . . he put it by again . . . he put it the third time by.' The outcome is catastrophic – a sudden switch of direction at the divergent climax – but this time (it is a narrow squeak) for Caesar, not for the Republic:

---

[8] See Edward Hall, *Chronicle*, 1548, ed. H. Ellis (1809; 1965), p. 374.

> And still as he refused it, the rabblement hooted, and clapped their chopped hands, and threw up their sweaty night-caps, and uttered such a deal of stinking breath because Caesar refused the crown, that it had almost choked Caesar, for he swounded and fell down at it.
>
> (I. ii. 243–9)

The 'tag-rag people' cast their caps into the air in frantic applause of a popular hero. Caesar, recovering from the falling sickness, is able, through the crowd's sympathetic response, to turn even that weakness to advantage:

> when he came to himself again, he said, if he had done anything amiss, he desired their worships to think it was his infirmity. Three or four wenches, were I stood, cried 'Alas, good soul!' and forgave him with all their hearts . . . If Caesar had stabbed their mothers, they would have done no less.
>
> (I. ii. 269–75)

Neither Shakespeare's Richard of Gloucester nor Plutarch's Caesar are allowed such histrionic rapport with their publics. The populace, therefore, even while it cheers its hero for refusing the crown, assists in and assists at the creation of the titanic Caesar who aspires to it. Caesar uses his histrionic abilities to satisfy his audience's expectations, contriving to make himself appear not only more god-like but also more human than ordinary mortals. That tense and ambivalent relationship between the public and its leader can make or unmake tyrants; it is ready to go either way – the divergence effect of catastrophe theory. Because the people are satisfied as spectators it seems that they acquiesce in, or participate in, the casual terror of Caesar's regime. Flavius and Murellus, we learn, 'for pulling scarfs off Caesar's images are put to silence' (I. ii. 285–6); we do not, in the play, know how.

It is not, however, the vast and popular audience alone that makes demands on Caesar the actor in history's theatre of catastrophe. He performs also before an intimate coterie audience that includes Antony: 'I rather tell thee what is to be fear'd / Than what I fear; for always I am Caesar.' Most men of ordinary pitch, if they are deaf in one ear, might be expected to make the point apologetically. But the player of Caesar, speaking imperiously, may well make his disability occasion for command: 'for always I am Caesar. / Come on my right hand, for this ear is deaf' (we supermen are like that). Perhaps on this occasion, as on others, however, Caesar's god-posture falters enough to reveal the theatrical artifice which sustains it. Playing on a later occasion before Calpurnia, in a far from full house, he will manage for a little to keep it going even in face of wifely solicitude:

What can be avoided
Whose end is purpos'd by the mighty gods?
Yet Caesar shall go forth.
(II. ii. 26–8)

That looks like submission to the gods, not a god-posture. But Caesar identifies his will with that of the gods and makes their choice his, as if he matches up to them with his more than human resolution, before lapsing into his domestic nature and saying what any of us might say:

Mark Antony shall say I am not well
And for your humour I will stay at home.
(II. ii. 55–6)

Caesar the god, then, is multiply created out of ordinary human clay – he is crowd-created, coterie-created and self-created.

He is created as well as destroyed by the conspirators under the sway of Brutus, activated by Cassius. The destructive energies of the play gather primarily in the mind, in the secret exchanges between the conspirators, and in Brutus's soliloquies. Caesar does not soliloquize and Brutus makes only one sustained public appearance. Through Brutus Shakespeare more closely explores the febrile theatre of the mind. As we see in *Titus Andronicus*, ghosts and madness and feverish obsessions were familiar preoccupations of Senecal plays, and Shakespeare found in North's Plutarch a lot of material suitable for Senecal treatment. But nightmares, atrocities, 'unlucky signs', ruptures in the natural order and vengeful apparitions are in Plutarch matters of reported fact. In the play they reach us through the consciousness of the conspirators and are related to their fears of the prodigious growth of Caesar; hence the 'unaccustomed terror of the night', the superstitious and apprehensive Casca (on his way to Pompey's theatre) and the sleepless anxiety of Brutus. The intimacy of the orchard-scene finds its starting-point in Plutarch ('But when night came that he was in his own house, then he was clean changed'). With the coming and going of the boy Lucius Shakespeare domesticates and familiarizes the insomnia of Brutus without diminishing its moral and political significance. Brutus's insomniac soliloquy is a climax and a growing-point in Shakespeare's art and in his understanding of the relationship between political society and individual consciousness:

Between the acting of a dreadful thing
And the first motion, all the interim is
Like a phantasma or a hideous dream.
The Genius and the mortal instruments
Are then in council, and the state of man

> Like to a little kingdom, suffers then
> The nature of an insurrection.
>
> (II. i. 63–9)

Brutus and the Roman state together are in a condition of catastrophic instability. The noble Roman is rehearsing an ignoble act, from the noblest of motives. In time this same soliloquy will tell us much about *Macbeth*, being a germ from which that play grows. In both plays the phantasmagoric imagination prompts the destruction of the kingdom and state of man, and then recoils upon the destroyer. Macbeth's thought, however, is made by Shakespeare from a language more evidently feverish than Brutus's. Brutus apparently remains Roman and rational in the Stoic way – recognizing self-transcending principles and allegiances, seemingly putting political imperatives before personal ones, acknowledging the need for public vindication of his act, and for private vindication in a public language. Yet in killing others both Brutus and Macbeth kill something in themselves. Brutus by his act crosses that gap of conscience or consciousness that comes between the acting of a dreadful deed and the first motion. So, through a more complex series of stages, does Macbeth.[9] There is no solace in the consequent condition of life, in the 'tale told by an idiot'. His isolation is total and the death of his wife of no significance. Shakespeare may have remembered in the later play Brutus's curiously inert reception of the two reports of his wife's death. It is a gloss on the Stoic *apathia*, the condition of freedom, of freedom from feeling, that Brutus attains, or lapses into, after the killing of Caesar.

It is also a fascinating exercise in the comparative dynamics of human consciousness to compare Macbeth's 'If it were done when 'tis done' soliloquy with Brutus's, 'It must be by his death.' The instabilities of Macbeth's thought are sufficiently indicated by its opening memory of Christ's words to Judas at the last supper. 'What thou doest, do quickly' (Duncan's last supper is being prepared by servants backstage).[10] The instabilities of Brutus's meditation appear the moment we recognize that he begins his argument with his conclusion and then goes in search of its beginning. His revolutionary resolve is reached through orderly treacheries of thought:

> So Caesar may;
> Then lest he may, prevent. And since the quarrel
> Will bear no colour for the thing he is,
> Fashion it thus: that what he is, augmented,

---

[9] The allusion is developed by Roy Walker in *The Time Is Free: A Study of Macbeth* (1949).

[10] See below, p. 158.

Would run to these and these extremities;
And therefore think him as a serpent's egg,
Which, hatch'd, would as his kind grow mischievous,
And kill him in the shell.

(II. i. 27–34)

Brutus reaches a catastrophic formulation ('what he is, augmented /
Would run to these and these extremities') and predicts a catastrophic
metamorphosis. Yet Caesar by this account is not a tyrant but a potential
tyrant – he must be killed in his shell, and in the play he is most tyrannical
in the shell-like imaginations of Cassius and Brutus.

Caesar in his own shell, acting the part that imperial Rome asks of him,
is a god. Brutus, the ancestral republican, in process of denying Caesar's
god-ship, falls on his knees to Caesar, kills him, then sets himself up as a
priest. This priestly role of Brutus is very much Shakespeare's invention –
there is no trace of it in the sources, nor in the many other plays and
Roman histories of the time that scholarship has brought to my notice.
'Let's be sacrificers, but not butchers', 'O that we could come by Caesar's
spirit, / And not dismember Caesar! But alas, Caesar must bleed for it.'
This is a moment of catastrophic self-deception. It is so whether we think
of Brutus as the 'gentle friend' of Caesar, or as a republican assassin, or as
a religious philosopher acknowledging supreme moral presences or 'gods'.
Brutus makes no attempt to 'come by Caesar's spirit'; he is devoted to the
butchery and the sacrifice. What he represents to himself and others as a
measured, reluctant movement towards the death-solution is a powerful
undertow of his own obscure but characteristically Roman consciousness.

There is also a convergence in the play between Brutus's delusion that
he is a priest, ministering the divine will, and Caesar's subscription to
flattering images of his own sanctity. Here, as in *King Lear*, Shakespeare
keeps watch on the proximities of superstition to religious belief, and of
our beliefs to our consciousness of reality. Casca says of Caesar, 'he is
superstitious grown of late', and he should have stayed that way. But his
compulsion to act as if he were steadfast and invulnerable overcomes his
nervousness about augury. When Decius Brutus comes to tease Caesar,
with a show of familiar good sense, out of his night-gowned timidity, he is
also determined to set the colossus upon his pedestal again and wheel him
off to market. Once more the audience is poised upon a catastrophic
boundary, the going-one-way yielding suddenly to going-the-other. Caesar
plays his part in the conspiracy by assuming once again the god's
prerogatives, as the conspirators deliberately create, or re-create, the god-
figure they are out to destroy. Again we recognize, in the proximity of the
king-slayer and king-maker, the catastrophic divergence effect. Shakespeare's
insight here has Plutarch's authority: 'even they that most hated him were

no less favourers and furtherers of his honours, then they that most flattered him: because they might have greater occasion to rise, and that it appeared they had just cause and colour to attempt what they did against him.' The conspirators stage-manage Caesar's last and most hubristic performance. They tell him the Senate 'have concluded this day to give a crown to mighty Caesar' and they provoke from him the superhuman attitudinizing that licenses his slaughter. Decius Brutus makes of the interpretation of dreams a political skill and seduces Caesar by representing defiance of augury as a sign of resolute Roman virtue. Primarily, however, Caesar gives way to the most extravagant of adulatory metaphors – the one that makes him less a sacrifice to the gods than a self-sacrificing god:

> Your statue spouting blood in many pipes,
> In which so many smiling Romans bath'd
> Signifies that from you great Rome shall suck
> Reviving blood, and that great men shall press
> For tinctures, stains, relics and cognizance.
>   (II. ii. 85–9)

Shakespeare remembers the practices through which saints and martyrs were honoured in his own day. Caesar, some psychoanalysts might say, is excellent quarry for the kind of operation Decius Brutus carries out on him. He has a narcissistic personality, made up of a 'grandiose self' which seeks to dominate the world, and an 'infantile self' perpetually looking for admiration and sympathy. His god-acting persists in his responses to the soothsayer and to Artemidorus, and even on the stage of Brutus's imagination at Sardis. In his revived god-posture, Caesar goes to the Capitol and is cut down; his blood then seems ordinary enough.

But our consciousness of it soon ceases to be ordinary. The blood becomes first what Brutus makes of it in his strange priestly ritual:

> Stoop, Romans, stoop,
> And let us bathe our hands in Caesar's blood
> Up to the elbows, and besmear our swords;
> Then walk we forth, even to the market-place
> And waving our red weapons o'er our heads,
> Let's all cry, 'Peace, freedom, and liberty.'
>   (III. i. 105–10)

In Plutarch, the conspirators all wound Caesar as a sign of common commitment, but there is no blood-rite. It is Shakespeare's Brutus who makes a sacrificial ritual out of the assassination and voices that mood of moral and political exaltation which carries the conspirators into a visionary future. It is most visionary in the theatre, as Brutus and Cassius try to appropriate the laws of tragedy to serve their own political purpose:

> How many ages hence
> Shall this our lofty scene be acted o'er
> In states unborn and accents yet unknown.
>
> (III. i. 111–13)

The scene, however, is less noble than Cassius supposes. In the immediate Roman future an ugly, catastrophic process has still to work itself out.

At this, half-way, point of the play, Antony's servant kneels before Brutus and the action is suspended between divergent possibilities. The tragedy, acted in the Capitol and staged in the imaginations of Brutus and Cassius, will prove only an episode in that contrived by Antony. He shakes bloody hands with each conspirator in turn, but the effect is to diminish pity for the general wrong of Rome, and leave for the play (as for Antony's credit) a choice of 'two bad ways' on 'slippery ground'.

For Brutus, political catastrophe would attend the unchallenged supremacy of Caesar: 'So let high-sighted tyranny range on, / Till each man drop by lottery,' and he plots and stages a tragedy of the sacrificial kind, to appease the gods and redeem the Roman republic. For Antony, political catastrophe attends the cutting-down and cutting-up of Caesar, the bleeding piece of earth, and the tragedy he devises is of the atrocity-and-revenge kind:

> Blood and destruction shall be so in use,
> And dreadful objects so familiar,
> That mothers shall but smile when they behold
> Their infants quarter'd with the hands of war;
> All pity chok'd with custom of fell deeds;
> And Caesar's spirit, ranging for revenge,
> With Ate from his side come hot from hell,
> Shall in these confines with a monarch's voice
> Cry 'Havoc!' and let slip the dogs of war,
> That this foul deed shall smell above the earth
> With carrion men, groaning for burial.
>
> (III. i. 265–75)

There is much Shakespearian conviction here, much to remind us of the Roses Wars, and something to make us now remember that civil war was to come again, in England and in Europe, in the next generation. It recalls Northumberland's response to the news of Hotspur's death:

> Let heaven kiss earth! now let not Nature's hand
> Keep the wide flood confin'd! Let order die!
> And let the world no longer be a stage
> To feed contention in a ling'ring act;
> But let one spirit of the first-born Cain
> Reign in all bosoms, that each heart being set

On bloody courses, the rude scene may end
And darkness be the burier of the dead.

(2 Henry IV, I. i. 153–60)

Like the nihilistic imprecations of Northumberland, of Clifford in *2 Henry VI*, v. i. 31–60, and of the Bastard in *King John*, IV. iii. 144–54, Antony's is generated out of grief, the most inhuman propensities out of the most human; distress and rage together precipitate the divergence effect. Antony's, however, is also, in Lord Bardolph's phrase about Northumberland's, 'a strained passion', touched by a sophisticated Roman relish for cataclysm. The play demonstrates his determinaton to bring about the destruction he pretends to fear.

In the Forum scene Brutus behaves as if the play were over and the people free to resume their ordinary and rational lives. But the catastrophe of Antony's play is still to come, and his histrionic abilities awaken the pity of the Roman audience in a way that makes it totally pitiless. From his personal grief there is generated, with a theatrical art that creates the illusion of spontaneity, a hot communal ferocity which serves a cold political purpose. Through incremental repetition ('all, honourable men'), his oration, covertly exploiting the crowd's natural revulsion, switches the collective responses of stage and theatre audiences from one set of emotions and allegiances to another, changing the political disposition of the crowd, and with it the future course of Rome. The 'tide in the affairs of men,' to adapt the play's own metaphor for historical process, 'running to the mark runs faster out.' But it is a tide that submits for a season to Antony's detached influence: 'Mischief, thou art afoot, / Take thou what course thou wilt!' (III. ii. 259–60). Mischief afoot requires Cinna the poet to die without ceremony, enabling Shakespeare's art to create yet another divergence effect as the mob hesitates before the cry goes up, 'Kill him for his bad verses!' Had he or another shouted 'On to the Capitol!' all might have been well.

The dislocations and uncertainties that damage both the Stoic confidence of Brutus (in the tides in the affairs of men) and the Epicurean confidence of Cassius (in human initiatives) are aptly epitomized in the quarrel-scene. The episode averts, however, the catastrophe it courts – the gods are ready with their thunderbolts but no one is dashed to pieces. But it also prefigures the destructive misunderstandings of Philippi. Brutus's tactics are owed to his plotting of the catastrophic equation:

The enemy increaseth every day;
We, at the height, are ready to decline.
There is a tide in the affairs of men
Which taken at the flood, leads on to fortune;

> Omitted, all the voyage of their life
> Is bound in shallows and in miseries.
>
> (IV. iii. 216–21)

In the last phase of the play we watch the recession of tragedy into history. For tragedy is concerned with the finitude of human life, while history is aware that (somehow) it keeps going. As a tragedy the play persuades us that, with the deaths of Brutus and Cassius, poignant personal experiences, of historical significance, are complete. The wisdom by which they and Portia once lived can create a Roman style for dying. The tragic catastrophe is made to feel like an historical truth about the decline and fall of the Roman Republic: the community which makes god-like leaders and then sacrifices them cannot but be unstable. How can it stabilize itself? Brutus in heroic self-righteousness brings to Rome the traumatic ordeal he affected to avert: 'So let high-sighted tyranny range on / Till each man drop by lottery.' But the men drop by lottery in the proscription-scene of the play he has helped to set.

What then, if a Caesar threatens us, must we do? In politics, I like to think, I am a Shakespearian. We must take our Caesars and our Brutuses to see plays like *Julius Caesar*, in order, just a little, to diminish our pretensions to make ourselves gods or god-slayers. The play was, and remains, capable of awakening its audiences to a fuller and more sympathetic understanding of the catastrophic dynamics of human community. But if it teaches us to distrust our rulers, it also teaches us to distrust the distrusters.

7 Myth and History in Shakespeare's Rome

There is a moment in the live dialogue of the past where one of Shakespeare's historical characters is speaking to another about a third, more dubiously historical character from another play. Cicero, in his *Brutus*, is talking with Brutus about Coriolanus, in the company of the Roman historian Atticus.[1] Cicero has reason to make some comparisons between Themistocles of Athens and Coriolanus of Rome; both, he says, were great men in their respective civilizations or states (Cicero's word is 'men' *civis*); each was unjustly exiled by an ungrateful populace; each went over to the enemy, yet each relented and chose to meet a voluntary death. At this point Cicero breaks off and appeals to Atticus: 'I know that you tell a different story, but allow me to believe that this was indeed the way he died' (*Brutus*, p. 42).

Atticus, whose very name declares his rational disengagement from the catastrophic history of Rome, chooses to tease Cicero a little: 'As you please, for rhetoricians are allowed to distort history a little in order to give more point to their stories.' And he adds that the story Cicero believed about Themistocles was itself an invention by Clitarchus or Stratocles. Thucydides, a distinguished Athenian historian close in date to Themistocles, says he died a natural death and only 'rumour' or 'suspicion' put it about that he took his own life by poison. It is 'the others', according to Atticus, who claim that 'on sacrificing a bullock, he drank a bowl of its blood and from that draught fell dead.' 'That's the sort of death,' we are told, 'that gave them the chance for rhetorical and tragic embellishment, the ordinary natural death gave them no such opportunity.' And so, with strictly Attic urbanity, he approaches the end of Coriolanus: 'Since it squares with your

[1] Cicero, *Brutus*, with an English translation by G. L. Hendrickson (1952).

taste to make everything the same in the careers of Themistocles and Coriolanus, take the bowl too with my leave – I will even provide a sacrificial host in order to make Coriolanus a second Themistocles.' Cicero is disarmed, and undertakes in future to touch on historical matters with more caution.

Unfortunately the *Liber Annalis* of Atticus has not come down to us and we cannot know exactly what he said about Coriolanus' death. We may reasonably assume, however, that his account was close to that reported by Livy out of Fabius, that he lived until he was an old man and that 'oftentimes in his latter days he used to utter this speech, "A heavie case and most wretched, for an aged man to live banisht"' (Holland's *Livy*, in Bullough, v, p. 505). Cicero's discourse, therefore, brings us to the point of inception of a kind of myth. Atticus, by Cicero's account the most scrupulous (*religiosissimum*) of Roman historians, pretends to be ready to visit the facts with a fiction in order to give the story a more tragic significance. Cicero is artful. He uses Atticus' easy-going scepticism to sustain in the dialogue the claim that rhetoric has always exercised great influence on the course of history; and not only on its course, but also on our way of narrating it – how indeed can we know one from the other? The stories that offer to inform us about the past take form from and give form to our present experience; thus the creative instabilities of the language take us by surprise when we attempt to talk objectively about inFORMation, SIGNificance and hiSTORY.

By the time it reached Shakespeare the Coriolanus story had been shaped by Plutarch's mentors, by Plutarch himself and by his French and English translators to an outcome that was ripe for transmutation into theatre. It was ripe not merely because the man Shakespeare found it so, but also because certain traditions of language, theatre and civilization were poised and ready for a fresh articulation and re-creation of Rome and its sustaining stories. The story of Coriolanus began to be told, some 2,500 years ago when, it has been rumoured, the Romans laid siege to Corioli. It was still being told when Günter Grass wrote *Die Plebeier proben den Aufstand*, attending to Brecht and the work-norm riots in East Berlin; and John Osborne's *A Place Calling Itself Rome* took it into Belfast and the war-cults of our own time. A full story of the myth would take in the Roman and Greek annals, the paintings of Poussin and Tiepolo, the operas by Frederick the Great and a dozen others, the music of Beethoven and Wagner, and the scores of plays and adaptations that make up its history in the theatre. It would engage the leading motives and values of the political past of Europe – war and survival, fame, honour and prosperity, the integrity of state and populace, the class prerogatives of power, and changing notions of warrior-virtue and the properties of government. And it would show that different cultures and national traditions have, over successive generations, used the story to clarify and dramatize vital truths about their own political

condition. The story of the myth might itself be made something of a myth
– attributing to the muddled, dark discontinuities of the past rather more
luminous order than can be found in unprocessed chronicled fact.

Each of Shakespeare's plays from Plutarch opens three perspectives of
significance – into antiquity, into Shakespeare's own time, and into our
own state of awareness. *Coriolanus*, for example, is about a critical episode
in the history of the Roman city-state and of Roman democracy. But it is
also about martial and political virtues as the court and the populace of
Shakespeare's London understood them. And now, in the course of
articulating and informing our responses to the play, we must take into
account the creating and uncreating proclivities of our own perceptions.
Moving in a larger Rome, but not in a larger space of consciousness, *Julius
Caesar* is about a crisis in the history of the Republic, and *Antony and
Cleopatra* about a critical passage in the history of the Roman Empire. But
it is still appropriate to remember that Essex, 'the General of our gracious
Empress' is in *Henry V* expected to return as a 'conquering Caesar' from
Ireland in 1599, to 'the Mayor and all his brethren' with 'the plebeians
swarming at their heels' (v. i. 23–34); or to recall Elizabethan or Jacobean
barges that rivalled Cleopatra's in their splendour. Both these plays too
have a continuing potency, and very varying significances, in the diverse
countries and cultures of the modern world.

Amyot's Preface to Plutarch's *Lives* contributes much to our recognition
of the value and excitement of old stories and old histories told afresh. We
are, he says, in the version familiar to Shakespeare:

> ravished with delight and wondering, to behold the state of
> mankind, and the true success of things, which antiquity hath and
> doth bring forth from the beginning of the world, as the setting
> up of empires, the overthrow of monarchies, the rising and falling
> of kingdoms, and all things else worthy of admiration, and the
> same lively set forth in the fair, rich, and true table of eloquence?
> And that so lively, as in the very reading of them we see our minds
> to be so touched by them, not as though the things were already
> done and past, but as though they were even then presently in
> doing, and we find ourselves carried away with gladness and grief
> through fear or hope, well near as though we were then at the
> doing of them.[2]

North has followed Amyot to the point where the reader of the story is
about to become the spectator of the re-created staged event. It is the point
that Shakespeare reached in the late 1580s when he began to turn Holinshed's

---

[2] Jacques Amyot, Preface to *Plutarch's Lives Englished by Sir Thomas North*, ed.
W. H. D. Rouse, 10 vols. (1898; reprinted 1908, 1910), I, p. 19.

narrative into the plays of *Henry VI*, and ten thousand spectators, according to Thomas Nash, could imagine they beheld Talbot 'fresh-bleeding'.[3] The dynamics of historical theatre are not essentially discursive or philosophic but affective and imaginative; 'we are carried away with the gladness and the grief, through fear and hope' of past events, 'well near as though we were then at the doing of them'.

Shakespeare's Roman plays are not merely history and myth, they are also theatrical experiences. 'Gladness and grief', 'fear and hope' are more urgently experienced and more sharply focused upon the theatre's 'table of eloquence', and they will not always answer to a rational account. While they are intensely and personally felt, the processes that shape them (often clarified in the theatre) are often obscure and impersonal – unconscious, cultural, biological – even when they find rational pretext and occasion. Thus there are truths about human consciousness and community, and about the relationship between them, which can be expressed in the languages of poetry and theatre, and can be fully expressed in no other way. The most interesting manifestations of the literary and theatrical imagination are not to be explained in terms that diminish their autonomy. Explanations derived from theories of economic history, for example, undervalue those complexities of response to money, property and power that theatre at its best anatomizes; and psychological explanations are apt to neglect those large and impersonal structures and processes of society that can be expressed in the design of a play.

It is convenient to remember that *Julius Caesar* is likely to have been the first play performed at the opening of the first Globe Theatre in 1599 and can therefore be said to mark a climactic point in the development of Shakespeare's art, in the history of theatre, and in the history of our consciousness of Rome. It offers insight into the Roman psyche and the Roman community, mediated through the renascent English language and its re-created structures, both verbal and material, of tragic theatre. The Globe was large enough to hold over 2,500 spectators, and small enough to keep them all within easy talking-distance of its front-centre stage. It created audiences for both private and public speech; it could eavesdrop on intimate conversation and self-communing soliloquy, or it could offer platform and audience for political exhortation. By directly engaging the responses of our isolated or communal selves, the Globe play can change the relationship between them.

Shakespeare in his plays from Plutarch is very conscious of that relationship; he explores it in the state and he exploits it in the theatre. In *Julius Caesar* Shakespeare opens pinhole perspectives into Plutarch's

---

[3] See ch. 4, 'The Frame of Disorder', p. 80.

narrative that are at once transient and revelatory. In the three-hour traffic of the Globe stage on this occasion, Cicero, our leading meditator on myth and history, is allowed but three minutes. The distance between his response to events and Casca's is first measured in the second scene: 'Did Cicero say anything? – Ay, he spoke Greek – To what effect? – Nay, and I tell you that, I'll ne'er look you i' th' face again. But those that understood him smiled at one another, and shook their heads; but, for mine own part, it was Greek to me.' Shakespeare has Casca relate the cataclysmic portents that Plutarch recalls from Strabo, but Cicero receives them with sceptical detachment: 'Why, saw you anything more wonderful?'

> Indeed, it is a strange-disposed time;
> But men may construe things after their fashion,
> Clean from the purpose of the things themselves
> (I. iii. 33–5)

He is a rational man, and concedes that 'this disturbed sky is not to walk in.' Cassius, on the other hand, under the same disturbed sky, works on Casca's vulnerable fantasy with more 'instruments of fear and warning / Unto some monstrous state' (I. iii. 70–1). Thus the play's Cicero diagnoses, and its Cassius manipulates, Casca's mythopoeic consciousness.

Throughout the play's first movement Shakespeare assimilates what North's margin calls the 'Predictions and Foreshews of Caesar's Death' into the 'ideot self', the private, phantasmagoric awareness of the conspirators. The catastrophic processes of the play are both publicly and intimately generated, the afflictions of the society have both a private and a communal pathology. 'Since Cassius first did whet me against Caesar, I have not slept'; Brutus's insomnia reached Shakespeare as a matter of historical report: 'care did wake him against his will when he would have slept.' Imaginative attentiveness to what North calls Brutus's 'deep thoughts' (Bullough, II, p. 98) helps to account for Shakespeare's quickening ability to move into obscure areas of human and verbal consciousness. The 'phantasma' or 'hideous dream' that troubles Brutus prefigures the tormented state-of-Scotland and state-of-mind that make *Macbeth*. The disarming truth that Shakespeare had no opportunity to read Freud should not prevent us from recognizing that Shakespeare's language has its own way of keeping in touch with what we now call the unconscious, while at the same time retaining its capacity to play upon the responses of a public audience. The Roman plays move across the territories of the community, the 'self', and of the mediating language. Without attending systematically to the doctrines, if I may so call them, of Lacan, I would like to take advantage of a few of his formulations that have a bearing on Shakespeare's treatment of myth and history. Listening to Brutus's soliloquies or to Macbeth's, we have often reason to reflect that 'the unconscious is structured like a language';

and keeping track of Brutus's exchanges with Cassius we can find our own reasons, if not Lacan's, for saying that 'the unconscious of the subject is the discourse of the other.'[4] Cassius' discourse is addresed to Brutus's unconscious; hence the obscure and private dispositions of the assassins assist in the determination of public events. They assist in creating an image, or a myth, of Caesar, and then they destroy it. 'What private griefs they have, alas, I know not, / That made them do it' (III. ii. 213–14) is Antony's calculatingly guileless reflection. The play invites us to look for motives that are not objectively political. Cassius' memories of Caesar, for example, have a personal as well as a public significance (I. ii. 90–131); and Brutus's ancestral consciousness (II. i. 46–58) is not transmitted through merely political channels. The conspirators are personal mediators of public consciousness, makers of myth and history: 'the eye sees not itself / But by reflection, by some other things.' While Cassius forges in Brutus's mind the Caesar 'that bestrides the narrow world' (I. ii. 135), the populace are clapping and hissing their festive hero as if he were a player in the theatre. Thus Caesar, the man of ordinary clay, grows prodigious in the acclaim of the tag-rag people and in the fears of the conspirators. Cassius both creates and uncreates the myth of Caesar, and it is apt enough that he should mythologize his personal relationship with Caesar by remembering Aeneas's rescue of Anchises – he finds a place for himself in the fabled history of Virgil's Rome (I. ii. 112–15). Shakespeare's theatre is revealing something of that process of screening which memories undergo both in the 'single and peculiar life' and in the memorializing history of the state.[5]

Despite the glance at Virgil, however, the characteristic mode of fiction that shapes the catastrophic movement of events in *Julius Caesar* is not epical but tragical. The king-slaying is, in a range of senses, acted out and staged. Caesar, in both Shakespeare's play and Plutarch's story, dies at the foot of Pompey's statue. Political history requires that the imperial spirit of Rome should erect such giant forms and that its republican spirit should pull them down. In personal and domestic perspective the imperial spirit looks like grotesque vanity and the republican one like emulous spite. From both political and intimate experience of the process of assassination, the history play is made for tragic theatre. The 'history' and the 'tragedy' are

---

[4] Jacques Lacan, Écrits: *A Selection*, tr. Alan Sheridan Tavistock Publications (1977), p. 55.

[5] I borrow the term 'screen memories' here and elsewhere from the psychoanalysts. Re-creative fictional distortions of memory occur both in the individual's history and in that of the state (which does not always write its annals true – *Coriolanus*, v. vi. 113). Renaissance theories of history as an analogue of memory respond usefully to this sophistication. See also Lacan, *Écrits*, p. 47.

not co-extensive, and we are made to see that a disposition to make tragedy is part of the history.

Shakespeare makes no use of Plutarch's report that Romans made Caesar dictator because they hoped that to be 'ruled by one man alone' would be 'a good means for them to take breath a little' after the civil wars. On the contrary, he allows no scope for the judicial weighing of possibilities, and expresses its suppression through the conspirators' treatment of Cicero. 'It shall be said his judgement ruled our hands', says Metellus, 'and all be buried in his gravity'. 'Oh name him not,' says Brutus, 'let us not break with him' (take him into our confidence). The Roman community is therefore given over to irrational sacrificial practices and satisfactions that Shakespeare, no doubt with the assistance of Seneca, had taught himself to recognize as 'Roman' in *Titus Andronicus*. Marcus Brutus sees himself as priest and Caesar as host ('Let us be sacrificers, but not butchers'); and Decius Brutus visits the mythopoeic dreaming consciousness of Caesar to persuade him that from him great Rome 'shall suck reviving blood'. That final convulsion of adulation sends Caesar forth in the confidence of his own divinity. Marcus Brutus sees himself as saviour and priest in the eye of Cassius; Caesar takes himself for saviour and martyr in the eye of Decius Brutus. Since Brutus's 'ideal itself' is generated from family tradition ('awake and see thyself') and since Caesar is aspiring to meet expectations that Pompey once satisfied, the convergence of their roles has a political as well as a private significance.

Caesar has a part to play in both Brutus's tragedy and Antony's; but the assassination which is the climax of Brutus's tragedy is only a turning-point in Antony's. Antony's in-touchness with the driving motives of Roman consciousness is more profound than Brutus's, in ways that the play makes us understand, both through the character and persona of Antony and, more obliquely, through internal structural analogues which will respond to formal theatrical and political analysis. Antony makes his crucial appearance at the centre of the play, and he might be said to reverse its flow. Peripeteia, actual, imminent, or potential, is in this play a recurring structural device. I have suggested in chapter 6 that we can usefully borrow a phrase or two, and a certain disposition of mind, from catastrophe theory in mathematics. In the human world as in the mathematically describable one, incremental changes can have more than incremental effects; little-by-little they can bring human consciousness and behaviour into crises from which there is no little-by-little recovery. One useful phrase is 'divergence effect', describing what happens when the tracks of one of Thom's seven equations, shifting in one or more of its variables, carries it towards a sudden change of configuration. *Julius Caesar* has many such instabilities and divergences, catastrophically poised before they are resolved.[6] All may

[6] See ch. 6, '*Julius Caesar* and the Catastrophes of History'.

be said (from the evidence at Shakespeare's disposal) to convey historical truths; and all may be said to satisfy the laws of theatre (and therefore of fiction, and therefore of myth).

It is Antony's oration over Caesar's body that offers the keenest divergence effect of the play. His authentic grief is transmuted by theatrical art into political manipulation, and the natural distress of the populace is perverted into communal savagery. Antony's mythopoeic skill finds starting-points in Plutarch as he takes, for example, 'Caesar's gown all bloody in his hand'; and it embellishes his rhetoric with touches of what might be called 'fictional fact' or screen memories – 'That day he overcame the Nervii', 'See what a rent the envious Casca made.' But by this moment the damage has already been done, inflicted by an incremental rhetorical device: the eight-times repeated and finally dispossessed word 'honourable'. The populace now become indeed the 'cruel men of Rome' Murellus saw in the first scene, will soon be lynching Cinna the poet. The 'dogs of war' Antony lets slip are visceral reactions to Caesar 'the bleeding piece of earth', sacrificed by Brutus in the fulfilment of his republican duty to his ideal self (his ego-ideal). Both Brutus and Antony bring about the catastrophes they affect to fear – each performs his tragic play. The deaths of Brutus and Cassius have a tragic significance in both the conspirators' play and in Antony's; but the battle of Philippi and emergence of the triumvirate reach us primarily as historical events in the continuing life of Rome.

It was a life, we may reflect, that in the history and in the theatre had to be carried on without Cicero. His judicious, Attic good sense – the sort that might in the play have come by the spirit of Caesar without the shedding of blood – is summarily disposed of: 'Mine speak of seventy senators that died / By their proscriptions, Cicero being one – Cicero one? – Cicero is dead.' The historian Atticus, we may notice in passing, had by this time returned to Greece, where he was able to offer asylum to some of the victims of Antony's imperial affections. Cicero died a victim to the tragic sense of life, about which he wrote so teasingly in the dialogue of *Brutus* and which Brutus himself so fully embodied. 'Which only goes to show,' if I may again subvert Lacan, 'that the offering to obscure gods of an object of sacrifice is something to which few subjects can resist succumbing, as if under some monstrous spell.'[7]

The Rome of *Coriolanus* is under a different spell, cast in a different Roman English. But this play too is highly conscious of the relationship between the processes of history and those of theatre, between annals and myths. Plutarch's story, to return to Cicero's phrase, gave Shakespeare

[7] Jacques Lacan, *The Four Fundamental Concepts of Psycho-Analysis*, tr. Alan Sheridan (1977), p. 275.

ample chance for 'rhetorical and tragic embellishment'. In a later passage of *Brutus* Cicero commends the rhetorical accomplishment of another Mark Antony – the orator who died in 87 BC as a victim of the Marian proscription. Cicero is finding Roman virtue in the close consonance of word and action:

> If we divide delivery into gesture and voice, Antonius's gesture did not seek to reflect words merely, but agreed with the course of his thought – hands, shoulders, chest, stamp of the foot, posture in repose and in movement, all harmonizing with his words and thoughts; voice sustained, but with a touch of huskiness. This defect, however, he had the skill to turn to advantage . . . You can see how all this bears out the saying attributed to Demosthenes who, when asked what was first in oratory replied 'action', what second, 'action', and again what third, 'action'. Nothing else so penetrates the mind, shapes, moulds, turns it, and causes the orator to seem such a man as he wills to seem. (*Brutus*, p. 142)

'Penetrat in animos, fingit format flectit, qualis ipsi se videre volunt': the Latin phrases might well evoke the language and gesture of Shakespeare's *Coriolanus* the play and the man. 'Fingit format flectit'; language (again I concur with Lacan) is not a sign,[8] and at its most fully active it does more than communicate; it makes. It informs and shapes a man as he wills to seem, and it penetrates 'in animos':

> you may as well
> Strike at the heavens with your staves as lift them
> Against the Roman state, whose course will on
> The way it takes, cracking ten thousand curbs
> Of more strong link asunder than can ever
> Appear in your impediment.
>
> (I. i. 67–72)

That is the state embodied in Caius Martius, rhetorically at the disposal of his surrogate father, Menenius. But three bodies-politic make the Roman scene: one with fat enough upon it to make the belly smile – *rhetor* and politic survivor; another erect, rigorous, invincible – the state warrior in the warrior state; and the third 'the beast with many heads', the 'voices', 'rubbing the poor itch of their opinion to make themselves scabs.'

The language and spectacle of the theatre create from the metaphor of the 'body-politic' a range of impacts and effects quite out of reach of the narrative sources and reflective analogues (in John of Salisbury, for example). Shakespeare's abilities as a poet are fully engaged in creating those responses to language that are most intimately related to the warrior cult of the body.

---

[8] Lacan, *Écrits*, p. 83.

We are at verbal risk if we call the playwright's art in this mode 'mythopoeic'; yet it is so if it is more fully realizing the potency of a fiction that has great significance for the state. As Cominius says of Martius when he leads the Volscians against Rome, 'He is their god; he leads them like a thing / Made by some other deity than Nature, / That shapes men better.' If we ask what desires are satisfied and what values articulated by Martius' heroic drives, the responses we get from the play are political, but not merely political; and they are Roman, but not merely Roman. In the history of the unified, heroic state, we recognize the dependence of the city upon Martius for its continuing life and identity. Were he not shaped better than other men, the battle for Corioles would have been lost (Cominius' temperate virtues could not have won it), and Rome would have undergone the subjugation and dissolution that the Volscians suffer at the end of Plutarch's story. In the history of the divided, multiple community, however, those same heroic drives are activating a malignant class war between (there are many ways of putting it) 'Rome and her rats', the eaters and the eaten, those who 'run reeking o'er the lives of men' and the 'quarter'd slaves'.

The play's more intimate structure offers analogous antinomies, the brutal street and battlefield confrontations transposed into a cultivated domestic retreat. Yet here, it may be claimed, is the genesis of the warrior myth-of-state: 'If my son were my husband,' says Volumnia at the scene's start, 'I should freelier rejoice in that absence wherein he won honour than in the embracements of his bed where he should show most love; and a few moments later she visibly and audibly rejoices as if her son were indeed her husband:

> Methinks I hear your husband's drum;
> See him pluck Aufidius down by th' hair,
> As children from a bear, the Volsces shunning him.
> Methinks I see him stamp thus, and call thus:
> 'Come on, you cowards, you were got in fear
> Though you were born in Rome!' His bloody brow
> With his mailed hand then wiping, forth he goes
> Like to a harvest-man that's task'd to mow
> Or all, or lose his hire.
>
> (I. iii. 29–37)

Volumnia's is the voice and language, as well as the 'honoured mould', that bred Martius and brought him into the world, better shaped than other men, to sustain a warrior-caste society that evidently (we learn in passing) treats its harvest-workers pretty rigorously. The war-delight is sexually informed, the language creating vicarious battle-excitements more satisfying than remembered 'embracements' of a dead husband's bed. But that war-delight, as Shakespeare had reason to know, has a more spacious history

than Volumnia's widowed state affords it. He glances back to Homer's
Troy, culls material from Elizabethan classical literature of Sparta, and
keeps a close watch on his Jacobean audience's readiness to make idols,
both in the theatre and in the streets, of men of blood, whether fact or
fiction, long dead or still alive. Plutarch's *Moralia* includes a story about a
Spartan mother proclaiming her sons finer pieces of work than the most
costly and curious piece of tapestry. Volumnia thus flaunts her son and her
grandson to Virgilia, silent at her embroidery. In the warrior-state the
husbands die in battle and sons displace them, and the widowed mother
must find her sexual joy, her *jouissance*, in her vicarious, language-shaped
ecstasy of battle ('penetrat in animos, fingit format flectit . . .'). Cominius'
great oration ('the deeds of Coriolanus / Should not be utter'd feebly') is
largely made from the words of North; but, coming upon it fresh from
Volumnia's cruel raptures ('The breasts of Hecuba / When she did suckle
Hector, look'd not lovelier / Than Hector's forehead when it spit forth
blood'), we pick up the subliminal sexuality and seem to know why Tullus's
rapt heart dances when he embraces the body that has so often splintered
his grained ash. It would be possible to evoke more significances from the
language and the latencies of our awareness, from the gates of Corioles
'bringing forth' their youth, to the 'lonely dragon in the fen' come to ravish
the daughters of Rome, and to the father wishing his son to 'stick i' th'
wars / Like a great sea-mark, standing every flaw and saving those that eye
him.' Those darknesses of the mind are more searchingly explored in
Macbeth where Murder 'with Tarquin's ravishing strides' moves like a
ghost; and more directly in *The Rape of Lucrece* where Tarquin extinguishes
the light before his 'proud flesh' metaphorically batters down the consecrated
walls of the city. (I break off, before exposing my own unconscious to
diagnostic inquisition.)

I have concentrated on some of the energies and structures of two plays,
with the intention of relating instabilities of the Roman state to persisting,
if not perennial, instabilities of human consciousness, the sort that might
still find life-transcending virtue in contempt for life, in the heroic service
of the community. I am tempted to say that the state-of-the-state is matter
of history, and the state-of-consciousness matter of myth. But the words
'myth' and 'history' never have stood still and never will – they will continue
to run up and down and in and out on a great diversity of errands. I'll
keep them at heel long enough, however, to let them say that Shakespeare
the playwright, poet and historian, simultaneously exploring and celebrating
states-of-mind and minds-of-states, makes historical myths of lasting
significance.

Yet let me deny myself that rhetorical coda and re-open the box I
pretended to close. The term 'historical myth' is often used about fictions
that are felt to be useful in the interpretation of history. *Coriolanus* is in

this sense too a historical myth. The historian J. B. Black, writing on *The Reign of Elizabeth* in 1936, tells us that the queen was 'little likely . . . to entrust the destiny of the state' to the Earl of Essex, 'a man whose genius shone on the battle-field, and not in the counsels of peace.' 'The earl,' he says, 'could not change his nature. He could not school his imperious mind to the give and take of politics, or share responsibility at the council table.' He could not move 'from the casque to the cushion'; Professor Black is writing Aufidius' history of England. Perhaps his responses had been tuned by Lytton Strachey, who in *Elizabeth and Essex* commends the General of the Horse at Zutphen for giving 'all men great hope of his noble forwardness in arms'; but commends the queen for succeeding 'by virtue of all the qualities which every hero should be without –dissimulation, flexibility, independence, procrastination, parsimony'. I am not re-issuing that old invitation to 'identify' Shakespeare's great warriors with Essex, but recognizing that *Coriolanus* brings to a climax that conflict of values which persisted through Shakespeare's lifetime in the court and city with which he was acquainted, between 'noble forwardness' and 'dissimulation'.

Both 'nobility' and 'dissimulation' change their meanings in *Antony and Cleopatra*, and rhetorical tactics must allow it a mere postscript on the ground that it is not only a Roman play but also an Egyptian one. It is also a different kind of 'myth'. In the course of resolving the historical and political tensions of the Roman Empire into a unified experience of the affections, Shakespeare calls upon the arts of rhetoric and on the myths of Isis, Dionysos, Venus and Mars. When Antony says, 'Unarm Eros, the long day's task is done, / And we must sleep', Shakespeare takes the chronicled name (Eros) into a pagan mystery of the Renaissance – Mars is again disarmed by Venus. When Cleopatra says, 'His legs bestrid the ocean', Shakespeare and she are making myth out of history; for what cannot be true of Antony's legs ('gentle madam, no') is true of Roman arms; love, like the empire, is required to span the Mediterranean.

8 Shakespeare's Language of the Unconscious: The Psychogenesis of Terrorism

Like the Weaver's dream this discourse has no bottom. What I have to say is about Shakespeare, and it could probably be said without the assistance of the concept of 'the unconscious'. Nevertheless I shall use it and I begin by taking my bearings from Freud, Jung and Lacan, not to approach them, but in order to keep my proper, respectful distance.

Shakespeare shared with Freud the insight that all events have an intimate as well as a public history. He shared with Jung an awareness of the impersonal imaginative inheritance that has come down to us from the more remote past. And he shared with Lacan a keen sensitivity to the hidden complexities and perplexities of language. These are the preoccupations that I shall keep in mind as I trace one strain of Shakespeare's interest in the more elusive processes of our thought and language – those that go to the making of the terrorist, from Clifford to Brutus and Macbeth.

It is probable that Shakespeare began by writing the plays of Henry VI, and it is in the second of the series that he first sharpens his awareness of those obscure processes of consciousness that go to the shaping of historical events. At the centre of this cataclysmic phase of England's past we know that he found in the chronicles a desolating but highly theatrical atrocity, when, at the Battle of Wakefield, the Duke of York endures a mock coronation and crucifixion, his face splashed derisively with the blood of his son, the Earl of Rutland, freshly slaughtered in the play by the Lancastrian, Lord Clifford. Shakespeare wrote up this scene while making

This is a modified version of a paper given to a seminar of the Royal Society of Medicine in April 1987 and published in the Society's *Journal*, 81 (April 1988), pp. 195–9).

Part 3 (i. iii), but there is evidence that he returned from it to re-write an episode in *Part 2*'s version of the Battle of St Albans. At the start of *Part 3* it is reported that Clifford's father 'was by the swords of common soldiers slain', but in *Part 2* as it has come down to us, he is killed by York, and his death is made occasion for an apocalyptic invocation of pity and terror – one of the imaginative climaxes of the Roses plays (*2 Henry VI*, v. ii. 31–65).[1] Shakespeare went back to trace one of the confluent sources of the event by probing Clifford's consciousness and clarifying his motives, and throughout the scene we watch the process by which impersonal, ideological violence is generated out of private grief

> Shame and confusion! all is on the rout,
> Fear frames disorder, and disorder wounds
> Where it should guard. O war thou son of Hell
> Whom angry heavens do make their minister,
> Throw in the frozen bosoms of our part
> Hot coals of vengeance!

'Disorder wounds where it should guard'; that comprehensive generalization aptly describes the failure of all chivalrous obligation in the heat of battle and it is not hard to recognize in it a version of Holinshed's report that in a later encounter in fog and snow at Ferrybridge the troops were killing their own side. Thus language, by way of transfigured experience, is conditioned to express a self-effacing, transcendent commitment to the values of war:

> Let no soldier fly.
> He that is truly dedicate to war
> Hath no self-love; nor he that loves himself
> Hath not essentially but by circumstance
> The name of valour.

At this point, says the editorial stage direction, Clifford 'sees his dead father':

> O, let the vile world end,
> And the premised flames of the last day
> Knit earth and heaven together!
> Now let the general trumpet blow his blast,
> Particularities and petty sounds
> To cease!

The 'premised flames of the last day' knitting heaven and earth together is an image from biblical tradition, but again, like the 'angry heavens', it is

---

[1] For treatment of the speech in a wider historical perspective see ch. 4.

caught up from reported conditions at Ferrybridge, while the 'general trumpet' is prefigured by the trumpets we have just been hearing on the theatre's battlefield. An access of tenderness gives a fresh focus to his destructive passion:

> Wast thou ordained, dear father,
> To lose thy youth in peace, and to achieve
> The silver livery of advised age,
> And in thy reverence, and thy chair-days, thus
> To die in ruffian battle? Even at this sight
> My heart is turn'd to stone; and while 'tis mine
> It shall be stony.

This is not merely war, it is dynastic war – the prevailing condition, in Clifford's awareness, not of the battlefield only, but of the whole frame of things. 'Essentially', it appears, and not 'by circumstance', the old Earl was 'ordained' to meet a violent end, and Clifford contrives to see his own 'flaming wrath' as a divine kindling of the 'premised flames of the last day'. Rutland, poor lad, didn't stand a chance (you can see him trying in *Part 3*, I. iii); but Shakespeare, I believe, understood why only when he had re-created this history of the consciousness of a committed terrorist.

'Consciousness', however, not 'the unconscious'. Clifford is very deliberately creating a cosmic perspective for his mutilated affections; the biblical resonance, together with the classical allusions to Medea's dismemberment of her brother Absyrtus, and to Aeneas carrying his father out of Troy are obviously owed to a Renaissance education very like Shakespeare's. But much of his language has been hammered out in the white heat of the poet's consciousness, in what the chorus of *Henry V* calls 'the quick forge and working house of thought'. Elsewhere in the play Shakespeare attends in a more conventional way to the ordeals of consciousness or, to use the Elizabethan word for it, 'conscience'.

In his dedicatory preface to *A Treatise of Melancholie*, published in 1586 (perhaps three years before the Henry VI plays were written), Timothy Bright makes a distinction which no doubt is still being made in different words:

> I haue layd open howe the bodie, and corporall things affect the
> soule, and how the body is affected of it againe: what the difference
> is between natural melancholie, and that heauy hand of God vpon
> the afflicted conscience, tormented with remorse of sinne, & feare
> of his iudgement.

Shakespeare's victim of the 'heavy hand of God' is Cardinal Beaufort. At his death (in Act III, sc. iii) he cannot recognize the King at his bedside and his mind returns phantasmagorically to the murder of Gloucester:

> He hath no eyes, the dust hath blinded them,
> Comb down his hair; look, look, it stands upright,
> Like lime-twigs set to catch my wingèd soul.

While working within a convention, Shakespeare is enriching it, as a comparison with Nathaniel Woods's *Conflict of Conscience* will show to those with leisure enough to consider curiously.[2]

It may be a comment on the workings of Shakespeare's own unconscious that some fifteen years later he assimilated certain elements of *2 Henry VI* into the play *Macbeth*: not only Clifford's dedicated violence and Beaufort's moral distress, but also the witches and the equivocations of fiends.

Looking for a link between afflicted consciousness and the fiends, furies and fates, in superstition, story and theatre, I find it in the destructive constraints that the past imposes on the present. When the Duchess of Gloucester in *2 Henry VI*, I. iv. consults the witch Margery Jordan and the false priests Hume and Southwell, she is looking for ways of satisfying frustrated political ambitions; but what she gets are oracular pronouncements about the fates awaiting certain delinquent barons. Following the chronicles, Shakespeare aligns the prophecies with the retributive processes of history. Thus it comes about that present freedoms are restricted both by processes within the mind and processes outside it; but both kinds are obscure and both affect us as covert, impersonal pressures – both appear to operate, through puns and equivocations, by way of the unconscious.

Macbeth is a more complex expression of this range of truths, but this is not essentially what it is. It is a tragedy and its truth is festive, not analytical. Like the old pagan festivals, but in a more complex society, it celebrates the mysteries of life and death. It remains 'pagan' because it has to do with that natural world in which 'good things of day begin to droop and drowse', but it is also about a specific monarchical state with sophisticated 'urban' characteristics, and about 'supernatural solicitings' bred from the imaginatively energized relationship between the two. Like the England of the Roses plays, Macbeth's Scotland is a warrior society in which power owes much to dynastic succession. We are reminded too that King James, who almost certainly saw the play, was directly descended from Banquo.

Lady Macbeth never meets the weird sisters, but Shakespeare uses her to establish early in the play the link between what reaches us as supernatural soliciting, and obsessive political ambition:

> Come you spirits
> That tend on mortal thoughts, unsex me here
> And fill me from the crown to the toe topful

---

[2] The play is reprinted in W. C. Hazlitt's edition of Dodsley's *Old Plays* (1874), vol. VI.

> Of direst cruelty! Make thick my blood,
> Stop up th' access and passage to remorse,
> That no compunctious visitings of nature
> Shake my fell purpose, nor keep peace between
> The effect and it.
>
> *(Macbeth*, I. v. 40–7)

Where, in the earlier play, Clifford's cruelty is precipitated by pity, here a span of consciousness, between the fell purpose and its effect, has to be erased if the deed is to be accomplished. Shakespeare had interested himself in this space a few years earlier where Brutus meditates on Caesar's murder:[3]

> Between the acting of a dreadful thing
> And the first motion, all the interim is
> Like a phantasma, or a hideous dream.
> The Genius and the mortal instruments
> Are then in council; and the state of a man,
> Like to a little kingdom, suffers then
> The nature of an insurrection.
>
> *(Julius Caesar*, II. i. 63–8)

The play is shaped by the charting of that 'interim', the phantasmic domain of consciousness that breeds its language. The first movement is the interim between the murder of Duncan (II. ii) and its first promptings, and the second to the slaughter of Banquo (III. iii). The third is proclaimed in Macbeth's words:

> The flighty purpose never is o'ertook
> Unless the deed go with it. From this moment,
> The very firstlings of my heart shall be
> The firstlings of my hand. And even now,
> To crown my thoughts with acts, be it thought and done:
> The castle of Macduff I will surprise,
> Seize upon Fife, give to th' edge o' th' sword
> His wife, his babes, and all unfortunate souls
> That trace him in his line.
>
> *(Macbeth*, IV. i. 145–53)

It does not escape attention that 'firstling' is 'first-born'. Some years ago Lionel Knights did much to challenge one tradition of criticism by making mock of Andrew Bradley's ingenuous question, 'How many children had Lady Macbeth?' But the time may have come to ask it again, perhaps at Freud's invitation, and to be content with the answer that there are none

---

[3] See above, p. 134.

living – a severe constraint under a dynastic dispensation.

The execution of the deed, the killing of the children, is accomplished in Act IV, ii. The gap is closed, but the condition in which he finds himself is expressed by his response to his wife's death:

> She should have died hereafter,
> There would have been a time for such a word.
> To-morrow, and to-morrow, and to-morrow,
> Creeps in this petty pace from day to day,
> To the last syllable of recorded time;
> And all our yesterdays have lighted fools
> The way to dusty death. Out, out, brief candle!
> Life's but a walking shadow, a poor player,
> That struts and frets his hour upon the stage,
> And then is heard no more. It is a tale
> Told by an idiot, full of sound and fury,
> Signifying nothing.
>
> *(Macbeth*, v. v. 17–28)

I have suggested elsewhere that Shakespeare is recollecting Brutus's reception of Portia's death after the assassination. But the *apathia* we are invited to wonder at in the earlier play is here stripped of its Stoic fur. The execution of the deed, the firstling of thought, prefigured by Lady Macbeth's readiness to offer her milk for gall and to pluck her nipple from the babe's boneless gums, has left time uniformly punctuated and therefore without significance.

In offering this account of the play's structure I am not wishing to set aside others. Much is rightly made, for example, of its Morality form; 'hell is murky', the fiends equivocate, and Macbeth's ordeal is a kind of moral distress. But Shakespeare, in this play more than any other, is interested in confluent pressures upon consciousness, obscure in their origins, but within the playwright's (as distinct from the character's) capacity to clarify.

At the start of Act I, sc. vii the direction prescribes 'dishes and service over the stage', and it is to Duncan's last supper that Macbeth speaks the celebrated soliloquy. 'If it were done, when 'tis done'.

We confront at the start the routine paradox that the language is at once Shakespeare's and Macbeth's. Macbeth is not a poet; the dramatized consciousness must be attributed to the character, the power to articulate it, to the poet. A few years ago the distinguished actor Bob Peck attempted to perform this speech as if it were addressed in an explanatory and soldierly manner, directly to the audience. The director, Howard Davies, treated the play as if it were a Brechtian exercise in social analysis. He denied the language its mystery, and therefore, I believe, cut off its access to our darker, more ambiguous, understanding. This is not a man speaking to men. It is pre-social speech, the words and thoughts still emerging, surfacing, from, to borrow Eliot's phrase, the mixing of memory and desire.

> If it were done, when 'tis done, then t' were well
> It were done quickly. If th' assassination
> Could trammel up the consequence, and catch
> With his surcease, success; that but this blow
> 5 Might be the be-all and the end-all – here,
> But here, upon this bank and [Schoole] of time,
> We'ld jump the life to come. But in these cases
> We still have judgement here, that we but teach
> Bloody instructions, which, being taught, return
> 10 To plague th' inventor. This even-handed justice
> Commends th' ingredience of our poison'd chalice
> To our own lips. He's here in double trust. . . .

The opening lines recall Jesus's words to Judas at another last supper ('What thou doest, do quickly'), anticipating the 'poison'd chalice' in line 11, the rancorous 'vessel of my peace' recalled at III. i. 66, and the cup of wine with which Banquo is toasted in III. iv. 87 for 'th' general joy of the whole assembly'; we receive the anticipations as Shakespeare's, the recollections as Macbeth's.[4] It is among those configurations in the play that relate it intimately to Christian metaphor and story, apparently reaching Macbeth obliquely and unidentified from the shadows of the mind. For if it were a consciously controlled allusion (like Clifford's to 'the last day') he could be expected to recognize it as a moral constraint upon his freedom. As it is, once identified, it is cheekily blasphemous, making Jesus tell him not to hang about but to get on with it – as if both betrayals were ordained. As a highly unstable moment of the play it relates to others. It is said of the 'merciless Macdonwald', for example, that 'the multiplying villainies of nature do swarm upon him' (I. ii. 9–12), meaning that he is by nature capable of any villainy; but the metaphor works in a contrary direction, exposing him to the torment of swarming insects. In a world, or at least in the fog and filthy air of a Scottish climate, where fair is foul and foul is fair, it is hard to distinguish the agent of evil from the victim; or, as in the present passage, the clarities of conscious resolution from a discomposing response to the promptings of the unconscious, an unconscious that has assimilated much from a personal past of interest to Freud and an impersonal inheritance that might concern Jung.

'The unconscious,' says Lacan, many times, and I, after him, almost as

---

[4] I have used this touchstone of Shakespeare's art elsewhere, and give a briefer account of the speech in the Foreword ('Shakespeare's Aeolian Mode') to *Mutative Metaphors in Psychotherapy: The Aeolian Mode*, by Murray Cox and Alice Theilgaard (1987).

many, 'is structured like a language.' The oracle alights revealingly on
'catch / With his surcease, success', a trenchant but unstable pun mixing
death, accomplishment (something over and done with), triumph and
succession. The words are tied to each other and surface simultaneously.

In line 6 the word in square brackets is given in the Folio reading, but
was treated by Theobald as a variant spelling of 'shoal', which stands in
most modern texts. Glancing back to 'bank', we take the impression of
shifting sands and insecurity, a hazardous base in space and time from
which to 'jump' or 'risk' the life to come. But when we look forward to
'teach / Bloody instructions', the 'Schoole' comes back to us and the 'bank'
begins to sound like a school bench. Even Peck's determination could not
turn the shift of thought into plain speech. The language betrays and reveals
more than it expresses. Such a paraphrase as 'We have to face retributive
judgement here, in this life; by using violence we teach others to use it
and they retort it on us', forfeits the ambiguities which are the vehicle for
the equivocating fiends. In one perspective, it might be said, the
equivocations are indeed the fiends. In the phantasmagoric movement of
the soliloquy, Macbeth slips from the poise of measure for bloody measure,
by way of the equitable scales of justice, to the passing of the cup at the
communal feast.

Lines 12–19, however, are lucid, fully articulated, and perfectly fitted
for social discourse, including Bob Peck's direct talk to the audience:

> He's here in double trust:
> First, as I am his kinsman and his subject,
> Strong both against the deed; then, as his host
> 15 Who should against his murtherer shut the door
> Not bear the knife myself. Besides, this Duncan
> Hath borne his faculties so meek, hath been
> So clear in his great office, that his virtues
> Will plead like angels . . . .

They can be heard, rather than overheard; but while they clarify the
offence, they serve also momentarily to illuminate one of the play's central,
dark paradoxes. The virtue that keeps Duncan clear in his great office is
not meekness; we know from the second and fourth scenes that he owes
his ascendancy and security to his 'good and hardy soldiers' and his 'valiant
captains'. They do not reach us, however, in this innocent language, but
again in the phantasmagoric recollections of the battlefield, the 'two spent
swimmers that do cling together / And choke their art' where 'the Norweyan
banners flout the sky / And fan our people cold'. As for Macbeth's virtue,
Shakespeare recalls, as he did in *Hamlet* (II. ii. 471–82). Pyrrhus's slaughter
and mutilation of Priam, described by Marlowe:

> Then from the navel to the throat at once
> He ripp'd old Priam; at whose latter gasp
> Jove's marble statue gan to bend the brow,
> As loathing Pyrrhus for this wicked act.
>   (*Dido Queen of Carthage*, II. i. 255–8)

In an age in which, to borrow words that Shakespeare in *Coriolanus* adapted from Plutarch, 'valour is the chiefest virtue and most dignifies the haver' Macbeth's virtue is de-stabilized, not only by the allusion (if that is what it is) but again by an incongruous and revealing metaphor:

> For brave Macbeth (well he deserves that name),
> Disdaining Fortune, with his brandish'd steel,
> Which smok'd with bloody execution,
> (like Valour's minion) carv'd out his passage
> Till he fac'd the slave;
> Which ne'er shook hands, nor bade farewell to him,
> Till he unseam'd him from the nave to the chops,
> And fix'd his head upon our battlements.
>   (*Macbeth*, I. ii. 16–23)

The odd courtesy of 'shook hands' and 'bade farewell' grotesquely intensifies the outrageous and unchivalrous inhumanity of the swordsman's virtuosity and virtue. The impaling of heads (like the plucking out of eyes) was, from earliest times to the Restoration, a routine way of proclaiming the triumph of virtue.

The radical sense of 'virtue' – 'manliness', readily related to sexual potency – is covertly and sometimes openly enlisted in both *Macbeth* and *Coriolanus*, most significantly by the women:

> Art thou afeard
> To be the same in thine own act and valour
> As thou art in desire?
>   (*Macbeth*, I. vii. 39–41)

To which Macbeth responds, 'I dare do all that may become a man; / Who dares do more is none.' 'Why did you wish me milder?' Coriolanus asks of Volumnia, 'Would you have me / False to my nature? Rather say, I play / The man I am.' (*Coriolanus*, III. ii. 14–16). The self-destructive momentum of warrior virtue touches climactic moments in both plays, and we reach one in the last movement of Macbeth's soliloquy.

Lines 19–25 are responding again to obscure memories and pressures. The heaven's cherubin are the horsemen of the Apocalypse; but the naked new-born babe has a more intimate genesis, and leaves editors wondering whether the plural or (as elsewhere in Shakespeare) the singular is intended by 'cherubin':

> trumpet-tongu'd, against
> The deep damnation of his taking-off;
> And pity, like a naked new-born babe,
> Striding the blast, or heaven's cherubin, hors'd
> Upon the sightless couriers of the air,
> Shall blow the horrid deed in every eye,
> That tears shall drown the wind.

The babe is recalled to our imaginations a few minutes later in the 'boneless gums' plucked from Lady Macbeth's breast, and will return in the 'Second Apparition, *a bloody child*', prefiguring Macduff in Act IV, sc. i. In the soliloquy it relates to the vulnerability of the King, but it primarily expresses the potency of innocence. 'Sightless' does not mean 'blind', as Blake in his marvellous water-colour supposed, but 'invisible'. Both pity and the wind bring tears to the eyes, and the metaphor transforms both into a purgative, violent force. 'Like a naked new-born babe / Striding the blast' – a highly improbable conjunction of words, when we reflect upon it, wholly inappropriate to ordinary talk, in spite of the disarming 'like'. But it offers the right bridge to the image that every pestered schoolboy knows and every actor in my experience mispronounces. For what we usually hear in the theatre is:

> I have no spur
> To prick the sides of my intent, but only
> Vaulting *ambition*, which o'erleaps itself,
> And falls on th' other.
>
> (I. vii. 25–8)

What we ought to hear is '*vaulting* ambition'. Macbeth speaks as a horseman, responding to the baby striding the blast, and says he has no means to spur himself on. He hasn't that kind of ambition, but only the vaulting sort. We may remember, as Shakespeare may have done, Vernon's report of Prince Hal at Shrewsbury:

> I saw young Harry with his beaver on,
> His cushes on his thighs, gallantly arm'd,
> Rise from the ground like feathered Mercury,
> And vaulted with such ease into his seat
> As if an angel dropp'd down from the clouds
> To turn and wind a fiery Pegasus.
>
> (*1 Henry IV*, IV. i. 104–9)

Hal in Vernon's romantically chivalrous perception is not contending with the angels, but emulating them. Macbeth finds himself exposed to an image of virtue divided against itself; as a practised horseman, moreover, he knows that the hazard of vaulting ambition is going over the top and crashing down on the other side.

Like Clifford's invocation, but more subtly and variously, Macbeth's soliloquy exposes the hidden processes of the criminal consciousness of an heroic leader and now childless father in a warring dynastic monarchy. A state of the psyche, we might say, in a warrior state – Brutus's 'state of a man' and Macbeth's 'single state of man'.

I have focused on language, within a dramatic structure related to the articulated experience of the 'character' Macbeth. I remembered only for a moment that *Macbeth* is a festive play; it is related to communal seasonal rites that celebrate the natural processes of growth and maturity violated by, and denied to, Macbeth, and related also to Hallowe'en, when Christendom is most attentive to 'the one half world' where 'nature seems dead' and 'Witchcraft celebrates Pale Hecat's off'rings.' Reflections on those relationships, however, would require a different understanding of the operations of 'the unconscious' in art, to be set in an anthropological perspective, and in the history of theatre from the *Ajax* to *The Spanish Tragedy*.

I set out to show that Shakespeare recognized that public events have covert personal histories, that an impersonal imaginative inheritance from a remoter past contributes to our comprehension and apprehension of experience, and that the equivocations, the slips and slides of language are instrumental in the creation and betrayal of the values by which we live. There are other modes of terror in Shakespeare's plays (in *Richard III*, for example, *Troilus and Cressida* and *King Lear*) and other territories of operation for the covert processes of consciousness – love, money and war.[5]

Some poets (Blake and Keats, for example) resemble Shakespeare in delighting in the duplicity of words, while others (in the line from Ben Jonson) would have words do as they are told, one thing at a time. I have referred to Steven Booth's distinguished edition of the Sonnets as Finnegans Sonnets, trying to recognize that Joyce and Freud have changed our way of hearing and reading Shakespeare's language and perhaps put the poems more satisfyingly in touch with our genital and phallic dispositions. But what the poet left out of sight now surfaces for all to see.[6]

When the Bastard in *King John* watches Hubert take up the body of the dead Arthur he charts the catastrophes to come:

[5] See above, p. 59 and below, p. 228.
[6] "The Semiotics of Shakespeare's Sonnets', *TLS*, 23 June 1978, pp. 606–7.

> Go bear him in thine arms.
> I am amaz'd, methinks, and lose my way
> Among the thorns and dangers of this world
> How easy dost thou take all England up
> From forth this morsel of dead royalty!
> The life, the right, and truth of all this realm
> Is fled to heaven . . .
> Now powers from home and discontents at home
> Meet in one line; and vast confusion waits
> As doth a raven on a sick-fall'n, beast,
> The imminent decay of wrested pomp.
>   (*King John*, iv. iii. 139–45, 151–5)

His responses are finely and ambiguously balanced, but where Clifford had cried, 'In cruelty I'll seek out my fame', Falconbridge does what he can to salvage the integrity of the kingdom that the young prince will inherit from the old king. I would hope that a fuller recognition of the perverse verbal and affective processes – private and political – through which terror is derived from pity and 'virtue' might assist in finding a way through the thorns and dangers of what is still the Bastard's world.

Part III

Tragic Sacrifice

9 Hamlet the Bonesetter

'The time is out of joint. O cursed spite / That ever I was born to set it right!' It is Hamlet's *moira*, his pitiless lot, that he is cast as bonesetter to the time, and he does not look upon it as a privileged role. The play *Hamlet* is, in one dimension of Aristotle's thought, a goat-song, and in what follows I shall be importunately concerned with the lines of continuity between the tragic play and its primordial spectre, the sacrificial ritual.[1] An interest in Shakespeare cannot in itself be expected to shed light on perplexities that have for so long engaged and divided classical scholars and anthropologists, but when some of Shakespeare's plays are viewed with such perplexities in mind, certain features of their structure and process become, I believe, distinctly visible. In attempting such a perspective there is no necessity to begin with *Hamlet*. *Titus Andronicus*, for example, in its anthropological as distinct from its historical setting, looks back to rituals of human sacrifice and exemplifies a primitive logic and elemental feeling carried unexpectedly in the vehicle of a decorated and sophisticated art. But the continuities that persist in Shakespeare's maturity are both more obscure and more profound, and to trace them I take my point of departure from a celebrated passage in Gilbert Murray's *Five Stages of Greek Religion*.[2]

> At the great spring Drômenon the tribe and the growing earth were renovated together: the earth arises afresh from her dead seeds, the tribe from its dead ancestors; and the whole process, charged as it is with the emotion of pressing human desire, projects its anthropomorphic god or daemon. A vegetation spirit we call him, very inadequately; he is a divine Kouros, a Year-Daemon, a spirit

[1] I am indebted to the indirect encouragement offered to pursue this theme by Walter Burkert, 'Greek Tragedy and Sacrificial Ritual', *Greek, Roman and Byzantine Studies* (1966), pp. 83–121.

[2] I quote from the 1935 version of the second edition.

that in the first stage is living, then dies with each year, then thirdly rises again from the dead, raising the whole dead world with him – the Greeks call him in this phase 'the Third One', or the 'Saviour'. The renovation ceremonies were accompanied by a casting off of the old year, the old garments, and everything that is polluted by the infection of death. And not only of death; but clearly I think, in spite of the protests of some Hellenists, of guilt or sin also. For the life of the Year-Daemon, as it seems to be reflected in Tragedy, is generally a story of Pride and Punishment. Each Year arrives, waxes great, commits the sin of Hubris, and then is slain. The death is deserved; but the slaying is a sin: hence comes the next Year as Avenger, or as the Wronged One re-risen. 'All things pay retribution for their injustice one to another according to the ordinance of time.' It is this range of ideas, half suppressed during the classical period, but evidently still current among the ruder and less Hellenized peoples, which supplied St Paul with some of his most famous and deep-reaching metaphors. 'Thou fool, that which thou sowest is not quickened except it die.' 'As he was raised from the dead we may walk with Him in newness of life.' And this renovation must be preceded by a casting out and killing of the old polluted life – 'the old man in us must first be crucified.'

There may be much here that pedantry, or indeed scholarship, would seek to set aside as speculative, but a little reflection upon the literary evidence will convince us that the modes of thought that Murray attributes to ancient ritual are still at work in the tragic, religious and political experience of much later phases in the history of civilization, including our own. The closing sentences of the passage, for example, could remind us that the two parts of *Henry IV* teach us what it means to whip the offending Adam both out of the realm and out of our frail natures. *Henry IV* confesses its debt to the Morality Play, *Titus Andronicus* betrays one to Ovid and to Seneca, and we may recognize in Shakespeare a convergence of traditions analogous to that which Gilbert Murray observes in St Paul. Because St Paul had assimilated the insights of Greek tragedy into an experience of the significance of Christ (the point could be put the other way round), it becomes possible for us to claim that *Hamlet* is not only a Renaissance tragedy but also a sacrificial tragedy in a tradition older than Christendom, reaching back to Aeschylus and even, perhaps, to the Drômenon. It is, as others have observed, in certain crucial respects like the *Oedipus Rex* of Sophocles,[3] either because Shakespeare knew a version or because he took from Seneca

---

[3] See, e.g., Francis Fergusson, *The Idea of a Theater* (1949).

and his English imitators certain imaginative understandings that had also reached him by another route – through the metaphors, teachings and theatre of Christianity.

In both Sophocles' play and Shakespeare's, the survival of the state is threatened by a specific disaster – plague or invasion – which has its source in some more obscure evil which has to be brought to light and eradicated. In the opening lines of *Hamlet* men on guard are a very precise expression of an urgent threat to the state, and offer just the right opportunity for the voicing of misgivings both vague and specific about the nature and direction of a threat which is in the largest sense political – touching the very survival of the *polis*. Coleridge has gone before to admire the detail: the self-control of the guardsmen imposed by a routine ceremony; the disquieting attentiveness to the exact time; the mouse; the impress of shipwrights; the irony of 'long live the king'; the ominous resonance of 'sick at heart'. Horatio's vision dominates – Renaissance sceptic but skilled in medieval ways of thought, comparing Claudius's Denmark with Caesar's Rome, alive to the supernatural signs that prefigure political disaster, knowledgeable about ghosts. A blight is already upon the state of Denmark whose court we meet in the second scene. Turning an ingenuous eye for resemblances upon the *Oedipus Rex*, we may recognize a comparable prelude. This is the priest speaking, in Yeats's translation: 'We all stand here because the city stumbles towards death, hardly able to raise up its head. A blight has fallen upon the fruitful blossoms of the land, a blight upon flock and field and upon the bed of marriage – plague ravages the city.' 'Flock and field' have little place in *Hamlet* (although we may remember the 'mildew'd ear / Blasting his wholesome brother'), but the analogue is clear, and it happens in both plays that the roots of infection are revealed by a sudden dramatic discovery or *anagnorisis*. The messenger in the *Oedipus*, and the ghost in *Hamlet*, reveal murder and incest at the head of state.

In the elemental logic of the *Oedipus* it follows that if the state is to survive and renew its failing life, the king must be deposed. We may find the argument metaphoric rather than literal, for it would be surprising (I imagine, even to enlightened ancients) if plague virus responded so directly to a change in government. But the metaphor is powerful (particularly in the theatre) and it seems to express a valid claim about the ultimate connection between public and private events. In *Hamlet*, 'The cease of majesty / Dies not alone, but like a gulf doth draw / What's near it with it.' The invasion threat from Fortinbras's 'lawless resolutes' is not directly a consequence of the new king's guilt, but since the death of the elder Hamlet the state has appropriately been supposed 'disjoint and out of frame'. A resemblance to the *Oedipus*, however, must not be allowed to mask conspicuous differences. Oedipus is his own scourge and minister; he bears the guilt and undertakes to purge it, but where the sacrificial role in

Sophocles' play is single, in Shakespeare's it is double. From one point of view it is indeed the death of Claudius that restores the equilibrium of the Danish state and (we might add) of the English audience; from another, it is the death of Hamlet, for at his fall a role appears to have been perfected, an end to have been fully shaped. The killing of Claudius is not merely, however, a personal judgement upon the murderer and hypocrite, it is the destruction of the whole moral and political world which he represents and over which he presides – the Denmark of Gertrude, Polonius, Laertes, Rosencrantz and Guildenstern, and even Ophelia – and of all the things their words, and our response to them, endorse. Hamlet takes into his consciousness the sins of the realm for which Claudius is responsible. We are made intimately aware of the processes of Hamlet's consciousness, or 'conscience', to use the play's word at a moment in its history when it was particularly ambiguous. It is this intimate transmission of inner consciousness and awareness that calls for the full exercise of Shakespeare's mastery of the conventions of soliloquy, through which so much of Hamlet's presence in the play is expressed. The second scene, which opens with the assured public voice of Claudius, ends with the private, seemingly obsessed, inward-looking utterances of Hamlet. Thus the two great figures of the play are not only made the 'mighty opposites' of the tragic narrative, they reach us through contrasting theatre-conventions, made to engage the attention of the audience in radically different ways. From this point of view the play turns itself about. The first court scene shows us Claudius as a great image of authority, enthroned against the façade, and finishes with Hamlet front-stage, speaking words we are allowed less to hear than to overhear, filling the theatre with the chaos of his mind, already the 'distracted globe'. At the start, to make the same point more archaically, there is apparent order in the macrocosm and disorder in the microcosm. But at the play's end, the most memorable passages suggest quiescence and calm within the mind of Hamlet while the spectacle presents total confusion in the court of Claudius. In the meantime we watch Claudius grow active in self-inquisition; his masks slip and his language, as he begins to soliloquize, grows more like Hamlet's:

> My stronger guilt defeats my sharp intent,
> And, like a man to double business bound,
> I stand in pause where I shall first begin,
> And both neglect.

(III. iii. 40–3)

Under pressure from Hamlet the contrast steepens between what the king seems to be in public and what he reveals himself to be in private, and he becomes, however inadequately, a scourge and minister to his own condition. But for most of the play Claudius is a representative figure, not only because he is the head of state, a crucial fact in an apparently vigorous monarchy, but also because he exemplifies the characteristic moral affliction of Denmark, the hypocrisy which makes moral realities inaccessible.

Hamlet is representative in quite another way, one which invites another comparison with the *Oedipus Rex*. When Sophocles' Oedipus approaches the tragic discovery of his own guilt he has a choice between stopping short, and letting the matter drop without further questioning, or persisting until he masters the full horror of the moral catastrophe. Jocasta, the Shepherd and even Tiresias advise him to take the tactful, politic course and to drop the whole inquiry; but Oedipus owes his tragic stature precisely to his decision to tear off all the veils, to expose the total, desolating predicament, and to take on himself the full consequences both in action and suffering. Jocasta's suicide denies her a tragic death, but Oedipus tears out his eyes and lives on until he is morally fit to die. In *Hamlet* it is the king who tries to cover and the prince to discover the full measure of the realm's distress. Claudius is most guilty, we may say naîvely, but Hamlet has the keenest sense of guilt. Hamlet exposes his sensibilities to the moral afflictions of the realm, through the mediation of the ghost (unseen by the guilty), through his experience of the events of the play, and through his exercises in introspection. He takes in, not his mother's guilt and his uncle's only, but the pervasive evils of the community:

> The pangs of despis'd love, the law's delay,
> The insolence of office, and the spurns
> That patient merit of th' unworthy takes.
>
> (III. i. 72–4)

'But to the quick of th' ulcer,' says Claudius to Laertes, 'Hamlet comes back.' He intends only to 'get to the point', but the play's language works upon our consciousness to remind us that Hamlet returns to probe the inward corruption of the outward condition that Claudius struggles to sustain. For Hamlet, surgeon and bonesetter, not king and queen alone but Polonius and Laertes, Ophelia and himself too, are awry: 'What should such fellows as I do crawling between earth and heaven? We are arrant knaves all; believe none of us. Go thy ways to a nunnery.' If Hamlet's wit here as elsewhere seems malicious, it is because it inflicts pain; but that pain is of the moral kind – consciousness of guilt – and that consciousness, by any religious account in the Western tradition and by many ethical wisdoms, has both a destructive and a redemptive energy. In the *Pilgrim's Progress* it is Christian's prerogative to carry his great burden, for many less morally aware figures (including Worldy Wiseman) are without it; but it is also his privilege to shed the burden, since no felicity can be won with it.

In calling the word 'moral' so often into service I do not wish to overlook certain elementary complexities. 'The death is deserved,' says Gilbert Murray of the Year-Daemon, 'but the slaying is a sin', and we know the paradox to be fundamental in many plays from the *Agamemnon* to the *Revenger's Tragedy*. In *Hamlet* its application to Claudius and the prince is clear enough, but Shakespeare adroitly allows it also a kind of retrospective force. It is only in Hamlet's vision that his father is unequivocally 'so excellent a king'; by the Ghost's account he is 'confin'd to fast in fires, / Till the foul crimes done in my days of nature / Are burnt and purg'd away.' He recedes into the dawn sky as the glow-worm pales his rival 'uneffectual fires', to submit to a process of spiritual purification which transcends and encompasses the infected bed, body and 'ear' of Denmark. In this perspective Claudius looks like the agent as well as the victim of a continuing and universal sacrificial process. In the *Oedipus Rex* the king is guilty but (I would try to insist) blameless; in *Hamlet* the king is culpable but so, in the operation of the play's language, are we all. With this qualification we may observe of *Hamlet* that the moral imperatives of the plot do not push it towards an act of murderous revenge in obedience to the Ghost and all he stands for, but towards the discovery and assimilation of a communal guilt, in obedience to that higher tragic law which Shakespeare has mastered in the course of shaping the play. Incitement to guilt – that is the motive of the nunnery-scene, the play-scene and the bedroom-scene; and when guilt is everywhere manifest, dis-covered, Hamlet quietens and sheds his more febrile resolution, 'the readiness is all.' He goes into the last scene prepared to die; not prepared to murder. The Ghost, who voices the old revenge law, even while undergoing his purification by fire, fades from the play after failing to 'whet' Hamlet's 'almost blunted purpose', and when the killing of Claudius and the death of Hamlet come at last, they come by accident.

But is it accident? In ancient tragedy, and possibly too in more ancient ritual, there is some recognition or claim that the ultimate moral laws are transcendent and cannot be subdued by the human will. Gilbert Murray locates the mystery in those metaphors of dying-into-life which can be related to the diurnal and seasonal rhythms, and to human mortality. Horatio at the end of the play speaks of 'accidental' events, but his words will bear more than one construction:

> So shall you hear
> Of carnal, bloody and unnatural acts;
> Of accidental judgements, casual slaughters;
> Of deaths put on by cunning and forc'd cause;
> And, in this upshot, purposes mistook
> Fall'n on th' inventors' heads.
>
> (v. ii. 380–5)

'Accidental judgements' may mean 'fortuitous miscalculations' – a lot of things going wrong by chance; or it can mean 'contingent punishments', as if some ineluctable process worked through accidental circumstance towards a fuller realization of justice in the human world. In some moods we might call such a process 'history'; the play speaks of 'a divinity that shapes our ends'. Much happens in the play by significant accident. When Hamlet tries to kill the king, for instance, his sword finds Polonius. Behind the accident and the arras it is possible to glimpse a moral order and even to claim moral cause and effect: Polonius the eavesdropper has been betrayed into hysteria as he witnesses Hamlet's inquisition of his mother. But if Polonius deserves to die, his deserts are not to be found in the Ghost's ethic and command, but only in the larger perspectives in which the Ghost himself is tormented; we *all* deserve to die, as we all deserve whipping.

The tragic effects of both *Hamlet* and the *Oedipus Rex* may be set down, therefore, to a sacrificial law, working through 'accidents' as well as through human choice and disposition, towards the discovery and purgation of guilt. It may be that it needs no ghost come from the grave to tell us that. Gilbert Murray himself, indeed, has been this way before, and among his many heirs and critics I am particularly indebted to Francis Fergusson.[4] But it remains true, I believe, that many of the alleged problems of the play, which persist at least in academic and pedagogic discourse, are much diminished when we attend to them with this tragic structural principle in mind.

Among the first mechanical or technical questions that arise about *Hamlet* is, why is it so long? And the first answer would seem to have little to do with the claims pursued so far: 'Because it is built on a structure of analogues; not on a narrative.' Of these, the most important is that between the world and the stage. If we ask why Shakespeare takes up so much time with the players and their play, we have immediately to acknowledge that their narrative purpose could have been served in, say, a quarter of the lines allowed. The narrative requires that Hamlet should use the mousetrap to catch the conscience of the king, but the structure requires that Shakespeare should use it to explore Hamlet's situation and make the audience more alive to its moral and histrionic complexity. Such is the motive for the scene attending to Hamlet's advice to the players, to their rehearsal, and to the attendant soliloquy. All make us more alert for reflections cast in that mirror held up to nature, the 'abstract and brief chronicle', the Gonzago play. It is often overlooked and underrated, taken to be Shakespeare's sport at the expense of its predecessors. In fact, its bleak, keen, arid rhymes bear the burden of the whole. Whatever defects

[4] *Idea of a Theater*, pp. 124–5.

are attributed to the art of the players' (and Hamlet's) play, Shakespeare's own art, as Fergusson has shown us, is in command. Thus when the Player King speaks of the dislocation between human purpose and accomplishment:

> Our wills and fates do so contrary run
> That our devices still are overthrown,
> Our thoughts are ours, their ends none of our own
> (III. ii. 211–13)

we can find analogues through the play. Thus Laertes to Ophelia:

> but you must fear
> His greatness weighed, his will is not his own.
> (I. iii. 16–17)

And Hamlet's words to Laertes:

> Was't Hamlet wronged Laertes? Never Hamlet.
> . . . Hamlet denies it.
> Who does it then? His madness.
> (V. ii. 233, 236–7)

Or again, Claudius's:

> My stronger guilt defeats my sharp intent.
> (III. iii. 40)

But most important, the Player King's conclusion is re-echoed by Horatio at the close of the play, from the 'overthrown devices' to 'purposes mistook.'

Similarly, the Player King is nervous about the transcience of human purpose:

> What to ourselves in passion we propose,
> The passion ending, doth the purpose lose.
> (III. ii. 194–5)

It is a spent version of Claudius's still live admonition to Laertes:

> That we would do,
> We should do when we would; for this 'would' changes
> And hath abatements and delays as many
> As there are tongues, are hands, are accidents.
> (IV. vii. 118–21)

Again, the Player King speaks in Hamlet's voice when he finds that:

> Purpose is but the slave to memory
> Of violent birth but poor validity.
> (III. ii. 188–9)

And from the same speech:

The violence of either grief or joy
Their own enactures with themselves destroy,
(III. ii. 196–7)

is an oblique comment on Hamlet, Laertes, Claudius and Ophelia. The Player King, then, reminds us that *Hamlet* is a play about failing human wills and passions, about the need to sustain purpose in face of fading memory and frail resolution; but also, and ironically, about the futility of purposeful action in a society insufficiently aware of the nature and extent of its plight. There are no short cuts. 'Readiness', to use Hamlet's word, comes only when, to linger on the common phrase, 'the time is ripe'; thus, once again, the Player King:

Which now, the fruit unripe, sticks on the tree
But fall unshaken when they mellow be.
(III. ii. 190–1)

Nothing in the play goes according to plan, but everything happens by significant accident and when the time is ripe, when the society and the individual, the *polis* and the *ideotes* (to put it more obscurely), are aware and 'ready'.

The play, in ways that I do not pretend to have exhausted, imitates the situation in the Danish court; but then the situation is reversed, and the prince begins to mimic the play. The Player King speaks, as Fergusson aptly says, with the clarity and helplessness of the dead; but Lucianus, the king-slayer, momentarily animates, and his reflections upon a deed of darkness, 'Thoughts black, hands apt, drugs fit, and time agreeing; / Confederate season, else no creature seeing', are transposed into Hamlet's soliloquy a few minutes later, ''Tis now the very witching time of night' and 'Now could I drink hot blood.' Shakespeare contrives that the Ghost, the Gonzago play and the traditions of English Seneca should chime together, all converging on the same idea of moral justice, of dramatic decorum and of behavioural imperative. Thus Hamlet assumes the role of Senecal avenger (English style) and in it he encounters Claudius at prayer and in the same role he spares him. There is no occasion to question Hamlet's sincerity. To obey the Ghost's command Hamlet must by an immense histrionic effort transform himself into a Lucianus, and thus transformed he cannot bring himself to kill his victim at his prayers. The episode becomes yet another in the pattern of self-frustrated purposes, overthrown devices.

It is necessary critical commonplace about the play that from the moment Hamlet cries, 'These are actions that a man might play', to his, 'Ere I could make a prologue to my brains they had begun the play', we are kept sharply aware of the equivocal compulsion to 'act', meaning both to do something, somehow, to some effect, and to act a part, fulfil a role. Shakespeare's amplitude has this occasion, therefore, that within the larger dramatic rite he mounts a smaller, to an analogous end. But it has other occasions too, some of which can be subsumed by asking again the question that academic courtesy should perhaps never again allow – why does Hamlet delay? Alfred Harbage once reduced two hundred and fifty years of answers to a basic twelve,[5] but I must offer a stingier abstract. Some have argued a psychological defect in Hamlet's character; he is squeamish, or sick with melancholy, or immature, or cowardly, or stricken by an Oedipus complex; all assuming that neither Shakespeare nor the spectator need to challenge the moral authority of the Ghost whom Hamlet would have obeyed if only he had had it in him. A second group find not a psychological but a moral flaw in Hamlet; he resents the call of duty, or is too philosophical to act. A third kind of answer blames the Ghost, finding Hamlet nauseated by the primitive compulsions of a brutal injunction, too sensitive to do as he is told. A fourth set finds neither Hamlet nor the Ghost culpable but points to the obstructions that need to be objectively negotiated before Hamlet can get on with his job – he must test the Ghost's truth, sort out the succession problem or win the populace to his side. The solutions thus curtly surveyed (leaving much patient and sensitive work unacknowledged) appeal to the character and speeches of Hamlet himself. Of solutions appealing to the design of the play the most celebrated is the briskest – 'No delay; no play'. But a meaningless delay, we may reflect in the Philistine temper that Stoll's aphorism induces, is not only bad art but also bad box-office. We must persist with the question in another form, recognizing that Hamlet is not a man but an artefact. Why does Shakespeare make Hamlet delay and, to begin with, what explanations for delay does he make explicit in the speeches he gives to Hamlet himself? These come readily to mind – the Ghost must be tested through the mousetrap and Claudius must not be killed while he is praying, while in soliloquy Hamlet muses on 'Bestial oblivion or some craven scruple / Of thinking too precisely on th' event'. From this excursion it would appear that Shakespeare designed the delay to appear as a problem to Hamlet's own bewildered consciousness, and also that the time taken up with this problem is quite short.

'Time taken up' – it is Shakespeare who delays in this sense, not Hamlet. It is he who gives sustained attention to those episodes and speeches not directly connected with the Ghost's command. For Shakespeare takes only a limited interest in Hamlet as an avenger. His deeper interest is in Hamlet the tragic-hero, required to take upon himself the moral distress of the whole community. The delay in *Hamlet* is not of the stock kind associated

---

[5] *As They Liked It* (1947), pp. 1, 6.

with the revenge tradition in which Kyd and Marston were active. Shakespeare makes Hamlet delay to say, 'O what a rogue and peasant slave am I', or 'Or my imaginations are as foul as Vulcan's smithy', or 'What is this quintessence of dust?' or 'As if increase of appetite had grown by what it fed on' or 'I am very proud, revengeful, ambitious.' He delays to voice his sense of guilt and to make personal the evils and vulnerabilities of the society about him. The process is at work both in the detail of the play's language and in the disposition of its episodes. Thus Hamlet addressing Horatio glances at the sycophancy of the court:

> Why should the poor be flatter'd?
> No, let the candied tongue lick absurd pomp,
> And crook the pregnant hinges of the knee
> Where thrift may follow fawning.
>
> (III. ii. 59–62)

It is an almost subliminal dialect, and to be effective it must find us very quick to perceive the connection between the proclivities of courtiers and the proclivities of dogs – for the dogs breathe in the lines, unnamed. The play's many digressive episodes owe their unity to a related principle, for all mediate between the audience's sense of the human condition and the stage Denmark's accommodation of it.

If, for example, we ask why Shakespeare gives us a scene between Reynaldo and Polonius about Laertes, we find it among the play's many instances of espionage. Spy-traps are set by Polonius and Claudius upon Hamlet, Rosencrantz and Guildenstern upon him, and Polonius again; Hamlet and Horatio upon the king; the Ghost, if we will, upon Hamlet and the queen; and Hamlet upon Rosencrantz and Guildenstern, opening the packet and devising a new commission. But all these are examples of court intrigue, while the Reynaldo scene is outside the narrative intrigues and shows us the routine of Danish manners. While it is not relevant to the story it is relevant to the action. We find the dramatic Denmark a spacious and various society; we know the quality of its guards, gravediggers, courtiers, students, young women and old men, of its leisure, its social habits, its entertainments, literary criticism and proverbial wisdom. The Polonius family scenes yield many graceful, mannered, worldly felicities that are still admired by a wide public and must from the beginning have been capable of winning to a high degree the audience's assent in a norm of privileged domestic behaviour. This is not to deny his public significance; for there is a sense in which he may be constrained in one scholar's stereotype of 'the tyrant's ears',[6] and it is entertaining to see that parallels

---

[6] L. B. Campbell, in *J. Q. Adams Memorial Studies*, ed. J. B. McManaway and others (1948).

can be alleged between Polonius' speeches and Burleigh's letter to Oxford of 23 April 1576.[7] But the elegance and worldiness of the wisdom so admired by Dr Johnson gives place in the scene with Reynaldo to an exposition of the significant difference between whoring and drabbing, and of the art of taking truth with a bait of falsehood. Like the scene in which Hamlet meets the Norwegian captain, it contributes to Shakespeare's anatomy of the 'imposthume of much wealth and peace, / That inward breaks, and shows no cause without / Why the man dies'. In the reflecting but unrepeating mirrors of the play's structure the Reynaldo scene is also one of many to reveal facets of the father–son relationship in Claudius's Denmark. By the image of the causes of both Laertes and Fortinbras Hamlet on different occasions sees the portraiture of his; Hamlet delays a little time to reflect on them, but Shakespeare delays much to present them.

The talk with Reynaldo relates, in another range of the play's analogues, to the process by which Hamlet's sense of his mother's sexual guilt is extended to Ophelia, setting a blister on the fair forehead of an innocent love. Polonius expects Laertes to behave in France much as that young man behaved on St Valentine's eve in the ballad-snatches of the mad Ophelia:

> Then up he rose, and donn'd his clothes,
> And dupp'd the chamber door;
> Let in the maid that out a maid
> Never departed more.

> (IV. v. 52–5)

Once again, the relevance is to the action but not to the story. The ballad fragments can tell us nothing about what has happened, only about what is always happening. In the poignancy of her distraction she allows the dead old man ('His beard was as white as snow') the Christian valediction that she herself will be denied in the 'maimed rites' accorded her by the church of the stage Denmark. The bits of popular song and flower lore are the only resources she has to mediate between her catastrophic experience of the general guilt (Hamlet has done to her what Claudius did to Hamlet) and her naïve incomprehension of it.

Many complex analogues, some meeting in Ophelia's madness, connect the episodes, speeches and characters expressing human approaches to the experience of death. Between them they display what we may feel as the play enlarges to be an almost exhaustive range of attitudes and apprehensions, from the high social decorum of Gertrude's and Claudius's consolatory speeches of the second scene to the habituated professional jocularity of the gravediggers, with many modes of fear, pain, nostalgia, exhaustion, protest

---

[7] Percy Allen, *De Vere as Shakespeare* (1930).

and acceptance in the moods of Hamlet's soliloquies, and almost as many theological and moral speculations attending the shifts of their thought. Once we content ourselves with this aspect of the play's amplitude, many problems about relevance disappear. We can see, for example, why Hamlet lugs the guts of Polonius into a neighbouring room and leaves him to be nosed out by the stairs into the lobby, and why Gertrude is so long a spectator to Ophelia's muddy death. Questioning the logic of the narrative we get comical answers: Hamlet was hoping to conceal from Claudius a murder his wife had witnessed, and the queen was too preoccupied with composing the felicitous verses she hoped to speak in court to spare time to take a grip on Ophelia's weedy trophies and haul her out. But analogical imperatives, reaching into comprehensive areas of the society and of consciousness, require that death receives alike a brutal presentation and a lyrical. It means, among many other things, a body to be disposed of before it offends the senses, and it can occasion a 'melodious lay' upon the dissolution of a creature native and indued to the element that consumes her. And the same range of analogues takes in Imperious Caesar, the jester and his painted mistress, and those twenty thousand who 'go to their graves like beds, fight for a plot / Whereon the numbers cannot try the cause'. The techniques of the tragic play, worked out in a Renaissance theatre capable of touching both public and intimate responses, has found new ways of expressing the communities of both human society and human mortality; the Drômenon is left a long way behind, but its functions are not abdicated.

That Shakespeare was more than usually conscious of the functions of the tragic play within the larger society, and specifically within a monarchy, is clear from the extended attention he gives to the production of the Gonzago play whose thematic content we have already discussed, and I come to the worrying, if slightly gratuitous, problem: did Claudius see the dumb-show, and if not why not? According to Dover Wilson, Shakespeare needed the dumb-show to signal Hamlet's intention to the audience, but as Hamlet did not need it, he treats it as a meddling intervention on the part of the players.[8] According to S. L. Bethell, Wilson's account is too subtle and makes too severe a demand on the actors' powers of communication.[9] The Elizabethan audience, he thinks, enjoyed a double consciousness of the functions of art: they would know the dumb-show was one thing to the spectators in the Globe (alerting them to a close watch on Claudius), and another for the stage audience of Danes, who would see an 'inexplicable dumb-show', an obscure ritual disclosing little about the Gonzago plot. And certainly Ophelia's question, 'What means this, my lord?' and her

---

[8] *What Happens in 'Hamlet'* (1935).
[9] *Shakespeare and the Popular Dramatic Tradition* (1944).

observation, 'Belike this show imports the argument of the play', do seem ingenuous and banal when we assume she sees exactly what we see. Nevertheless I find it hard to believe that she sees anything else, and Shakespeare's purpose in measuring more than one distance between art and life seems to have a transparent effect if not a disarming purpose. Hamlet's 'miching mallecho' comment and his, 'the players cannot keep counsel; they'll tell all' are spoken, not with alarmed resentment, as Dover Wilson supposes, but with mounting eagerness. Claudius endures the silent, puppet-like enactment of his crime, but his nerve breaks as the analogues are pressed home in speech. By a process of intensifying articulation the art of the players serves its discovering purpose. Shakespeare is deftly allegorizing the function of his own craft, for this 'abstract and brief chronicle' is meant, in the tirelessly interrelating language of the play, to 'Make mad the guilty, and appal the free'.

The ambition to 'Make mad the guilty' proves an equivocal and reflexive one, connnecting Hamlet's first determination to assume 'an antic disposition' and his confession that he was 'punish'd with a sore distraction' when he 'wrong'd Laertes'. In the flux of the play the movements between the antic wit and the madness which is 'poor Hamlet's enemy' leave complicated tracks through territories of moral ambiguity where, for example, 'Our indiscretion sometimes serves us well, / When our deep plots do pall.' And Shakespeare, very aware of the malignant potential of consciousness-of-guilt (not quite co-extensive with 'guilty conscience'), attributes to Hamlet many of the characteristics of the Jacobean malcontent or melancholiac, fated to live in a world that is 'weary, stale, flat and unprofitable' even before the Ghost gives specific shape to the general malaise. The personal malaise has been generally described as an incapacity for adult living,[10] and more specifically diagnosed as an 'Oedipus complex'. Ernest Jones's study remains interesting, perhaps, as an event in the history of psychoanalytical criticism, but it is worth re-visiting in the present context because it pursues a connection with the Oedipus story quite different from that which might relate *Hamlet* to the plays of Seneca and Sophocles.[11] For Jones it is Hamlet's moral duty to which his father exhorts him,

> to put an end to the incestuous activities of his mother (by killing Claudius), but his unconscious does not want to put an end to them (he being identified with Claudius in the situation), and so he cannot. His lashings of self-reproach and remorse are ultimately because of this very failure, i.e. the refusal of his guilty wishes to

[10] See e.g. G. Wilson Knight, *The Imperial Theme* (1931), and L. C. Knights, *An Approach to 'Hamlet'* (1960).
[11] *Hamlet and Oedipus* (1949).

undo the sin. By refusing to abandon his own incestuous wishes he perpetuates the sin and so must endure the stings of torturing conscience.

The postulated nature of the 'unconscious' being what it is, and the word 'ultimately' putting the point at such a distance, there can be no accessible evidence to demonstrate Shakespeare's complicity, as it were, in Ernest Jones's understanding. We are left to assume some obscure collaboration between the unconscious responses of playwright, of character and of audience. Without wishing to rule out this possibility (evidence for its truth might be argued, for example, from Hamlet's double playing of King-slayer and nephew when he identifies with Lucianus), I would suppose this too intimate and too non-political an interpretation of the play, and the point may be pursued through a further comparison withe the *Oedipus Rex*. From a reading of Sophocles we may distinguish between the impact of the play and the impact of the myth, and if we ask if the play manifests an understanding of the obscurer sources of the myth in human consciousness, the answer would seem to be emphatically reassuring. Jocasta warns Oedipus not to trouble about the rumours he hears:

Nor need this mother-marrying frighten you;
Many a man has dreamed as much.[12]

and Oedipus experiences the revulsions that are attributed uniquely to the double crime of patricide and incest, compounding 'All horrors that are wrought beneath the sun'.[13] Sophocles' treatment does nothing to diminish the force of the myth (for example, by convicting the king of carelessness) and everything to clarify it. The therapy for which the story is made ready, however, is not the private, clinical kind of Dr Jones's day, but the public, tragic kind we may attribute to the Athenian theatre with the aid of Aristotle's term *catharsis*. The tragedy works upon the communities of both human society and human mortality. In Theban society the trap is sprung by the irony which makes Oedipus the state's judge of his own case. In the mortal community, the trap catches every man, inescapably born, as he is, into the basic triangular family situation, inclining him toward excessive love of the mother and an answering jealousy of the father. None can be held responsible for such biologically induced desires, but society holds culpable any who manifest them beyond a certain point. Hence, to ensure social survival, the desires must be repressed, and in the story of the play, the king must abdicate or be deposed, undertaking an ordeal of physical blindness appropriate to the moral blindness with which human

---

[12]*Oedipus Tyrannus*, lines 981–4 (E.F. Watling's translation).
[13]*Oedipus Tyrannus*, line 1409 (F. Storr's translation).

circumstance has afflicted him. Freudian treatment of the Oedipus myth therefore cannot yield a complete account of the play; the *Oedipus Rex* is about king and city as well as about mother and son. Similarly, Jones's interpretation of *Hamlet* attends too exclusively to the personal relationship between Hamlet and Claudius. He has it that Hamlet's own evil prevents him from completely denouncing his uncle's, 'his moral fate is bound up with his uncle's for good or ill. In reality his uncle incorporates the deepest and most buried parts of his own personality, so that he cannot kill him without also killing himself.' The play, it is true, seems often to reach towards deep and buried parts of personality, but Shakespeare so constructs it that the relationship between the personal state, the human state and (if the pun can be allowed its relevance) the Danish state, is frequently acknowledged and regulated in language and episode. He does not let the intrigues of king and prince shape the play and determine its sequence of scenes. Through the personal ordeal of Ophelia, for example, we glimpse the folk-lore and folk-experience of the larger society, and make a discovery about the nature of mortality. Ophelia's destruction in the play-world of *Hamlet* entails her idiocy, her isolation from the community, family and lover whose discords have fractured the complex and delicate relationship between what we conveniently call the individual and the society, or between the personal and social self, the *polites* and *ideotes*. In Shakespeare's presentation of Ophelia's madness there is much to remind us that as spectators to a play, like the stage audience before whom the alienated girl 'performs', our attention is engaged in changing emotional perspectives. We may be a community watching a community, a family watching a family, or individuals caught up with individuals in the artist's modulation of our personal sympathies. Shakespeare's control of the relationship between the several modes of audience response is what makes the acting of the play a kind of ritual; and it is this control and this range of response that makes it difficult either to acquiesce in Ernest Jones's indifference to the issue of state or to share Arnold Kettle's readiness to set aside the experience of Hamlet the son, as distinct from Hamlet the prince of Denmark. ('This sort of thing,' he says, referring to the murder, usurpation and marriage, 'was not, after all, so very unusual.')[14] For Kettle, Hamlet's protest against the 'feudal world' is manifesting the kind of humanist feeling which was to erupt some thirty years later in the egalitarian aspirations of Cromwell's army. It may well be so, but the play insists that Claudius has usurped the roles of both king and father, figures that have related but not identical claims upon respect, allegiance and love. It is not therefore true that the tragedy is valid only for an archaic monarchy, for any 'father-figure' that a

[14] *Hamlet and History* (1971).

society projects as its authority – whether a king or a prime minister – could call into operation a similar range of experiences and ironies. The play offers no reassurance that men in power may not smile and smile and be villains in other dispensations and other regimes, and the problems of deposing kings may differ only technically from those of deposing, say, presidents and party chairmen. For the son of a king, however, the experience is sharply focused, and in *Hamlet* Shakespeare's control of it is the more certain because the play comes both at a critical moment in the history of the English monarchy and at a moment of maximum expressiveness in the history of a theatre both large enough and small enough for Shakespeare's purpose, capable of providing public spectacle and of being filled with private thought.

Jones treats 'Revenge this foul and most unnatural murder' as if it were the obviously dutiful thing to do. What decent chap wouldn't? And what neurotic outsider wouldn't, after a spell upon the surgery couch? Jones has the powerful ethical tradition of the nordic sources behind him, but it is a tradition that Shakespeare resists. He has no need of that little maxim in the *Atheist's Tragedy*, 'Attend with patience the success of things / And leave revenge unto the King of Kings', for an equivalent principle has forged his design. The Ghost's awareness of the choices before Hamlet expresses Shakespeare's. The Ghost makes his last appearance precisely when it appears that Hamlet has made the wrong choice; assuming the Lucianus-like posture of killer, he has spared Claudius at his prayers, and committed himself to the rival activity that the Ghost had proscribed:

Taint not thy mind, nor let thy soul contrive
Against thy mother aught; leave her to heaven,
And to those thorns that in her bosom lodge
To prick and sting her.

In the event, it is the revenge that is left to the 'divinity that shapes our ends', and the mind-tainting contrivances of the soul that are acted out. When the thorns are lodged, there is a sense in which the work is done. Hamlet and the audience submit to a providential movement of events towards what, in a qualified sense of the word, is a sacrificial outcome. The play's shaping providence does not answer to naïve expectations – there is nothing miraculous about it. While little happens in the last act in obedience to human design, nothing happens either of which no human account can be given; events take form from propensities, not from purposes. Hamlet's searching inquisition of himself and others has compelled the community to undergo a process of moral catharsis.

The word 'sacrificial' is treacherous and complex and must not be barbarously used to impose upon civilized accomplishment an archaic and irrelevant paradigm,[15] yet to call *Hamlet* a 'revenge play' is more culpably to do just that. The point is not that the play is imitating the old rituals but that, with immeasurably greater spiritual and political subtlety, tragic art in the time of both Sophocles and Shakespeare continued in one of its aspects (not all) to acknowledge the persistence of the old mysteries of sin and death. I do not know if anything is gained from calling Hamlet a *pharmakos* or scapegoat, for if we do that we must recognize that he wears his rue with a difference. Like other tragic heroes, he is a victim to the comedy of innocence, whereby we find it necessary to impute guilt to those we kill.[16] The play's leading victim becomes one of its killers, and the cruel discourtesies of his wit do damage to his own humanity. Shakespeare contributes another episode to the history of goat-song, bringing it a long way from its beginnings. For it is finally, not in Denmark's stage court but on the stage of Shakespeare's theatre that the 'sacrifice' of Hamlet and Claudius takes place. Through the attraction and alienation of our sympathies, it is the audience's capacity for life that from generation to generation has been renewed, not that of Fortinbras's fictional state. Hamlet is sacrificed, not because Claudius disposes of him in the interests of Denmark, but because Shakespeare kills him to allow us the satisfaction and exaltation of tragic catharsis.

[15] I have examined some aspects of the word in 'Upon Such Sacrifices', *British Academy Annual Shakespeare Lecture*, 1976 (ch. 12 below).
[16] Burkert, 'Greek Tragedy and Sacrificial Ritual', pp. 106–9.

10 Blood and Wine: Tragic Ritual from Aeschylus to Soyinka

To get good wine, George Herbert tells us, we must trample upon God made flesh; the agony of the press and the vinous delights meet in religious ecstasy: 'Love is that liquor sweet and most divine, / Which my God feels as blood; but I, as wine' ('The Agonie'). Shakespeare is rarely so explicit about the contiguities of cannibalism and the communion service, yet there are in his theatre many equivalent radical insights. What we may take to be remote, pagan and even barbaric rites persist and flourish in complex urban civilizations and in finely tempered urbane communities like that of Herbert's Little Gidding, or that to which Timon supposes himself to belong in the Athens of Apemantus.

Little is to be gained by considering Shakespeare in relation to the theatre of our own time unless we recognize that the continuing traditions of tragedy have primordial as well as literary sources, and that its literary history of some twenty-five hundred years in the Western world is, in an anthropological perspective, quite brief. This does not mean that it is the business of criticism and scholarship to return the complexities of civilized theatrical art to the apparent simplicities of its speculative beginnings. Our primordial selves are a present as well as a past reality; we all, as it were, grow from seed, and some of the most powerful dispositions of human consciousness continue to manifest themselves in ways that certainly would not have surprised Aeschylus, and probably would not be wholly strange to the Neanderthals either. If we are to encourage the slow, perplexed growth of a more adequate humanism, the ritual processes still at work in our own societies urgently need to be understood and revalued. Nigeria is well placed to make a formidable contribution to this understanding, through its cultural history and through its new-made theatre.

The plays of Wole Soyinka are a revelation of the way in which theatre can reach into the heart of a community and make vital, amusing and distressing discoveries about its ordeals and its capacities for life.[1] They therefore invite fresh responses – very much of our own time – to the plays of ancient Athens and of the English Renaissance; the twentieth-century playwright clarifies paradigms of tragic art that span perhaps a hundred generations. It is not merely that Shakespeare and the Greeks have had an influence upon Soyinka; it is rather that influences – currents and flowings-in from the remote past – are by his work made more accessible to us in plays that have gone before. Because there are persisting strains in our nature certain tragic structures are apt to recur, but it does not therefore follow that they are archetypal and unchanging. Tragic art is an instrument for changing human nature, not for impaling it on rigorously conceived necessities. The paradigms on which I shall focus attention are related to the ritual figure of the 'carrier' and to the festivals of Dionysus.

Soyinka's *The Strong Breed* (1966) is about a school-teacher in an African village who dies in his attempt to save a simple-minded child from becoming the symbolic victim of a festive rite. We may discern in the play three sets of moral imperatives, each of which makes a distinctive contribution to its theatrical structure and to the expressiveness of its language. Two sets relate to differing versions of the carrier ritual. In Yoruba culture the tradition by which a specially selected figure 'carries' away the evils of the community takes a variety of forms, and Soyinka here distinguishes between the ritual practice of the hero's home village, where for many years his father was 'carrier', and the different but related practice of the village where he is a newcomer, working in its school and living with a nurse who is the chief's daughter. Both forms of the ritual are expiatory, but the one honours the carrier who bears away the village's afflictions, while the other, for comparable ritual ends, humiliates him. In the several visionary retrospects of the play we find that the old man, year after year obeying the imperatives of his community, carrying the ritual boat to the water, is allowed enough strength and clarity of purpose to perfect with dignity what Soyinka elsewhere calls 'the monstrous cycle of regeneration'. He knows, and the village knows, that one day he will not return from the ceremony but will die in the performance of it, but in the meantime he performs his role with pride. 'I have taken down each year's evils for over twenty years,' he tells his son Eman (whose name means 'saviour'). 'I hoped you would follow me.' But Eman has left his father's domain and when, caught in a human predicament, he comes to offer himself as carrier, it is to a community with significantly different practices. The host village afflicts its

---

[1] I quote throughout from Wole Soyinka, *Collected Plays* (2 vols. Oxford, 1973).

stranger-carrier with ritual beatings and abuse, driving him out. Because Eman does not endure his ordeal acceptingly, he fails to satisfy the ritual imperatives of the host community, and the headman, Jaguna, is contemptuous of a carrier who lacks the manly virtues: 'He had not even gone through one compound before he bolted. Did he think he was taken round the people to be blessed? A woman, that is all he is.' Oroge, the assistant master of ceremonies, responds more perceptively: 'He would let himself be stoned until he dropped dead.' The answer to Jaguna's question 'What made him run?' is to be sought not in Oroge's glance at the 'unhinged' mind of the unprepared carrier but in the third set of human and ritual imperatives dramatized actively in the play's present, and retrospectively in its flashbacks. Eman, in refusing to submit to a certain kind of humiliation, knowingly brings about his own death. He flees for his life, but also for all life; he makes from the rite, and he makes a human get-away. Many complexities attend the ambiguities of Eman's flight in the play, but the human imperatives are readily outlined. At the start of the play Eman cannot bring himself either to take Sunma, the chief's daughter, away with him or to leave her behind at the festival. He stays, and offers himself as carrier, in order to save Ifada, the idiot, from being frightened to death. In the course of the play we learn that he fled his father's village years ago, because there he had found the solemnities of the circumcision ritual corrupted by a lecherous tutor. Eman in the play's last phase goes to his death in an act of fidelity to his father, in the role of carrier, towards the life-sustaining river of death, into the trap which Jaguna has prepared for him. He is in flight from the ritual but, in an unexpectedly human way, he honours it – he dies to save the child.

From Jaguna's point of view the ritual is a failure because both the carrier and his communal hunters, lacking virtue, were womanish and craven: 'I am sick to the heart of the cowardice I have seen tonight.' But in the play's human perspectives we can see that Jaguna's own priestly role is contaminated. He is provoked into malice both by his daughter's association with Eman and by Eman's challenge to the custom of enlisting a stranger: 'A village which cannot produce its own carrier contains no men.' The community, infected by its chief's malice, generates ferocities and revulsions of its own until it finally recoils from the climax of its own ritual excitement – Eman hanged from a tree. 'But did you see them?' asks Jaguna, 'One and all they looked up at the man and words died in their throats.' 'It was no common sight,' says Oroge, referring not merely to the spectacle of the hanged man (words dead in his throat) but to the villagers' response. 'Women could not have behaved so shamefully,' says Jaguna. 'One by one they crept off like sick dogs. Not one could raise a curse!' Eman's sacrifice of himself (it is made to feel like that) belongs to neither of the old ritual patterns. His death, however lyrically conveyed as he runs to keep pace with his dead father, is finally an atrocity that shames the community – 'they crept off like sick dogs'. At the end of the play the moral energies of the community seem exhausted and the acting out of the old ritual has brought it to a stop. The victim has moved humanity a step forward, for the ugly victimization of Eman, the enlightened school-teacher trying to save an imbecile child, works ironically in the manner of a carrier ritual; the sick dogs will in time be ready for a fresh start.

In the opening chorus of the *Agamemnon* of Aeschylus the story is told of the king's submission to pressures and pieties requiring him to sacrific his daughter, Iphigenia, to prosper 'a war waged to avenge a woman'. This is not a seasonal rite but an occasional one, and Iphigenia, although a sacrifice, is not precisely a carrier; she is not bearing away the evils of the society or carrying messages of appeasement to the gods. While his ships are rotting and his soldiers starving, Agamemnon is told by Calchas that the wind will change only if he offers his own daughter to Artemis, the daughter of Zeus. Aeschylus recovers the pathos and ceremony of the event but he shouts too, in pained and ironical protest against the inhuman outrage enacted by priest and king (*Agamemnon*, 217–54).[2] In this play, as in Soyinka's, there is an apparent conflict of human and ritual imperatives. Without in any way diminishing the heroic stature of Agamemnon, and fully exploiting the imaginative potency of the old stories, Aeschylus exposes the values of which the stories are an expression – the pieties, commitments to war, revenge and sacrifice – to severe sceptical analysis.

The analysis is not of the discursive kind; it works through poetry, using all the resources of the language, upon our sympathetic imaginations and upon the obscurities of our verbal awareness. As in the plays of Shakespeare (and Soyinka) the language makes covert connections between one range of values and another, and between the fabulous event and the ordinariness of human experience. Thus Agamemnon's readiness to give his daughter to the war is still vivid to the audience's memory when the chorus later tells of the trading of men for dust at the quayside as the Greek dead are sent back from Troy (*Agamemnon*, 432–55). Through a series of exquisitely painful equivocations war is compared with a gold-merchant. Ares, bartering the bodies of men for gold, holds his balance in the poised spears of the battlefield and scrupulously offers the Greeks value for money. From Ilium he sends back those who have passed through his refining fire – a heavy weight of precious dust for the price of a man, and at home the women marvel at their jars of gold, their urns of dust – 'How skilled in battle! Fallen nobly in the carnage!' Moving against the tide of acquiescent eloquence is a protesting undertow: 'grief charged with resentment spreads

[2] References to Aeschylus are to the Loeb edition, ed. H. W. Smyth, (2 vols., 1946).

stealthily against the sons of Atreus.' The earlier responses to the grand sacrifice of Iphigenia are generalized in all their instability. Sacrifice is ubiquitous in war, and the tragic poet both commemorates and repudiates it.

Neither kings nor gods are exempt from the playwright's imaginative and ethical scrutiny, for the poet knows that the gods and sanctities of human piety and government are the creation of the human imagination. From the old values re-created and freshly imagined, Aeschylus assists in the making of those new, transmuted values that were in process of being embodied, however imperfectly, in the laws and customs of a new city-culture. Thus the series of plays which begins with a tale of human sacrifice ends with a joyous invocation to the presiding goddess of the city of Athens. But, while it ends upon a festive note, the tragic festival of the theatre leaves us as conscious of the destructive as of the creative potencies of human consciousness. Thus the Trojan war, belonging then as now to the distant past, belongs also to Aeschylus' time and to our own; the play endeavours to see the last of an all-too-present condition. The passage of the trilogy from sacrificial song to civic rejoicing is, in Soyinka's phrase, its 'threnodic essence'.

In the plays of Euripides the ritual affirmation is exposed to a more intimate (but not more profound) human inspection. In *Iphigenia at Aulis* Euripides gives us not only the threnodic essence of Iphigenia's sacrifice, but also its human comedy. We are brought close to the personal, familial, political and theocratic roles of Agamemnon, who is shocked by the deed of sacrifice but also drawn to it. Iphigenia herself voices the antinomies of tragic response – recoiling from the cruelty and arbitrariness of premature death:

> Below, there's nothing: he's mad who prays to die.
> Even base living profits more than noble death;
> $(1250–2)^3$

yet attracted, under the pressure of necessity, by its apparently sublime significance (1368–1401, 1420). For an analogous attraction and repulsion we could go to Shakespeare's *Measure for Measure* (from 'I will encounter darkness as a bride' to 'Ay, but to die, and go we know not where', III, i. 85, 119) but more directly, to a choice of tragic victims in the plays of Soyinka – Eman, for example, in *The Strong Breed*, or Elesin in *The Death of the King's Horseman* (1975). Iphigenia is snatched from the altar by Artemis, Elesin snatched from his suicide dance, at once willingly and

---

[3] References to Euripides are to the Loeb edition, ed. A. S. Way, (4 vols, 1919). The translation of these lines is from D. J. Conacher, *Euripidean Drama* (Toronto and London, 1967), p. 259.

unwillingly, by Pilkings, the District Officer. Both get-aways are evasions of the tragic festival. In Soyinka's play the Praise Singer is denied his natural and communal role when the son is impelled to die in his father's place: 'this young shoot has poured its sap into the parent stalk, and we know this is not the way of life. Our world is tumbling in the void of strangers, Elesin.' But Soyinka gives to his theatre audience the tragic catharsis that the District Officer denies the villagers watching the death-dance. Elesin strangles himself in a *coup de théâtre*, his bride closes his eyes, and the playwright contrives his own valedictory dirge. The *Iphigenia at Aulis* reaches a differently equivocal crisis; she whom the gods love is carried away to live with the gods (1610–13) leaving Clytemnestra to wonder if report is 'but a sweet lie to heal the broken heart' (1617–18) and the audience to wonder if the play is a tragedy or a melodrama. Euripides' interest in the inhumanity of the death rites persists in the *Iphigenia in Tauris* where Iphigenia on the island of Artemis is required to preside over continuing sacrifices even more arbitrary than her own. Her get-away silences the tragic death music and leaves King Thoas to make the best of 'a doom reversed and a life re-won'.

Unlike Aeschylus, Euripides and Soyinka, Shakespeare seldom deals directly with ritual deaths. Only in *Titus Andronicus* is human sacrifice ('T'appease their groaning shadows that are gone') assimilated into the narrative and there through the juxtaposition of Roman and Gothic rites, it is associated with barbarism, the state from which Rome arose and into which it declined. In Shakespeare's more mature tragedies, the several traditions that converge from Greek and Latin theatre, from the Christian Church and from the literature of the Bible, find more oblique expression. But in this ample perspective it may be said of all Shakespeare's tragedies that they have a 'threnodic form' which sings out about the 'dying-into-life' process, and a dissenting form which cries out against it. Thus in *Romeo and Juliet* a poignantly lyrical death, of some redemptive significance to the community, is also a disgraceful outrage brought about by human malignancies and inadequacies. In *Julius Caesar* and in *Othello* the heroes preside like priests over acts of butchery which they represent to themselves and to the gods as sacrifices, before taking their own lives in acts of tragic suicide. In relating Shakespeare's tragic forms to Soyinka's, however, I take the very different instances of *King Lear* and *Anthony and Cleopatra*.

King Lear may still come back to us in the form of an old tale, told by the fireside: 'There was once a king and he had three daughters. One day, grown old and tired, he divided his kingdom into three parts and called his daughters to him. "Which of you," he asked, "loves me most?" . . .' The old tale, before Shakespeare lays hands on it, moves to a consolatory outcome: 'The youngest daughter defeated her sisters in battle and gave the kingdom back to her father. He reigned over it for the last happy years of his life, and when he died, the daughter that had truly loved him reigned in his place.' Shakespeare's tale says: 'But her sisters defeated her in battle and they cast the king and his youngest daughter into prison. The youngest daughter was hanged and the king died of age, pain and grief.' Keeping these folk-story simplicities in mind, it is possible to see the fundamental nature of Shakespeare's defiance of one range of his audience's expectations. The old *Leir* might have been reshaped into a Last Play, a melodrama, with the formal solace of song and masque. But in *King Lear* Shakespeare plots the deaths of king and daughter and leaves the kingdom desolate. Why? The question is capable of many answers,[4] but it is apt to reopen it with other tragic rituals in mind.

In the Iphigenia story the king's daughter 'dies' in order that his armies may in time prevail against Troy, and the king himself dies in the feuds attending the city's advance towards a better understanding of divine justice. In *The Strong Breed* the Old Man and his son die in order that the life of the village (i.e. pagan) community should, in a variety of senses, be renewed. Christian rituals celebrate 'the Lamb of God that taketh away the sins of the world', and Christ, by this metaphor, was the greatest and last of the carriers. Audiences of Shakespeare's play then (and even now) would be familiar with an earlier carrier, in the fifty-third chapter of Isaiah:

> Surely he hath borne our griefs and carried our sorrows . . . But he was wounded for our transgressions, he was bruised for our iniquities . . . He was oppressed, and he was afflicted, yet he opened not his mouth; he is brought as a lamb to the slaughter, and as a sheep before her shearers is dumb, so he openeth not his mouth. He was taken from prison and from judgement . . . cut off out of the land of the living.

There is no allusion to Isaiah in *King Lear* but a reading of the prophet alongside the play creates tantalizing prospects for our moral and aesthetic sensibilities, and this passage is a reminder of the transcendent moral status that, in one tradition of human understanding, we allow to the unprotesting victims we beat up. In the play's first scene the exalted response is that which the old ritual figure – the sheep before the shearer – once elicitied: 'What can you say . . .? Nothing, my lord . . . Nothing? . . . Nothing.' Shakespeare's intervention in the old story recovers the values at work in the old Hebraic and Christian carrier rite, but not without qualification. Cordelia is brought to judgement again in the last scene, and the play's structure first admits and then denies the solace of its ritual. The triumphant cry 'Come, let's away to prison' affords to Shakespeare's audience something

---

[4] I have attempted some answers in 'Upon Such Sacrifices', British Academy Annual Shakespeare Lecture, 1976 ch. 12 below.

of the satisfying exaltation that Soyinka's village communities look for in their carrier rites, an effect that might be played more poignantly if Lear, to 'take upon's the mystery of things', literally carried Cordelia off in his arms. The interlude that follows is made out of another set of traditional ritual confidences, as Edgar prevails over Edmund in trial by combat. But the evils of the kingdom have not been carried away. '*Enter Lear with Cordelia in his arms*' says the stage direction. The carrier has come back. There is no transcendent exaltation, no snatching away of a Cordelia loved by the gods. The atrocity is more conspicuous than the sacrifice, the play's dissenting form prevails over its threnodic form.

The figure in Isaiah is said to 'bear the sins of many'. Shakespeare's assimilation of the ritual compels us to keep watch over the disintegration of the king and his kingdom. The old kingdom from which Lear abdicates was sustained by certain allegiances, appropriately associated with the old feudal order, still kept up in the play by the best of its survivors – Kent, Edgar, the Fool, and (with a difference) Gloucester and Albany. The division of the kingdom entails its dissolution, but Lear in the storm finds that the old kingdom was divided before he divided it. There were (and are) communities of the oppressors and of the oppressed, of the rich and the poor, the torturers and the tortured, the protected and the exposed, the masters and the servants, the knaves and the fools, and the governed and the ungoverned. They are not stable communities either – they shift about, collapse and destroy each other; and a man's history can take him into many communities. So it is with Lear's history, which is of his exposure to the arrogances and distresses of the multiple community, within the largest community of all – that of human mortality. It is not a history of exposure only, however, but of inward assimilation. Lear takes his kingdom into his inmost consciousness and Shakespeare through him takes it into ours.

In the ritual of the theatre the audience is required to go through what Lear goes through, and the progressive destruction of the old king and his 'own kingdom' exposes us to fresh insights into our common humanity and mortality. One instance of the oblique immediacy of Shakespeare's theatrical art will serve to suggest the ways in which the play creates a new relationship between the king's consciousness of his power and his recognition of weakness. At the start of the play Lear, at his most absolute, threatens Kent with an imaginary bow and arrow: 'The bow is bent and drawn; make from the shaft!' (I, i. 143). Much later, when the king himself has been exposed to 'feel what wretches feel', we meet that bow and arrow again.[5] Lear, who 'lacks soldiers', imagines himself as the warrior king

[5] I owe this observation to conversation with Dr. A. C. Charity of the University of York.

again, pressing conscripts into his army. 'That fellow,' he says, catching sight of Edgar, 'handles his bow like a crow-keeper; draw me a clothier's yard' (IV, vi. 87). Lear presumably draws his imagined bow again, in proud full stretch. Then his memory fails him and he looks helplessly at his left hand, pointing like an arrow, and at his right, held inexplicably in space. The straying mind finds reason first for the arrow-hand – 'Look, look, a mouse!' and his voice drops to a whisper as he wanders between the two auditory senses of the word 'peace' before he can explain the other hand: 'Peace, peace, this piece of toasted cheese will do't.' As he feeds the mouse, the oscillations between terror and solicitude start up again. The player-king may even choose to crush the mouse with his gauntlet as it falls into the cheese-trap – 'There's my gauntlet; I'll prove it on a giant.' In the phantasmagoria of Lear's consciousness life is paying a forfeit to the warrior's power.

An analogous account of tragic processes, large and small, might be given of Soyinka's *The Road* and of his *Madmen and Specialists*. Other modes of tragedy, however, invite a different account. When the National Theatre in 1972 commissioned from Soyinka a new version of *The Bacchae* of Euripides, it was in the fully realized expectation that the distance between ancient Greece and modern Nigeria would be readily diminished; the resulting play still belongs to ancient Athens, to the Yoruba, and to us. The story is told again virtually unchanged, and its commanding metaphors are retained, with much the same significance for our understanding of society and consciousness. Dionysos is welcomed to Thebes in human form, but repression is soon seen at work in the community, as the king jails the revellers, and in Pentheus' own psyche as he attempts to shut up the god himself; he is unable to control the instinctual life because it takes precisely the violent animal character he attributes to it – symbolized by the escaping bull. Euripides' play, beginning with serene and joyful song and dance in honour of Dionysos, ends in savage horror under the dominion of the same god, and the king is lynched in festive frenzy by the woman who bore him. Soyinka keeps the plot with a more muted opening movement. In both versions certain life-delighting and life-sustaining impulses turn sour and self-destructive. Both Euripides and Soyinka honour the old stories and the old pieties while exposing them to fresh experiential tests of their validity, and both put authority, order and regiment upon trial. But Soyinka's Nigerian play shows that the old turbulent energies, delights and excitements, instinctual aspirations and malignancies have assumed new disguises, put on new masks. The scourging scene, the sack-cloth and ashes, the chorus of slaves, and many other episodes and images, extend the play's scope into Christian and socialist references and values. More strikingly, moreover, the human perspective changes. The play gets even closer than Euripides to the pathos and absurdity of human ordinariness, while at the same time being sophisticated and knowing in its treatment of the old Greek, Christian and African rituals.

When Tiresias, in Soyinka's version, picks himself up from the procession of revellers who are featuring him in what is meant to be a symbolic scourging of the old dispensation, covered in weals, he cries out in protest: 'Can't you bastards ever tell the difference between ritual and reality?' The theatre is neither ritual nor reality, but it is in a position to make a spectacle of both. It can also make a spectacle of itself (a trick Soyinka might have learned from Shakespeare) and set traps for its audience, including the academics in it, who can easily be tricked into talking like Tiresias ('I found that significant,' says Tiresias to Kadmos, who has just said 'foreskin' when he meant to say 'fawnskin'; 'when you start on significance,' says Kadmos, 'you lose me'). Throughout the play the tragic ritual is put under severe comic pressure. Some of the comedy comes from life picking itself up again (like Tiresias) when the ritual knocks it down. But some of it is inhuman, meant to amuse the gods rather than men, and if we enjoy it, the explanation is to be found in the kind of all-seeing aloofness which the theatre enables us to share with Dionysos.

The Bacchae of Soyinka is not in itself a particularly Shakespearian play, but it inherits from Euripides a myth and structure that clarify, without oversimplifying, the antinomies of energy and order that reach a high point of tragic and comic conflict in a number of Shakespeare's plays. When, for example, the blood-and-ale-intoxicated followers of Jack Cade process through the London streets with the heads of Lord Say and Cromer upon poles, we cannot precisely say that Dionysos is avenged upon Pentheus, but we can see that the energies of anarchy have been liberated in a community whose government has lapsed into oppressive disarray. The procession that scourges Tiresias in Soyinka's first scene moves through the afflicted landscape of a slave state, with crucified figures 'mostly in the skeletal stage) and green vines clinging to the charred ruins of the temple of Semele. It is not from Euripides (though it would not have been wholly unfamiliar to him), but from the Nigerian civil war, shadowed by Golgotha. Dionysos waits, relaxed 'as becomes divine self-assurance' in the ruins. The priests who intone a liturgy as they lead the revellers are the first tragedians, the first singers of goat-songs, trying to make harmony and rhythm (Aristotle's *melopeia*) out of what is in danger of becoming a suddenly ugly event. When Dionysos, an amused witness on stage, intervenes to save Tiresias from rough handling with the words, 'Sing death of the Old Year, and – welcome the new – god', we the off-stage audience recognize a seasonal rite; we too have read *The Golden Bough*. Dionysos, with the playwright's connivance, is out to save the song, the 'threnodic form' of the rite and the play.

The ritual form meets its dissenting challenge, however, both from the old Euripidean sources and from some new ones. 'Which of us is victim this year?' a herdsman asks, and is told, 'That old man of the king's household. The one who looks after the dogs.' The slave-leader's indignation (which has no counterpart in Euripides) is met by peasant fortitude: 'Suppose the old man dies?' – 'We all have to die sometime' – 'Flogged to death? In the name of some unspeakable rites?' – 'Someone must cleanse the new year of the rot of the old or, the world will die.' The slave-leader persists – 'Why us? Why always us?' – but the herdsman points to the crosses to remind him that 'The palace does not need the yearly Feast of Eleusis to deal with rebellious slaves.' The routine victims of the repressive, warring society are, by the wit of the play, related to its ritual victims.

In Shakespeare's *Henry IV* the Dionysiac figure of Falstaff is not a god, but an idol of the theatre, and his celebrants at the Boar's Head are without a liturgy; if we look for a ritual in the play we must make what we can of the scenes staged by 'the harlotry players' in anticipation of the king's repudiation of the flesh. The play, however, sets up its own set of relationships between life-delight, wine-delight, the readiness to die and the readiness to kill. As the nobles come 'like sacrifices in their trim', the expendables are tossed to 'fill a pit as well as better'.

Soyinka's theatrical analysis of the political dynamics of the play's community is not of a naïvely predictable kind. It is the slave leader who proves to be most excited by the apparition of the god, his sensitivity to the plight of others makes him the more vulnerable to the 'god of seven paths: oil, wine, blood, spring, rain, / Sap and sperm', and his revolutionary energies are diverted into destructive festive fury. The violence here, as in *Julius Caesar* where the crowd moves from 'O piteous spectacle!' to 'tear him to pieces' when it meets the poet Cinna, is generated out of human fellowship and humane indignation.

The play's divine comedy is more active in its early movements than in the last. Dionysos not only energizes the revolution, he also confronts old age and priestly celibacy with desolating insights into the inadequacy of human wisdom:

> Poor Tiresias, poor neither-nor, eternally tantalized psychic inter-mediary, poor agent of the gods through whom everything passes but nothing touches, what happened to you in the crowd, dressed and powdered by the hands of ecstatic women . . . You poor starved votary at the altar of the soul, what deep hunger unassuaged by a thousand lifelong surrogates drove you to this extreme self-sacrifice. Don't lie to a god, Tiresias.

Tiresias makes his confession. At first he claims political motives for playing the victim's role; it was touch and go with Thebes: 'if one more slave had been killed at the cleansing rites, or sacrificed to that insatiable altar of nation-building . . .' the state would have gone to pieces. But the god doesn't believe the politician; he looks for different flagellant impulses and finds them – those lashes did begin something, he feels 'a small crack in the dead crust' of his soul, and at the god's invitation he begins to dance. It would be possible to find many more such instances in the play of tragic ritual under comic inspection – a god's eye view of the pretensions of men – as when Kadmos grumbles about being an administrator: 'An administrator, Tiresias! Then an old-age pensioner on the court list. I who slew the dragon and bred a race of warriors from his teeth.' The comedy is addressed to a sophisticated audience that knows about the classics, but also to any Yoruba leader who until quite recently might have been the theme of fables.

Soyinka's play glances too at an aspect of Dionysos that is not conspicuous in Euripides' version – his role at weddings. The action is broken in upon by two nuptials, in which Dionysos offers Pentheus a glimpse of 'the past and future legends of Dionysos'. In the first, a feast breaks up in disorder as the groom makes off with the wine-girl under the spell of Dionysos and the influence of drink; in the second, Dionysos is manifest in the figure of Christ at the feast of Cana, turning the water into wine. The large point made in the fable about the contrary potentials of Dionysos – violent and tranquil – is thus repeated in the familiar sacrament and festival of marriage. Dionysos is a perennial and ubiquitous presence, assuming many forms.

This is a necessary reflection as we look again from Soyinka to Shakespeare. While there are no sustained processional pagan rituals in Shakespeare's plays, and nothing directly equivalent to *The Bacchae*, there are sacrifices, lynchings, dances, drunken parties and other manifestations of the savage divinity. And there are figures to keep Dionysos and Falstaff company (Autolycus among them), with others to challenge their destructive skills, like Prince Hal, Prince John and Octavius Caesar. In *Antony and Cleopatra*, the Romans 'dance . . . the Egyptian Bacchanals' and drink themselves into a stupor:

> Come, let's all take hands,
> Till that the conquering wine hath steep'd our sense
> In soft and delicate Lethe.

(II, vii. 104–6)

But the play does not invite us, as *The Bacchae* does, to revalue the cult of Dionysos, Shakespeare's 'monarch of the vine, / Plumpy Bacchus with pink eyne!' The old wisdoms that are exposed to scrutiny have a more complex presence in its theatre, and our humanity is differently discomposed and reordered. Like the *Bacchae* plays, the action of *Antony and Cleopatra* is bounded by the comprehensive and inescapable catastrophic process by which we are all born, flourish and die, and the poet articulates that elemental cycle through which life reverts to the slime which breeds it ('let the water-flies / Blow me into abhorring') and then starts up again with the help of erotic agriculture ('he ploughed her and she cropped').

That way of putting it does not account for the scale of the play, however. Unlike Euripides and Soyinka in their Bacchic plays, Shakespeare is looking for his *agons* not in the story of a ritual but in the history of an empire. *Antony and Cleopatra* spans the epic space that imperial ambitions opened up between the power and values of Rome on the one hand and Egypt on the other. The play's threnodic form, however, still requires us to perceive that Antony and Cleopatra die because (like Soyinka's Elesin) they are completely caught up in the cycle of regeneration whose law is a perpetual dying-into-life; Cleopatra's 'celerity in dying' is itself an expression of her life-delight. Caesar, the survivor, is, to borrow a phrase from Eliot, 'outside the scheme of generation'; being Fortune's 'nave' and 'knave' he does not go round with the wheel. Pentheus, on the other hand, is impaled on the wheel, a spectacular sacrifice to the cycle whose festive drives he tried to arrest. There are, of course, other perspectives to be constructed for the play. One strain in the Roman view of Antony, for example, looks back through Plutarch to the cult of *sophrosyne* in Greek ethical traditions, and it is apt enough that Caesar's sophronistic regulative virtues should be revalued in a Jacobean court which had its own imperial aspirations. The Egyptian range of energies and insights is less capable of systematic exposition but there was much to respond to it in the taste and culture of the Jacobean court, including the exuberance of Shakespeare's own theatre and poetry.

The continuities of theatre and ritual, however, retain their own distinctive importance – when, for example, Apemantus grieves 'to see so many dip their meat in one man's blood', or Perdita plays as she has 'seen them do / In Whitsun pastorals', or Feeble reflects that 'he that dies this year is quit for the next.' Some valuable explorations of Shakespeare's assimilations of ritual form have found their starting-points in Freud, or in Nietzsche's *Birth of Tragedy from the Spirit of Music*, but we nevertheless do well to call on the lively analogues, close and distant, that the history of theatre itself affords. Soyinka's *Bacchae* ends:

Tiresias   What is it Kadmos? What is it?
Kadmos   Again blood, Tiresias. Nothing but blood.
Tiresias   [*He feels his way nearer the fount. A spray hits him and he holds out a hand, catches some of the fluid and sniffs. Tastes it.*]
No. It's wine.

George Herbert would have understood that.

11   The Theatre of *Othello*

A great play can only be made when the time is ripe, when the language and experience of the community are ready for it, and when the traditions of literature and theatre coalesce at the right moment in the art and imagination of the playwright. It happens not infrequently that a masterpiece brings into new conflict and harmony forms and insights whose history had previously been divided. *Othello* is at the confluence of several theatrical and literary traditions, moral, heroic, comic and domestic, and therefore, also, of the corresponding traditions of human values.

In *Shakespeare and the Allegory of Evil* Bernard Spivack, like others before him, traced the origins of much that we find in the play to the old Moralities and interludes of medieval and early Tudor England.[1] The destruction of Othello's reputation and occupation is a fall from grace, and Iago is an agent of that fall – the amoral Vice or, some would say, the Devil himself. We can seem to be staying still within the biblical traditions of drama if we say that the fall must be atoned by sacrifice. Othello, like Brutus in *Julius Caesar*, at the climax and nadir of his own fall sees himself not as a murderer but as a sacrificer; he kills Desdemona after assuming the role of confessor and priest.

But we do not know Othello merely as Iago's gull; a lover, murderer and deluded sacrificer, we also know him as a noble warrior who has 'done the state some service'; and such figures are not to be found in the old Morality Plays. They belong to a rival, heroic tradition.

Neither the noble soldier nor the sacrificer are to be found in the story by Giraldo Cinthio from which Shakespeare adapted his play. In it 'the Moor' (he is not called Othello) is a garrison captain but not a leading power in the state, and the murder is a squalid piece of butchery faked to

---

Earlier versions of this paper were given in Ilorin, Nigeria, in Aleppo, and at the Shakespeare Institute.
[1] Bernard Spivack, *Shakespeare and the Allegory of Evil* (1958).

look like a suicide. The elements that make the play heroic, therefore, and that make it aspire to atonement and sacrifice, are to be looked for, not in the narrative source, but in the history of theatre.

For the elements of its comedy there are precedents in the *commedia dell'arte*,[2] in Ben Jonson, and conspicuously in Shakespeare's own art. In its stage-technique and its insight into domestic jealousy, the *Merry Wives of Windsor* anticipates *Othello*: 'Good plots, they are laid, and our revolted wives share damnation together.' Shakespeare had read in San Giovanni's *Il Pecorone* a story about a Professor who inadvertently teaches a student how to seduce his young and beautiful wife and used it to make his only English comedy, in which Francis Ford, driven frantically jealous as he promotes the seduction of his own wife, in the end proves her chaste and himself (to borrow Iago's phrase) 'egregiously an ass'.

There is a complex web of conventions, therefore, in which the warrior protagonist of the heroic play is exposed to the Vice of the Morality, in the black comedy of a garrison town. Theatre conventions can be looked upon as signs, and each established genre, under pressure of expectation or in response to principles of decorum, tends, even aspires, to become an autonomous sign-system, exempt from challenge and change, and therefore an apt vehicle for established attitudes and ideologies. But conventions are derived by a degree of common consent from the shared experience they signify. Not the characters only, but their sustaining modes of expression meet in *Othello*, representing attitudes to life, ranges of moral values, responses to reality which Shakespeare found diverging and conflicting in Renaissance Europe. The play does not consolidate the conventions it inherits but re-creates them.

Ethical and imaginative values in Shakespeare's plays are apt to have a topography as well as a theatrical history. Different territories of the Mediterranean in particular are often given a distinctive ethos and significance: Rome and Egypt in *Antony and Cleopatra*, Italy and Tunis in *The Tempest*, Tyre and Antioch, Tarsus and Mytilene in *Pericles*. Jealousy takes recognizable but different forms in the Garter Inn of Windsor, the courts of Messina and Sicily, and the fortified island of Cyprus. The action of *Othello* is (following Cinthio) in Mediterranean suspense between Venice and North Africa. Its hero is exotically African and its 'demi-devil' a sophisticated Italian.

The link between Africa and the heroic imagination was first forged outside the formal theatre. The evidence is in the account books for the Lord Mayor's midsummer shows.[3] They tell us that the black, or tawny,

[2] See Barbara Heliodora C. de Mendoça, '"Othello": a Tragedy Built on a Comic Structure', *Shakespeare Survey*, 21 (1968), pp. 31–9.
[3] *A Calendar of Dramatic Records in the Books of the Livery Companies of London*

soldier-hero was a figure in festivals long before he reached the Elizabethan stage. The 1519 accounts include what seems to be the first reference to a popular African pageant which was to become a regular feature of the annual shows and carnivals. We are told that two shillings and tenpence was paid to those who led the horses of the 'Sowden' or 'Sultan', the Jewess and the Gaoler. Two years later, the King of the Moors and sixty 'morians' appeared in another extravagant procession whose account records the loan of 'a dummy lance that the King of the Moors pavillion was born upon, over his head.'

These moorish shows were resplendent, soldierly and sensual. 'Woman,' said Nietszche, in *Thus Spake Zarathustra*, 'is born for the sport and amusement of warrior man.' The king of moors or the Sultan, expensively got up in red satin and silver foil, rode in high style under his gilded pavilion, with a mighty pageant of soldiers, slaves and concubines behind him. His function was to overawe the crowd and prepare them for the plays and shows that were to follow. He was there as much for his own sake as for anyone else's, but we can attribute to him a distant political significance, as a festive representative of power and sexual potency in the early stages of Tudor empire.

These regal black and tawny men show that Africa and the Mediterranean had a special place in the Tudor imagination long before Shakespeare made *Othello* and before Christopher Marlowe made his play about the 'rare and wonderful conquests of *Tamburlaine the Great*'. From the beginning of the century, the role of the Moor in public spectacle was to enrich the public conception of power, wealth and sensual splendour, valued by a community that still honoured John the Baptist, the life of Christ and the lives of the saints.

In its moments of festival, when 'our noble and valiant general' would have 'every man put himself into triumph' both for the 'perdition of the Turkish fleet' and in 'celebration of his nuptial', *Othello* looks back to the processional and pageant theatre of *Tamburlaine*. Marlowe, turning spectacle into word, reached beyond the silver paper, dummy lances and fireworks, but in the same direction – towards the glorification of military power, earthly sovereignty, and conquest in love and war. The Scythian Tamburlaine is heard:

> Threatening the world with high astounding terms
> And scourging kingdoms with his conquering sword.
>
> (*1 Tamburlaine*, Prologue, 5–6)

The 'high astounding terms', themselves occasioning much wonder and

---

1485–1640, ed. D. J. Gordon and Jean Robertson, Malone Society Collections, III (1954).

delight, are modulated out of the soldier's voice into the lover's:

> in this sweet and curious harmony,
> The God that tunes this music to our souls:
> Holds out his hand in highest majesty
> To entertain divine Zenocrate.
>
> (*2 Tamburlaine*, ii. iv. 30–3)

And there is some intimation of that marvellous, lucid purity which will characterize the love speech of Othello:

> The christall springs whose taste illuminates
> Refined eyes with an eternal sight,
> Like tried silver runs through Paradise
> To entertain divine Zenocrate.
>
> (ii. iv. 22–5)

Marlowe in his later plays was to set aside his golden trumpet, but others with less skill took it up in plays, including Greene's *Selimus* and *Orlando Furioso*, which recall *Tamburlaine* and shadowily anticipate *Othello*.

For the theatrical genesis of Iago we may look in the Mystery and Morality Plays and in Shakespeare's earlier work for two distinctive attributes – his diabolical disposition and his trick of establishing a special and intimate relationship with the audience. There is an early instance in the Tudor interlude *Lusty Juventus*.[4] In it a young man, called simply 'Youth' is led astray by a number of treacherous companions including 'Hypocrisy'. Hypocrisy is sent by the devil to approach Youth in the name of 'Friendship', 'Simple and rude of fashion'. But before he talks to Youth, he confides to the audience that he means to tempt him into riotous living. When Hypocrisy joins Youth it is like Iago talking to Cassio, friend accosting friend; but the audience, with all the phrase implies, is 'in the know'. A number of figures in the old Moralities, with names like Dissimulation, Fraud and Ambidexter, are double-dealers endowed with this special (strictly hypocritical) acting skill – seeming to be what they are not – and they all have this Satanic privilege of intimacy with the audience. In increasingly elaborate and sophisticated forms, the same privilege is allowed by Shakespeare to the Duke of York, Richard of Gloucester, Edmund in *King Lear* and, finally, to Iago.

Thus along several lines, from pageant and heroic play, Miracle and Morality, history and tragedy we might come to a nexus in *Othello*. There is no need to trace more refined interconnections of convention (such as the use of overheard dialogue) in order to recognize that formal lineaments

---

[4] *An Enterlude called Lusty Juventus*, in *Four Tudor Interludes*, ed. J. A. B. Somerset (1974).

of theatre control (though they do not determine) our response to the play. What we make of it, of course, may depend in part upon whether we are 'valiant servitors', 'curled darlings of the nation' or 'toged consuls', masters of 'bookish theoric', but it depends too upon the way in which we connect the values of theatre to those of human relationships, and that connection is itself freshly explored in every performance of *Othello*.

It is usual to refer to the third scene of the third act as the temptation or corruption scene. If we see it as one of many such in Tudor drama, then the play does indeed look like a Morality, and Othello's credulity and fall, in face of the negative and trivial skills of the tempter Iago, is damnably culpable; to anticipate a later metaphor (v, ii. 283) a 'rash and unfortunate man' is poisoned by a 'viper'. But Iago is not merely corrupting Everyman or leading Youth astray. He is contriving the destruction of the community's warrior-hero, and he is neither Vice nor Devil, but a searchingly anatomized disaffected soldier 'trimmed in forms and visages of duty'. While his arts relate to those of the old theatre-figure of Hypocrisy, they are shown to be the active histrionic arts of an at-once familiar and amazing moral world. We are compelled to recognize too that Othello's very virtues, bonded to his defects, make him vulnerable to Iago's performance.

Tamburlaine overcomes his enemies by the sword and by words. But his 'great and thundering speech' does not merely intimidate, it casts a spell. Shakespeare in *Othello* takes up again the instrument that Marlowe had set aside, but in the interim he had attended to another voice of Africa. It is in the Prince of Morocco's splendid (but still comic) vaunts that he brings his language closest to Marlowe's:

> Mislike me not for my complexion,
> The shadow'd livery of the burnish'd sun,
> To whom I am a neighbour and near bred.
> Bring me the fairest creature northward born,
> Where Phoebus' fire scarce draws the icicles,
> And let us make incision for your love,
> To prove whose blood is reddest, his or mine.
> I tell thee, lady, this aspect of mine
> Hath fear'd the valiant; by my love, I swear
> The best-regarded virgins of our clime
> Have lov'd it too.
>   (*Merchant of Venice* ii. i. 1–11)

There is one of the imaginative points of departure for the later play. Keen swords, red blood, pure virgins – these are the elements of the Afro-Marlovian chemistry of passion and war in the sun's fertile climate. The 'Hyrcanian deserts and the vasty wilds of wide Arabia' (*Merchant*, ii, vii. 41–2) are as much the territories of Othello's as of Tamburlaine's and

Morocco's valiancy and love. Seeing the plays in the same season one might reflect that all three warriors have 'golden minds', rate high in their own estimation, and might be supposed apt choosers of the golden casket, and that Iago would have Desdemona react to Othello as Portia does to Morocco, and not 'love him for bragging and telling her fantastical lies'.

Stimulated by his reading of Cinthio, and thinking again about Africa and Mediterranean war, Shakespeare therefore returned to test the vitality of the heroic tradition and its associated declamatory style of poetry – the 'high astounding terms' that Iago hears as 'bombast circumstance / Horribly stuffed with epithets of war'. What happens to Tamburlaine and Zenocrate when Ambidexter gets to work on them? What becomes of the exotic, sovereign, warrior-lover when he is confronted by a morality Satan (or Satan's modern human counterpart, the skilled destructive hypocrite), and what becomes of his language, his passions and his reputation? For the full significance of these questions to be brought home to us it is necessary that we have some sympathy of response to the heroic side of Othello, and it happens that neither heroic aspiration nor the declamations that express it are likely to be highly valued in an age of spuriously heroic propaganda and squalid military actions.

Yet it is clear than an appreciation of *Othello* which is not responsive to its war-music must be defective. The stage history, while it will not open our ears to the Othello music (to use Wilson Knight's felicitous phrase) warns us against closing them to it. The campaign against the Turks, moreover, had for Shakespeare's contemporaries some of the significance of the crusades – wars in the cause of Christendom, and the Venetian victory at the Battle of Lepanto had been commemorated in verse by King James.[5] The survival of the Venetian state (as in some degree the survival of the English one) depended upon the valour of its warriors, and some of its bravest were recruited from Africa.

The poet Keats did not need to have his ears opened to the Othello music. The celebrated line 'Keep up your bright swords, for the dew will rust them' expresses the magnanimity of Othello, and the brilliance and vulnerability of the violence he can easily command and from which he can impressively refrain. When Edmund Kean spoke it, says Keats: 'it was as if his voice had commanded where swords were as thick as reeds. From eternal risk he speaks as though his body were unassailable.'[6] Again, writing to his brother and sister, he catches the clash between two modes of moral judgement in precisely the relevant phrase of the play:

[5] See Emrys Jones, '"Othello", "Lepanto" and the Cyprus Wars', *Shakespeare Survey*, 21 (1968), pp. 47–53.
[6] Review for the *Champion*, 1818; see Sidney Colvin, *Life of John Keats* (1918), p. 243.

> Do you deny that there is anything in the Pride, Pomp and
> Circumstance of glorious war, that makes ambition virtue . . . in
> the eyes of admiring multitudes? Is it a paradox of my creating
> that 'one murder makes a villain, millions a hero'?[7]

Ambition is a vice, indeed a Vice, in one of the play's tributary theatre
traditions – the Morality; and a virtue in another – the heroic play. The
clause 'in the eyes of admiring multitudes' is pertinent too: Elizabethan
multitudes would admire the Pride, Pomp and Circumstance readily enough,
and grant that they make ambition virtue. Even in our time the audience's
heroic sense of community can still be stirred, if only nostalgically, by the
warrior-hero. But audiences past and present also know that 'one murder
makes a villain'. The disciplined hero who serves the state is corrupted to
murderer through the agency of that persistent and malignant heir of the
morality devil. Or, from another point of view, we witness the corruption
of African virtue by the vices of Christendom.

Published critical opinion for many years polarized between the views of
Coleridge and Bradley on the one hand, and those of T. S. Eliot and F.
R. Leavis on the other.[8] 'Motiveless malignity,' said Coleridge in awe, of
Iago, a being 'next to devil, only not quite devil'. For him, as for Bradley,
a noble and innocent man is destroyed by diabolical cunning. Othello didn't
stand a chance. He was 'too good' to believe his ensign capable of such
deceit. It says much for one set of the play's impressions and effects that
such a view of it cannot be wholly set aside. But on reflection, at a little
distance from the play, we may think it an odd nobility and innocence that
makes a man more ready to believe his bride an adulteress than her detractor
a liar, and we may not be appeased by E. E. Stoll's innumerable instances
from old tales of the 'slanderer believed'.[9]

F. R. Leavis, in his essay 'Diabolical Intellect and the Noble Hero'
retorted by dismissing Iago as 'not much more than a necessary piece of
dramatic mechanism'; 'The mind that undoes him is his own,' he says of
Othello, 'the essential traitor is within the gates.' Othello in his last speech,
is, in T. S. Eliot's ears *cheering himself up*. He is endeavouring to escape
reality, he has ceased to think about Desdemona, and is thinking about

---

[7] *The Letters of John Keats*, ed. Maurice Buxton Forman (1935 / 1947), p. 309.

[8] T. S. Eliot, 'Shakespeare and the Stoicism of Seneca', in *Selected Essays*, 3rd
edn (1951), pp. 126–40; F. R. Leavis, 'Diabolical Intellect and the Noble Hero',
in *The Common Pursuit* (1952), pp. 136–59; A. C. Bradley, *Shakespearean Tragedy*
(1904), pp. 207–42; S. T. Coleridge, *Shakespeare Criticism*, ed. T. M. Raysor
(1960).

[9] E. E. Stoll, '"Othello": An Historical and Comparative Study', in *Studies in
Language and Literature, No. 2*, (University of Minnesota, 1915); and *Art and
Artifice in Shakespeare* (1933).

himself . . . He takes in the spectator, but the human motive primarily is
to take in himself.' Leavis is less reductive. He too finds 'self-dramatization'
at the end, 'as un-self-comprehending as before', but of the recollection of
Aleppo and the self-stabbing, he says, 'with that double force, a *coup de
théâtre*, it is a peculiarly right ending to the tragedy of Othello . . . The
final blow is as real as the blow it re-enacts, and the histrionic intent
symbolically affirms the reality: Othello dies belonging to the world of
action in which his true part lay.'

In finding 'the poetic skill at one with the dramatic' Leavis speaks of
Shakespeare's art, not Othello's; 'if characters in poetic drama speak poetry
we ought to be able to notice the fact without concluding that they are
poets.' In this play, however, histrionic and rhetorical skills do appear to
be attributed in very different modes, to Iago and Othello. The audience
is engaged more closely than it might otherwise have been in the play's
conflict, through the changing relationships between it and the players. The
conflict is between the heroic and magnanimous view of life, whose
spokesman is Othello, in high eloquent speech, casting his spell over stage
and theatre; and the anti-heroic, whose spokesman is Iago, harsh and
colloquial, front-stage, holding the audience in a cynical acceptance of what
human nature boils down to. It is more than usually difficult for us to
disengage our theatrical from our moral responses. While Othello and Iago
are both performers, however, their characters are not co-extensive with
their performances. There are covert effects of language that express the
characters without sustaining their images of themselves. These effects will
not be the same for all witnesses on all occasions, but they can still be
perceived as latencies of the text.

In his second speech of the play Iago tells us that he has been passed
over for promotion in favour of the 'great arithmetician' Cassio. This way
of putting it gives a representative status to Iago's manifest and explicit
jealousy; in the armies of the Renaissance officers had to be capable of
calculating trajectories for the new artillery, and the prospects of old-style
soldiers were often frustrated. The professional jealousy, however, is charged
with more intimate resentments that turn on the relationship between Cassio
and Othello. A Shakespearian purpose is served in the allusion to 'horribly
stuffed' language – it stirs wary expectations about the bombast to come;
but it also gives Iago a verbal bone to worry and bite on, and is the first
of many signals of a destructive sexual nausea blighting his affections, and
correlating with that with which he poisons Othello. His intrigue, ostensibly
on Roderigo's behalf, serves his own perverted and perverting design.
Virulent feelings infect his roles as the frankly honest anatomist of society
who has taken the measure of the moral squalor of Venice, and as the
accomplished hypocrite, capable of flourishing the 'flag and sign of love, /
Which is indeed but sign':

> O, sir, content you.
> I follow him to serve my turn upon him:
> We cannot all be masters, nor all masters
> Cannot be truly followed. You shall mark
> Many a duteous and knee-crooking knave
> That, doting on his own obsequious bondage,
> Wears out his time, much like his master's ass,
> For nought but provender.
>
> (I. i. 41–8)

While the first scene is staged in Iago's theatre, the second is dominantly, and the third pre-eminently, in Othello's: 'My services that I have done the signiory / Shall out-tongue his complaints.' In the streets he refrains from the bright sword and before his sagittary audience with comparable magnanimity he refrains from words until the Duke offers him his cue. When he does speak, the 'round unvarnished tale' of his 'whole course of love' reaches us, as it does the senators, as an exalted and modulated performance. It is not the hypocrite's performance, but if we are bent on giving a reductive account of it we might recall his own sideways glance at 'boasting' (I, ii. 20), together with Iago's jeers at the Moor's 'bombast circumstance' or (still to come) at his 'bragging' and 'fantastical lies'. If we choose to share Iago's response to Othello's rhetoric we are likely to yield to much in T. S. Eliot's view of the play. Othello, he says of the last scene, 'has ceased to think about Desdemona, and is thinking about himself . . . Humility is the most difficult of all virtues to achieve . . . nothing dies harder than the desire to think well of oneself.' But the heroic tradition is not concerned with humility in that Christian sense which is so important in the morality plays. Its *virtue* is close to the root sense of the word – manliness – and looks back to classical Rome when, as Cominius puts it in *Coriolanus*, 'Valour was the chiefest virtue / And most dignified the haver.' This kind of virtue thrives on a confidence remote from diffidence and humility.

Eliot says that Othello at his death had quite forgotten Desdemona; but what is Desdemona apart from her love for Othello? And what is that love if it is not a passionate acquiescence in Othello's heroic image of himself? Our enjoyment of the play, and our recognition of the Othello range of virtues, cultivated in the service of the state, depends upon our sharing a Desdemona-like simplicity of response to the spell of the nostalgic rhetoric of Mediterranean ware:

> Her father lov'd me, oft invited me;
> Still question'd me the story of my life
> From year to year – the battles, sieges, fortunes,
> That I have pass'd.

I ran it through, even from my boyish days
To th' very moment that he bade me tell it;
Wherein I spoke of most disastrous chances:
Of moving accidents by flood and field,
Of hair-breadth scapes i' th' imminent deadly breach,
Of being taken by the insolent foe
And sold to slavery, of my redemption thence
And portance in my travels' history;
Wherein of antres vast and deserts idle,
Rough quarries, rocks, and hills whose heads touch heaven,
It was my hint to speak – such was my process –
And of the Cannibals that each other eat.
The Anthropophagi, and men whose heads
Do grow beneath their shoulders. These things to hear
Would Desdemona seriously incline.

(I. iii. 128–46)

Eternal and continuing risk in the extravagant landscape of North Africa, extremities of ordeal and fortitude, cast their enchantment upon the listening girl, distracted by 'house affairs', but returning to 'the dilated pilgrimage'. 'She loved me for the dangers I had passed / And I loved her that she did pity them.' There is a boy and a slave to be pitied and a liberated hero to be admired. Harmonies of tenderness and triumph resound in a characteristically echoing verbal space, to the satisfaction, it must be said, not of Desdemona only, but of Brabantio, the senators and, supremely, of Othello himself. Othello tells his story in a way that moves him ("twas wondrous pitiful') and satisfies his imagination. Tamburlaine's cry, 'What is beauty saith my suffering then?' is a comparably transcendent, if more abstract, reaching after perfection. Put more ominously, the story creates an ideal and unreal image of the self. Othello does know about the power of words – a soldier's words, heard in a domestic setting, to stir a girl's affections, and he knows how to hold an audience. His rhetoric is not false, and is endowed with generous, simple meanings by Desdemona's response. But when he says 'rude am I in my speech, / And little bless'd with the soft phrase of peace', he speaks with the assured voice of one who plays a leading role in the theatre of war.

'I would not my unhoused free condition / Put into circumscription and confine / For the sea's worth'; but in the course of the play Othello's condition is circumscribed and confined. From the golden world of his creation, Iago delivers a brazen – exactly reversing what Sidney took to be the function of a poet. The world to which Iago reduces the spaciousness of Othello's is ugly enough but only too familiar to the experience of the audience. At the end of the third scene we revert to Iago's world and theatre. He is given his first soliloquy, as Shakespeare from the vicious hypocrite breeds the Vice, Hypocrisy.

Direct deployment of the Morality convention is used to express Iago's growing confidence in his histrionic and manipulative powers. But while it is apt at this point to recall the Vice analogues, the Devil and *Satan Tentatus* from early plays,[10] they do not displace the disaffected Ensign whose jealousy is at once intensified, betrayed and masked by the play-acting and play-making abilities he chooses to cultivate. The play that is taking shape, Iago's within Shakespeare's, is a Morality. Iago's version, allegorically speaking and by his own account, will be the Devil's. But humanly speaking, in Shakespeare's version, it appears as the destructive operation of frustrated affections and a damaged ego. Allegorically, the Devil must recognize the virtues and understand the weaknesses of his victims; humanly, jealousy covertly admires its objects and is sensitive to their propensities: 'Cassio's a proper man . . . The Moor is of a free and open nature / That thinks men honest that but seem to be so.' Iago enlists the allegory into his own service, as Shakespeare's Prince Hal had done before him, in his soliloquy at the end of *1 Henry IV*, i, ii., but the Prince plays for redemption, his Moorship's ancient, for damnation: 'It is engender'd. Hell and night / Must bring this monstrous birth to the world's light.' In the grim, intimate comedy of *Othello* Iago's play-making wit is meant to confound a life of the affections in which he is denied a place. It has no large political purpose. But it does have the political consequence of reducing the hero of the society to his meanest possible condition – cutting him down to size. The heroic virtues of the valiant and aspiring Othello prove vulnerable to the corrosive techniques of Iago. A more ordinary man would have been less destructible. 'The mind that undoes him is his own.' as F. R. Leavis puts it; he is destroyed both from within and from without. From within, because Shakespeare discovers the instabilities of the heroic imagination; from without, by the operation of Iago's plot.

Cinthio, like Shakespeare, moves the action from Venice to Cyprus; but by inventing the storm that separates the lovers at sea Shakespeare gives occasion for a poignant reunion:

> Oh my soul's joy!
> If after every tempest come such calms,
> May the winds blow till they have waken'd death,
> And let the labouring bark climb hills of seas
> Olympus high, and duck again as low

---

[10] See Leah Scragg, 'Iago – Vice or Devil?', *Shakespeare Survey*, 21 (1968), pp. 53–67.

As hell's from heaven. If it were now to die,
'Twere now to be most happy.

(<small>II</small>, i. 184–90)

From this glimpse of heroic voyaging, we take again the sense of exalted calm, of having won through. But the violent motions of the sea, like the risks to which the soldier is exposed among 'hills whose heads touch heaven', make an ominous climax to the lovers' embrace, witnessed by Iago on the quayside.

Othello has arrived again in the theatre of the devil and the double-dealer (it is as if Tamburlaine comes to the Malta of Marlowe's Barabas and Ithamore). Iago is allowed a still-growing histrionic zest, fully exhibited in the notorious 'motive-hunting' soliloquy at the end of the scene. The audience is offered a choice of possible motives. Knowing, like Iago, just how rotten people are, being 'honest', as he is, about the nasty mess we all live in, we are invited to join the theatrical game of finding an apt 'motive' for the behaviour of the characters in his play. The manner is remote from that used to Roderigo in the first scene. 'That Cassio loves her, I do well believe it' is not readily spoken with sincere intensity, but to suggest 'that's plausible enough'. And the same play-making, musing tone can be heard in 'That she loves him, 'tis apt and of great credit.' Then he wryly faces the awkward facts that might put a stop to his plot:

The Moor, howbeit that I endure him not,
Is of a constant, loving, noble nature;
And I dare think he'll prove to Desdemona
A most dear husband.

(<small>II</small>. i. 288–91)

But there are other possibilities, and his histrionic wit toys with them:

Now I do love her too;
Not out of absolute lust, though peradventure
I stand accountant for as great a sin.

(<small>II</small>. i. 291–3)

There is that possibility, archly and lightly dismissed, but he has thought of something better, a motive to get him going, and to allow him to rehearse with full ferocity the role of avenger:

But partly led to diet my revenge
For that I do suspect the lusty Moore
Hath leap'd into my seat. The thought whereof
Doth like a poisonous mineral gnaw my inwards;

And nothing can nor shall content my soul
Till I am even with him, wife for wife.

(II. i. 294–8)

The play is so designed that we cannot take seriously the rumour (I, iii. 370) that the 'constant, loving noble' Moor has done Iago's 'office' between his sheets, nor that Emilia is for Iago an object of jealous concern, as Cassio and Othello manifestly are. The choice of motives here becomes the choice of the actor, Hypocrisy, as Iago seeks to put himself more fully in control both of his own spontaneous drives and of his plot. There is no character equivalent for the soliloquy outside the theatre (no ensign, for example, trying out his roles in front of a mirror) but, again like Hal's soliloquy, it expresses a deliberately disengaged manipulative disposition; where Hal works with the Morality's large design, however, Iago works with the destructive one that is conventionally frustrated within it. At the end of the soliloquy he breaks off with:

'Tis here but yet confus'd,
Knavery's plain face is never seen till us'd.

(II. i. 311–12)

A couple of minutes later, his plot is clarifying and a soliloquy explains its next phase to the audience. The requisite dramatic sensations are readily awakened on the platform by allowing Iago, moving between the audience and Othello, to appear at once as a spectator to the play and its director. He proposes to 'put our Cassio in some action / That may offend the isle' and breaks off again – 'but here they come.' (II, iii. 60–1) Having confided in the audience as intriguer and devil, he now rejoins the action in his role of 'Dissimulation' – exactly the Morality pattern.

But the pattern intrudes upon and mutilates the martial and bridal triumph invoked by Cassio on the quayside and required by the romantically heroic side of the play:

Great Jove Othello guard
And swell his sail with thine own powerful breath,
That he may bless this bay with his tall ship,
Make love's quick pants in Desdemona's arms,
Give renewed fire to our extincted spirits,
And bring all Cyprus comfort.

(II. i. 77–82)

It is a rendering of Othello's proud, ecstatic ascendancy that stays in the imagination but remains unrealized in the garrison conditions we meet in the scenes that follow. The soldierly chat between Cassio and Iago tells us that Othello 'has not yet made wanton the night', reminding us that in the dominant time-scheme of the play 'the black ram' is not allowed to 'tup'

Brabantio's 'white ewe'. The 'noble swelling spirits, / That hold their honours in a wary distance' (II, iii. 55) simultaneously desecrate the bridal consummation and fright 'the isle from her propriety'. Othello is discomposed: 'passion, having my best judgement collied, / Assays to lead the way' (II, iii. 206–7).

The openly manifest cause of Othello's fall is in the plot, dominated by Iago's role-playing through the patiently fabricated false selves that win the respect and confidence of Cassio, Othello and Desdemona. The anti-heroic convictions of the audience are as deeply engaged as their heroic convictions. The process is focused in the two contrary statements on 'reputation': the anti-heroic to Cassio, 'Reputation is an idle and most false imposition, oft got without merit, and lost without deserving'; and the heroic to Othello, 'Good name in man and woman, dear my lord, / Is the immediate jewel of their souls.' Both are traded as free and honest advice 'probal to thinking'. From Othello, however, it stirs the same wariness about honour that has just precipitated the brawl among other 'noble swelling spirits' on the island and exposed Desdemona to the hazards of the 'soldier's life': 'By heaven, I'll know thy thoughts!' He has begun to slip into the way of thinking of the 'general camp', to 'duck again as low as hell's from heaven', from:

> Excellent wretch! Perdition catch my soul
> But I do love thee; and when I love thee not
> Chaos is come again.
>
> (III. iii. 90–1)

to 'Damn her, lewd minx! O damn her, damn her!' (III, iii. 476).

Iago the Vice is in control of Othello's grosser reactions ('Villain, be sure thou prove my love a whore') but the self-destructive potency of Othello's marine imagination is outside his scope and belongs to the heroic dimension of the play. His sense of reality and the nature of his affections are conditioned by his heroic commitment to battle, and by the moods and motions of water:

> Like to the Pontic Sea,
> Whose icy current and compulsive course
> Ne'er feels retiring ebb, but keeps due on
> To the Propontic and the Hellespont;
> Even so my bloody thoughts, with violent pace,
> Shall ne'er look back, ne'er ebb to humble love,
> Till that a capable and wide revenge
> Swallow them up.
>
> (III. iii. 453–460)

Here, figuratively speaking, is the inner plot of the play in a sentence which acts out the movement of the tragedy. That movement is no longer wave-like, but a tirelessly accelerating current. It is a remarkable instance of visionary geography. For, borrowing from Pliny,[11] Shakespeare has found in the natural world exactly the marine motions which best express Othello's perverted passions. The cold water of the Black Sea moves into the sea of Marmara, the Propontic, the narrow strait of the Hellespont and the Mediterranean. Othello's gathering feeling and revulsion is inseparable from a metaphor which not only expresses the current of his passions but creates it. A simple comparison introduces the first four lines, and 'Even so' the second four. But words more appropriate to Othello's 'bloody thoughts' are insinuated into the sea-half of the simile: the current 'ne'er feels retiring ebb'. The effect is to give 'icy' and 'compulsive' an emotional force too, attaching them in advance to 'bloody thoughts'. Similarly the four lines about 'thoughts' carry the sea-words still: 'with violent pace', 'ne'er ebb to humble love', until we reach not the 'capable and wide' sea, which we would expect ('capable' meaning 'capacious'), but 'capable and wide revenge'. Thus Othello's commitment to the sea has, through his feverish imagination, committed him more intensely to revenge. 'Humble love' is one of the states of magnanimity to which he must bid farewell in the temptation scene; the other is the pride, pomp and circumstance of glorious war. He loses command – of his language, of his spontaneous drives, and of the garrison.

To Iago, 'a trifle light as air', an instrument for gulling Othello with a trick from the old comedy: 'thus credulous fools are caught', but Othello's credulity is of a piece with the the delight in miraculous accomplishment that embellishes his story and finds magic in the web of the handkerchief:

A sibyl that had numb'red in the world
The sun to course two hundred compasses
In her prophetic fury sew'd the work.
(III. iv. 70–2)

The truth about Othello and the language in which it is expressed ('antres vast and deserts idle') is itself fabulous, and moves at the periphery of what Iago calls 'fantastical lies' (including perhaps – how can we tell – 'men whose heads do grow beneath their shoulders'). It is therefore fragile and unstable.

The Marlovian rhetoric that aspires to create a divine and eternalized Desdemona is exposed to shock-waves. Her own dedication of herself ('to

---

[11]'And the sea Pontus evermore floweth and runneth out into Propontius, but the sea never retireth back again within Pontus' (II. 97); 'Out of Pontus the sea always floweth, and never ebbeth again' (IV. 13), Pliny, *Naturalis Historia*, tr. Philemon Holland, 1601. [*Othello*, ed. Norman Sanders ad loc.] G. B. Shaw quotes the speech to exemplify the splendour of *Othello's* 'word-music'. 'The words do not convey ideas: they are streaming ensigns and tossing branches to make the passion visible.' *Shaw on Shakespeare*, ed. E. Wilson, New York 1961, London 1969.

his honours and his valiant parts / Did I my soul and fortunes consecrate')
is by the turn of events represented as a flaw in 'one entire and perfect
chrysolite', but the flaw is not in her, but in the honours and the parts.
Cassio marvels at her transcendence of the stresses to which Othello is
exposed by (in Iago's phrase) 'the elements that clip us round about':

> Tempests themselves, high seas, and howling winds,
> The gutter'd rocks and congregated sands,
> Traitors ensteep'd to clog the guiltless keel,
> As having sense of beauty do omit
> Their mortal natures, letting go safely by
> The divine Desdemona.
>
> (II. i. 68–73)

But he is expressing in another proleptic figure the course of a mortal
nature betrayed to Iago's treachery.

Even those of us who lack the qualifications to make clinical judgements
can recognize in certain Shakespearian plays the fictional equivalent of the
case-history. Thus *Much Ado*, *The Merry Wives of Windsor*, *The Winter's
Tale* and *Othello* can be seen as essays in what Freud called paranoiac
jealousy.[12] A narrative psychoanalysis of the plays would attend to the
complicated emotional bondings detectable between man and man, and man
and woman. A theatrical analysis, however, must be concerned with the
objectifying insight of the Devil/Vice and his real-life analogues, and with
the correlated response of his victims. With the preternatural skill of the
jealous man Iago homes in on the visible and covert vulnerabilities of
Othello, Roderigo, Cassio and Desdemona. Like the Egyptian charmer who
endowed the handkerchief with such significance, he can 'almost read the
thoughts of people'. Othello's complex consciousness is both that of the
common soldier ready to interpret the token passed from an officer to his
trull, and that of the rare warrior. His heroic endeavour is intimately
committed to an ideal of immaculate chastity that, fearing its contamination,
he tries to hold outside the diurnal and menstrual routines of time:

> Thinks't thou I'ld make a life of jealousy?
> To follow still the changes of the wat'ry moon
> With fresh suspicions? No! to be once in doubt
> Is once to be resolv'd.
>
> (III. iii. 177–80)

Like Hotspur he would not live 'upon a dial's point' (*1 Henry IV*. v. ii.

---

[12] See 'Some Neurotic Mechanisms in Jealousy, Paranoia, and Homosexuality', in
Sigmund Freud, *Collected Papers*, International Psycho-analytical Library (5 vols.
1924–57), II, paper 19.

83) nor be 'the fixed figure for the time of scorn / To point his slow unmoving finger at' (IV, ii. 54–5).

His unfitness for the sublunar world prompts him to interpret Iago's 'tricks of custom' (the hypocrisies of everyday life) as 'close dilations' of the heart (III, iii. 123). He cultivates with his Ensign (who can be expected to know what's going on in the camp) a barrack-room intimacy that usurps Desdemona's dedicated devotion to his self-image, and he reads her eagerness to assist Cassio as evidence of guilt. Leontes' 'is whispering nothing?', after watching Hermione's innocently hospitable courtship of Polixenes, is of a piece with Claudio's much ado about nothing (punning upon 'noting'), and with Othello's demand for 'ocular proof' before he too is 'noting' (Iago calls it 'scatt'ring and unsure observance') and turning lies into objective 'truth'. Ford in *The Merry Wives* plays Iago to his own Othello but is allowed only the objective evidence of Falstaff's designs upon innocence. He would bring down on Windsor the 'curse of marriage' of Othello's fantasy, 'That we can call these delicate creatures ours / And not their appetites.' Othello's fantasies, however, cannot be called to account by the laws of comedy. Claudio's touchiness about his honour is discovered for what it is by those who are free of vanity, or whose vanities have been collapsed into love. Ford is not allowed in the eyes of the audience the ascendancy he believes himself to enjoy as an actor and a plot-maker. Nor can he flaunt that heroic pride that leads Othello to see his condition as 'the plague of great ones'. Leontes, who is a 'great one', does grievous damage to himself and to others in a world that owes its powers of recovery to a process which mirrors the regenerative passage of the seasons; it is not a process available within the expressive conventions of *Othello*.

Caught in the handkerchief trap, Othello falls into a fit, attended by Iago's Jonsonian comic moral – 'thus credulous fools are caught.' The Othello music is silenced. The 'capable and wide sea' becomes:

> The fountain from which my current runs
> Or else dries up, to be discarded thence!
> Or keep it as a cistern for foul toads
> To knot and gender in.

(IV. ii. 59–62)

'Drink the water of thy cistern,' says the Geneva version of Proverbs 5: 15–18, 'Let thy fountain be blessed, and rejoice with the wife of thy youth', and in the margin, 'God blesseth marriage and curseth whoredom.' The catastrophic ethical switch from blessing to curse is expressed in an image of contaminated breeding, the creative flow (in Lawrentian terms) confounded with the excremental flow, the old clarities fouled and mudded.

Othello, in a 'horrible fantasy', playing a kind of Iago to himself, devises an episode of reductive theatre with Emilia in the role of brothel-keeper.

'Something sure of state hath puddled his clear spirit,' says Desdemona, in an exchange between the women which tries to make sense of Othello's behaviour and, as it were, confine it within the boundaries of domestic comedy. In Emilia's experience the green-eyed monster is 'begot upon itself': 'They are not ever jealous for the cause, / But jealous for they're jealous'; but she also takes a larger view of marital frailty – 'it is their husbands' faults if wives do fail.' Desdemona's gossip ('Lodovico is a proper man . . . He speaks well') keeps her in touch with the manners of Venetian ladies and recalls her dealings with Cassio, but as her imagination tries to take hold of events she, like Ophelia, is haunted by fragments of song whose sharper insights ('If I court moe women, you'll couch with moe men') are subdued by pathos ('The fresh streams ran by her and murmured her moans'). The equilibrium recovered by Emilia's good sense and Desdemona's simplicity cannot, however, recall the play to the temper of *The Merry Wives*. Emilia's more desperate perception ('The Moor's abused by some most villainous knave') stays active, and Desdemona's passivity ('even his stubbornness, his checks, his frowns – / Prithee, unpin me – have grace and favour in them') is ominously unstable.

Desdemona sets the final scene ('Lay on my bed my wedding sheets') over which Othello presides in the style of the hero who had once excited her imagination: 'It is the cause, it is the cause, my soul / Let me not name it to you, you chaste stars.' The word sounds again in the play's echoing space, 'It is the cause', signifying both his wife's imagined offence, and the cause to which the soldier dedicates his violence. Transposed from Othello's theatre of war to Desdemona's bridal bed, his rhetoric is tuned to respond to her exquisitely vulnerable living presence:

> When I have pluck'd thy rose,
> I cannot give it vital growth again,
> It needs must wither. I'll smell thee on the tree.
> [*kisses her*]
> O balmy breath, that dost almost persuade
> Justice to break her sword!
>
> (v. ii. 13–17)

The lover's kisses aspire in the sacrificer's fantasy to a climactic death, exempting love from time and change:

> Once more, once more.
> Be thus when thou art dead, and I will kill thee
> And love thee after. Once more, and that's the last.
> So sweet was ne'er so fatal.
>
> (v. ii. 17–19)

Yet his Olympian vision and dialect find occasion, not for the compassion they seem to court, but for an awed self-pity:

> I must weep,
> But they are cruel tears. This sorrow's heavenly,
> It strikes where it doth love.

He is, to anticipate a later phrase, seeking to keep murder in tune. Like Tamburlaine he would have 'some holy trance' convey his thoughts 'up to the palace of th' empyreal heaven'. The trance, however, owes nothing to 'the drowsy syrups of the world'; it is verbally induced. John Dee, translating Vitruvius, speaks of the 'sounding vessels' of the ancient theatres, used to amplify the 'convenient voice' of the players and bring it 'more clear and pleasant, to the ears of the lookers on'. The clarified harmonies of voice expressed the relationship between the aspiring soul and 'the most *mervaillous* frame of the whole world.'[13] Murderous discords wait upon sacrificial concords, but Shakespeare under the constraints of his own art cannot supply them. In the neighbouring theatrical territory of Illyria 'Caesario' would 'most jocund, apt and willingly' die to appease 'a savage jealousy tht sometimes savours nobly' (*Twelfth Night*, v, i. 119–20), but that was under a different dispensation, in a play written for a topsy-turvy occasion. Desdemona does not submit without protest to her sacrificial role, but Othello, under the spell of his own exalted delusions, shows immense powers of resistance to the everyday testimony and evidence with which she, like Emilia, tries to confront him.

Othello's strictly lunatic imagination ('Dian's visage', 'the very error of the moon', 'pale as her smock') looks for a cosmic catastrophe: 'Methinks it should be now a huge eclipse of sun and moon.' The words invite an actor's voice for the sounding vessels. But Emilia (as it were, trading his helmet for a housewife's skillet) will only concede him a domestic disaster ('O gull! O dolt! as ignorant as dirt'). When Desdemona asserts her innocence she tries, in response to Emilia's importunate practical question, to redeem Othello's image of himself by once again consecrating herself to it: 'A guiltless death I die . . . O, who hath done this deed? . . . Nobody; I myself. Farewell! / Commend me to my kind lord!' But the effect, as he persists in damning the lewd minx, is to pitch Othello again 'as low as hell's from heaven'.

After the confused denouements of Iago's miscarried plot and Othello's, the problem for both the maker of the play and its hero is to retrieve the tragedy from the 'slime that sticks on filthy deeds'. Words and swords must be freshly deployed, to round up his story:

[13] Frances A. Yates, *Theatre of the World* (1969), pp. 25–6, 14.

Be not afraid, though you do see me weapon'd:
Here is my journey's end, here is my butt
And very sea-mark of my utmost sail.
(v. ii. 266–8)

The dilated pilgrimage and tempestuous voyage reach a point of arrival. Shakespeare in *Coriolanus* will use an amplified form of the image to express constancy in the turbulence of battle:

The god of soldiers,

With the consent of supreme Jove, inform
Thy thoughts with nobleness, that thou mays't prove
To shame unvulnerable, and stick i' th' wars
Like a great sea-mark, standing every flaw,
And saving those that eye thee!
(v. iii. 70–4)

Othello's 'sea-mark', not without resonances of thoughts informed with nobleness, glances too at the sword (of 'the ice brook's temper'), towards Desdemona's body ('Cold, cold, my girl') and at his own death.

His last words take the form of a speech to the parting Venetians ('Soft you, a word or two before you go') and offer them for the re-telling, a version of his tale that tranquilizes his own imagination, and will satisfy that of theatre audiences in so far as it reflects their experience of the play:

Then must you speak

Of one who lov'd not wisely but too well;
Of one not easily jealous but, being wrought,
Perplex'd in the extreme.
(v. ii. 343–6)

That he loved 'not wisely' all must agree; that he loved 'too well' cannot be said in terms that the dead and dying women and our sympathies for them would allow. But the rhetorical grammar is potently deceptive, and allows little scope for moral reflection. Again, its claims cannot be separated from the expressive resonances of language. Paraphrased into Emilia's practical and domestic talk they would collapse. As it is, his assurance that he was 'not easily jealous' covertly enlists the warrior's constancy in place of the lover's. 'Can he be angry?' Iago asks, when Othello's jealous wrath is reported to him.

I have seen the cannon
When it hath blown his ranks into the air,
And like the devil from his very arm
Puff'd his own brother – and is he angry?
(III. iv. 134–7)

Othello is not easily discomposed and is in that sense 'to shame unvulnerable'.

Because that kind of constancy first awakened Desdemona's love and pity, and because there is no doubting his being 'wrought' and 'Perplex'd in the extreme', we may submit, transiently at least, to the spell of 'not easily jealous'.

Othello's Venetian and Jacobean English audiences, however, are offered not last words only, but a final performance, in the theatre of his memory.

> Set you down this;
> And say besides, that in Aleppo once,
> Where a malignant and a turban'd Turk
> Beat a Venetian and traduc'd the state,
> I took him by the throat the circumcised dog,
> And smote him – thus.
>
> (v. ii. 351–6)

Othello's story is of a life to be remembered both for its devotion to the cause of love and for service to the state. As he recalls it he is courting Desdemona once more and, like Coriolanus, he is looking for a place in the annals. Desdemona, unlike Othello, is not a culpable victim, and we are not required to read her 'Nobody, I myself' as an admission of responsibility. Her 'downright violence and storm of fortune', however, is at one with her awed, marvelling dismay at the soldier's exotically cruel history (including, no doubt, such fortuitously grotesque touches as the choking of a circumcized dog). The sword-stroke (the *'coup de théâtre'*), is for the annals; the dying kiss is the lover's atonement:

> I kiss'd thee ere I kill'd thee. No way but this
> Killing my self, to die upon a kiss.

'No way but this.' Exactly so. The virtue recovered at the end of the play can only be that which is affirmed in its most resounding language, here to do with exotic, violent, soldierly love. The enemy to the state and to love (not a battle enemy, but something more like a street brawler) is now become himself, the capable and wide revenge is self-slaughter. Within the code of honour by which he tried to live, what purifies or redeems the soldier does the same service for the dead lover.

Iago must survive the play. All that the Morality Devil stands for is lasting, and aptly therefore represented as immortal. But although derived from the devil, Iago is not a devil. He is the embittered ensign and the common soldier still. Shakespeare's job was not to find new ways of presenting the devil but rather to find new ways of representing what the devil represents. 'To you, Lord Governer,' says Lodovico, 'Remains the censure of this hellish villain.' The Morality allegory is there, but Lodovico is using a soldier's language. He does not receive Othello's suicide as an act of sacrificial purification or honourable atonement. He is a man tidying up the stupid, ugly mess (the bed that 'poisons sight') as best he can. But it is not merely a mess. Lodovico has not seen the play that we have seen, in which heroic theatre, Morality and comedy have not destroyed each other, but have created a new perspective of human values. Othello is in Emilia's eyes and Iago's 'a great black fool'. But in the heroic traditions of theatre:

> every warrior that is rapt with love
> Of fame, of valour, and of victory
> Must needs have beauty beat on his conceits.
> (*1 Tamburlaine*)

His desires, like Tamburlaine's 'lift upwards and divine'. He does in two senses deserve to die. Because he has committed a crime he deserves death as a punishment; and because he vindicates himself in the only way his great virtues as soldier and lover allow, he deserves death as a reward, as a point of arrival.

12 'Upon Such Sacrifices' – *King Lear*

Upon such sacrifices, my Cordelia,
The Gods themselves throw incense.

The words, and those coming before and after, are familiar. It is my hope
to make them a little less so, by setting them in a variety of perspectives,
some spacious and some narrow, and by casting upon them a changing,
polarizing light. We have reached an imaginative crux of the play, and a
critical moment in the story of Lear's senility. Consciousness – Lear's and
ours – is, to adapt Regan's phrase, on the very verge of its confine. Where
we might have expected a cry of pain, the language, out of defeat and
desolation, seems to be generating immense heroic solace, and the scene
grows rich in unparaphrasable discoveries that will not stay for rational
questioning. It is one of the great movements of European tragedy and
these words, spoken in a kind of madness, are its climax. 'Have I caught
thee?' we ourselves ask of the play, wondering what haunts its elusive
speculations, what we are meant wholly to see and what only to glimpse.
What does Lear mean by 'such sacrifices' and is Shakespeare's meaning co-
extensive with the King's? We need to persist with such questions because
the processes of tragic sacrifice are not primordial merely; in raw, masked,
or sublimated form they are still active and still need to be understood. 'It
is certainly victims that move humanity forward,' said Trotsky, and his
own tragic history was to vindicate him.

   Bradley's eloquent account has persuaded many to see in 'such sacrifices',
'that serene renunciation of the world, with its power and glory and
resentments and revenges' expressed in the speech before: 'Come let's away
to prison.'[1] Others have supposed Lear to respond to Cordelia's 'For thee,

---

[1] A. C. Bradley, *Shakespearean Tragedy* (1904), p. 289.

oppressed king, am I cast down.' In a choice of ways we could abbreviate the dialogue and win in clarity what is lost in evocative obscurity, but we would discover that the disjunctions and lapses are essential to the expressive effect. Shakespeare is compelling us to undergo the central tragic experience of the play through the language of a demented consciousness.

Looking upon these prison speeches with the cool and alien eyes of some critics, we see the 'radical incoherence',[2] the desolation and the impotence; but to an eager eye the signs are brighter and open upon 'a new world'[3] and 'a most delicate music'.[4] Any attempt to anatomize such fragile mysteries must move in the difficult territory which joins and divides the literary critic and the psychoanalyst, and I wish in particular to keep in mind Lacan's claim that 'the unconscious is structured like a language.' Lacan, it is said, 'supposes an unconscious discourse interfering with the conscious discourse, and responsible for the distortions and gaps in that discourse.[5] He supposes much else; but since Shakespeare was ignorant of Lacan, I prefer to recall from A Midsummer Night's Dream that 'The lunatic, the lover and the poet, / Are of imagination all compact.' Antony and Cleopatra proclaims the compact of the lover's imagination and the poet's; in King Lear it is the lunatic's and the poet's. The vulnerabilities and incapacities of the distressed and senile mind are enlisted into the service of the poet's art. Theseus' writ runs even on the battlefield of Lear's Dover: 'The best in this kind are but shadows; and the worst are no worse if imagination amend them.' Lear's shadowing thought, at once expressing the mind's decay and the poet's insight, puts our amending imaginations to a severe test.

The scene, the play's last in the Folio text, opens with the voice of repression:

Some officers take them away: good guard,
Until their greater pleasure first be known
That are to censure them.

Edmund speaks as a minor officer of state, disposing of delinquents to be dealt with later by the top brass on a day of judgement – a 'doomsday' we might be surprised into saying, noticing his appropriation of the language of sovereignty to debased purpose.[6] Cordelia's response may be taken as a

---

[2] H. A. Mason, Cambridge Quarterly, 2 (1967), p. 222.
[3] B. McElroy, Shakespeare's Mature Tragedies (Princeton, 1973), p. 200.
[4] Francis Fergusson, Shakespeare, The Pattern in his Carpet (1970), p. 235.
[5] Jacques Lacan, The Language of the Self, tr. Anthony Wilden (1968), p. 262.
[6] For the importance of doomsday in the play, see Mary Lascelles, '"King Lear" and Doomsday', Shakespeare Survey, 26 (1973), pp. 69–79.

sententious vaunt,[7] its rhymes carrying it a little above the flux of events:

> We are not the first
> Who, with best meaning, have incurr'd the worst.
> For thee, oppressed King, I am cast down;
> Myself could else outfrown false Fortune's frown.

In a less active and complex dramatic context the stoic solace would seem conventional enough, and indeed the last line is remembered from Neville's translation of Seneca's *Oedipus*. Seen under the polarizing light of the play's imaginative evocations, these plain words will disclose hidden structures, but they do not immediately do so. In the passing moment it is enough that they declare Cordelia's invincible independence of spirit and lead easily into a sharp and live challenge to Edmund's insolence: 'Shall we not see these daughters and these sisters?'

Lear himself neither protests nor acquiesces. By an effort of language he dismisses and apparently transcends all possibilities of resistance:

> No, no, no, no! Come, let's away to prison;
> We two alone will sing like birds i' th' cage:
> When thou dost ask me blessing, I'll kneel down,
> And ask of thee forgiveness: so we'll live,
> And pray, and sing, and tell old tales, and laugh
> At gilded butterflies, and hear poor rogues
> Talk of court news; and we'll talk with them too,
> Who loses and who wins; who's in, who's out;
> And take upon's the mystery of things,
> As if we were God's spies: and we'll wear out,
> In a wall'd prison, packs and sects of great ones
> That ebb and flow by th' moon.
>
> (v. iii. 8–19)

A reductive paraphrase makes clear the embarrassing inadequacies of Lear's reaction to a human and political situation that is too much for him: 'Let us go to prison where we can bless and forgive one another, tell stories, pray a little, laugh at the butterflies, and chat with the other prisoners about the ups and downs of the world.' The space between the poet's accomplishment and its reductive travesty is more readily recognized than explained and charted.

Among the many testaments and metaphors that find a kind of freedom in the prisoner's condition I know of none which makes a greater claim on

---

[7] I suppose Cordelia to mean that she has suffered defeat and been cast down by Fortune in Lear's service. But it is possible to confine her meaning to, 'Only for your sake did I consent to be taken prisoner – otherwise I could have got away.' The figurative sense, making Cordelia downcast or dejected on Lear's account but defiant on her own, is improbable at this date (see *OED* s.v. *downcast*).

our attention than this. The language of the play and of the king seem liberated at the moment of incarceration, with Lear's simplicities keeping pace with Shakespeare's complexities. Thus, 'Come, let's away' is an easy, light invitation to freedom that itself is released from impalement between the precipitating negations 'No, no, no, no!' and the terminal word 'prison'. In the same transport the words 'alone' and 'will' are lifted upon a movement that translates the bird's privilege of flight into a privilege of song, taking freedom into the cage. Shakespeare then remembers the scene in the old play where Lear and Cordella kneel to one another in ecstasies of forgiveness. Rapturous mutuality becomes the tenor of life itself, carried on the equable tide of the syntax: 'so we'll live, / And pray, and sing, and tell old tales, and laugh / At gilded butterflies.' If those butterflies at once surprise and delight us as an image of inconsequential freedom, they do so because subliminally they have been prepared for in the quick, wayward flight of Lear's psyche and Shakespeare's. Knowledge, says Sidney, can 'lift up the minde from the dungeon of the bodie, to the enjoying his owne divine essence.'[8] Psyche, we may remember, was the Greek word for 'breath' and a word for the soul and for a butterfly. Laughing at butterflies is like praying and singing and the telling of old tales – all are the breath of life, and what Keats bid farewell to when he read *King Lear*, 'golden tongued romance', is here recalled to the centre of the play's ordeal. In the setting of the whole *oeuvre* we may think of the last plays – of *The Winter's Tale*, *Pericles*, and in particular of *The Tempest*, where the banished father tells his daughter the story of their afflicted lives. The old tale, we are persuaded, is all that Sidney claimed it to be, a vehicle of truth. Lear's and Cordelia's lives themselves become a remote old tale of fluctuating fortunes that might bring comfort to men in cages. Sidney's own *Arcadia* supplied many others, including the tale of Leonatus which Shakespeare used in his story of Gloucester. Lear and Cordelia are 'not the first / Who, with best meaning, have incurr'd the worst'.

'The poet's eye in a fine frenzy rolling / Doth glance from heaven to earth, from earth to heaven.' The glance from 'gilded butterflies' to 'poor rogues' changes the sense of 'butterflies' and suggests fly courtiers down on their luck. The solace is not now in song but in talk: 'hear poor rogues / Talk of court news'. In *King John* the Dauphin speaks in scorn of the culpable innocence:

> That never saw the giant world enrag'd
> Nor met with fortune other than at feasts,
> Full warm of blood, of mirth, of gossiping.
> (v. ii. 57–9)

[8] *Works*, ed. A. Feuillerat (Cambridge, 1923), III, p. 11.

The immunity of the feast, at which mirth and gossip can make light of the instabilities of the world, is in the later play carried into the prison. The walls momentarily seem a protection against mutability, a state of maximum security. But by the implications of the moon metaphor a kind of power is still exercised in the imprisoned state. Shakespeare once made Falstaff and Hal share a joke about night-robbers, 'minions of the moon' that 'ebb and flow like the sea'. In Lear's fantasy the conceit and its precision are lost to the larger resonance; their triumphant, freshly renewed intimacy ('We two alone . . . we'll live . . . we'll wear out') will have power to outstay and exhaust the moon that, in Yeat's aptly Renaissance phrase, 'pitches common things about'.

For all its tenderness and intimacy, however, Lear's 'fine frenzy' retains something of the Orphic ambition of the storm-scenes, looking for power outside Edmund's dominion, derived from a kingdom not of this world. He looks for a kind of ecstatic detachment that hovers between the penultimate catastrophe – imprisonment, and the ultimate one – death. 'God's spies' was supposed by Johnson to mean 'angels commissioned to survey and report the lives of men', and most editors have followed, prefering that to Warburton's more worrying notion that they are 'spies placed over God Almighty to watch his motions'. But both 'angels' and 'God almighty' are alien to Lear's discourse. If its effect is to be fully felt, 'spies' must call back the talk with 'poor rogues'; Lear is stuck in a cell finding things out from the other political prisoners. But the 'spies and speculations intelligent of our state' reported by Kent in Act III are the servants of France, while these are God's servants, intelligencers of a divine order.

At much the same time that *Lear* was written, William Perkins wrote his *Commentary on Galatians*, published in 1604. He distinguishes three ways in which we can be 'spies of the better sort':

> First, we are to be spies, in respect of our owne sinnes and corruptions, to spie them out. *Lam*, 3. 40 *Let us search our waies, and inquire, and turne againe to the Lord*. Againe, we are to play the spies in respect of our spiritual enemies, that we may find out the temptations of the flesh, the world and the divell. Thirdly, we must be spies, in searching of the Scriptures, *Ioh*. 5. 39 that we may understand the words of the Law of God, and find comfort · to our soules.[9]

I am not claiming that Lear read Perkins or that Shakespeare did, or even that I have, more than a little. But Perkins reminds us that the spy's vigilance could be commended as a spiritual virtue. Shakespeare would

[9] *Works* (London, 1617), II, p. 192.

have known too the text in Galatians that Perkins allegorized and adapted:

> For all the false brethren that crept in: who came in prively to spie
> out our libertie, which we have in Christ Jesus, that they might
> bring us into bondage.[10]

Again, there is no allusion. But the connection can be made at some level
of awareness between the 'liberty' which is a divine privilege, the bondage
inflicted by 'false brethren', and the treacherous function of the spy,
transformed by Perkins and by Shakespeare into a creative one. There is
no need to suppose with William Elton, therefore, that the speech at this
point carries 'presumptuous or blasphemous overtones'.[11] And with or
without the help of Perkins we may glimpse 'god's spies' in Shakespeare's
theatre, in the figures of Prospero and of the Duke in *Measure for Measure*,
metaphors of the playwright's art.

At this point Edmund, frigid spectator to the scene, says 'Take them
away.' The gaoler's imperative arrests the flight of affirmations; but they
break free again:

> Upon such sacrifices, my Cordelia,
> The Gods themselves throw incense. Have I caught thee?
> He that parts us shall bring a brand from heaven,
> And fire us hence like foxes. Wipe thine eyes;
> The good years shall devour them, flesh and fell,
> Ere they shall make us weep; we'll see 'em starv'd first.
> Come.
>
> (v. iii. 20–6)

Kenneth Muir tells us that he found 'in an old notebook' (belonging to
God's spy?) 'the suggestion, perhaps based on T. Carter's *Shakespeare and
Holy Scriptures* . . . that underlying Lear's speech there are echoes of
several Old Testament stories – of Jephthah's daughter, who was sacrificed,
and of the destruction of Sodom by a brand from heaven, of Samson and
the foxes, of Pharaoh's dream of the good and bad years.'[12] Northrop Frye,
writing on Blake, picks up the same range of references (perhaps from the
same source) and hazards an explication:

> Here the word 'sacrifices,' the central idea which the Old Testament
> deals with, has suggested something in it to Lear, probably the
> story of Jephthah's daughter. From there he jumps to the story of

[10] Ibid., p. 191 (Galatians 2: 4).
[11] *King Lear and the Gods* (Huntington, 1966), p. 250.
[12] *King Lear* (Arden Shakespeare, 1963), p. 201.

Sodom and the story of Samson and the foxes, thence to Pharaoh's dream of the lean kine who ate up the fat ones or 'good years'; and the meaning of the whole chain is: the world shall burn and the golden age come back before our enemies can triumph over us. Of course these are the uncontrolled associations of a vague and wandering mind, but after all *King Lear* is a play, and Shakespeare must have expected from his audience something of the allusive agility that the reading of Blake demands.[13]

Northrop Frye is himself something of a divine intelligencer, but I am not confident that Shakespeare was expecting an 'allusive agility' from his audience. The process and effect of the art are more obscure; the poet takes us into recesses of language and significance that cannot be probed by the sort of vigilance that recognizes allusions. 'There is an unconscious subject,' as Lacan has it, 'seeking to address itself to another unconscious subject',[14] and an audience alert to the effects of the art is not necessarily aware of its imaginative genesis.

Had William Perkins, however, been at Whitehall when the play was first presented before the king, he could have entertained all Northrop Frye's allusions, and more. But about the first – that to Jephthah's daughter – he would have felt uncomfortable; for he is nervous of the old tale in Judges which tells of the king keeping his vow by making a burnt offering of his daughter when she is the first to welcome him home from victory. Dismayed by a God who could demand such sacrifices, Perkins works to prove that '*Iephte* did not offer up his daughter in sacrifice, but only set her apart, to live a single life, to the honour and service of God.'[15] Resistance to the ancient cult of sacrifice is an important and necessary strain in both humanist and Christian tradition; and Bradley is in the same tradition as Perkins when he chooses to find in 'such sacrifices' only the renunciation of the world, with Cordelia 'set apart' in prison.

Once we know the play, however, and these words have become part of its total design as well as of its unfolding process, we are keenly aware of the continuities between this catastrophe and the next. Kenneth Muir speaks of 'an underlying suggestion of human sacrifice, which looks forward to the murder of Cordelia'. The 'underlying suggestion' could be no more than a metaphor, 'In being cast down for my sake you offer to the gods a sacrifice they approve'; but if we allow the words to look forward to the murder of Cordelia, the consolatory metaphor yields to the barbaric fact. Spoken over the dead Cordelia they would be intolerable. For her murder is an atrocity.

[13] *Fearful Symmetry* (Princeton, 1947), p. 374.
[14] *The Language of the Self*, p. 262.
[15] *Works* (1617), ii, p. 98.

What gods would throw incense on that?

The answer must be that Shakespeare expected us to. For it is he who contrives the sacrifice of Cordelia. Geoffrey of Monmouth and Holinshed tell of Cordelia's victory, and say that after Lear had been restored two years, she reigned for five before being deposed by men who resented the regiment of women.[16] In a sense, at this moment of the play, Shakespeare was still free to end it without sacrifice. But the chronicles go on to tell of Cordelia's being cast into prison where, 'being a woman of manlie courage, and despairing to recover libertie, there she slue herself'. Spenser tells us she hanged herself. In *King Lear* the despair and self-destruction are diverted to the Gloucester story, but it is the poignant after-history of Cordelia that presumably impels the playwright to kill her in Lear's lifetime, to the playgoer's great awe and satisfaction. Lear at this point may mean what Bradley means by 'sacrifices' but Shakespeare means more.

In almost all its two dozen contexts in his work 'sacrifice' signifies not 'renunciation' but blood sacrifice and burnt offering, and in probing this mystery we are not perversely far from Shakespeare's own preoccupations in, for example, *Titus Andronicus*, *Julius Caesar* and *Othello*. A sacrifice, these plays tell us, cannot but be a murder and is apt to be an atrocity, in which the cruelty of the crime is an element in its motivation. Shakespeare's probings are both psychological and anthropological: what kind of society, with what values and religious traditions, found a central place for sacrifice? Answers about Lear's Britain, as for Cymbeline's, were to be found in William Harrison's *Description of Britain*, printed in Holinshed's *Chronicle*. The ancient religion of Albion, says Harrison, offered 'mankind' to some of its gods 'in lieu of sheep and oxen'; offenders, prisoners 'and also their owne children' were consumed to ashes and reputed to be 'the most acceptable sacrifice that could be made unto their idols'.[17] Lear and Cordelia were by this account liable to be made 'acceptable sacrifices', and a plain chronicle-play, seeking to re-create what Harrison calls the 'great decaie' of the realm of Albion,[18] would make that the theme of Lear's exclamations – 'Let's away to prison and be sacrificed to the gods.' Shakespeare could have known of similar practices among the Carthaginians, from Plutarch,[19] and among the Mexicans, from Montaigne; Montaigne even tells of the ecstatic delight of the victims.[20]

But *King Lear* is not a plain chronicle, it makes little of the formalities

---

[16] See Geoffrey Bullough, *Narrative and Dramatic Sources of Shakespeare* VII (London, 1973), pp. 316, 319.

[17] *Hol.*, I, p. 39.

[18] Cf. *Lear*, v, iii. 298.

[19] Plutarch's *Morals*, tr. Philemon Holland (1603), p. 268.

[20] *Essayes*, tr. John Florio, ed. T. Seccombe (1908), I, 252.

of the religion of Albion and requires no priest to preside at the murder of
Cordelia, seeking atonement and propitiation of the gods. Edmund, its
instigator, has motives remote from Brutus's (Let's be sacrificers, but not
butchers, Caius') and from Othello's ('thou . . . mak'st me call what I
intend to do / A murder, which I thought a sacrifice'). 'Know thou this,'
he says to Cordelia's hangman, 'that men / Are as the time is.' The 'time'
is not that of 'Druiysh and Bardike ceremonies' which Harrison speaks of,
it is the perennial time of malignant political importunity. Shakespeare
knew it from his staging of the slaughter of the boy Rutland at Wakefield,
or he could have known it from Ulysses' hounding to death of the boy
Astyanax in the *Troades* of Seneca, and it is of little consequence that the
one is naked atrocity while the other pretends to be a sacrifice. He could
have known it too from contemporary outrages, such as the Darnley murder,
which Lilian Winstanley thought *King Lear* to be about. The play's perennial
time reaches to our own. When Edmund disposes of Lear and Cordelia the
pretext – to pre-empt any rallying of forces under the spell of their names,
is much the same as Lenin's and Sverdlov's for the murder of the Tsar
and his family: they would not 'leave the Whites a live banner to rally
round'.[21] Still more recently, the eight-year-old son of Sheik Mujib was
gunned to pieces at Dacca.[22] In such perspectives, talk of 'sacrifice' can
seem at once sentimental and barbaric, but it need not be so, and there
are other perspectives.

Ancient Albion, as described by Harrison, numbered amongst its idols
the play's Jupiter and Apollo and also the god Hercules. Having already
shaped out of Ovid and Seneca the madness of *Titus Andronicus*,
Shakespeare, with or without the cue from Harrison, could have made his
way back to the *Hercules Furens* where Hercules casts incense upon the
burning remains of the tyrant Lycus, and speaks words that were to be
quoted and translated by Milton, when he was justifying the Christian
sacrifice of King James's son in *The Tenure of Kings and Magistrates*:[23]

> there can be slain
> No sacrifice to God more acceptable
> Than an unjust and wicked King.

If Shakespeare were alluding to that, Lear's words would look back upon
himself; he would be the unjust and wicked king about to be sacrificed.
Can we be quite sure that he is not? The sense would stretch that way
under pressure, but there is no pressure. While it is true that *King Lear*

---

[21] *Trotsky's Diary in Exile* 1935, tr. Elena Zarudnaya (1959), p. 80.
[22] The murder of the Sheik and certain members of his family was acclaimed by
the new president as an 'heroic act'; see the London *Times*, 16–19 August 1975.
[23] *Prose Works* (New Haven, 1962), III. p. 213.

seems to come appropriately in English history at a time of approaching crisis for the monarchy – the play does little to increase our confidence in the British governing class[24] – the focus is not at this point upon the king's failures. If there is in the speech a relationship with Seneca, it is where we hear still some stirring of purging wrath in Lear's distraction. 'Purgare terras propero,' cries Hercules, clubbing to death his wife and children: 'I am in haste to purge the earth.' Lear's 'I shall do such things, / What they are, yet I know not, but they shall be / The terrors of the earth', and his, 'Let the great gods that keep this dreadful pudder o'er our heads / Find out their enemies now', are not derived from Seneca but they are in the same temper as the invocations of the *Hercules Furens* – titanic and retributive rage taken to a point of madness under the sway of Jove the Thunderer.

The Seneca recollection, however, would not consort with the intimacy of Lear's cry. To find those that do we can look again to the New Testament and the Old. Among the opening injunctions of Hebrews 13 is one to 'Remember them that are in bondes, as though ye were bonde with them.' There is prison 'bondage' and there is the human 'bond'. So in the prison scene of *Lear*; there are bonds about the king and his daughter and there is a bond between them. 'In burnt offerings,' says the text, alluding to bulls and goats, God has 'no pleasure':

> To do good and to distribute forget not:
> for with suche sacrifices God is pleased.

> Obey them that have the oversight of you, and
> submit yourselves: for they watch for your soules,
> as they may do it with ioye, and not with griefe:
> for that is unprofitable for you.
> (Hebrews 13: 16–17; Geneva version)

'With such sacrifices God is pleased', 'Obey them that have the oversight of you', 'for they watch for your souls', 'do it with joy' – it is not hard to receive these phrases (from the Geneva version) to an honoured place in the theatre of Lear's mind, to keep company with 'upon such sacrifices', 'let's away to prison', 'God's spies' and 'wipe thine eyes', but they are not allowed unambiguously to take command of Shakespeare's play. Other insights and energies are active too, and in detailed application there are ironies. 'Obey them that have the oversight of you' comes in the play to mean, 'Do what Edmund tells you', while the other half of the text, 'for they watch for your souls', unexpectedly chimes with 'God's spies'. This

---

[24] See Rosalie L. Colie, 'Reason and Need: *King Lear* and the "Crisis" of the Aristocracy', in *Some Facets of King Lear*, ed. R. L. Colie and F. T. Flahiff (Toronto and London, 1974).

excursion into the New Testament could bring Lear's meaning closer to Bradley's 'serene renunciation of the world': 'Let us go forth therefore out of the camp . . . for here we have no continuing citie: but we seke one to come.' But in Edmund's plot and in Shakespeare's imprisonment is a move towards murder, towards the 'human sacrifice' that the text from Hebrews finds needless.

Thomas Adams in *The Sacrifice of Thankfulnesse*, first published in 1616, takes his text from Psalm 118, 'God is the Lord, which hath showed us Light: bind the Sacrifice with Cordes, even unto the Hornes of the Altar.'[25] He distinguished 'expiatory' and 'gratulatory' sacrifices. The first is either 'to acknowledge *Peccati stipendium mortem*; that Death was the wages of sinne; due to the Sacrificers, layed on the Sacrificed', or 'Mystically and symbolically to prefigure the killing of the *Lambe of God*, that taketh away the sinnes of the world.' But,' says Adams, quoting Hebrews, 'those sacrifices are abolished in Christ who offered our Sacrifice for Sinnes for ever.'[26] A full account of Christian sacrifice in relation to the history of theatre would enable us to make the same point in a different way. In the so-called N. Town cycle of Miracle Plays, for example, Abel's sacrifice of a Lamb prefigures that of Christ, and versions of the Abraham and Isaac story agree in taking comfort from the fact that God on this occasion did not, after all, require a human sacrifice but provided himself with an animal one; it is the arrested human sacrifice, nevertheless, that in some of these plays prefigures the sacrifice of the son of God. Ultimately God required the sacrifice of the word made flesh.

If we think of the play's final scene as, in Helen Gardner's words, 'a secular *Pietà*',[27] Christian assumptions about the nature of Sacrifice are at hazard. For, although it belongs to the fictional pre-Christian past of the chronicles, we do not see Cordelia's death as a prefiguration, we experience it as a representative event of human history. Later contemporaries of John Foxe, watching *Lear*'s first performance on the day of the first martyr (at whose stoning Paul himself assisted) could reflect on the many that had been stretched, squashed, mangled, boiled, burnt, and hanged for Christ's sake. But not, it may be objected, *sacrificed*. Here, do what we will, certain ambiguities persist; but before returning to the play, there is a need to recognize a point of convergence in Christian and classical understanding of sacrifice.

The crucifixion of Christ, the stoning of Stephen, the burning of Thomas Cranmer and the execution of Thomas More (to name two of direct interest to Shakespeare), unlike Abraham's offering of Isaac, were not acts of piety

---

[25] *Works* (1630), p. 82.
[26] *Works*, p. 89.
[27] *King Lear* (John Coffin Memorial Lecture, London, 1967).

and devotion, but judicial murders.[28] In each case, where sanctity and devotion are to be found, it is in the heroic submissiveness of the victims. Where sacrifice moves us as a tragic event it is because the victim has made himself fit to die and dies for something greater than himself. From Greek and Latin tragedy we could take many instances – Iphigenia, Polyxena, Amphitryon, to name three that Shakespeare could have known from Seneca. But for Christendom, the history of sacrificial humility finds its source most often in the figure in the fifty-third chapter of Isaiah, 'taken from prison and from judgement, cut off out of the land of the living'. There, we may think, is Cordelia's history. 'For the transgression of my people was he stricken,' says the old God in the old book. Does the playwright say otherwise in the new play?

Thomas Adams advises us that 'gratulatory sacrifice' is symbolic and spiritual in character: 'Christ is our *Altar*, let ourselves be the *Sacrifice*: the Fire that kindles it, the love of God, the Smoake that goes up, the consumption of our sinnes.'[29] Adams writes in a religious tradition that finds one of its fullest early expressions in Psalm 51, where deliverance from blood guiltiness is in the sacrifice of 'a broken spirit: a broken and a contrite heart'. Tragedy too invites imaginative identification with the victim. For Adams, a true sacrifice consists not only in doing ('Faciendo'), but also in dying, in suffering ('Patiendo') for Christ, without 'gall of bitternesse' or 'honie of self-complacencie'. This too is capable of a kind of translation into Shakespeare's theatre: 'For thee, oppressed King, am I cast down' is not a quotation from St Paul to the Corinthians, 'Persecuted, but not forsaken; cast down, but not destroyed . . . for we which live are always delivered unto death for Jesus' sake', but it is under the same dispensation. Adams could without blasphemy have commended Cordelia's sacrifice of herself out of love for an 'oppressed king', even if he did detect in her character a taste of honey and a touch of gall. Desdemona dies, in spite of Othello, by the same feat of self-sacrifice: 'Who hath done this deed? – Nobody, I myself. Farewell.'

If the play were not conspicuously about father and daughter I doubt if any thought of Jephthah's sacrifice would come to mind, but for those sufficiently familiar with Bible story the association may be prompted by the spectacle, for this can play a significant part in the scene's shadowing of the catastrophe to come. Between the more violent invocations, 'such sacrifices' and the 'brand from heaven', comes the strangely tantalizing phrase, 'Have I caught thee?' The eagerness and perhaps the tenderness of it a little reduce the banal possibilities of significance, such as, 'Have I

---

[28] Cf. *Winter's Tale*, ii, iii. 113–14, 'It is an heretic that makes the fire, / Not she which burns in it.
[29] *Works* (1630), pp. 89–90.

caught your meaning?', or even, 'Have I got you into this?' But because Shakespeare once had Falstaff quote in the *Merry Wives* the second song of Sidney's *Astrophel and Stella*, and because the poetry of *Lear* has made our associative processes so active, our amending imaginations feel free to follow 'Have I caught thee?' with 'my heav'nly jewell'. It is the more likely if Lear at this point takes Cordelia in his arms. Were she to swoon – and she does not speak through Lear's declamations – the next line of the song may haunt us too: 'Teaching sleepe most fair to be?' But, whatever the importance of the song, there is an advantage in having Lear leave centre-stage with Cordelia live but relaxed in his arms, later to return with her dead, in a double image of the father's solicitude and distress. The narrative and imaginative continuity between the apprehended sacrifice and the murder would be accented by the symbolic tableau. We may think of the two great Bellini images in the Accademia at Venice, the one a Madonna and sleeping child, the other a *pietà*, each reflecting the dispositions of the other.[30]

After the thought of sacrifice, Lear's imprecations retreat into elusive allusion. What fragments, to borrow Eliot's phrase, does the King shore against his ruins? Sodom was destroyed by fire, the commentaries remind us, Samson tied firebrands to the tails of foxes, 'the thinne eares devoured the seven good eares' when, in Pharaoh's dream, the Egyptians are threatened with famine.[31] It is characteristic of all these associations that none is necessary but none, once entertained, can be quite dismissed. In this speech, as distinct from the last, there is not opportunity for song. 'After ye were illuminated,' says the Epistle to Hebrews, 'ye endured a great fight of afflictions.'[32] Lear's fragments are glimpses of afflictions: the purging wrath of the Lord, the violence and cunning of God's servants, the catastrophic instability of the harvest. The Old Testament is called to witness that divine interventions in human history have left its stress and pain undiminished. But it does not help to apply the allusions too specifically; it is the errant, straying mind that is losing and finding its way. Joseph, we may or may not remember, was in prison when he was called on to interpret the King's dream, but Shakespeare is not testing our 'allusive agility'. Lear is a fond father – mad, affectionate, and protective. He is reverting to childhood, to Cordelia's greatest vulnerability and to the sources of his own simplicity. His talk here can as well take us back to the nursery as into the commentaries of Cambridge divines. The word 'good-year', says the *OED*, delightfully, 'came to be used in imprecatory phrases as denoting

---

[30]Giovanni Bellini: *Madonna col Bambino dormiente, La Pietà*. See Francesco Valcanover, *Gallerie dell' Accademia di Venezia*, (Novara, 1955), pp. 34, 43.
[31]Genesis 19, 41; Judges 15.
[32]Hebrews 10: 32.

some undefined and malefic power or agency'. Beyond the voice of apocalyptic terror can be heard the voice of the father comforting the child, 'Don't be afraid . . . I won't go away . . . Stop crying . . . Don't worry about those nasty people, the bogey-man will eat them all up.' But such ingenuous tenderness would not in itself suffice; the obscurity, the scale, and the terror are necessary to keep alive another range of implications. For the Senecal God of Thunder meets the God of Hebrews in the play's final images of doom: 'Yet once more I shall shake, not the earth onely, but also heaven . . . For even our God is a consuming fyre.'[33]

It may be supposed that my many appeals to the Bible and to biblical exegesis are attempts to subdue the playwright's art by priestcraft. But the relationship I wish to gloss between Shakespeare's poetry and Christian metaphor and understanding is not of that kind. Leon Trotsky, whose own history I earlier called 'tragic', says of Shakespeare's tragedies that they 'would be entirely unthinkable without the Reformation.'[34]

> As a result of the Reformation religion became individualistic. The religious symbols of art having had their cord cut from the heavens, fell on their heads and sought support in the uncertain mysticism of individual consciousness . . . But in every one of Shakespeare's dramas, the individual passion is carried to such a high degree of tension that it outgrows the individual, becomes super-personal, and is transformed into a fate of a certain kind.

In pursuing connections between the play and the Bible I do not mean to return Shakespeare's art to pre-Reformation times when, again to quote Trotsky, 'the Christian myth unified the monumental art of the Middle Ages and gave a significance not only to temples and the mysteries, but to all human relationships', and when a great art was made possible 'by the union of the religious point of view on life with an active participation in it'. I assume rather that the experience of both the Reformation and the Renaissance in England made possible, through a fuller and more direct personal access to the Bible, a recovery of the imaginative inheritance of Hebraic and Christian literature as distinct from its institutional, doctrinal and ritual inheritance; and I would contend for the view that in the Middle Ages there is a dominant movement out of imaginative truth towards doctrine, while in the Renaissance the movement is the other way. My account of *Lear* is meant in part as a contribution to that contention. Many theologies are voiced, tested, and found expendable within the arduous imaginative experience of the play. The God of Deuteronomy and Hebrews, like Lear's, bringing a brand from heaven, is a consuming fire. A 'consuming

---

[33] Hebrews 12: 26–9 (Geneva).
[34] *Literature and Revolution*, tr. Rose Strunsky (1925), p. 242.

fire' is what Keats found the play to be, and I shall now turn aside from the imprisonment scene to ask more generally about the play, what is consumed and how.

Keats saw himself submitting to a process of self-destruction and self-renewal which, remembering Psalm 51 ('Purge me with hyssop, and I shall be clean'), might again be called sacrificial:

> Adieu! for, once again, the fierce dispute
> Betwixt damnation and impassion'd clay
> Must I burn through; once more assay
> The bitter-sweet of this Shakespearean fruit.
>
> But, when I am consumed in the fire
> Give me new Phoenix wings to fly at my desire.

Keats's phrases 'consuming fire' and 'impassioned clay' are themselves generated in the poetry of the play, which we now recall from Act I sc. iv, when Lear rages upon Goneril about fifty of his followers gone 'at a clap':

> Life and death! I am asham'd
> That thou hast power to shake my manhood thus,
> That these hot tears, which break from me perforce,
> Should make thee worth them. Blasts and fogs upon thee!
> Th' untented woundings of a father's curse
> Pierce every sense about thee! Old fond eyes,
> Beweep this cause again, I'll pluck ye out,
> And cast you, with the waters that you loose,
> To temper clay. Yea, is't come to this?
> Ha! Let it be so: I have another daughter,
> Who, I am sure, is kind and comfortable:
> When she shall hear this of thee, with her nails
> She'll flay thy wolvish visage. Thou shalt find
> That I'll resume the shape which thou dost think
> I have cast off for ever.
>
> (I. iv. 296–310)

The habit of command is still behind the sway of the verse, but the 'power to shake' has recoiled upon his own self, his trembling body, his 'manhood'; his hot tears, owed to hurt pride, inflict a moral distress which feels like a physical one; frustrated retributive malice turns first upon his daughter's senses, then back upon his own. 'If thine eye offend thee, pluck it out'; the text characteristically goes astray, for it is the eyes' capacity to betray feeling that offends Lear. The plucked eyes and their tears cast to 'temper clay' (Keats's 'impassioned clay') will be remembered later when Gloucester fears for Lear's eyes and then loses his own, and the hot tears return with a changed significance when Lear wakes from sleep at Dover, supposing himself resurrected to judgement. The deep wound and the piercing of every sense also have their subliminal after-life in the play. The word 'pierce' which here relishes pain inflicted, will later register pain endured ('a pigmy's straw doth pierce it') and find its apotheosis in Edgar's cry when he sees the king crowned with nettles, 'O thou side-piercing sight'. Lear's vertiginous oscillation between his love of security and his passion for vengeance breeds in his imagination the morally grotesque 'kind and comfortable' daughter who will 'flay' her sister's 'wolvish visage', manifesting one of the huge fluctuations of mood that ultimately bereave Lear of his senses. The last cry threatens a resurrection of the thunderer-self, absolute monarch, uncompromising father. But in senses that Lear is not yet ready to understand, that shape is indeed cast off for ever. 'If the whole of the individual's being cannot be defended,' Laing writes in *The Divided Self*, 'the individual retracts his lines of defence until he withdraws within a central citadel. He is prepared to write off everything he is, except his "self". But the tragic paradox is that the more the self is defended in this way, the more it is destroyed'.[35]

The closeness of some aspects of art to case-history registers very clearly in Shakespeare's treatment of both Lear and Gloucester. Lear has been formally diagnosed as 'a case of senile dementia' by practising psychiatrists in our own time,[36] and by Goneril in ancient Britain:

> The best and soundest of his time hath been but rash; then must
> we look from his age, to receive not alone the imperfections of
> long-engraffed condition, but therewithal the unruly waywardness
> that infirm and choleric years bring with them.
>
> (I. i. 295–9)

Gloucester has invited less professional attention, but in Act IV, sc. vi. by the acting-out of what Harsnett called a 'devil play',[37] he is exorcised of his suicidal despair. Spectators to the plight of Lear and Gloucester, we may wonder what connection there is between 'self-destruction' and 'self-sacrifice'. Shakespeare invites our wonder. 'Selves' are precipitated by Lear's initial self-promoting love plot, and more selves are generated in the course of the play in response to domestic and political circumstance. A 'character' may have more than one 'self', and the purging of selves is at once a psychological and a social process. I cannot hope to establish the truth of such an

[35] R. D. Laing, *The Divided Self* (1960), pp. 80–1.

[36] John G. Howells and M. Livia Osborn, 'A Case of Senile Dementia – King Lear', *History of Medicine* (Oct. 1973), pp. 30–1.

[37] Samuel Harsnett, *A Declaration of Egregious Popish Impostures* (1603), chs. 1 and 5.

ambiguous and ambitious generalization, but only to catch glimpses of its operation.

Ideas of self-sacrifice often take their inspiration from the New Testament: 'our old man is crucified with him, that the body of sin might be destroyed.'[38] St Paul's metaphor is a terrifying one for all who are, as it were, exposed to it. 'Exposed' is prompted by the metaphor of the play. Lear and Gloucester are shut out of the castle, with all its false securities, to undergo the 'tempest of the mind' and a 'blind pilgrimage'. Thus exposed they are, in a sense, crucified. Yet had they been wiser and better men they would not have so suffered. Lear would have kept his kingdom, taken Albany for viceroy, and spent his holidays hunting in Burgundy. Gloucester would have dabbled in astrology and let his legitimate and only son run the estate. That would have been prudential virtue of the kind that Edgar as the Bedlam beggar prescribes:

> Take heed o' th' foul fiend. Obey thy parents; keep thy word's justice; swear not; commit not with man's sworn spouse; set not thy sweet heart on proud array. Tom's a cold.
>
> (III. iv. 80–3)

The price for breaking the commandments is exposure to the weather, and in mockery of his father's history, Edgar assumes the afflictions of a self-indulgent court parasite (a gilded butterfly) who has lost his place for want of rectitude; the moral imperatives protect the securities of the society. Prudential wisdom has a treacherously complex life in this play, as we also find when we catch ourselves thinking Goneril's or Regan's thoughts about their father.

The other possibility is folly; for folly disdains security, puts the self at risk, and often destroys it. The word and the condition are richly polarized (to use the optical metaphor again) throughout the play, but I am concerned to see them only in the light of 'such sacrifices'. There is a complex of imaginative links between Cordelia's, 'For thee, oppressed King, am I cast down', and the Fool's advice to Kent in the stocks:

> Let go thy hold when a great wheel runs down a hill, lest it break they neck with following; but the great one that goes upward, let him draw thee after. When a wise man gives thee better counsel, give me mine again: I would have none but knaves follow it, since a Fool gives it.
>
> (II. iv. 71–7)

Cordelia, Kent, the Fool, and Edgar all fail to let go of the great wheel

---

[38] Romans 6: 6.

running down hill and, as Lear reports in a line of uncertain reference, 'my poor fool is hanged'.

Erasmus and Montaigne were among those who, like Shakespeare, gave fresh life to the old insights into the nature of folly. The fool puts himself in jeopardy, goes where things are to be known; he does not stay in the castle.[39] That is not true of every kind of fool, but of the play's kind, and of those that Erasmus and St Paul admired, who are 'fools for Christ's sake'.[40]

The transition from folly to madness is an easy one, in the language and in fact, in the play and outside it. From Montaigne many commentators on *Lear* have caught up passages about madness, folly, and the loss of the senses. According to Montaigne's highly sceptical account of moral growth – sceptical because it allows so slight a validity to human reason – man moves out of a state of self-deception through a state of madness into a state of vision:

> Dares not Philosophie thinke that men produce their greatest effects, and nearest approching to divinity, when they are besides themselves, furious, and madde? We amend ourselves by the privation of reason, and by her drooping. The two naturall waies, to enter the cabinet of the Gods, and there to foresee the course of the destinies, are furie and sleepe. This is very pleasing to be considered. By the dislocation that passions bring unto our reason, we become vertuous; by the extirpation which either fury or the image of death bringeth us, we become Prophets and Divines.[41]

In another dimension of his thought, Montaigne teaches us the treachery of our senses. He imagines a philosopher suspended from a tower of Notre Dame in an iron cage. 'He shall, by evident reason, perceive that it is impossible he should fall downe out of it; yet he cannot chuse . . . but the sight of that exceeding height must needs dazle his sight and amaze or turne his senses.'[42] And Montaigne confesses his own horror in face of the 'infinite precipices and steepy downfalls' of the Italian Alps.[43] The senses, runs the irony of the argument, 'do often master our discourse' and force us to receive impressions we know to be false. Turning from Montaigne to the cliff-scene at Dover we recognize that Shakespeare is indeed taking us to the edge of an abyss, creating new insecurities. The marvellously

---

[39] Cf. *Moriae encomium*, 'A foole in jeopardyng, and goyng presently where thynges are to be knowne, gathereth (unles I am deceived) the perfect true prudence'. (Translated Chaloner, London [1549], 1900.)

[40] I Corinthians 4: 10.

[41] *Essayes*, ed. Seccombe, II. 349.

[42] Ibid., p. 389.

[43] Ibid., p. 390.

simulated vertigo contrived by Shakespeare and by Edgar has a blind man as its auditor. Nicholas Brook finds that the 'leisured expansive rhythm and detailed imagery all enforce the sense of an ordered world, whose petty strifes are ridiculous if not invisible to the distant viewer'.[44] But these are precarious serenities. The diminutions which accent the spaciousness of the scene testify to its mocking unreality: 'Methinks he seems no bigger than his head'; the 'murmuring surge, / That on th' unnumber'd idle pebble chafes', so richly evoked to Keats's delight, 'cannot be heard'; the fishermen look like mice. It is not an ordered world but a fading one and the senses give a false account of it:

> and yond tall anchoring bark
> Diminish'd to her cock, her cock a buoy
> Amost too small for sight.
>
> (IV. vi. 18–20)

Montaigne has his own way of touching the same range of experiences. He quotes a Latin description of the Alps, which Florio translates, 'So as they cannot look down without giddinesse both of eyes and mindes'; and follows it with a glance at a 'worthy philosopher' who 'pulled out his eyes, that so he might discharge his soule of the seducing and diverting he received by them'.[45] Montaigne with ruthless good humour, of the sort he keeps for philosophers, says that he 'should also have stopped his ears, which are the most dangerous instruments we have to receive violent and sudden impressions to trouble and alter us; and should, in the end, have deprived himself of all his other senses, that is to say, both of his being, and life. For they have the power to command our discourses and sway our mind.'

From the start of the cliff-scene Edgar has worked to disable Gloucester's senses. 'Look how we labour' – 'Methinks the ground is even' – 'Horrible steep'; 'Do you hear the sea?' – 'No truly' – 'Why then your other senses grow imperfect / By your eyes' anguish' – 'So it may be indeed.' The growing imperfection of Gloucester's senses is a delusion artificially contrived by Edgar, with the explanation,

> Why I do trifle thus with his despair
> Is done to cure it.

Gloucester rehearses for himself a Stoic death, meant to keep intact the citadel of his being, in dignified submission. But he is exorcized of his Epicurean confidence – his trust in the senses, and preserved for a different death. Edgar persuades his father that back upon the cliff top from which he has 'fallen' he has left a phantasmagoric thing: 'methought his eyes /

---

[44] *Shakespeare: King Lear* (London, 1963), p. 43.
[45] *Essayes*, II. 390.

Were two full moons; he had a thousand noses, / Horns whelk'd and wav'd like the enridged sea.' Compounded of bits of demonic superstition and images of the sea, the figure is a fantastic projection of the old Gloucester, the old self, that Edgar is exorcizing. Another kind of contextual enquiry could take us back to Thomas Adams, who said vertigo was the bodily infirmity corresponding to the 'disease of the soule called Inconstancie'.[46] But our most convenient farewell to the episode is Harry Levin's comment that the ultimate meaning of Gloucester's fall 'is its symbolic gesture of expiation'.[47]

Guilt and expiation are elements of the sacrificial order – offence, guilt, expiation, atonement, renewal; which also, commonly, compose the tragic order. For tragedy is goat-song, as Walter Burkert has reminded us, in a paper, 'Greek Tragedy and Sacrificial Ritual',[48] which has done much to refresh and to vindicate many of the insights of Nietzsche and some of the findings of Gilbert Murray. The recognition that sacrifice persists as an elemental if not inescapable process of human consciousness may find many witnesses, from Aeschylus, St Paul and Shakespeare to Lawrence, Freud and Laing. But it is Shakespeare who does most, for those in touch with his poetry, to internalize the tragic-sacrificial experience, to realize it in the hidden structures of language and consciousness. The tragic *anagnorisis* is at once circumstantial and inward, for those caught up in the tragic process discover its validity and acknowledge the imminent destruction of the old self.

'I know that voice,' says Gloucester, listening to Lear at Dover. 'I know' comes back to Lear as 'ay' and 'no' in the active obscurities of his moral awareness:

> Ha! Goneril, with a white beard! They flattered me like a dog, and told me I had white hairs in my beard ere the black ones were there. To say 'ay' and 'no' to every thing that I said! 'Ay' and 'no' too was no good divinity.
>
> (IV. vi. 96–100)

This is an inexhaustible recognition scene, from Edgar's 'side-piercing sight', by way of Gloucester's, 'Is't not the King?', to 'I know thee well enough; thy name is Gloucester.' To see Goneril in a white beard is another kind of recognition, making one phantasmagoric image from a complex of insights. Gloucester is associated with the conspiracy of flattery which Goneril's treachery literally brings home to him. The conspiracy is provoked

[46] *Works*, p. 443.
[47] H. Levin, 'The Heights and Depths', in *More Talking of Shakespeare*, ed. J. Garrett (1959).
[48] In *Greek, Roman and Byzantine Studies*, 7 (1966), pp. 87–121.

by the very institution of monarchy, requiring total obedience to a commanding ego which is not allowed to mature, become other than itself, saying 'Ay' to 'I'.[49]

The nausea provoked by his 'pelican daughters' extends to the whole process of generation itself, 'But to the girdle do the gods inherit, beneath is all the fiend's.' In a kind of second abdication, of the kingdoms of the old *polis* and the old self, Lear releases the self-destructive passions of the whole society – 'Let copulation thrive.' Although in the society and in the psyche it is an abdication of reason, yet the habits and ferocity of command again persist, together with a purgative irony, learned from exposure, that can gape at the mangled face of Gloucester the old lecher and call him 'blind cupid', can move from the farmer's dog barking at a beggar to the 'great image of Authority – a dog's obeyed in office', and return again to Gloucester's sockets with the prescription, 'get thee glass eyes; / And like a scurvy politician, seem / To see the things that are not.' It is a comprehensive yet intensely personal indictment of the society.

In its last stage, Lear's recognition of Gloucester, the prophetic role of preacher is acknowledged:

> thy name is Gloucester;
> Thou must be patient; we came crying hither:
> Thou know'st the first time that we smell the air
> We wawl and cry. I will preach to thee: mark.

The mind slips from wawling to preaching, finds itself a text that Solomon himself would have been proud of, 'When we are born, we cry that we are come / To this great stage of fools.' Then, I suspect, Lear slips again from preaching to blessing, lays his hand on Gloucester's eyeless head and finds 'This' a 'good block' – good for shaping a hat on. The generation of the mutilated man from the crying child is a frightening glimpse of the nature of growth and evolution in the play. Lear's distress takes a tactical evasion, 'It were a delicate stratagem to shoe / a troop of horse with felt', but it gathers again its retributive violence, 'And when I have stol'n upon these sons-in-laws, / Then, kill, kill, kill, kill, kill, kill!' An element of tragic ritual has found its indirect way into the inner consciousness – the *bacchenein*, the 'intoxication of killing'.[50]

In the 'heaviness of sleep' Lear has (like Joshua) 'fresh garments' put

---

[49] Those interested in Shakespeare's imaginative history will find in Wilson's old play, *The Three Lords and Three Ladies of London*, that the lady who claims, 'I love you more than tongue can tell', is checked by Lady Conscience, 'I know that tongue, Lucre beware of Fraud.' Shakespeare's 'Fraud', Goneril, also speaks other hyperboles ('dearer than eyesight, space and liberty') which find new significance in the scene at Dover.

[50] Burkert, 'Greek Tragedy and Sacrificial Ritual, p. 116.

upon him and awakens to music and to his daughter's love. It is an essential element in the sacrificial experience that life should be renewed, refreshed, reawakened, resurrected. St Paul is strict on the point: 'If after the manner of men I have fought with beasts at Ephesus, what advantageth it me, if the dead rise not?'[51] In his own 'phantasma and hideous dream' Lear at first awakens to a delusion of judgement:

> You do me wrong to take me out o' th' grave;
> Thou are a soul in bliss; but I am bound
> Upon a wheel of fire, that mine own tears
> Do scald like molten lead.

The 'wheel of fire' and the 'molten lead', along with the rack, are not only instruments of torture in Lear's old kingdom of avenging wrath, they are also hallucinations precipitated in the mind by the hotness of his tears of contrition – the deceptive senses are at work again. The wheel of fire burns also in the Apocalypse of St Peter and the Second Book of the Sibylline Oracles, but those images of damnation must ultimately be owed, one feels, to experiences like Lear's. The play creates that experience and we keep watch on it. The scene acknowledges the senile vulnerabilities – 'I will not swear these are my hands', 'I am a very foolish fond old man' – before they reach their climax in the triumphant naming of Cordelia. His punitive, retributive moral logic, however, is not only spent in weakness, it is foiled in its workings by Shakespeare's felicitous tuning of the word 'cause':

> If you have poison for me, I will drink it.
> I know you do not love me; for your sisters
> Have, as I do remember, done me wrong:
> You have some cause they have not.
> > No cause, no cause.
> > (IV. vii. 71–4)

Lear asks, 'Am I in France?' and Kent answers, 'In your own kingdom, Sir.' Lear responds, 'Do not abuse me.'

In the old play Kent's answer would have been free from ambiguity, the old Lear is not mad and has, in modern jargon, no ontological insecurities, and had Shakespeare stuck to his sources the King would have been restored to power in his own country. But it is Lear's fitness for death that is finally tested, not his fitness for life. There can be no reversion to the kind of authority once exercised but now played out – that shape is cast off for ever. One response to Kent's 'In your own kingdom, Sir' is that, after the visionary madness at the cliff, the King is no longer in his kingdom; the kingdom, in all its fearful disorder, is in the King. Another might be 'my

---

[51] I Corinthians 15: 32.

kingdom is not of this world.' The defeat of Lear's party is a tragic imperative, not a political one, although I have no doubt that the first court audience could have been as dismayed by a play ending in a successful invasion as they were by one which began, 'Know I have divided in three our kingdom.'

The playwright is presiding over a sacrifice; and the playwright, in the span of the theatre's few hours, is himself the clearest god who makes honours of men's impossibilities. I find the scene between Lear's exit and his return much exposed to the strain of Shakespeare's complex commitments, and I cannot find it wholly satisfactory. In particular I would wish away some moments in Edmund's dilatory ineptitude about his pardon of Cordelia – not to save her, but to make her death more obviously owed to a process of human malice which has passed a point of no return. When Lear enters with Cordelia dead in his arms, however, the poet's art is at its most assured. I welcome the suggestion that Kent's question, 'Is this the promis'd end?' should read 'Is this the premis'd end?' as in Clifford's doomsday speech at St Albans.[52] Is this the premis'd end? . . . Or image of that horror?' The image is all we can have, for none can speak in knowledge of death and resurrection, only in shadows and metaphors. But Shakespeare takes art and language as close as it will go:

> She's gone for ever.
> I know when one is dead, and when one lives:
> She's dead as earth.
>
> (v. iii. 260–62)

But how can Lear know? On waking at Dover he had thought himself dead, 'I feel this pin-prick. Would I were assur'd of my condition.' The impulse to test his bereaved senses comes upon him again; he calls for a looking glass, watches for the feather to be stirred by Cordelia's breath, listens for her voice. By such touches the desolation is articulated and the prospect of resurrection dulled as he peers at his servant Caius. 'Dead and rotten' but now alive again as Kent. The failing senses and imperfect mind make their final effort – 'I'll see that straight' – to reach a last paroxysm of affliction and wonder:

> Thou'lt come no more,
> Never, never, never, never, never!
> Pray you, undo this button: thank you, Sir.

[52] Lascelles, *Shakespeare Survey*, 26 (1973), p. 79.

Do you see this? Look on her, look, her lips,
Look there, look there!

(v. iii. 308–12)

We are probably mistaken to ask whether Lear dies in ecstasy, believing Cordelia alive, or in exhausted disappointment, recognizing another delusion. For among the possible performances, none can dispense with the courtesy and solicitude of the last three lines; it is the tenderness that prevails. Lear's waking words at Dover may come again, 'I should e'en die with pity / To see another thus.' Lear dies 'with pity', and that access of pity, which in the play attends the dissolution of the senses and of the self, is a condition for the renewal of human life.

If, believing with Albany that 'All friends shall taste / The wages of their virtue', we wish that Cordelia could get up and walk away, we may have that solace too; for this is, after all, not a primordial sacrifice but a play. The boy who played her part no doubt survived to enjoy a Christian burial 'in hope of the resurrection to come'. If his voice had not cracked in the interim he might have played Hermione or Marina. But the success of the later plays does not diminish the tragic truth that, as Christopher Smart has it, 'man is between the pinchers while his soul is shaping and purifying.' Cordelia's death is an aspect of Lear's ordeal to which she is ready to submit. There is no need to associate with those who convict her of pride or perversity; for this is what is known in the old rituals as the 'comedy of innocence', when the goat was made to gnaw the vine so it could be held responsible for its own death.[53] Cordelia's innocence, we find in the theatre, and her readiness to put herself in jeopardy, are precisely what make her a fitting sacrifice.

[53] Burkert, 'Greek Tragedy and Sacrifical Ritual', p. 109.

Part IV

Comedy, Human and Divine

13 The Theatre of God's Judgements – *All's Well that Ends Well* and *Measure for Measure*

When the sick King of France in *All's Well that Ends Well* is miraculously cured of a fistula by the daughter of a dead physician, the cultivated nobleman Lafeu is made to read to us from what appears to be the title of a street ballad, 'A showing of a heavenly effect in an earthly actor'. It might be said of the play as a whole that it is a showing of heavenly effects in earthly actors, and if we pick up a pun on 'actors' as play-actors and as agents of a higher design, so much the better. When we go to the theatre we take with us our private and our public selves in order to exercise and to extend our own ways of being human. But we also go to enjoy, for a while, some of the privileges of being divine. 'There is no show like it,' say the gods of Erasmus's *In Praise of Folly*, looking down on the human scene, 'Good God, what a theatre!' It is one function of theatrical entertainment to enable us to indulge our humanity; another, to detach us from it and take, in time and in judicial space, a more comprehensive view of it. We look down upon ourselves.

A discussion of Shakespeare's human and divine comedy could begin with *The Comedy of Errors* and end with *The Tempest* but there are two plays, both gaining in popularity in our own time, in which Shakespeare is more than usually attentive to the relationships between human and divine theatre: *All's Well that Ends Well* and *Measure for Measure*. There

This paper has grown from two contributions to seminars at the Shakespeare Institute; the section on *Measure for Measure* retains some formulations from a review article, 'To a Saving Purpose' (*TLS*, 26 November 1976).

is a perspective in which we may locate these plays not only between Shakespeare's first comedy and his last, but also between two moments in the long history of theodicy, one in the sixth century, the other in the eighteenth. In his celebrated *Theodicy* (1710) Leibnitz set out to vindicate the divine order in a world apparently deformed by evil, and Pope obliquely followed him when he wrote:

> All nature is but art, unknown to thee
> All chance, direction, which thou can'st not see;
> All discord, harmony not understood;
> All partial evil, universal good;
> And, spite of pride, in erring reason's spite,
> One truth is clear, whatever is, is Right.[1]

Shakespeare was in touch, directly or indirectly, with analogous ideas and insights from Boethius who, while enduring imprisonment under Theodoric, consoled himself with the thought that processes which to their apparent victims manifest themselves as the waywardness of Fortune might, if a wider view could be taken of their effects and purposes, be seen as providentially ordained in a universe ordered by harmony and love. 'All shall be well, and all manner of things shall be well.'

Between Boethius and Leibnitz are many other theodicean exercises and enquiries, including *The Theatre of God's Judgements*, translated and augmented from a French source by Thomas Beard (Oliver Cromwell's tutor) in 1597.[2] Shakespeare may well have looked at it, for among its many anecdotes it includes an analogue to *Measure for Measure*; its significance, however, is more likely to be found, not in the story of the captain's wife who tried to save her husband by submitting to sexual intimidation, but in what it suggests about the theatrical and theological alignment of the late comedies. Its Preface seems to announce a theodicy:

> And unto [God] belongeth the direction and principall conduct of humane matters, in such sort, that nothing in the world commeth to passe by chance or adventure, but only and alwaies by the prescription of his wil; according to the which he ordereth and disposeth by a straight and direct motion, as wel the generall as the particular, and that after a strange and admirable order. And this a man may perceive if he would but marke and consider the whole body, but especially the end and issue of things.

In the pages that follow, however, while there is much about judgement,

---

[1] *An Essay on Man* (1734), I. 289–94.
[2] *The Theatre of God's Judgements: or, a Collection of Histories;* quotations are from the first edition, 1597 (*STC*, 1659).

there is little about art; the cosmos of Beard's account is morally ordered but not aesthetically satisfying. 'Pitiful spectacles' are 'exhibited to us' or 'set before our eyes', but they are meant to deter, not to delight: 'God hath propounded and laid open in this corrupt age a Theatre of his iudgements that every man might be warned thereby.'[3]

Had Shakespeare been attracted by the title he would have had reason to reflect wryly upon the claims of the Preface, for in the Bankside theatres the intelligence responsible for disposing chance and adventure into 'a strange and admirable order' is the playwright's; while the characters are often required to wait for 'the end and issue of things', and the audience may be privileged to 'marke and consider the whole'. There is therefore a kind of thinking about the ways of man and God that can only be carried on in the theatre, using the theatre itself as an instrument of thought. The forms of discursive rhetoric used by philosophers and theologians are not capable of exposing ideas to certain highly relevant stresses and tests which can be brought to bear on the stage. Skilled in such exposure, Shakespeare's confidence in the divine order is much less assured than that of Boethius, Leibnitz and Beard, but it is nevertheless there. His comedies, particularly *All's Well* to *The Tempest* often awaken expectations (not always fully honoured) that word, story and spectacle will 'find a harmony in things that are most strange to human reason.'[4]

In his history-plays Shakespeare had already used the theatre to exhibit, and to call into question, those providential laws that were thought by the chroniclers to operate in what they, like Beard, regarded as a theatre of God's judgements. Such laws, often bringing Nemesis and Divine Vengeance to bear upon those whose cruelty, negligence or weakness deserved it, owed as much to fiction as to recorded fact, and in Shakespeare's plays as a whole, intricate connections might be traced between those that are most attentive to the chronicle record and those that are apparently remote and visionary – between *Richard III*, for example, and *The Tempest*. God's retributive justice as enacted in the chronicles of Richard's reign, and imitated in the play, is exposed to protesting analysis by the Duke of Clarence, one of its culpable victims: 'He needs no indirect or lawless course to cut off those who hath offended him.' The ministers of the Divine Will in the history-play do indeed take indirect and lawless courses in the execution of a justice that would satisfy Thomas Beard, but whose spirit Shakespeare embodies in the repellent stage presence of Queen Margaret. Clarence, however, is also the dreamer whose marvellings about the submarine world anticipate the metamorphoses of which Ariel sings, as a

---

[3] Ibid., pp. 93, 183.
[4] Thomas Middleton, *Women Beware Women*, I, ii. 181–2.

'minister of Fate' in a very different showing of heavenly effects among earthly actors.

Beard at several points touches on material that interested Shakespeare. But when he reflects on the fates of Caesar, Brutus, Antony and Cleopatra, for example, he cannot be said to reveal in them the 'strange and admirable order' proclaimed in his Preface:

> Marke here the pitifull tragedies that following one another in the necke were so linckt together, that drawing and holding ech other, they drew with them a world of miseries to a most woful end: a most transparent and cleare glasse wherein the visages of Gods heavy iudgements upon all murderers are apparently deciphered. (p. 250)

'Strange and admirable' are words that Shakespeare himself uses, with very different evocations, in and about *A Midsummer Night's Dream*, where he displays the lovers' 'shaping fantasies that apprehend / More than cool reason ever comprehends.' His version of the Antony and Cleopatra story owes its outcome, on a greater scale, to the shaping fantasies of transfigured minds and to 'something of great constancy' outside the scope of Beard's imagination.[5] The space between the lovers in *Antony and Cleopatra* is the stretch of the Roman Empire across the Mediterranean; in *Troilus and Cressida* it is either side of the city walls in time of war; in *All's Well* it is a social distance, but of more than social consequence. Shakespeare's focus in the comedies is not on the larger movement of political events, but on love in relation to power, within the specific cultural conditions of court and city. Love, for Boethius as for Dante, is the ultimate unifying principle of the cosmos, but earthly versions must take in Dante's Paolo and Francesca, Chaucer's *Troilus and Criseyde*, and Shakespeare's Othello, Pandarus and Helena.

Chaucer, in *Troilus and Criseyde* allows his hero to believe with Boethius in 'Love, that of erthe and see hath governaunce', but he does not allow him a blissful theodicean retrospect. Troilus after a long ordeal looks down after death upon the human scene to find its governed not by love but by 'blinde lust'; compensated by rarer satisfactions, he scorns the spectacle but finds it amusing; it seems that (unlike Chaucer's readers) he is not delighted by the love tale as Chaucer tells it when, among 'the erratik sterres, herkeninge armonye / With sownes fulle of hevenish melodye', he sees 'with full avysement':

---

[5] See *A Midsummer Night's Dream*, v, i. 26, and for a fuller discussion of *Antony and Cleopatra* see ch. 7.

And doun from thennes faste he gan avyse
This litel spot of erthe, that with the see
Enbraced is, and fully gan despyse
This wrecched world, and held all vanitee
To respect of the pleyn felicitee
That is in hevene above; and at the laste
Ther he was slayn, his looking doun he caste;

And in himself he lough right at the wo
Of hem that wepten for his deeth so faste;
And dampned al our werk that folweth so
The blinde lust, the which that may not laste.
(*Troilus and Criseyde*, V. stanzas 260–1)

Shakespeare's Troilus is not allowed that privilege, but it could be said that the theatre spectators are free to look down and laugh. Not, however, in the same spirit; there is no glimpse of plain felicity in heaven, and they are denied a lyrical outcome for the love-story, whether in a comic mode (*Much Ado*) or a tragic one (*Romeo and Juliet*). What they are most directly offered is a reductive and sardonic comedy, taking its bearings from Thersites and Pandarus. If there is another possibility, sustaining the values of love, government and chivalry in a mutilated world and sounding harmony where discord prevails, it must be clarified through the subtler symmetries and structures of Shakespeare's art in the play as a whole.[6]

All's Well can be treated as another comedy of the marriage market (like *Much Ado* or *The Taming of the Shrew*); 'Get thee a good husband,' says Parolles to Helena, 'and use him as he uses thee.' But the language and action of the play is suspended between importunate practical considerations and wonderful ones. Its terse and cryptic sentences are tuned to remote evocations – subjection and authority, virtue and power, wisdom and mortality, the living and the dead, the old and the young, sorrow and affection. But the King's illness, Bertram's disaffection and Helena's distress are the here-and-now stuff of comedy. The man Helena is after is so far above her that she cannot at first hope to marry him. Cosmically speaking, he is out of her sphere, and animally speaking:

Th' ambition in my love thus plagues itself:
The hind that would be mated by the lion
Must die for love.
(I. i. 90–2)

In an ordinary, familiar voice she says she is ready to lose her virginity 'to her own liking', but in another of her voices she contributes to the play's

[6]A topic pursued in ch. 3.

high, sententious musings on the nature of divine order and human freedom, and she cultivates a capacity to look down upon the human scene:

> Our remedies oft in ourselves do lie
> Which we ascribe to heaven. The fated sky
> Gives us free scope, only doth backward pull
> Our slow designs when we ourselves are dull.
>
> (I. i. 216–19)

No comparable elbow room for human endeavour is allowed in the theatre of God's judgements. Shakespeare's theatre offers a radical challenge to Beard's, but unlike *Measure for Measure*, *All's Well* does not directly test Beard's solution to the perplexities of theodicy. From the earlier plays it would be reasonable to predict that the comedies would come to probe more fully our 'free scope' under a 'fated sky', together with that of the characters performing under the playwright's direction. Helena designs to win Bertram and her design contributes momentously to Shakespeare's own plot, which from the start has its divine and human aspects. To the sick King of France Helena seems 'heaven sent', but the audience (seeing all) is not allowed to forget that her true motive for curing him is to move her virginity up-market and to lie with a lord.

The connections between Helena as a saviour or instrument of the Divine Will, and Helena as man-hunter are subtly as well as openly made. She tells the King that among the 'receipts' her father gave her was one:

> Which as the dearest issue of his practice
> And of his old experience th' only darling,
> He bade me store up, as a triple eye,
> Safer than mine own two, more dear.
>
> (II. i. 106–9)

Shakespeare may well be recalling Criseyde's lament when she looks back upon Troy and Troilus at the end of the story:[7]

> 'To late is now to speke of this matere;
> Prudence, allas! oon of thyn eyen three
> Me lakked alwey, er that I cam here;
> On tyme y-passed, wel remembred me;
> And present tyme eke coulde I wel y-see.
> But futur tyme, er I was in the snare,
> Coude I not seen; that causeth now my care.'
>   (*Troilus and Criseyde*, v. stanza 107)

The 'triple eye', or 'third eye', is an attribute of *Prudentia*. It makes pro-

---

[7] Quotations are from the text in *The Story of Troilus*, ed. R. K. Gordon (1964).

vision for the future, just as Providence itself, from *pro-videre*, is a way of looking forward. It has a place, therefore, in the divine comedy of the play, as indeed it has in the *Divina Commedia* of Dante.[8] For those in Shakespeare's audience who picked up the allusion to Prudence, however, and understood her to be an aspect of the divine will, there could be others to take the 'third eye' for a bawdy joke (as it is elsewhere in Jacobean drama) archly referring to Helena's virginity (knowing too, that she has to be prudent in her disposal of it). All would see that the father with his marketable remedy has made prudent and providential provision for his daughter.

Helena is sententious again, to a rhyming tune, as she tries to persuade the King to accept her divine ministrations:

> It is not so with Him that all things knows
> As 'tis with us that square our guess by shows;
> But most it is presumption in us when
> The help of heaven we count the act of men.
>
> (II. i. 149–52)

She expresses the Boethian insight into human incapacity to comprehend the divine order. But Shakespeare is himself squaring his guess by a show and allows his audience to know more than the King knows, and more than Helena admits to knowing. Thus, while Helena persuades the King that they are players in the Divine Comedy, we can see she is also playing in a very human one from which none of the players can wholly disengage. Her eager piety, which has its clarity and truth, is attended by her determination to go to bed with Bertram. When, a little later in the scene, she invites the King to punish her, should she fail, for her 'impudence' and her 'strumpets boldness' her words fit the human comedy only too well, taking it in the direction of Lafeu's unchivalrous innuendo, 'I am Cressid's uncle, / That dare leave two together. (II. i. 97–8).

When Helena's plot wins her the choice of 'a youthful parcel of noble bachelors' it is rich in the comedy of human frailty. Bertram is snobbishly but righteously indignant that a bride should be thrust upon him, Helena is mortified to be refused, and the King is angry and touchy about his honour. When Bertram submits to the will and power of the King, however, we may still discern, behind the prudence, the irony and the evasion, the shape of the divine plan. When the King says, 'Obey our will, which travails in thy good', he speaks as an instrument of Bertram's destiny, and the marriage can still be seen as the fitting climax of a miraculous and providential design. A design, however, from which Bertram, after a prudent

[8] Dante, *Purgatorio*, xx, 130–2. For further references see *All's Well*, ed. Russell Fraser, New Cambridge Shakespeare (1986), ad loc.

profession of obedience, struggles to free himself.

Squaring his guess by shows, he makes his get-away to the wars, leaving behind him a letter which, in one dimension of the play's comedy, is meant to keep him out of Helena's bed and affections for ever:

> 'When thou cans't get the ring upon my finger, which never shall come off, and shew me a child begotten of thy body that I am father to, then call me "husband": but in such a "then" I write a "never".
>
> (III. ii. 57–60)

The letter is intended as a snub and its dismissive wit, making the '[k]not eternal' as he writes to his mother, is meant to be free of ambiguities. But Helena, knowing like Chaucer's Criseyde that 'Goddes speken in amphibologyes', reads it as an oracle. In other late comedies – *Pericles*, *Cymbeline*, *The Winter's Tale* – oracular courses are 'ordered by Lady Fortune', by 'the fingers of the powers above', by Time, and 'great creating nature'; in *All's Well* they are ordered, tuned and ripened by Helena herself. She makes the last sentence of the letter the basis of her next design:

> 'Till I have no wife, I have nothing in France.'
> Nothing in France, until he has no wife!
> Thou shalt have none, Rossillion, none in France;
> Then hast thou all again.
>
> (III. ii. 99–102)

Bertram is overreached and outwitted by a lady who remains in her discomposure poised and objective enough to assume the role of the goddess and strumpet Fortune,[9] and to take Bertram as her hostage. The comic snare that she devises is not without its own 'amphibologyes'. Her cryptic letter to the Countess insinuates her own readiness to die a pilgrim-martyr's sacrificial death:

> 'He is too good and fair for death and me,
> Whom I myself embrace to set him free.'
> (III. iv. 16–17)

But in fact, she is not, as she claims, sanctifying his name with zealous fervour; she is footing it to Florence to spy on him. She is poignantly distressed that the prospect of marriage should have driven Bertram to the 'none-sparing war'. In the play, however, war has no point other than to display and test the manly virtue of those who take part in it (on either side), and manliness turns out to be a very ambiguous attribute. It is not the valiant hero she pursues and catches in Bertram, but the licentious and

[9]See above, pp. 47–9.

treacherous soldier. 'He goes to flesh his will in the spoils of her honour,' says the Second Lord, when Bertram thinks he is bedding Diana. The gross human comedy, however, is transfigured. Helena the designing woman, the strumpet Fortune, the adventurous pilgrim, the miraculous therapist, wittily transforms Bertram's disreputable lapse into the virtuous fulfilment of a sacred obligation:

> Let us assay our plot, which if it speed,
> Is wicked meaning in a lawful deed,
> And unlawful meaning in a lawful act
> Where both not sin, and yet a sinful fact.
> (III. vii. 44–7)

Helena's power over Bertram therefore is not merely the kind that Fortune might exercise, it is ministering the divine laws and sanctities of marriage. Yet, as Bertram experiences her, she is (as he later claims) 'a common gamester to the camp'. In this disguise he finds Helena 'pleasant' and she is delighted, wins his ring, bears him a child, and fulfils the oracle.

The comedy remains active at once in the territories of love and war, and of what we may call divine revelation – by processes outside their control characters are revealed for what they are. Bertram as Captain of the Horse consorting with 'a common gamester' is behaving like Cassio with Bianca in the audience's eyes and with Desdemona in Othello's, and like Diomedes with Cressida in Thersites' version. He is therefore as vulnerable to exposure as Parolles. The design of the Lords Dumaine upon Parolles keeps pace with Helena's design upon Bertram. Parolles is a wordy, swaggering pretender whose cowardice is comically brought home to us when he is delivered into the hands of his fellow officers, talking 'Bosnian' and pretending to be enemies. 'You do not know him as we do,' says the First Lord to Bertram, 'but when you find him out you have him ever after.' Parolles is found out. 'He was first smok'd by th' old lord Lafeu', says the First Lord, and when Parolles himself returns to court humiliated he tells Lafeu, 'O my good Lord, you were the first that found me.'

By this route we may return to Parolles' master and Helena's – to Bertram. Helena's first words to Bertram commit her to his service:

> I give
> Me and my service, even whilst I live,
> Into your guiding power.
> (II. iii. 102–4)

But he repudiates her service and tries to escape it. She becomes his unseen 'guiding power' and he too, like Parolles is 'found' for what he is. And when Helena has found him out she has him for ever. 'Be sure your sins will find you out,' says the Book of Numbers, in a text much favoured by Beard.

Shakespeare's version of 'finding out', however, is not like Beard's, or indeed, in this play, like that of the Old Testament. Here, as in the *Theatre of God's Judgements*, and in *Measure for Measure*, there is a constant keeping of judicial watch upon the principal characters. Among the play's characters we can distinguish the watchers and the watched, the judges and the judged, the finders and the found. But pre-eminently the watching, judging and finding prerogatives are allowed to the audience. Parolles and Bertram are exposed, stripped of their pretensions, and compelled to submit to the service of others. To put the point another way, however, they are returned, by way of the human judgements of the play's spectators, to their own humanity. They have both been 'crush'd with a plot', but 'there is place and means for every man alive', and as an audience we know that simply the things we are must make us live.

'All's well that ends well' is a proverb that proves in the play to be rather less reassuring than we might expect. It is full of solace when we hear it from Helena as she sets out for home from Florence: 'the time will bring on summer . . . / Our waggons are prepared and time revives us / All's well that ends well; still the fine's the crown.' But it is not the seasonal change that ends the course, it is the springing of Helena's trap. A good woman, the human comedy says, if she's a designing woman, will always catch a bad man out. The final reassurances are severely qualified: 'All yet *seems* well,' says the bewildered King. The ethical and aesthetic laws of courtship, marriage and comedy require that Jack should have Jill and naught should go ill, and 'if souls guide vows, if vows be sanctimonies, / If sanctimonies be the gods' delight' (*Troilus and Cressida* V. ii. 139–40), these same laws are 'divine'. But Helena at the end is wedded to a crushed Bertram and the King is ready to start the whole thing up again when he offers to let Diana take her choice from his parcel of Bachelors. These are sceptical and human glosses on the way in which the playwright and Helena between them have shaped a divine love-comedy, a kind of theodicy. The play's *Deus ex machina* does not belong to the pantheon of Beard's Theatre, but to a human world which has found fresh scope for the creative exercise of a woman's affections, vitality, knowledge and intelligence.

Measure for Measure is a later and more ambitious human and divine comedy, engaging more directly with the traditions and convictions represented by Thomas Beard. That it was indeed the later play (perhaps by a year) is indicated by the fact that the bed-trick, found in both, is in the sources of *All's Well*, but not in those of *Measure for Measure*.[10] The

---

[10] In Boccaccio, *Decameron*, Day III, Story 9, William Painter. 'The Palace of Pleasure' (1566–7, 1575); see Bullough, II, pp. 389–96.

bed-trick is as old as the Book of Genesis, where Jacob wakes in the morning to find that, owing to the cunning of his father-in-law, Laban, he has spent the night with his sister-in-law, Leah, instead of his wife, Rachel. In both Shakespeare's plays (not in the Bible) it is used to make sexual intercourse at one and the same time the consummation of a sacred relationship, and a flagrantly sensual adventure. (It also suggests that for men, given silence and darkness, one woman is much the same as another.)

Measure for Measure was made by Shakespeare from the stories, plays and teachings of others, and (more extensively than *All's Well*, which is largely confined to the court) from the language of the community. It invites us as playgoers and as readers, to reconcile in one experience, pleasure in old romantic tales, an understanding of the Christian Gospels, a knowledge of life and government in cities and states, and an awareness of our weaknesses. We are entertained by the wisdom of the Church, the wit of the hangman, the love of God and the love of the brothel, by the mess of human life and by perplexed intimations of divine order. If the play is a 'problem', it is because it is hard to keep pace with its art, both in Shakespeare's theatre and, figuratively, in the theatre of God's judgement.

In a chapter about persecutors of the Gospel Beard writes:

> For though it may seeme for a time that God sleepeth and regardeth not the wrong and oppressions of his servants yet he never faileth to carry a watchful eie upon them, and in his fittest time to revenge himself upon their enemies. (p. 56)

Beard, it seems, would have been a reasonably contented spectator at a play that from the start invites attention in three interrelated perspectives – divine, human and theatrical. The divine is evoked in the title's allusion to St Matthew: 'Judge not that ye be not judged'; 'With what judgement ye judge, ye shall be judged; and with what measure ye mete, it shall be measured to you again.' Under the sway of these texts the play-world is constructed in obedience to laws that are active in Beard's theatre – a watchful eye is kept upon the servants of God and on their enemies.

That same watchfulness, however, also opens up the play's human and theatrical perspectives into spaces ultimately outside the reach of Beard's perceptions. 'Of government the properties to unfold . . .' announces a formidably comprehensive theme. The Duke leaves the government of his city in order to put his Deputy's virtue on trial. Looked at one way, Angelo is required to assume the responsibilities and prerogatives that the Sovereign derived from God (Beard's chapter 6 is attentive to some of the corollaries – 'How the greatest Monarchs in the world ought to be subject to the law of God, and consequently the lawes of man and of nature'). Looked at another way, Angelo is a man like any other, and the withdrawal of the

Duke's power and presence is a necessary condition of creative human freedom:

> for if our virtues
> Did not go forth of us, 'twere all alike
> As if we had them not. Spirits are not finely touched
> But to fine issues.
>
> (I. i. 33–6)

'Let there be some more test made of my mettle,' says Angelo; and that test is carried out, in front of an audience made more than usually observant of human capacities and frailties.

But to what end? To what fine issue? The question might be posed either generally, in the manner of theodicy, about life at large, or specifically about those comedies that many, taking a hint from Polonius, are ready to call 'tragicomedies' because they encompass certain tragic effects before revealing that all ends well. At the turn of the century 'Mungrell tragicomedy', as Sidney once called it, enjoyed a refreshed and more sophisticated life under the critical sway of Guarini.[11] The genre may be said to include Whetstone's *Promos and Cassandra*, the principal source of *Measure for Measure*, and Shakespeare's own *Troilus and Cressida*, placed in the Folio between the histories and the tragedies, and often associated with the 'problem plays'. When potentially tragic happenings are brought under comic control by the presiding intelligence of the play its tragicomic form is ripe for theodicy.

The retributive laws of Beard's *Theatre*, 'punishing the world according to their demerits' are only intermittently at work in *Troilus and Cressida* – they are better satisfied by Henryson's version of the story, in which Criseyde is afflicted with leprosy. In *Measure for Measure* the comedy creates the conditions for their satisfaction and then disengages from them. Something similar might be said about a number of other comedies, including *The Merchant of Venice*, in which a city and its laws are under critical inspection, and whose plots turn on what Beard (writing 'Of Usurers and their Theft') calls 'unjust and crafty bargaining' (p. 413). The earlier play's discoveries about money and the affections in Venice, beautifully focused in the story of the bond, are made with irony and grace. But in

---

[11] For an account of Guarini's *Compendio della Poesia Tragicomica* (1601), see Madeleine Doran, *Endeavors of Art* (1954), pp. 203–8, and *Measure for Measure*, J. W. Lever ed. (1965), p. lxi: 'He supposed the form to take from tragedy "its great characters but not its great action; a likely story but not a true one; . . . delight, not sadness; danger, not death"; and from comedy "laughter that was not dissolute, modest attractions, a well-tied knot, a happy reversal, and above all, the comic order of things." This avoidance of extremes was said to be justified in the conditions of the modern world.'

Measure for Measure, concerned with the government of the city and of the passions in Vienna, the ironist's surgery probes more searchingly into the psyche, into society and into what men have taken to be the divine order of things.

The play's intimations of 'grace' are in touch with a greater range of Biblical doctrines and metaphors. Man has fallen, and is continually falling, from the state of grace and innocence in which he was created – which is a richly conventional way of saying that we have an apparently invincible tendency to make a mess of things. The totalitarian constraints of Vienna have collapsed through licentious neglect. The play's plot attends to the constraints of divine and civil order and its language expresses the destructive and creative energies of the unconstrained, free and licentious self. While the governors are unfit to govern, the governed can be ungovernable. It is Claudio who speaks most immediately for the governed – subject to the Divine law, to the state and to his own nature. In an encounter with Lucio, rich in companionable comedy, he takes the measure of all three: of the 'Authority' that invokes the 'words of heaven: On whom it will, it will; on whom it will not, so; yet still tis just' (I. ii. 122–3); of the new governor whose 'tyranny' awakes the 'enrolled penalties' that the Duke for 'nineteen zodiacs' has let hang by the wall; and of himself. The allusion to Romans 9: 15, 'I will have mercy on him to whom I shall show mercy' both exposes and accepts the arbitrariness of the Divine dispensation, and Claudio imposes the same, distinctly Calvinistic moral vision upon his own propensities. When Lucio playfully asks him, 'Whence comes this restraint?' Claudio speaks wisely under arrest:

> From too much liberty, my Lucio, liberty:
> As surfeit is the father of much fast,
> So every scope by the immoderate use
> Turns to restraint. Our natures do pursue,
> Like rats that ravin down their proper bane,
> A thirsty evil, and when we drink we die.
> (I. ii. 125–30)

Criticism has alighted with either satisfaction or bewilderment on the 'water' and the 'proper bane'.[12] It is a leading figure in the play's design, owing its verbal treachery primarily to the ugly truth about poisons which excite the thirst that kills the rats. The invitation to moderation is one that

[12] See Terence Hawkes, 'Take me to your Leda', *Shakespeare Survey*, 40 *(1987)*, *pp. 21–32;* William Empson, *Seven Types of Ambiguity* (1930) (1947), p. 184. Empson treats the 'rats that ravin' simile as an instance of the fifth type, 'lying between two things when the author is moving from one to the other'. But the instability here owes more to the phenomenon it describes than to the impression that the author 'is discovering his idea in the act of writing'.

Aristotelian tradition extends to free men in the confidence that his natural reason would prompt him to accept it. But by the metaphor the life-sustaining appetites are intimately bonded to the destructive ones; such, it might be said (speaking wisely), is our Fallen Condition. Speaking more ordinarily, we can see that some (like Claudio) are rigorously punished for behaving naturally when the law catches up with them, while others (like the Burghers who protect the City brothels) get away with it – or think they do.

The ambiguous energies that drive the natural, subject self, also drive the magisterial self. 'The Magistrate is or ought to be a Speaking law,' says Beard, 'and ought to maintain the authoritie and credit thereof, by the due and upright administration of Justice: for if he did not this, he were a dumb law and without life' (p. 13). The Magistrate must therefore enforce the law and obey it; but in the play's human perspective the Duke has failed to enforce it and his Deputy fails to obey it. As Beard says elsewhere, it is 'the dutie of an earthly prince to exercise not only clemencie and gentlenesse, but also sharpnesse and severitie, thereby by punishing and chastising malefactors to suppress all disorders in the Commonwealth' (p. 7). It is a truth that the Duke sees clearly when he looks back through the Friar's eyes:

> My business in this state
> Made me a looker-on here in Vienna,
> Where I have seen corruption boil and bubble
> Till it o'errun the stew. Laws for all faults,
> But faults so countenanced that the strong statutes
> Stand like the forfeits in a barber's shop,
> As much in mock as mark.
>
> (v. i. 316–22)

The Friar's access to the life of the community provides 'a most excellent looking glasse for kings to behold the sickleness and instabilitie of all their power and pompe' (p. 127). The Duke/Friar is the looker-on who, like Beard's God, 'never faileth to carry a watchful eie' upon 'the wrong and oppression of his servants'. It is also the playwright's watchful eye, and ours.

This theatrical perspective most conspicuously opens prospects for fresh thought about Divine order and human confusion. Shakespeare allows the Duke/Friar a prerogative similar to the playwright's own. Turgenev once told Henry James that he looked upon his characters as '*disponibles*', 'subject to the chance, the complication of existence.'[13] Playwrights and novelists

[13] Henry James, *The Portrait of a Lady* (1881), ed. Leon Edel (1968), Preface, pp. 15–16.

(like the ancient bards and god-smiths) create characters not merely to show us what they will do, but also to find out what they will do. So it is with both the Duke and Shakespeare, looking upon Angelo in Act I, sc. iii: 'Hence shall we see If power change purpose: what our seemers be.' They use the theatre in order to make a discovery about human nature – to show us something and to find something out. In the course of the play human dispositions are exposed to many experiential stresses and the responses are often both reassuringly natural and unreassuringly culpable. Characters are put to the test and they convincingly fail. As spectators, intimate or distant, we are moved or startled at the inability of human principles to keep control of human reactions. Shakespeare uses the theatre in order to make a discovery about human nature: he shows us something, and he finds something out.

When Shakespeare's King Henry V moves in disguise among his subjects, it happens casually, unannounced to the audience. But in *Measure for Measure* the device is advertised, flaunted almost, as a trick of the theatre. It is as if the Duke is expecting something to go wrong but does not quite know in what way or to what degree. Like Shakespeare, he has set the character in action and then keeps watch on it. This keeping watch – the presence on the stage for much of the time of the spectator-duke – makes a crucial difference to the way in which the audience experiences the first, catastrophic, movement of the play. 'There is a kind of character in thy life,' the Duke tells Angelo in the first scene, 'That to th' observer doth thy history / Fully unfold.' Through the first three acts the character in Angelo's life is more fully unfolded to the observer. And not his character only, but those of all engaged in the action. Keeping track of the re-created life of the human discourse – argument, cadence, rhythm and metaphor – it is impossible to allege any human improbability in the scenes that bring on the play's central predicament. The process starts with Lucio, coming fresh from the brothels to the nunnery to enlist Isabella's help for her brother:

> Fewness and truth, 'tis thus:
> Your brother and his lover have embraced,
> As those that feed grow full, as blossoming time
> That from the seedness the bare fallow brings
> To teeming foison, even so her plenteous womb
> Expresseth his full tilth and husbandry.
>
> (I. iv. 39–44)

Here, if anywhere, is the play's version of the precarious state of innocence, turning the Fall into a procreative miracle. Isabella initially takes the offence lightly ('O, let him marry her'), and later, although conceding, under doctrinal pressure from Angelo, that to 'coin heaven's image / In stamps that are forbid' is as mortal a sin as murder, she adds a significant reservation: ' 'Tis set down so in heaven, but not in earth.' The old story of the Fall brings death and procreation into the world at the moment when human freedom is first exercised, and it creates immense stresses and difficulties when translated into dogma and law. Human love as expressed in sexual procreation is contingent upon the Fall. Lucio's Shakespearian eloquence about great creating nature does not dwell upon the theology, but it stirs instinctual sympathies, and his prompting of Isabella when she intercedes with Angelo ('Ay, touch him, there's the vein') forges a significant link between one kind of warmth of feeling and another, between the lovers' sexuality on the one part, and companionable or filial compassion on the other. We are made aware of the multiple ways in which we may obey the imperative, 'love one another.'

Moving in this territory of human experience *Measure for Measure* probes those vulnerable spots of language and awareness that Beard (p. 9) calls the 'most secret thoughts' of 'conscience':

> God hath bestowed upon every one a certaine knowledge and iudgement of good and evill, which being naturally engraved in the tables of mans heart, is commonly called The law of nature: whereby every mans owne conscience giveth sufficient testimony unto itselfe, when in his most secret thoughts it either accuseth or excuseth him.

Angelo's capacity to put himself in another's place (one aspect of 'conscience') is tested by Escalus, inviting him to ask if he too could not have offended, 'Had time cohered with place or place with wishing.' But it is only when he listens to Isabella's superb moral exhortations and is sexually excited by them that he is betrayed by the treacheries of the language and of his own nature: 'She speaks, and 'tis / Such sense that my sense breeds with it.' Her moral exaltation, animated by what her brother calls her 'prone and speechless dialect', awakens a response which is instantly contaminated, and he desires 'her foully for those things / That make her good.' Given the right performer and performance his excitement is shared by the audience.

Shakespeare's art in this movement of the play is in an intimately convincing flux of word and feeling, close in style, as in date, to *Hamlet*:

> What's this? What's this? Is this her fault or mine?
> The tempter, or the tempted, who sins most? Ha?
> Not she, nor doth she tempt; but it is I
> That, lying by the violet in the sun,
> Do as the carrion does, not as the flower,
> Corrupt with virtuous season.

> (II. ii. 162–7)

He is like dead flesh growing rotten in the sun. The coherence of time and place spring upon Angelo a kind of existential trap. Similar traps are prepared for Isabella and Claudio.

Under another of the great religious metaphors, Isabella would become a 'bride of Christ'. Her intense and absolute moral commitment breeds in her what Leavis called 'a sensuality of martyrdom':

> Th' impression of keen whips I'ld wear as rubies,
> And strip myself to death, as to a bed
> That longing have been sick for, ere I'ld yield
> My body up to shame.
>
> (II. iv. 101–4)

The commonplace truth is that a preoccupation with chastity is inseparable from a preoccupation with sexuality. The greater mystery, the 'plague spot' as Keats called it,[14] connecting 'goatish winnyish lustful love' with 'the abstract adoration of the deity' is made exquisitely clear in the warmth that Isabella's pleading gathers from her responses to Lucio. Out of Lucio's love of vice there is generated the kind of virtue that Angelo sins in loving. Lucio is a sort of Pandar trying to procure Claudio's pardon by vicariously seducing Angelo from the strict course of law. Once it is planted there is no way of arresting the 'strong and swelling evil' of Angelo's 'conception'.

The trap that is sprung upon Claudio is the death-sentence. The austere Stoic consolation (remote in spirit from Boethius) which the Duke offers him takes from biblical tradition the desolating recognition that 'all things here below are vain' without the contrary conviction that we must make cheerful use of what we have,[15] and from classical tradition its temper and manner recall Juvenal rather than Horace, Virgil or Lucretius:

> Reason thus with life:
> If I do lose thee, I do lose a thing
> That none but fools would keep.

[14]'Here is the old plague spot; the pestilence, the raw scrofula. I mean that there is nothing disgraces me in my own eyes so much as being one of a race of eyes nose and mouth beings in a planet call'd the earth who all from Plato to Wesley have always mingled goatish winnyish lustful love with the abstract adoration of the deity. I don't understand Greek – is the love of God and the love of women expressed by the same word in Greek? I hope my little mind is wrong – if not I could – Has Plato separated these loves? Ha! I see how they endeavour to divide – but there appears to be a horrid relationship.' As Claude E. Finney remarks (*The Evolution of Keats's Poetry*, Cambridge, Mass., 1930), at the time he wrote this note on 'Love's beginning, Object, Definition, Division' in his copy of Burton's *Anatomy*, Keats seems not to have read the *Symposium*, where he would have found Plato's distinction between the Uranian and Pandemian Aphrodites.
[15]Ecclesiastes 1, 2: 24.

....

> Thou hast nor youth nor age,
> But as it were an after-dinner's sleep,
> Dreaming on both, for all thy blessed youth
> Becomes as aged, and doth beg the alms
> Of palsied eld; and when thou art old and rich,
> Thou has neither heat, affection, limb, nor beauty
> To make thy riches pleasant.
>
> (III. i. 6–8, 32–8)

Claudio is apparently persuaded: 'To sue to live, I find I seek to die, / And seeking death, find life. Let it come on.' But Claudio's acquiescence in the Duke's version of the *ars moriendi* is owed to the punitive frustration of his life-delight; the death-rhetoric casts its spell only while there is no prospect of renewed life.

The decisive trial of both Isabella's and Claudio's humanity comes when they meet, and Claudio glimpses the possibility of a reprieve – he may yet live if she yields to amorous intimidation (submits to rape). Neither can respond fully to the intensity of the other's distress. The moral imperative (the need to be good) confronts the vital imperative (the need to live). 'Death is a fearful thing,' cries Claudio; 'And shameful life a hateful,' retorts Isabella. Each stance has its history, in the play and in the wider traditions from which the play was made. But the passionate momentum of the encounter allows no scope for reflection. The votary of St Clare, for example, might have learned from St Augustine that no lesser sin may serve to avoid commission of a greater, but Isabella, caught by a cruel vortex in the currents of filial affection, is not capable of deploying text and dogma in the manner of her first encounter with Angelo. Claudio exercises his ratiocinative skills only to humanize Angelo and his pragmatism stops short of recognizing that a man who makes such a bargain is unlikely to keep it.

Taking different liberties with the source material, and in some respects keeping closer to them,[16] a sentimental playwright might have devised a very different scenario. Isabella (turned transient heretic in her ordeal)

---

[16] Cinthio's Epitia, after much moral debate, yields to Juriste (the counterpart of Angelo), to save her brother from execution for rape, but it apparently proceeds. The Emperor requires Juriste to marry Epitia, but she forgives her husband only when a captain reveals that he substituted the head of a condemned fratricide (see Bullough, II, pp. 402–3, 420–42). After condemning Andrugio to death for an offence resembling Claudio's, Promos takes Cassandra to bed but fails to keep his bargain with her. She reports to the King, who requires Promos to marry her before being punished by death; it turns out that her brother's gaoler had substituted 'A dead man's head, that suffered the other day', and all ends well within what Guarini calls 'the comic order of things'. (See Bullough, II, 406–7, 445–515).

might have been made ready to sacrifice her prospects of salvation to save her brother; while Claudio, absolute for death, would resolutely forbid her. Angelo, moved by such a demonstration of self-effacing affection and honour, would have relented, repented and graciously surrendered his office. As it is, Claudio's natural impulse to cling to life is impaled upon Isabella's equally natural indictment of his honour – 'Wilt thou be made a man out of my vice?' Isabella's dedicated preoccupation with her chastity, frustrated by filial obtuseness, corrupts her solicitude into childish fratricidal nausea:

> O you beast!
> Take my defiance!
> Die, perish! Might but my bending down
> Reprieve thee from thy fate, it should proceed.
> I'll pray a thousand prayers for thy death,
> No word to save thee.
>
> (III. i. 135, 142–6)

A predicament has been created for which there is no human solution.

Shakespeare's solution waits in the watchful presence of Duke Vincentio, whose problem is exactly analogous to the playwright's own, and if this were the world's globe and not the Globe Theatre, the problem, for a theodicean, would be God's. The Duke, who has just prepared Claudio to die, sees him reassume his unhappy free self and plead naturally, if ignominiously, for his life. In a number of other plays and stories of Shakespeare's time a ruler moves about his country in disguise, but it is consistent with Shakespeare's earlier plays that he should here be disguised as a friar. Shakespeare had used friars to try to sort out human confusions before – in *Much Ado*, where Friar Francis has only modest success, and in *Romeo and Juliet*, where Friar Lawrence in the end has none. In *Measure for Measure* it is as if Shakespeare resolves into a single figure Friar Lawrence and Prince Escalus of Verona. The role of the Friar, like that of the Votaress, gives the playwright easy access to the words of the Gospel and the teaching of the Church, together with the privilege of intimacy with certain characters, while the roles of Duke and Deputy put Renaissance theories of law and government, together with the machinery of the state, at his disposal. The disguise convention itself enables Shakespeare to create a theatre-world informed by an omniscient and omnipresent omnipotence. Under these conditions the comedic catastrophe should be assured, but it will remain, to say the least, vitally unstable.

Both as Duke and Friar, Vincentio is brought close the playwright and helps Shakespeare to make his own art manifest to the audience, *Measure for Measure* teases us into and out of an awareness of the analogy between divine and human creators in the world and in the theatre, allowing it sometimes a solemn validity, as when Angelo says, 'I perceive your grace, like power divine / Hast looked upon my passes'; and sometimes making mock of it, as when Lucio describes Vincentio as 'the fantastical Duke of dark corners'. Between the god and the fantastic comes the Duke as compassionate father, liberal ruler, frustrated plotter and meddler, but all of them keep in touch with Shakespeare the playwright. Shakespeare is aware that he can no more leave his characters than can the Duke his subjects, to work out their own salvation. Conscience will not serve to regulate the city or the passions, because Angelo's immensely active conscience does not deter him from his vices. Humane government will not serve either, since Escalus continues to be taken in by the Deputy. Nor can the populace be trusted, because they are committed to false logic and mostly make their living in the city's brothels.

Any account of the divine and human comedy of *Measure for Measure* must recognize that, when in Act III, sc. i. l. 150, the Duke comes forward in his disguise as friar, the action changes its mode, its conventions, its perspective; verse gives place to prose; and intrigue, leisured and measured, displaces the tensions and *agons* of the first movement. The aesthetic shock is considerable. We pass from Shakespeare's poetry at its most urgent and exploratory to the easy lies and evasions of the Duke's 'crafty' talk; from Claudio's keenly apprehended terror of death to the Duke's apparently facile reassurances; from:

> Ay, but to die, and go we know not where;
> To lie in cold obstruction and to rot
> This sensible warm motion to become
> A kneaded clod; and the delighted spirit
> To bathe in fiery floods, or to reside
> In thrilling regions of thick-ribbed ice;
> (III. i. 117–21)

to this:

> Son, I have overheard what hath passed between you and your sister. Angelo had never the purpose to corrupt her; only he hath made an assay of her virtue to practice his judgement with the disposition of natures. She (having the truth of honour in her) hath made him that gracious denial which he is most glad to receive. I am confessor to Angelo, and I know this to be true; therefore prepare yourself to death.
> (III. i. 159–67)

But the change of style is one for which Shakespeare has made very careful provision by keeping the Duke on stage as spectator to the intimate events. The Duke's lies are white lies, meant to save the situation for the time being. But they also carry some of the play's truths. 'He hath made an assay of her virtue to practice his judgement with the disposition of natures', is not true of Angelo about Isabella, but it is true of the Duke about Angelo, and of Shakespeare about both Angelo and Isabella. He is, of course, the romantic playwright, using Romance tricks to recover order from human disarray. But even as theatre-goers we may continue to see the Duke as we see the friars of the earlier plays, as the sum of the many well-meaning devices that people employ in order to save each other from the consequences of crime, passion and folly.

The ugly predicament created by Angelo compels the Duke to enter into an imperfectly convincing conspiracy of creative deception with Isabella and Mariana. In doing so he may be said, like Shakespeare, to be finding a theatrical solution to an otherwise insoluble human problem. It is as if he invents the moated grange, the character of Mariana and Angelo's pre-contract of marriage with her, for their existence could not have been disclosed under the conventions operating at the start of the play without the Duke appearing a calculating manipulator. As it is, 'Craft against vice I must apply' is neither a proclamation of omnipotence nor an elementary confession of human opportunism.

The craft is as much the playwright's as his character's, and in the last act it is deployed with great skill. The theatrical solution which the playwright finds for the human problem is not arbitrary (much less so than the text from Romans 9: 15 would warrant); it keeps in touch with all the human values and verities exhibited in the play – justice, mercy, chastity and love, with the necessary vindications and qualifications. 'The "resolution of the plot", is ballet-like in its patterned formality and masterly in stagecraft.' says F. R. Leavis.[17] Shakespeare is taking advantage of the range of conventions which the Jacobean theatre used in masque to allegorize the elusive ways of the gods. Isabella's version of the human spectacle becomes Shakespeare's:

> But man, proud man,
> Dress'd in a little brief authority,
> Most ignorant of what he's most assur'd,
> His glassy essence, like an angry ape
> Plays such fantastic tricks before high heaven
> As makes the angel's weep.
>
> (II. ii. 117–22)

The fantastical Duke is a trickster too, and Shakespeare a trickster, but the tricks are played to a saving purpose, with all the resourcefulness of the

[17] 'The Greatness of *Measure for Measure*,' reprinted from *Scrutiny* in *The Common Pursuit* (1952), pp. 160–73.

old Romance tales and of the theatre.

Shakespeare moves with disarming skill from the 'human' to the 'divine' perspectives, and from the divine to the 'theatrical'. By switching our perceptions from one to the other we can see some of the specific 'problems' for what they are. It has, for example, been thought inhuman of the Duke that he should so long delay telling Isabella that her brother is still alive. But Shakespeare's theatre is still putting Isabella to the test. When she finally kneels to plead for Angelo's life, her solicitude is a fuller exercise of the Gospel ethic than it would otherwise have been:

> Look, if it please you, on this man condemn'd
> As if my brother liv'd. I partly think
> A due sincerity governed his deeds,
> Till he did look on me.
>
> (v. i. 443–7)

A playful theological irony, too, moves the Duke to give Isabella a very human explanation of the failure of his omnipotence to save her brother's life:

> O most kind maid,
> It was the swift celerity of his death,
> Which I did think with slower foot came on,
> That brain'd my purpose.
>
> (v. i. 393–6)

If we think of the Duke as a man, he is telling a plausible lie. His plan almost miscarried in the way he describes. If we think of him as 'power divine', we are reminded of how difficult it is for God to keep pace with human wickedness. Beard in his Preface marvels at the 'wonderfull and incomprehensible wisedom of God, when by the due ordering of things so different and so many, he commeth still to one and the same marke . . . to wit, the punishment of the world according to their demerits'. It is a skill any playwright might envy as he tries to emulate it. The Duke does succeed in saving Claudio, however, while at the same time exposing Isabella to the experience of losing him. That experience is not too closely explored, and we do not take Isabella's distress too seriously because as playgoers we see that the playwright has the remedy in his hands. The Duke is made to say:

> But I will keep her ignorant of her good,
> To make her heavenly comforts of despair,
> When it is least expected.
>
> (IV. iii. 109–11)

The punishment of Angelo and the satisfaction of Isabella are postponed to the last moment of the last act – to the play's denouement and a last judgement.

In one tradition of response to the play its religious or anagogical significance prevails unambiguously.[18] Nevill Coghill proposes a version that Dante might have approved. Shakespeare, he reminds us, 'has turned Whetstone's Cassandra, who is described merely as "a very virtuous and bewtiful woman", into Isabella, about to enter the cloister and to become a votaress of St Clare, and the Bride of Christ.' In the play's final *Paradiso*, as he calls it, as the Te Deums soar and the trumpets blow 'over one sinner that repenteth', Isabella is apparently to become bride to the Duke, who 'has withdrawn himself into invisibility from the world of which he is the Lord', remaining 'as it were, omnipresent and omniscient . . . seeking to draw good out of evil', and reappearing 'like power divine' to preside over the judgements of the last scene. The 'devious Lucio', on the other hand, is a version of Lucifer or the devil: he is the 'cunning enemy that, to catch a saint / With saints dost bait thy hook.' Both the Duke and Lucio, however, work under too many theatrical constraints for Coghill's anagogical design to be more than intermittently and ironically present.

The Duke is a fit mouthpiece for the Gospel wisdom and the efficient agent of Divine judgement. But if he is allowed to be a more than ordinary character it is not because he is meant to be a god but because Shakespeare allows him some of his own privileges. From the point of view of Angelo, those privileges look like 'power divine' because Angelo can do nothing that the playwright-duke doesn't know about. Beard can yield a Divine apologia, however, for the Duke's cat-and-mouse game with Angelo in the last act: 'if at any time he defer the punishment of the wicked, it is for no other end, but to expose the fullnesse of their sinne and to make them more inexcusable . . . And thus the vengeance of God marcheth but a soft pace . . . to the end to double and aggravate the punishment for the slacknesse thereof' (p. 467). Angelo's false self holds out until the last moment – the suggestion is that we do not confess our sins until we have to – but the false self is finally put to death and he is allowed to make a fresh start (if not to be born again).

In one respect Shakespeare keeps his distance from the Duke: he is more ready to consort with publicans and sinners. The populace of Vienna is allowed a lot of untameable vitality, and where the Duke is frustrated by the freedom exercised by his obstinately human subjects, Shakespeare makes

[18] See Nevill Coghill, 'Comic Form in *Measure for Measure*', *Shakespeare Survey*, 8 (1955), pp. 14–27; R. W. Battenhouse, '*Measure for Measure* and Christian Doctrine of the Atonement', *PMLA*, 61 (1946), pp. 1029–59. Wilson Knight's celebrated essay, '*Measure for Measure* and the Gospels' is in *The Wheel of Fire* (1930), ch. 4.

way for it. Like Claudio, the substitute Barnadine proves very unready to die at the hands of the new hangman lately recruited from the brothels. The Duke, disguised as friar, calls on Barnadine, as once on Claudio, to prepare him for his end:

Sir, induc'd by my charity, and hearing how hastily you are to depart, I am come to advise you, comfort you and pray with you.

Barnadine Friar, not I; I have been drinking hard all night, and I will have more time to prepare me, or they shall beat out my brains with billets. I will not consent to die this day, that's certain.

Duke O sir, you must; and therefore I beseech you Look forward on the journey you shall go.

Barnadine I swear I will not die today for any man's persuasion.

It is a radical instance of a character getting out of hand, and of that vital imperative – the need to live – which prevails in the play.

The anagogical or religious design is live enough, but the play does not come to rest in it. The anagogical way of putting it argues that if it were not for Lucio, representing the devil as instrument of God, Angelo and Isabella would never have been tested. But the human way argues that without his lecherous friend Lucio, Claudio would have lost his head. In its treatment of Lucio, however, the play yields much to both kinds of analysis. His scurrility and his quick affections co-exist, and his gossiping habits, his licentious talk, give fresh life to the text in St Matthew, 'Every idle word that men shall speak, they should give account thereof in the day of judgement' – the day of judgement again coinciding with the play's denouement. But, humanly speaking, it becomes more important to believe in the damage that Lucio the man can do than in the damage the devil can do. Those who think the Duke vindictive in requiring Lucio to marry the punk on whom he has fathered a child would do better to keep their sympathy for the punk.

The play ends with a prospect of the Duke's marriage to Isabella, a prospect that Coghill and others see as a prefiguration of divine wedding – the votaress become the bride of Christ. It is more readily taken as a recall of both the Duke and Isabella to an ordinary humanity; the Duke's 'complete bosom' slily pierced by the 'dribbling dart of love', and Isabella too amazed by the play's ethical intricacies to know how to respond.

The attention that the psychiatrist Eric Berne has given to 'Games People Play' may with advantage be diverted to Shakespeare's comedies.[19] We discover that in the comedies some use plots, trickery, disguise, eavesdropping and lies destructively while others use them creatively. There is not a comedy which does not make ample use of creative deception. But 'games'

[19]Eric Berne, *Games People Play* (1966).

are not quite the same as 'plays'; games are played, in Berne's account, in order to win, while plays are framed for order and delight. This is finally what *Measure for Measure* affords – order and delight. The wonder is that it assimilates so much human confusion and waste into its order. And *Measure for Measure* remains one of the best defences we have against many kinds of attack upon civilized values, whether from the puritanical rigour and totalitarian tyranny represented by Angelo, the liberal free-for-all and the verbal treachery represented by Lucio, or the retributive cosmic theocracy advanced by Oliver Cromwell's tutor. As for the play and the Gospels, it is itself a parable in that high tradition, rich in paradoxes and ironies, and it achieves its demonstration: 'Judge not, that ye be not judged', for 'With what judgement ye judge, ye shall be judged; and with what measure ye mete, it shall be measured to you again.'

'In his fittest time,' says Beard, God will revenge himself upon the enemies of his servants. That 'fittest time' in the theatre of God's judgement is doomsday. In Shakespeare's theatre it is the denouement of the last act, when all the festive conventions of comedy demand that things be put right. A theatre-goer familiar with Beard's austere retributive theology could recognize in Shakespeare's play, if he dared to do so, an adroit turning-of-the-tables. Those who choose to believe that God works in a mysterious way his wonders to perform are met by the tantalizing question – 'You mean this way?'

14 History and Histrionics in *Cymbeline*

The sources of *Cymbeline* are sufficiently known. What now are we to do with them? Source-hunting offers its own satisfactions and it is an acceptable mode of conspicuous leisure, but it should be possible still to bring it to bear more closely on the problems of literary criticism.[1] Its bearing, however, may differ from play to play. It is salutary, for instance, to recognize that striking debt owed by *The Tempest* to travel literature.[2] When we find that Shakespeare's contemporaries allegorized the historical event we may more readily discount E. E. Stoll's scepticism about allegory in the play. I think, too, that the play sheds a backward light upon its sources, making us more alive to their dramatic and poetic potential.

Cymbeline is a different problem. It is not so self-evident a masterpiece. There is the common passage and there is the strain of rareness. The sources and analogues could be used to explain away whatever fails to make an immediate, effacing impression. But they have too, I think, a more positive value. They can show that many of the play's uniquely impressive effects could have been won only out of that specific area of convention that Shakespeare chose to explore. Within this area we can distinguish something like a dramatic genre, and as a label we might take Polonius' infelicity 'historical-pastoral' or, in deference to received opinion, 'historical romance'. Such labels are useful because they tell us what sort of conventions to look out for, although each play is apt to define its own area, make its own map. My emphasis will be on the 'historical', for there is, I think, a

[1] I have in mind Hardin Craig's observations in 'Motivation in Shakespeare's Choice of Materials', *Shakespeare Survey*, 4 (1951). For the *Cymbeline* sources see J. M. Nosworthy's Arden edition (1955).

[2] The material of *The Tempest* is reprinted in Frank Kermode's Arden edition (1954).

way of reading the sources which lends support to Wilson Knight's claim that *Cymbeline* is to be regarded 'mainly as an historical play'.[3] Criticism may fault his quite remarkable 'interpretation' for trying to evoke a maximum pregnancy from conventions that are insufficiently transmuted from their chronicle and theatrical analogues; but it cannot fault him for recognizing that the fictions of *Cymbeline*, while owing nothing to the factual disciplines commonly called 'historical', seek nevertheless to express certain truths about the processes which have shaped the past of Britain. I shall argue that even the 'romantic significance' of the play is worth mastering,[4] and that we can best master it by way of the chronicle sources.

To initiate the appropriate dialogue between the play and its sources, we might say that *Cymbeline* is about a golden world delivered from a brazen by the agency of a miraculous providence. That archaic formulation would not have startled Shakespeare's contemporaries, and it might equally preface a discussion of the play's alleged transcendent meaning or of its manifest indebtedness to convention. I mean to use it first, however, as a clue to track Shakespeare's reading through the labyrinth of Holinshed.[5]

Holinshed's brief notice of the reign of Kymbeline reads like an old tale, and Shakespeare clearly felt no obligation to treat it as fact. He distinguished firmly between the Tudor material, whose documentary force he retained in the earlier histories, and the Brutan, with which he took the fullest liberties in *Lear* and *Cymbeline*.

There is, however, no obvious reason why he should have turned his attention unhesitatingly to Kymbeline, and since the names of the characters are scattered over a wide span of pages in the second edition of Holinshed, we may be confident that he was widely read in the Brutan phase of the history, that he began at the beginning, and that he read it quite early, culling the name 'Iago' in its course. We may indeed regard *Cymbeline* and *Henry VIII* as the last fruits of the Brutan and Tudor chronicles in Shakespeare's dramatic art. They might be presented as complemental plays – a fantastical history and an historical fantasy, but the exercise would be premature without some excursion into the reading behind *Cymbeline*.

The first chapter of the *Second Booke of the Historie of England* did most, I think, to determine the form and tenor of the play. It tells of the descent and early life of Brute, and includes this passage:

[3] G. Wilson Knight, *The Crown of Life*, 2nd edn (1948), p. 129.

[4] Cf. F. R. Leavis, 'Shakespeare . . . has taken over a romantic convention and has done little to give it anything other than a romantic significance.' *The Common Pursuit* (1952), p. 177.

[5] I have assumed that Shakespeare used the 1587 *Holinshed* and have ignored a few passages in lesser-known chronicles which might be faintly nearer to the play. My longer quotations are of material not reprinted by Nosworthy or by W. G. Boswell-Stone in *Shakespeare's Holinshed* (1896).

To this opinion Giouan Villani a Florentine in his vniuersall historie, speaking of Aeneas and his ofspring kings in Italie, seemeth to agree, where he saith: 'Siluis (the sonne of Aeneas by his wife Lauinia) fell in loue with a neece of his mother Lauinia, and by hir had a sonne, of whom she died in trauell, and therefore was called Brutus, who after as he grew in some stature, and hunting in a forrest slue his father vnwares, and therevpon for feare of his grandfather Siluius Posthumus he fled the countrie, and with a retinue of such as followed him, passing through diuers seas, at length he arriued in the Ile of Britaine.'

Concerning therefore our Brute, whether his father Iulius was sonne to Ascanius the sonne of Aeneas by his wife Creusa, or sonne to Posthumus called also Ascanius, and sonne to Aeneas by his wife Lauinia, we will not further stand. But this, we find, that when he came to the age of 15. yeeres, so that he was now able to ride abrode with his father into the forrests and chases, he fortuned (either by mishap, or by God's prouidence) to strike his father with an arrow, in shooting at a deere, of which wound he also died. His grandfather (whether the same was Posthumus, or his elder brother) hearing of this great misfortune that had chanced to his sonne Siluius, liued not long after, but died for verie greefe and sorow (as is supposed) which he conceiued thereof. And the yoong gentleman, immediatlie after he had slaine his father (in manner before alledged) was banished his countrie, and therevpon got him into Grecia, where trauelling the countrie, he lighted by chance among some of the Troian ofspring, and associating himselfe with them, grew by meanes of the linage (whereof he was descended) in proces of time into great reputation among them: chieflie by reason they were yet diuers of the Troian race, and that of great authoritie in that countrie.[6]

There is little here that would be admitted as a 'source' by the criteria of Boswell-Stone, but Shakespeare may well have recognized an opportunity to deploy the conventions of Romance in a play made from one or other of the Brutan legends. His story of the lost princes as it has finally reached us is an invention not owed to, but consonant with, the strange adventures of Brute. And *Cymbeline* touches, in a different order and to changed effect, the motifs of mysterious descent, hunting, murder (a boy killing a prince), banishment, and chance (or providential) encounter with offspring of the same lineage. There is a kind of obligation here, and in his choice of the names of Posthumus and Innogen (the wife of Brute) Shakespeare

[6]*Holinshed* (1587), i, H.E., p. 7/B.

seems to offer a playful salute of acknowledgement.

The second chapter offers another piece of ready-made theatrical apparatus. Brute and Innogen 'arrive in Leogitia' and 'aske counsell of an oracle where they shall inhabit'. Brute kneels, 'holding in his right hand a boll prepared for sacrifice full of wine, and the bloude of a white hinde', and after he has done his 'praier and ceremonie . . . according to the pagane rite and custome', he falls asleep. The goddess Diana speaks Latin verses (which the chronicle translates) sending him to an isle 'farre by-west beyond the Gallike land'. 'After he awaked out of sleepe,' the chronicle goes on, 'and had called his dreame to remembrance, he first doubted whether it were a verie dreame, or a true vision, the goddess hauing spoken to him with liuelie voice.' Once again, the vision is not a source but an occasion. It may have licensed the vision of Posthumus – a stage theophany in a play which, like the myth, is concerned with the ancestral virtue and destiny of Britain. Shakespeare drew of course on his own experience of the theatre and perhaps on a memory of *The Rare Triumphs* for the specific form of the theophany, but whether by chance or design the verse form is oddly consonant with the chronicle.[7]

These early passages are important because they reveal most clearly the romantic, numinous aspect of Geoffrey of Monmouth's myth. But Geoffrey was also something of a tactical political moralist, and for him the high magical destiny of Britain was needlessly thwarted by emulation, 'revenging' and 'dividing'. In the chapters between Brute and Kymbeline Shakespeare would have passed much material already exploited to serve a political moral by the authors of *Locrine, Leir, Gorboduc* and the pseudo-historical part of *Nobody and Somebody* – reigns which for the most part ask to be treated in the spirit of Richard Harvey's *Philadelphus*, as tracts for the times.[8]

The *Third Booke* opens with an account of Mulmucius Dunwallō, the law-giver, named in *Cymbeline* but evidently more fully celebrated in a lost play called after him.[9] Whether he took it from the old play or the chronicle, the name Cloten (given by Harrison to the father of Mulmucius[10]) may

[7] Cf. 'An Ile which with the ocean seas inclosed is about, Where giants dwelt sometime, but now is desert ground.' (*Holinshed* (1587), I, H.E., p. 9/A.)

[8] Richard Harvey, *Philadelphus, or a defence of Brutes and the Brutan history* (1593). It argues that the Brutans did exist as they show the qualities (mostly bad) that Aristotle leads us to expect from human nature. Harvey took from the history the cautionary politics Geoffrey put into it.

[9] Other lost Brutan plays were the *Conquest of Brute (Brute Greenshield)* and *Uther Pendragon*. Had they survived we might have been better placed to recognize the conventions behind *Cymbeline*.

[10] *Holinshed* (1587), I, Description, p. 117/A. Boswell-Stone cites a later page where 'Cloten' and 'Clotenus' are named. But Harrison has 'Cloten' with a 'Morgan' nearby. Shakespeare may have known chapter 22 of the 'Description of Britaine'; it gives an abstract of the whole history.

have had for Shakespeare a sly historical as well as articulatory propriety. The brassy Cloten and his mother are hypostatized versions of the arbitrary spleen and malevolence that Geoffrey often found antecedent to the rule of law.

Of the fifty or so rulers between Mulmucius and Cassibelane, Holinshed briefly describes a quarter and catalogues the rest. Only one (Elidure) seems to have been touched by the playwrights, but Shakespeare ignored them and his interest was not quickened again until he reached the point where Geoffrey is confronted by Caesar, the old tale foiled by the modern history, fantasy by fact, romance by Rome. Shakespeare accepted the challenge to admit both, and I think J. M. Nosworthy mistaken in wishing he had done otherwise.[11] For had he done otherwise we might never have heard that 'odd and distinctive music' which F. R. Leavis derives from *Cymbeline's* 'interplay of contrasting themes and modes'.

Kymbeline is named at the centre of a long section dealing with the Roman conquest and the tribute variously yielded and denied by the line from Cassibelane to Arviragus. Shakespeare's readiness to see the tribute as a momentous historical symbol is clear enough from the play, but before we begin to admire and analyse it is worth remarking that he was not alone in trying by supernatural stage machinery and symbolic verse to give something like apocalyptic scale to the tribute settlement. Jasper Fisher's academic play *The True Trojanes*, probably later than *Cymbeline* but apparently independent, testifies equally to a contemporary interest in the conflict and reconciliation of the two 'valorous races' represented by Cassibelane and Caesar.[12] But Shakespeare's treatment yields far more of the potential of Geoffrey's myth than Fisher's.

So far then, Shakespeare's reading offers a paradigm for an action which makes the reconciliation with Rome a high event in the magical movement of British history from the vision of Brute to the golden prospect of the vision of Cadwallader. But it is substance rather for a pageant or a masque than a play. To give it a richer content Shakespeare had to rely in the end on his own resources, but he had scope still to exercise his imagination on other elements in the chronicle. In pursuit of that 'odd and distinctive music' he chose to modulate from the Brutan into the Roman key and from the Roman into the Renaissance Italian. The exercise is exquisitely playful, but what prompted him to attempt it?

Holinshed does not often chime well with Boccaccio; Geoffrey's 'romance' was not the sort which delighted sophisticated Italy. And yet it happens, oddly, that the chronicle can supply a gloss to Iachimo's confession in the last act: the dullness of Britain and the subtlety of Italy are Harrison's

---

[11] Arden *Cymbeline* (1955), p. 1.
[12] The play is printed in Hazlitt's *Dodsley*, 4th edn (1875), vol. 22.

themes in chapter 20 of his *Description of Britaine*. 'For that we dwell northward,' he says, 'we are commonly taken . . . to be men of great strength and little policie, much courage and small shift'; and after entertaining and dismissing several versions of the same criticism he finished by giving it a sharp twist to Britain's advantage.[13]

> For if it be a vertue to deale vprightlie with singlenesse of mind, sincerelie and plainlie, without anie such suspicious fetches in all our dealings, as they commonlie practise in their affaires, then are our countrimen to be accompted wise and vertuous. But if it be a vice to colour craftinesse, subtile practises, doublenesse, and hollow behaviour, with a cloake of policie, amitie and wisedome: then are Comineus and his countrimen to be reputed vicious.

Harrison would have found Wilson Knight's emphasis on Posthumus as 'the simple islander in danger of moral ruin' entirely congenial.[14] The conventional sentiment of the chronicle is concerned with the national character as well as the national destiny. Shakespeare may have seen in Boccaccio an opportunity to mediate the two.

There may have been a second little motive for calling *The Decameron* and *Frederick of Jennen* into the play. W. W. Lawrence compares Posthumus in Italy with 'a young Englishman making the grand tour at the end of the sixteenth century', and the allegedly absurd anachronism might be lightly excused by a Chronicle passage used for one of Cymbeline's speeches:[15]

> it is reported, that Kymbeline being brought vp in Rome, & knighted in the court of Augustus, euer shewed himselfe a friend to the Romans, & chieflie was loth to breake with them, because the youth of the Britaine nation should not be depriued of the benefit to be trained and brought vp among the Romans, whereby they might learne both to behaue themselues like ciuill men, and to atteine to the knowledge of feats of warre.

Within the spacious perspectives of *Cymbeline* the integrity of Britain is at once nourished and jeopardized by the 'civilizing' impact of ancient Rome and modern Italy upon its heroic and innocent but vulnerable youth.

The play's preoccupation with natural and sophisticated man is, however, something far more searching than anything the sources can suggest to jaded modern eyes. But we can get an inkling of how it might have struck

[13] *Holinshed* (1587), I, Description, p. 115/A.

[14] *The Crown of Life* (1948), p. 147. Other points made there could be illustrated from the Description, bk. 2, ch. 7.

[15] W. W. Lawrence, *Shakespeare's Problem Comedies* (1931), p. 188. The *Holinshed* passage (I, H.E., p. 33/A) is quoted by Boswell-Stone; cf. *Cymbeline*, III, i. 70.

Shakespeare from John Speed's *History* of 1611. Kymbeline himself was not much more for Speed than a name on a coin, but the period of his reign was a theme for rhapsody; it was the time that Christ was born and Augustus ruled in Rome. 'Then were the times that great Kings and Prophets desired to see, but saw them not, when the Wolfe and the Lambe, the Leopard and the Kid, the Calfe and the Lyon fed together.'[16] In a later passage Speed celebrates the marvellous correspondences between Virgilian and Messianic prophecy: 'hee vseth the very words of the *Prophets* in speaking of *a Maid*, and *a Child of a new progenie borne and sent downe from heaven*, by whom the brassy and iron-like world should cease, and a pure *golden age* succeed.' Even had it been published earlier, there would be no reason to suppose that Shakespeare read the *History*. The point is that the sceptical historian was a theologian still and could see fit to display these high conventional sentiments at this moment of his account of Britain. Holinshed's (or Fabyan's) brevities noticing the birth of Christ and the rule of Augustus may have stimulated in Shakespeare's imagination a comparable range of thought; hence what Wilson Knight calls the 'theological impressionism' of *Cymbeline*.

The same part of Speed's *History* offers reflections on the 'Originals of Particular Nations', comparing them on the one hand with 'that first beginning of the universall prosemination of Mankind . . . simple and far from those artificiall fraudes, which some call *Wit* and *cunning*', and on the other to 'that first neglective condition' to which men would revolve if 'Lawes, discipline, and Customes' did not restrain them.[17] It is a polarity retained but greatly complicated in the play where the episodes of Cloten and the princes explore very nicely the possibilities of man exempt from the rule of law.

That fussy phrase 'historical-pastoral' invites in this context a theological exegesis, but Shakespeare tactfully subdues his material to honour the decorum of the theatre rather than that of theological history. Finding that within the span of Kymbeline's reign he could sustain the spell of Brute's, he undertook to charm Boccaccio and Caesar into the same 'system of life'.

It is one of the tasks of criticism to observe the poise of the dialogue, to adapt Derek Traversi's phrase, 'between convention and analysis'. But the poise registers, too, in the handling of stage conventions; the calculated anachronisms of the play as history are matched by a calculated naïvety in its theatrical technique: 'the art that displays art', as Granville-Barker has it. It seems possible that this springs from small beginnings in the chronicle too. An analysis of the peculiar use made of disguise and garments in *Cymbeline* might fairly open with Harrison's observation, 'Oh how much

[16] John Speed, *The History of Great Britaine* (1611), p. 174. See also p. 189.
[17] Speed, *History* (1611), p. 179.

cost is bestowed now adaies vpon our bodies and how little vpon our soules! how manie sutes of apparell hath the one and how little furniture hath the other?'[18] And it might pass to Holinshed's story of Hamo 'apparelling himselfe like a Britaine' to kill Guiderius and of Arviragus who 'caused himselfe to be adorned with the kings cote armour'; and then to the Scottish chronicle where Haie (Shakespeare's model for Belarius and his sons in the battle-scene) refused the rich robes that the king offered him and 'was contented to go with the king in his old garments'.[19] Shakespeare could keep one eye here on the chronicle and the other on the fashionable theatre.

In turning from the history to the histrionics in the play, however, we must distinguish between that kind of theatrical virtuosity whose effects are merely startling and arbitrary, and that which serves a responsible purpose. The themes which the chronicle offered are portentous and had Shakespeare engaged with them too profoundly he would have tested the resources of the language and the responsiveness of the audience too severely. He would also have lost touch with the mood of the *Brut*, as he certainly does in *Lear*. He abstains therefore from using his giant's strength and allows certain points to be carried by a conventional gesture. His handling of disguise, soliloquy, stage situations, properties and even characters secures in turn an apt 'suspension of disbelief' and an equally apt 'suspension of belief'. Cloten and the Queen, for example, may be said to represent a range of complemental vices (roughly speaking, the boorish and sophisticated) which menace the natural integrity of the British court. But this is true only of the conventional configuration; they are never allowed to touch the audience deeply or urgently threaten their composure. 'The euils she hatch'd, were not effected', it is said of her Queen; and they are not effected because Shakespeare uses soliloquies and asides to make her guile transparent, and allows even her gulls to see right through her. *Cymbeline* indeed lets us into all the secrets, even into the secrets of the playmaker's craft. The 'inconsistency' of Cloten and the Queen is not analysed, for example, but simply exhibited; with a faint but distinct irony and a touch of burlesque their vices are made compatible with that minimal virtue of defiant patriotism they display before the Roman ambassador.[20] The tension (such as it is) is kept on the surface, while in that earlier instance of Queen Margaret in *Henry VI* it has to be dug out. If the characters were defined and explored

---

[18] *Holinshed* (1587), I, Description, p. 172/A.

[19] *Holinshed* (1587), II, H.S., P. 155/B. See also M. C. Bradbrook, 'Shakespeare and the Use of Disguise in Elizabethan Drama', *Essays in Criticism* II (1952), pp. 159–68.

[20] I think Warren D. Smith (*Studies in Philology*, 49 (1952), pp. 185–94) overstates his claim that Cloten is merely the 'vulgar, ill-mannered villain' in this scene. Shakespeare writes perhaps with some memory of Holinshed's Voadicia (H.E. Bk. 4, ch. II) as well as an eye on Jacobean courtly proprieties.

analytically the discordant potential of the material would fracture the play. It is indeed a tribute to the decorum of the piece that Posthumus cannot for long be compared with Othello, nor Iachimo with Iago, the Queen with Lady Macbeth or Margaret, Cymbeline with Lear, nor yet Cloten with Edmund or Faulconbridge. The stresses are less between good and evil characters than between the ingenuous and the disingenuous – the lighter way of putting it is the apter.

The play offers yet more daring sophistications of stage conventions than those deployed in the plots of the disarmed (and disarming) villains. The iteration, for instance, of the phrase 'his meanest garment' leading up to that grotesque mock-recognition scene. In a play which makes so much of deceptive appearances and false judgements, there is sly irony in making the innocent Imogen a false judge and in allowing Cloten's indignation to be vindicated after death. The prevailing transparency of artifice makes one suspect that the 'clotpole' stage head was deliberately displayed as a hollow property to give bizarre point to the lines introducing it, 'an empty purse, / There was no money in't', and it refines or civilizes the violent pagan force of the symbolic justice administered to 'That harsh, noble, simple, nothing', Cloten.

In detail as in large design the mode is self-confessedly artificial. The postulates are openly declared: 'Howsoere, 'tis strange, / Or that the negligence may well be laugh'd at : Yet is it true, sir'; 'do not play in Wench-like words with that / Which is so serious'; 'This was strange chance'; 'By accident I had a feigned Letter of my Masters / Then in my pocket', 'Shall's have a play of this? Thou scornful page, there lye thy part'; 'Let him shew his skill in the construction.' Other touches recall *A Midsummer Night's Dream* rather than *Love's Labour's Lost*: ''Twas but a bolt of nothing, shot at nothing / Which the Braine makes of Fumes'; 'What Fayeries haunt this ground?'; 'mine's beyond, beyond'. There are moments too of self-parody: when Cymbeline interrupts a more than usually mannered late-Shakespearian speech from Iachimo with 'I stand on fire. Come to the matter'; and again (one suspects) when the gaoler's 'fear no more Tauerne bils' might be Shakespeare's tongue-in-cheek backward glance at Imogen's obsequies. One needs to step lightly on these points; they are slender platforms for commentary. And much the same applies to the play's imagery; the patterns and iterations traced by Wilson Knight, Traversi and Nosworthy are undoubtedly there, but they are signs of opportunities lightly taken as occasion offers; they strike as sequences meant to be glimpsed rather than grasped.

All this does not mean that the entertainment is inconsequential. However conventional the frame of *Cymbeline*, it is still meaningful and it sets the more evocative and searching passages in the order of a significant design. But no matter how sharply cut the stones in the filigree, we are reminded that the skilled craftsman has the strength to crush the fabric at will. 'The best in this kind are but shadows.'

It remains true, however, that *Cymbeline* is not organized from 'a deep centre' like *The Winter's Tale*.[21] We are haunted by intimations of a profound significance, but it is constantly clear that the apocalyptic destiny of Britain cannot be reconciled with the form of pastoral-romance on any but the terms which Shakespeare offers.

We may sum up by taking a last glance at Imogen. Her votaries from Swinburne onwards may be allowed their extravagances and let pass with an "Ods pittikins' if they will admit that perfection is not, after all, indivisible. Imogen's perfection is playfully extended to her cookery – 'He cut our roots in characters.' But she remains in some sense, still, the centre of the play. It is fitting that she should voice most memorably a version of the Virgil verse transmitted through the chronicle, 'Et penitus toto diuisos orbe Britannos': 'I' th' worlds Volume Our Britaine seemed as of it, but not in't: In a great Poole, a Swannes-nest.'[22] She is a princess of Britain, yet theme for the praise of a Renaissance courtier; a pretty page for the Roman Lucius, yet aptly called a 'heavenly angel'. Her symbolic role is secured both by the dialogue (see the second Lord's speech just before the bedchamber scene) and by the spectacle: 'And be her Sense but as a Monument, / Thus in a Chappell lying.' When she lies 'dead' alongside the body of Cloten in the clothes of Posthumus, the spectacle is an evocative symbol of a triple sacrifice (though the word is too strong) – of an innocence that will revive, an animal barbarity which is properly exterminated and a duplicity (involving Posthumus) which has still to be purged.

Lucius is appropriately named after the first of the Christian kings of the British chronicle, and it happens that the political solution – the tribute allowed from sense of fitness and not won by force of arms – can endorse the ethical in a pageant finale announcing the Golden World with a touch of that 'pagane rite and custome' which opens the *Brut*: 'And let our crooked Smoakes climbe to their Nostrils From our blest Altars . . . And in the Temple of great Iupiter Our Peace wee'l ratifie.'

My conclusion perhaps resembles too closely the 'fierce abridgment' of the last act which 'distinction should be rich in'. But I would claim that substantially the same result could be reached through an enquiry into the theatrical analogues, from *The Rare Triumphs* through *Clyomon and Clamydes*, *James IV*, *Edward I*, *Common Conditions*, *The Wounds of Civil War*, *Tancred and Gismunda* and *The Dumb Knight* to the revived *Mucedorus*, the plays of Field and Beaumont and Fletcher to *The Second Maiden's Tragedy*. It might be shown, I think, that Shakespeare reconciled

[21] Leavis, *The Common Pursuit*, p. 174.
[22] *Holinshed* (1587), i, Description, p. 2/A.

the conventions of primitive and sophisticated romantic drama to express similar reconciliations accomplished in the substance of the plot.

15 *Pericles* and the Dream of Immortality

Criticism of Shakespeare's *Pericles* has most often concerned itself with those of the play's problems that might offer a solution to patient enquiry. If the results have been disappointing, they have been intelligibly so; and yet, were the evidence less fragmentary and indecisive, and we could reach confident conclusions about authorship, literary genesis, and the skills and frailties of compositors *A* and *B*, the essential mystery of the play might still elude us, for it has to do with the insights and devices by which art attempts to encompass human mortality. If we wonder why the plays of Shakespeare's time, flourishing as they do upon a medieval root, offer so little reassurance about personal survival in a life to come, we may reflect with Wittgenstein that 'Death is not an event of life. Death is not lived through.' The plays are pre-eminently about what is lived through.

The last pages of the *Tractatus Logico-Philosophicus* may remind us that doctrines of immortality cannot in any case do what they are meant to do:

> Is a riddle solved by the fact that I survive for ever?
> Is this eternal life not as enigmatic as our present one?
> The solution of the riddle of life in time and space lies outside space and time . . .
> The riddle does not exist . . .
> The solution to the problem of life is seen in the vanishing of this problem.
> (Is not this the reason why men to whom after long doubting the sense of life becomes clear, could not then say wherein this sense consisted?)[1]

Shakespeare's last plays seem both to touch upon the riddle and to set it

[1] Quotations are from the 1962 impression of the 1922 edition.

aside; to seek answers 'outside space and time' and yet to discount whatever
is adumbrated:

> Thou thy worldly task hast done,
> Home art gone, and ta'en thy wages . . .
> (*Cymbeline*, IV. ii. 261–2)

> We are such stuff
> As dreams are made on . . .
> (*Tempest*, IV. i. 156–7)

> The fixture of her eye has motion in't,
> As we are mock'd with art.
> (*Winter's Tale*, V. iii. 67–8)

The false deaths, the strange evaporations and the miraculous resurrections
of the last plays allow to our experience in the theatre some solace of
immortality that cannot readily take dogmatic form. 'Whereof one cannot
speak, thereof one must be silent'; but the poet is not under the philosopher's
obligation to keep silence – he finds a language to express the inexpressible.
What cannot be held by dogma or reached by systematic thought may be
intimated to the experience of our affections through the 'fine frenzy' of
metaphor and rhythm.

The intimations of *Pericles* may need no gloss – 'he that hath ears to
hear, let him hear'; but it is nevertheless of some consequence to our larger
perspective of literary understanding to notice that they have multiple
sources. The sources in part are perennial and experiential – in continuing
human endeavours to foil suffering and loss with dream and vision; but
they are also dramatic and literary, to be traced in Shakespeare's own art,
in the elements of romantic tale and (as F. D. Hoeniger has well observed)
in the traditions of the miracle play.[2]

For a rendering of the relevant human experience, it happens characteristically that we may look to Shakespeare's own art. When Clarence in *Richard
III* (I. iv.) tells Brackenbury of his ominous dream, death by drowning
finds a significantly resonant place in the play's poetry. The chronicle gave
but slender occasion for it. As a child Clarence had crossed the water to
meet Philip of Burgundy, and in the dream he is crossing to Burgundy
again, with Richard of Gloucester 'upon the giddy hatches'. The dream is
an intimation of risk ('Methought that Gloucester stumbled') and of the
coming-on of a Senecal doom ('that grim ferryman'); but returning to the
scene after reading *Pericles* the dream enables us to measure the distance

[2]*Pericles*, ed. F. D. Hoeniger, Arden Shakespeare (London, 1963), pp. lxxxvii-
xci.

of the dreamer's sense of reality from the political and human exigencies
of the mundane world. 'What was your dream?' asks Brackenbury, gaoler
to a political prisoner, 'I long to hear you tell it.' And Clarence tells of
'reflecting gems' that in scorn of eyes . . . woo'd the slimy bottom of the
deep', and of an ordeal of drowning, of belching, his soul seeking 'the vast
and wandering air'. It needs little prompting to recognize these tiny
prefigurations of the principal metaphors of *The Tempest* and of *Pericles*.
In *Richard III* they shadow forth, however transiently, the existence of an
imaginative world more spacious and elusive than that which Richard is
managing, and its mysterious processes of transmutation and renewal,
physical in themselves, seem haunted by a moral significance that receives
in this play no sustained expression. Clarence is drowned in a malmsey
butt, with little scope for allegoric tempest to his soul.

A history of Shakespearian metaphor might pass readily from Clarence's
'reflecting gems' to Ariel's, 'Those are pearls that were his eyes'. The sea-
change of *The Tempest* is a comprehensive metaphor, expressing those
strange mutations that can come about in the moral and political world
through the interventions of Prospero's magical skill. But natural processes,
the metaphor reminds us, are themselves strange and unpredictable,
particularly those that relate to death by sea. And in *The Tempest* the sea
is a moral agent in itself, whether clearing the mud from the beaches (v.
i. 79–82), or casting indigestible delinquents upon the shore:

> You are three men of sin, whom Destiny,
> That hath to instrument this lower world
> And what is in't, the never-surfeited sea
> Hath caus'd to belch up you.
>
> (III. iii. 53–6)

Man's spiritual nature, it might be claimed from *The Tempest*, is made
more comprehensible by Shakespeare's response to the nature of the sea,
and by his command of verbal expressions of the sea's movements. And so
it is in *Pericles*. *Pericles* is an old tale re-told within the comprehensive
metaphor of the sea.

It is unfortunate that we may not be able to attend to the tale as
Shakespeare first told it, for the text has, it seems, been sadly tempest-
tossed. Assumptions about the nature of its transmission are apt to qualify
one's account of the play, and there is therefore some need to say what
they are.[3] Although attributed to Shakespeare when first published in

---

[3] In what follows I have expressed a disposition but abstained from arguing a case.
The relevant data are very fully set out in *Narrative and Dramatic Sources of
Shakespeare*, VI (1966), ed. Geoffrey Bullough, and also discussed by Kenneth
Muir, *Shakespeare's Sources*, I (1957).

Quarto in 1609, with five reprints following in the years to 1635, it was mysteriously excluded from the 1623 Folio and admitted only to the third in 1664. Rowe omitted it but Malone with reluctance included it. Modern editors and critics have largely agreed in finding the first two acts less authentic than the last three, but they have differed in their diagnoses. It has been argued that the text is wholly a reported one, with one reporter (with a poor memory but a stickler for form) responsible for the first two acts, and another (with a better memory but careless of form) responsible for the last three.[4] Rival hypotheses see the play as divided in authorship, with Shakespeare responsible for the last acts and a minor figure for the first two. The slender and inadequate evidence allows us to believe alternatively that Shakespeare took up an old play and intervened with quickening interest and confidence until, by the time he reached the third act, he was virtually re-writing it; if the text were a good one we would need to accept as Shakespeare's responsibility both what he wrote and what he left, but as at several points the text is manifestly corrupt, our acceptance must remain discontented. I find it convenient to acquiesce in the notion of an old play re-written, because it consorts well with the impression that Shakespeare is offering an old tale re-told. When the play lapses from,

> The blind mole casts
> Copp'd hills towards heaven, to tell the earth is throng'd
> By man's oppression, and the poor worm doth die for't
> (I. i. 100–2)

to

> So puts himself unto the shipman's toil,
> With whom each minute threatens life or death
> (I. iii. 23–4)

we may assume either that the text is scarred by the reporter's memory, or that Shakespeare has allowed some voice other than his own still to be heard. But we may also believe that these 'inferior' lines come between the manner imitated from Gower:

> The lady shrieks, and, well-a-near,
> Does fall in travail with her fear
> (III. Chorus, 51–2)

and what the mature Shakespeare will make of it:

[4] By Philip Edwards, *Shakespeare Survey*, 5 (Cambridge, 1952), pp. 25–49.

> This world to me is as a lasting storm,
> Whirring me from my friends.
>   (IV. i. 19–20)

In some areas Shakespeare retails the wide-eyed gaucherie of his Romance sources, and in some he transmutes it to a revelatory simplicity.

Significantly enough, the play that was once a story was apparently turned again to story by George Wilkins in *The Painfull Adventures of Pericles Prince of Tyre* and its title-page tells us with satisfaction that it was 'excellently' presented in the theatre by 'the worthy and ancient Poet John Gower'. Whatever the history of the text, there is little doubt that Shakespeare was either content to take over the theatrical figure of Gower or that he invented him. He is used to mediate between the sophistication of the audience and the naïvety of the tale. Ben Jonson, skilled in the kind of comedy that by deftness of wit, subtlety of observation and controlled caricature, recalls us to norms of responsive social conduct, found nothing to admire in the 'mouldy tale' raked 'into the common tub' to 'keep up the Play-club'. Remembering what Samuel Johnson said of *Cymbeline* about wasting criticism upon 'unresisting imbecility', we must acknowledge that *Pericles* offers comparable resistance to good sense. The stage Gower could not appease everyone. Yet he is meant to appease; to disarm criticism, to invite the acquiescence of the modern intellect in an old eloquence. 'Thought with affection' (to adapt a phrase of Blake's) may take the play as Shakespeare took the verse of Gower and the prose of Laurence Twine, responding to its innocence and tolerant of its inconsequence, for these qualities seem here invincibly related; there are certain truths, Shakespeare seems to claim, that can only be conveyed in this archaic mode.

In a manner less conspicuously artless Shakespeare returns to a similar mode in *The Winter's Tale*. There is no story-teller, but the chorus and the wry and wondering allusions in the dialogue remind us that we are attending to an old tale:

2 Gentleman   What, pray you, became of Antigonus, that carried hence the child?

3 Gentleman   Like an old tale still, which will have matter to rehearse though credit be asleep and not an ear open: he was torn to pieces with a bear.
                                                        (V. ii. 57–61)

And a space is opened between what is true and what is credible:

> This news, which is call'd true, is so like an old tale
> that the verity of it is in strong suspicion.
>   (V. ii. 26–7)

Shakespeare's disposition to tell old tales was not, of course, a merely personal one. He had participated and collaborated (see *The Two Noble*

Kinsmen) in a Blackfriars fashion for revived Romance. For it happened at the beginning of the seventeenth century, and would happen again at the end of the eighteenth, that a society with a highly complex and civilized literary culture looked back to old tales and to the Middle Ages in search of rich simplicities, expressible in innocent speech and show. Shakespeare's Gower is an artefact corresponding to Chatterton's Rowley, and testifies to a similar nostalgia for an unspoiled innocence of imaginative understanding:

> To sing a song that old was sung,
> From ashes ancient Gower is come,
> Assuming man's infirmities,
> To glad your ear and please your eyes.
> It hath been sung at festivals,
> On ember-eves and holidays,
> And lords and ladies in their lives
> Have read it for restoratives.
>
> (I. Chorus. 1–8)

I have no difficulty in believing Shakespeare well pleased with such an opening. It is close to what literary history would invite us to call the romantic response to Romance. The old songs, sung at festivals and read by lords and ladies for restoratives, are those that Chatterton taught Keats to admire and in his own way to emulate.

When Keats exclaimed upon 'The Floure and the Lefe',

> Oh! what a power hath white Simplicity!
> What mighty power has this gentle story!

he was acclaiming qualities that Shakespeare may have recognized in the sources of *Pericles*. If we ask of the play, as Pericles asks of Marina, 'how achieved you these endowments, which you make more rich to owe?' we might find answers from the *Gesta Romanorum*, the *Confessio Amantis* and *The Patterne of Painfull Adventures*. These are the principal literary versions for Shakespeare of a tale that had, and still has, live currency in the oral traditions of Mediterranean Europe. How does Shakespeare discover or confer the 'power of white simplicity'? Apollonius in the story solves the incestuous riddle of the King of Antioch, takes to the seas in fear of revenge, finds a wife at Pentapolis, loses her in childbirth at sea, leaves the child at Tharsus and returns years later to learn that she has died; desolate and despairing he nevertheless clings to life to be miraculously reunited with his daughter, unspoiled by the pirates and the brothels, and with his wife, votaress of Diana at Ephesus. Shakespeare's interventions in the narrative are slight: he abbreviates the incest at Antioch, adds a second and third fisherman to greet Pericles from the sea, contrives the tournament for Simonides' daughter and enlarges the brothel episodes at Mytilene. More marginally, the name of Apollonius is changed to Pericles (recalling the Athenian Pericles from Plutarch, it has been suggested, and chiming with *periculum* for the sake of the dangerous voyaging); the daughter's name, Thaisa, is given to the mother to make way for the more precise and evocative 'Marina'. But the play's closeness to the narrative in structure and manner startle more than its divergencies of detail. The deaths of Antiochus and his daughter, for example, are reported with comparably brisk moral expedition in the play and the tale, and are not featured like the similar event in *A Looking Glass for London and England*. Gower's effacing, transparent fluency is sympathetically imitated by the play (if a little transposed into the manners of self-indulgent old age) and it offers the ground for the Shakespearian variations.

We may say of all Shakespeare's 'Last Plays' that each is about the renewal of creative life in an afflicted state of society. In each a miraculous providence works, through different agencies, to saving purpose. But in each an element of self-confessed artifice qualifies the auspicious outcome to remind us that the ultimately reassuring moral order that can be displayed to us in the theatre is indeed theatre; it cannot be transposed too promptly into 'fact' – the verity of it is under suspicion. *Pericles* is so contrived; its scenes of recognition and reunion that are the vehicles for the most expressive movements and metaphors of the poetry, are 'framed' in an old tale, by a particular technique of presentation. It is a technique that delights in spectacle and evades one kind of human reality in order to express another. We may take our cue from the stage Gower again:

> What pageantry, what feats, what shows,
> What minstrelsy and pretty din,
> The regent made in Mytilen,
> To greet the King.
>
> (v. ii. 6–9)

The play opens as a pageant, a feat and a show, with Gower to display the ranked heads of dedicate but uncomprehending princes; we must not ask why they failed to read so transparent a riddle – the convention of an antique tale will not stay to be questioned, but must be satisfied with the sudden moral dismay of the Prince who finds that 'she who comes apparell'd like the spring' is an 'eater of her mother's flesh'. The dismay is present enough for the purpose of the tale but it is not tragically realized; Gower's language could not have explored it, and the play's does not attempt to. Nevertheless, play and tale alike open with a blight upon a father and daughter relationship miraculously perfected 'in very sanctity'.

Without betraying Gower's large design, however, the play gathers little by little its own range of intensities and significances. The second scene opens with what might have been a self-questioning soliloquy in the manner of Hamlet, with the Prince musing upon the prevailing sins of the world and assuming a vicarious burden of tragic guilt. But it is not sustained – not, at least, in the version of the scene that reaches us through the eccentricities of transmission. The Lords of the Quarto bid farewell to Pericles before they can know that he is leaving and are promptly and inexplicably reprimanded for flattery. It may be that the authentic text provided a more decorous departure; as it is the play keeps the tale's peremptoriness ('Our Prince . . . Thus sodeinliche is fro ous went'),[5] while insinuating a more generous motive for flight than that he 'wolde his deth eschuie'. Pericles is moved by love for his subjects to evade the wrath of Antioch, to 'stop this tempest ere it came', and therefore 'puts himself into the shipman's toil'. The play is quick to initiate its dominant structural rhythm, its movement from the coast, the several territories of the 'mortal shore', to the high seas and back again.

The waywardness of the play, however accidental it may be, does nothing to diminish its consonance with the romance, and it a little enhances its continuity with miracle play. Antioch is a scene to exemplify one condition of life – where courtesy and grace are the masks of vice. Tyre exemplifies another, where lords in council about a good king seek his safety and that of the state. Tharsus is the opulent and proud society humiliated and brutalized by famine:

> All poverty was scorned, and pride so great
> The name of help grew odious to repeat . . .
> Those mothers who to nouzle up their babes
> Thought nought too curious are ready now
> To eat those little darlings whom they lov'd.
>
> (I. iv. 30–1, 42–4)

Pericles comes from the sea 'with attendants' bringing corn to the desolation of the streets. Oddly, though he speaks of going to Tharsus when he leaves Helicanus, Pericles does not then speak of the famine he means to relieve. Human purposes of that kind are not sustained in the play or in the tale; the circumstances of the story make the Prince bountiful, and bounty becomes his natural attribute, an aspect of his royal virtue. It is not necessary to claim that the Digby play of *Mary Magdalene* is a source, but F. D. Hoeniger is right to see it as an analogue: *Pericles* is a sequence of pageant episodes that attends as much to divine as to human purpose.

The second act opens with the narrative and the dumb-show that take Pericles from Tharsus and have him wrecked on the coast of Pentapolis. The dumb-show, which takes little time in the reading, can take much in the playing:

[5] Gower, *Confessio Amantis*, ed. G. C. Macaulay (Oxford, 1901), bk 8, I, 494.

Enter, at one door, PERICLES, *talking with* CLEON; *all the* Train *with them. Enter, at another door, a* Gentleman *with a letter to Pericles; Pericles shows the letter to Cleon. Pericles gives the Messenger a reward, and knights him. Exit Pericles at one door and Cleon at another.*

The symmetrical entrances and exits ('all the train with them') and the ceremony of knighting, together no doubt with 'minstrelsy and pretty din' keep the ugly facts at a distance without disguising them. It is hard to realize that one king is seeking to murder another; the greater reality is the voyage and the storm, the sense of an odyssey, of a continuing pilgimage.

We need not confine ourselves to those suggestions that the analogue with miracle play might prompt (the voyages of St Paul and of the King of Marcylle). Keats in a celebrated letter speaks of the world as 'The vale of Soul-making'.[6] 'Do you not see', he asks, 'how necessary a World of Pains and troublers is to school an Intelligence and make it a Soul?' Man is formed by circumstances, says Keats, and circumstances are the touchstones and provings of the heart that give *identity* to the intelligence that in itself has none. So it is in *Pericles*. The sea and the coast of Pentapolis test and find men, give identities to their intelligences. The Prince comes, wet, to the three Fishermen. The Fishermen are what they are because of the ordeals of their working lives, and Pericles what he is because of his exposure to the storm. This, surely, is a scene of Shakespeare's making – yet it keeps its continuity with what has gone before:

Pericles   May see the sea hath cast upon you coast –
2 Fisherman   What a drunken knave was the sea to cast thee in our way!
Pericles   A man whom both the waters and the wind
In that vast tennis-court hath made the ball
For them to play upon entreats you pity him;
He asks of you that never us'd to beg.
1 Fisherman   No, friend cannot you beg? Here's them in our country of
Greece gets more with begging that we can do with working.
2 Fisherman   Canst thou catch any fishes, then?
Pericles   I never practis'd it.
2 Fisherman   Nay, then thou wilt starve, sure; for here's nothing to be
got now-a-days unless thou canst fish for't.
Pericles   What I have been I have forgot to know:
But what I am want teaches me to think on:
A man throng'd up with cold.

(II. i. 56–73)

It is a tableau to be wondered at; Shakespeare musing again on

---

[6] *The Letters of John Keats*, ed. M. Buxton Forman (Oxford, 1947), p. 336.

unaccommodated man, with a naked king submitted to the resurrecting violence of the elements:

> Wind, rain and thunder, remember earthly man
> Is but a substance that must yield to you;
> And I, as fits my nature, do obey you.
> Alas, the sea hath cast me on the rocks,
> Wash'd me from shore to shore, and left me breath
> Nothing to think on but ensuing death.

(II. i. 2–7)

King and armour are belched from the sea (the 'wat'ry grave'), symbols of a harsh solicitude. But it is not merely tableau. Pericles is resurrected to the life of Pilch and Patchbreech. In the tradition that makes the lively talk of the shipman and his boy in the *Magdalene* play,[7] and in the track of the Romance reports commending the 'fisher' for his 'great pity', Shakespeare allows the affections to prevail in a state of desolation; on this occasion, the good-humoured, neighbourly affections expressed by the Fishermen's readiness to let Pericles share their lives. Life, to put the point solemnly, is renewed from a condition of death; the Fisherman puts it otherwise:

> Die keth-a? Now gods forbid't! And I have a gown here! Come, put it on; keep thee warm. Now, afore me, a handsome fellow! Come, thou shalt go home, and we'll have flesh for holidays, fish for fasting days, and moreo'er puddings and flapjacks; and thou shalt be welcome.

(II. i. 78–82)

In another aspect the community of king and fishermen has a political significance, Simonides, says Pericles, 'is a happy king, since he gains from his subjects the name of good by his government'. The first acts return several times to the responsibilities of kingship; yet they are acknowledged rather than dwelt upon. The qualities that Pericles ultimately embodies have little to do with government; they are constancy in endurance and constancy in the affections. These, we must say, borrowing the play's metaphor, are the jewels that survive the tempest.

Sympathetically regarded, the scenes that follow move deftly between the story and allegoric show. Where Gower tells of 'games' and Laurence Twine of the Prince's agility at tennis and his diligence in bathing the king, the play turns into a tableau and a tournament that have to do with the equality and the inequality of men. 'Every worth in show commends itself' and Pericles' sovereignty of nature is proved in honourable exercise. Shakespeare's gifts are not conspicuously present, but they seem to sound from far off:

---

[7] *The Digby Plays*, ed. F. J. Furnivall, EETS (1896), *Mary Magdalene*, ll. xxxx.

Whereby I see that Time's the king of men;
He's both their parent, and he is their grave.
And gives them what he will, not what they crave.

(II. iii. 45–7)

Pericles' subdued patience in face of time and circumstance is foiled by the clamorous armoured dance by which the King awakes him from his melancholy, and by the love that Thaisa so eagerly bestows upon him. The Prince's 'voice celestial' and his skill upon the harp, much admired by Gower, are not demonstrated in the play as it reaches us, but they are reported:

I am beholding to you
For your sweet music this last night. I do
Protest my ears were never better fed
With such delightful pleasing harmony.

(II. v. 25–8)

It is likely that 'minstrelsy did more than now appears to amplify the 'feats' and 'shows' of the first performances. As it is, music is much used both to superficial effect – the stage Gower's 'pretty din', and to profounder purpose, moving the imagination towards that moment when Pericles, his affections wholly reawakened and restored, hears the music of the spheres.[8]

The reawakening and restoring of the life of the affections after desolating loss is the continuing mystery, delight, preposterousness and satisfaction of the play. What is faintly prefigured in the first two acts is marvellously accomplished in the last three, partly through the fuller realization of the great central metaphor of the storm at sea, and partly through the exquisitely repetitious renderings of the tale of Marina – both are essential to the fulfilment of the play's dream of immortality.

The 'death' and burial of the queen at sea engage, as one might expect, the most generous resources of Shakespeare's art. When 'The sea-toss'd Pericles appears to speak', it is in a language whose sea-swell moves with formidable ease between cosmic awe and domestic intimacy, from, 'Thou god of this great vast, rebuke these surges, / Which wash both heaven and hell', to, 'O, how, Lychorida, / How does my queen?'. The exequy upon Thaisa finds its mysterious solace from a similar movement towards a more poignant solicitude:

A terrible childbed hast thou had, my dear;
No light, no fire. Th' unfriendly elements
Forgot thee utterly; nor have I time

---

[8] For a discussion of the music of *Pericles* and its analogues, see F. W. Sternfeld, *Music in Shakespearean Tragedy* (Oxford, 1963), pp. 244–9.

To give thee hallow'd to thy grave, but straight
Must cast thee, scarcely coffin'd, in the ooze;
Where, for a monument upon thy bones,
And aye-remaining lamps, the belching whale
And humming water must o'erwhelm thy corpse,
Lying with simple shells. O Lychorida,
Bid Nestor bring me spices, ink and paper,
My casket and my jewels.

(III. i. 56–66)

'A terrible childbed hast thou had, my dear' might be disarming domestic tenderness; and 'No light, no fire' could be the simple deprivations of birth at sea in a storm; but the terror and deprivation become momentous and cosmic with, 'Th' unfriendly elements / Forgot thee utterly', and by the submission of the sentiments to an implacable rhythm. Yet there is no despair. The protest is muted by the acceptance of necessity, and that necessity is made acceptable by the fuller recognitions of the sea's nature – the ooze, the belching whale, the humming water, the simple shells. The word 'ooze' gathered a rich significance in the later plays – Alonso in *The Tempest*, 'Therefore my son i' th' ooze is bedded', and Antony talking to Caesar about the Nile, 'as it ebbs, the seedsman / Upon the slime and ooze scatters his grain, / And shortly comes to harvest.' The 'ooze' is at once the end of life and its source, and to revert to it, we are made to feel, is almost a privilege. After touching in the fullness of its motion the huge elemental activities and sonorities of the sea – the belching whale and humming water – the verse comes to rest, with the dead Thaisa, in what is felt to be a condition of arrival – 'lying with simple shells'. As John Danby has said, it is the absolute *apathie* we both long for and disdain.[9] We may notice again the strange contiguity with the dream of Clarence. The 'aye-remaining lamps' here belong to the monument side of the metaphor, alluding to Roman sepulchres, but the lamps and the bones are not too remote from the 'in scorn of eyes, reflecting gems' of the dream, and it is fitting that Pericles should consign the jewels to Clarence's visionary slime.

The play's metaphor is elemental and its story elementary. We are fashioned from the elements, we are exposed to them, and we revert to them; hence the birth by sea, the many voyages, and the apparent death. Acceptance of the great elemental cycle is passingly expressed by Helicanus in an early scene:

[9] In *Poets on Fortune's Hill* (1952), p. 95.

We'll mingle our bloods together in the earth,
From whence we had our being and our birth.

                    (I. ii. 113–14)

But the process of Pericles' acceptance is more arduous; he must be schooled in patience:

Lychorida Here is a thing too young for such a place,
  Who, if it had conceit, would die, as I
  Am like to do. Take in your arms this piece
  Of your dead queen.
Pericles How, how, Lychorida?
Lychorida Patience, good sir; do not assist the storm.
  Here's all that is left living of your queen –
  A little daughter. For the sake of it,
  Be manly, and take comfort.

                    (III. i. 15–22)

The human simplicities prevail, but under protest:

Pericles   O you gods!
  Why do you make us love your goodly gifts,
  And snatch them right away? We here below
  Recall not what we give, and therein may
  Use honour with you.
Lychorida   Patience, good sir,
  Even for this charge.

                    (III. i. 26–7)

In the literary history of the story and its analogues, Pericles' protest sounds like a check to the reassuring theology of the *Golden Legend*. There, St Peter tells the stricken King of Marseilles to 'be not heavy if thy wife sleep, and the little child rest with her, for our Lord is almighty for to give to whom he will, and to take away that he hath given, and to re-establish and give again that he hath taken, and to turn all heaviness and weeping into joy'.[10] Without the miracle there is no reassurance, and Pericles' response depends not upon the 'gods' but upon Lychorida's affective human plea and invocation:

                Now, mild may be thy life!
  For a more blusterous birth had never babe;
  Quiet and gentle thy conditions! . . .
  Thou hast as chiding a nativity
  As fire, air, water, earth, and heaven, can make,

---

[10] William Caxton, *The Golden Legend*, Temple Classics, ed. F. S. Ellis (1900), IV. 80–1.

> To herald thee from the womb. [Poor inch of nature!][11]
> Even at the first thy loss is more than can
> Thy portage quit with all thou canst find here.
>
> (III. i. 27–9, 32–6)

It is apparently a generous patience, valuing his child's survival more than his own, for when the sailors ask, 'What courage, sir?' he can answer:

> Courage enough. I do not fear the flaw.
> It hath done to me the worst. Yet, for the love
> Of this poor infant, this fresh-new seafarer,
> I would it would be quiet.
>
> (III. i. 39–42)

Yet the worst of the ordeal is still to come, and 'patience' is not the only quality that will characterise the intelligence as it is fashioned into a soul.

If we ask what in the play assists in the recovery of life out of loss, we may take from it a diversity of answers: the sea, that casts up naked men, rusty armour and caskets; the skill of Cerimon at the miraculous first-aid post of Ephesus; the therapies of art and music; the human virtues of honour, fidelity and bounty exercised by several minor characters; and the astonishing powers of acceptance and endurance displayed by Pericles, hirsute and atrabilarian, upon the barge. But supremely, there is the buoyant and creative grace, wit, ferocity and patience of Marina in the brothel world of Mytilene. Mary Magdalene in the old play is seduced by the devil with the help of a taverner, 'luxsurya' and a 'galaunt',[12] Shakespeare's scenes have comparable vitality but an incomparably richer moral and theatrical impact – it is as if the saint herself (and not her frail unredeemed counterpart) were exposed to the luxurious energies of the fallen world:

> The nobleman would have dealt with her like a nobleman, and she
> sent him away as cold as a snowball; saying his prayers too.
>
> (IV. vi. 138–40)

Her qualities are not wholly of the passively resisting kind but receive a spacious testament, both in her own words,

> Proclaim that I can sing, weave, sew, and dance,
> With other virtues which I'll keep from boast;
>
> (IV. vi. 183–4)

and in the stage Gower's,

---

[11] I have followed Hoeniger in adapting from Wilkins the apostrophe in square brackets. See Hoeniger's note, Arden Shakespeare, III. i. 34.

[12] The Digby play of *Mary Magdalene*, I. viii.

She sings like one immortal, and she dances
As goddess like to her admired lays;
Deep clerks she dumbs; and with her needle composes
Nature's own shape of bud, bird, branch, or berry,
That even her art sisters the natural roses.

(v. Chorus 3–7)

Her attributes may look back to the sense of wonder that created the miracle plays and look about to the immediately contemporary Jacobean England, celebrated for its music and its embroidery; but they are mediated to Pericles, unwashed, hairy and dumb upon his barge, by the tale and its re-telling.

One of Keats's favourite speculations, he tells Benjamin Bailey, is 'that we shall enjoy ourselves here after by having what we call happiness on Earth repeated in a finer tone and so repeated'.[13] The play affords many repetitions (not always of happiness), and Marina's tale is several times told – by the stage Gower, by Shakespeare in the act of showing it, and by Marina within the play when she meets her father. The repetition is essential to the play's gathering significance, moving us away from the Gower without losing touch with 'the power of white simplicity'. Gower's craft is as innocent as his burden:

The unborn event
I do commend to your content;
Only I carry winged time
Post on the lame feet of my rhyme.

(IV. Chorus 45–8)

Events are 'commended', 'born' and, in recollection, born again. Repetitions return us to the central episodes with a transfiguring intensity, to be reflected on, wondered at, or energetically re-created. When Marina comes with violets and marigolds to the grave of Lychorida, her self-pity finds solace in poignantly stylized recollection:

Ay me, poor maid,
Born in a tempest, when my mother died,
This world to me is as a lasting storm,
Whirring me from my friends.

(IV. i. 17–20)

As her 'death' approaches at the hands of Leonine (we know of it but she does not) the reminiscences, owed no doubt to Lychorida but testifying to the presence of the past in her quick imagination, grow more circumstantial:

---

[13]*Letters*, ed. Forman, p. 68.

> When I was born,
> Never was waves nor wind more violent,
> And from the ladder-tackle washes off
> A canvas-climber.
>   (IV. i. 58–61)

When Marina comes at last to tell her tale again to Pericles it is in a language capable of immense perspectives, touching fortune, time and breeding, and great moral authority:

>   She speaks,
> My lord, that, may be, hath endur'd a grief
> Might equal yours, if both were justly weigh'd.
> Though wayward fortune did malign my state,
> My derivation was from ancestors
> Who stood equivalent with mighty kings;
> But time hath rooted out my parentage,
> And to the world and awkward casualties
> Bound me in servitude.
>   (v. i. 86–94)

The tale as Marina tells it literally awakens Pericles from his long trance.

'The Imagination,' says Keats, 'may be compared to Adam's dream – he awoke and found it truth.' Keats's eager speculations are not, in his own terms, to be known for truth by consecutive reasoning. Yet they offer insights consonant with our experience of the play:

> Adam's dream will do here and seems to be a conviction that Imagination and its empyreal reflection is the same as human life and its Spiritual repetition . . . the simple imaginative Mind may have its rewards in the repetition of its own silent Workings coming continually on the Spirit with a fine suddenness.[14]

In the impulsive sentences that follow Keats speaks of being 'surprised with an old Melody – in a delicious place – by a delicious voice' and of the image persuading him that 'the Prototype must be here after.' Forgiving the lapse into a sentimental mode (so much is 'delicious') and recalling the more tragic perceptions of the letter about the 'vale of soul-making', we may see in *Pericles* an answering experience. Pericles awakens to find his dream true, the silent workings of his mind (for much is made of his dumbness) surprised with a fine suddenness:

[14] Ibid.

> I am great with woe, and shall deliver weeping.
> My dearest wife was like this maid, and such a one
> My daughter might have been: my queen's square brows;
> Her stature to an inch; as wand-like straight;
> As silver voic'd.
>
> (v. i. 106–10)

It is not that Pericles believed wife and daughter to be alive still, but that Marina's presence in his imagination meets her presence in fact, with a rapture of recognition. The reality does not betray the dream but fulfils it – the paradisal experience that is denied to Lear when he awakens from his phantasmagoric hell at Dover, bound upon a wheel of fire, his tears scalding like molten lead. Recognition is a principal element in the story and the story is the vehicle of recognition; Pericles asks for more circumstance, and Marina tells him:

> If I should tell my history, it would seem
> Like lies, disdain'd in the reporting.
> (v. i. 118–19)

The realization (and how inescapable that word is) of Pericles' waking vision is exquisitely phased, for the tale offers an order of verities, attested by the beauty and virtue of the teller, and by her life in the affections:

> Prithee speak.
> Falseness cannot come from thee; for thou lookest
> Modest as Justice, and thou seem'st a palace
> For the crown'd Truth to dwell in. I will believe thee
> To make my senses credit thy relation
> To points that seem impossible; for thou lookest
> Like one I lov'd indeed.
> (v. i. 119–25)

The verities range from the remotely formulated kind, through the humane and intimate ('Modest as Justice'), to the satisfaction of the senses – both critical and physical. It is as if in all territories of experience the play had found the perfect voice and perfect auditor of its own story:

> Tell thy story;
> If thine consider'd prove the thousand part
> Of my endurance, thou art a man, and I
> Have suffered like a girl. Yet thou dost look
> Like Patience gazing on kings' graves, and smiling
> Extremity out of act.
> (v. i. 134–9)

The patience-upon-a-monument metaphor is a disquieting gloss on the spectacle just witnessed, for Pericles looks almost literally like one rising from the grave. But the moral discovery – distinguishing his own austere 'endurance' from the smiling 'Patience' of the 'fresh, new seafarer' is vital enough, and it is completed as the circumstance of the story is repeated in, as it were, 'a finer tone'. The climax of the revelation, a spiritual and sensual delirium, is expressed again by the sea metaphor, with drowning now become an ecstasy:

> put me to present pain,
> Lest this great sea of joys rushing upon me
> O'erbear the shores of my mortality,
> And drown me with their sweetness.
>   (v. i. 191–4)

and by a transparently riddling statement of the elements of the tale:

> O come hither
> Thou that beget'st him that did thee beget;
> Thou that was born at sea, buried at Tharsus,
> And found at sea again!
>   (v. i. 194–7)

These truths attained, the story recedes into that music of the spheres that Pericles (and the theatre audience) alone can hear. It entrances him into the sleep in which Diana appears, commanding him to give his 'crosses . . . repetition to the life', and to 'Awake and tell thy dream.' By the theatrical device of a vision the story is formally given what the poetry and the music have already conferred upon it – a supernal and subliminal authority. There is little left for the poet to do when Pericles goes to Ephesus, but he finds for Thaisa the quintessential formulation of the tale's mystery:

> Did you not name a tempest,
> A birth and death?
>   (v. iii. 33–4)

and the play is allowed to end with Pericles longing 'to hear the rest untold'.

It would be wrong to claim that *Pericles* as it reaches us is a consistently finished work of art, but it does fully express the potential of the material and tradition from which it was made; it rises higher than its sources and it does not muddy them. When the queen in Gower's story is retrieved from death, we are told how piteously,

> Sche spak and seide, 'Ha, where am I?
> Where is my lord, what world is this?'[15]

[15] *Confessio Amantis*, bk. 8, ll. 1207–8.

The play retains her words precisely, but with a transfiguring prelude, in which the most natural and spontaneous of effects – 'See how she gins to blow / Into life's flower again', is conjoined with the most artificial – 'the diamonds / Of a most praised water do appear, / To make the world twice rich'; it is a conjunction of eternity with life.

As for the play's experiential as distinct from literary sources, Keats a short while before his death wrote to Charles Brown a letter that intimately conveys the kind of human ordeal to which *Pericles* is foil:

> I wish for death every day and night to deliver me from these pains, and then I wish death away, for death would destroy even those pains which are better than nothing. Land and Sea, weakness and decline are great separators, but death is the great divorcer for ever . . . Is there another Life? Shall I awake and find all this a dream? There must be we cannot be created for this sort of suffering.[16]

Pericles offers its reassurances, creating a world in which death is an illusion and the dream of immortality is appeased without the postulate of an after-life.

T. S. Eliot, who found in *Pericles* 'the finest of all the "recognition scenes"',[17] was clearly thinking of Thaisa's waking words when he chose his epigraph for 'Marina' from the *Hercules Furens*: 'Quis hic locus, quae regio, quae mundi plaga?' In conjoining the tragic *anagnorisis* (Hercules awakens from his fury to find that he has slaughtered his family) with the infinitely auspicious recognitions of *Pericles*, Eliot puts both plays and poem into a vast perspective; one in which the crucial questions about death are not questions about survival, but questions about the ultimate awarenesses that the life lived enables and necessitates:

> What images return
> O my daughter.

In its 'sense of life' the poem's allusion to *Pericles* acknowledges a profound debt and that to Seneca measures a profound distance. For 'Marina' is an intense but muted response to the play – the woodthrush sings 'through the fog', the protagonist's expectations are held this side of ecstasy:

> let me
> Resign my life for this life, my speech for that unspoken,
> The awakened, lips parted, the hope, the new ships.

Pericles is vital in comparison, for it creates deaths that in the theatre can

---

[16] *Letters*, ed. Forman, p. 520.
[17] In the second unpublished lecture, 'The Development of Shakespeare's Verse', given at Edinburgh, 1937.

be 'lived through' to a gay and imaginatively satisfying outcome. It smiles extremity out of act.

16 The Tempest: Conventions of Art and Empire

There is enough self-conscious artifice in the last plays to allow us to suspect that Shakespeare is glancing at his own art when Alonso says:

> This is as strange a maze as e'er men trod;
> And there is in this business more than nature
> Was ever conduct of: some oracle
> Must rectify our knowledge.

And it may be that Prospero quietens the fretful oracles in his first audience with a tongue-in-cheek assurance:

> at pick'd leisure
> Which shall be shortly single, I'll resolve you,
> Which to you shall seem probable, of every
> These happen'd accidents; till when, be cheerful,
> And think of each thing well.

The tense marvellings of the play are oddly hospitable to moments of wry mockery. Things are never quite what they seem.

The play's mysteries, however, are authentic, not gratuitous; they touch our sense of wonder and they are accessible to thought; and we need no oracle, skilled in the subtleties and audacities of Renaissance speculation, to rectify our knowledge. We must nevertheless seek to attend, with the apt kind of attention, to get the perspectives right, and the tone. For, as often in the comedies, the perspectives and the tone are precisely secured, and it is only too easy to upset the balances of convention, of innocence and scepticism, that keep the allegory of the play at an appropriately unobtrusive distance.

There is a multiple, complex allegory. It has to do with the social and moral nature of man, with the natural world, with the ways of providence, and with the nature of art. Yet this very complexity is the source of the play's simplicity – of its power to entertain, to move, and to satisfy our playgoing and contemplative spirits.

The Tempest is about a human mess put right by a make-believe magician. Or, to recast the point in the suggestive neoplatonic phrases of Sidney, it is about a golden world delivered from the brazen by providence and miracle. But there remain more specific ways of saying what it is about. In relation to its immediate sources it touches the colonizing enterprise of Shakespeare's England. In relation to one strain of dramatic tradition it is a Morality, about the cure of evil and the foregiveness of sin; in relation to another, it is a pastoral entertainment, fit to celebrate the fertility and order of nature; and it owes to the masque its felicitous handling of illusion, spell and rite. In relation to Shakespeare's own art, it seems to recollect much that has gone before, and to shadow forth (Sidney's phrase) the playwright's role in the theatres of fantasy and reality.

The several kinds of expressiveness found in the play owe much to the fragmentary source material on the one hand and to the tactful management of stage convention on the other. Theatrical techniques are so used that they illuminate an area of Elizabethan consciousness that was expressing itself also in the activities and in the literature of exploration and empire. Long before we pursue 'meanings' (after the play, brooding upon it) we recognize that the allegory is anchored in the instant realities of human experience. Its etherial affirmations are hard-won, spun out of substantial material. The truths which offer themselves as perennial are made very specifically out of and for the England and the theatre of Shakespeare's own time. The play is as much about colonization as initiation, as much about the intrigues of men as the tricks of spirits.

The principal documents behind *The Tempest* are well known if not wholly easily accessible; they are William Strachey's *True Repertory of the Wracke*, published in *Purchas His Pilgrimes* together with an extract from the anonymous *True Declaration of Virginia*, and Sylvester Jourdan's *A*

---

[1] William Strachey's *True Repertory of the Wracke, and Redemption of Sir Thomas Gates, Knight* circulated in manuscript in 1610, but was not published until 1625, when it appeared in *Purchas His Pilgrimes*, vol. IV, ch. 6. Page references in this chapter of *True Repertory* and *True Declaration* are to the 1906 edition of *Purchas His Pilgrimes*. The text of Jourdan's *A Discovery of the Barmudas* (1610) is quoted from the 1812 edition of *Hakluyt's Voyages*, vol. V, but page references are to the more available modernized version in Louis B. Wright, *The Elizabethans' America* (Stratford-upon-Avon Library, 1965).

Discovery of the Barmudas.[1] The uses to which the play puts these materials would have been very different had it not been for the hospitality of the contemporary theatre (whose tastes Shakespeare himself did most to fashion) to the techniques and interest of the late comedies.

Strachey and Jourdan tell how Sir Thomas Gates and Sir George Summers were driven away from the rest of the fleet, bound for Virginia in June 1609, by a storm which finally lodged their ship – the *Sea Venture* – between two rocks off the coast of the Bermudas. After many 'rare and remarkable experiences' they built a new boat, the *Deliverance*, and a pinnace, *Patience*, and set sail for Virginia in May 1610. Their survival (like many another in the pages of Hakluyt) had about it something of the miraculous, and it invited as much comment on the ways of Providence as on the skill and resourcefulness of English sailors.

Shakespeare, with the storms of *Othello, The Winter's Tale* and *Pericles* freshly accomplished for the theatre, would recognize occasion enough for a play in the story of the Bermudas wreck. And the material offers itself most invitingly to a playwright whose interest in the ways of Providence, and in the conversion and salvation of man, had matured through long practice in allegoric, romantic comedy. The prose accounts of the wreck are constantly suggestive in ways that would be less noticeable were they read without knowledge of the play. It is often so. The masterpiece illuminates the sources, more than the sources the masterpiece. It is no longer possible to read the collections of Hakluyt and Purchas without recognizing that they offer as much to Shakespeare and to Coleridge as to Captain Cook.

In the *True Repertory* the storm is both a physical ordeal and a moral:

> a dreadfull storme and hideous began to blow from out the North-east, which swelling, and roaring as it were by fits, some houres with more violence than others, at length did beat all light from heaven; which like an hell of darkenesse turned blacke upon us, so much the more fuller of horror, as in such cases horror and feare use to overrunne the troubled, and overmastered sences of all, which (taken up with amazement) the eares lay so sensible to the terrible cries, and murmurs of the windes, and distraction of our Company, as who was most armed, and best prepared, was not a little shaken. (p. 6)

The 'unmercifull tempest' is a terrible leveller; death at sea comes 'uncapable of particularities of goodnesse and inward comforts', and gives the mind no 'free and quiet time, to use her judgement and Empire'. There are hints enough for the play's opening scene in which hope is confounded by the counterpointed roarings of crew, court, and elements; the dignities of seamanship and of prayer are subdued to 'A confused noise within'. For the dignity of Gonzalo's wit (that alone survives the horror and the test) there is no equivalent in the source. But Strachey has his own way of wondering at man's powers of survival:

> The Lord knoweth, I had as little hope, as desire of life in the storme, & in this, it went byeond my will; because beyond my reason, why we should labour to preserve life; yet we did, either because so deare are a few lingring houres of life in all mankinde, or that our Christian knowledges taught us, how much we owed to the rites of Nature, as bound, not to be false to our selves, or to neglect the meanes of our owne preservation; the most despairefull things amongst men, being matters of now wonder nor moment with him, who is the rich Fountaine and admirable Essence of all mercy. (p. 9)

And it is easy to see in retrospect how, at a touch, the observations, the marvellings and the pieties of Strachey might be transformed into the language of *The Tempest* with its capacity for dwelling upon the preservation of life, the rites of nature, and the 'admirable Essence of all mercy'.

The pieties of the prose accounts are more than conventional; they owe their awed intensity to the sequences of catastrophe and miracle that the voyagers endured. As often, Shakespeare's contemporaries allegorized the historical event. We need not hesitate to treat the play as allegory since that is how Shakespeare's contemporaries treated the actual event. After God has delivered the seamen from the 'most dreadfull Tempest' of 'tumultuous and malignant' winds, the authority of the Governor is required to deliver them from what *The True Declaration* calls 'the tempest of Dissention'. Reviewing the mutinies that threatened the survival of the Bermudas party, Strachey writes:

> In these dangers and divellish disquiets (whilest the almighty God wrought for us, and sent us miraculously delivered from the calamities of the Sea, all blessings upon the shoare, to content and binde us to gratefulnesse) thus inraged amongst our selves, to the destruction each of other, into what a mischiefe and misery had wee bin given up, had wee not had a Governour with his authority, to have suppressed the same? (p. 32)

Reading this passage (and some similar ones) with the poet's eye, we can see how Prospero might have taken shape. From his experience of the theatre Shakespeare's imagination and invention readily made a single figure out of the miraculous deliverer from the sea's calamities, and the 'Governour with his authority' stopping the victims of the wreck from killing one another. It is an apt opportunity to take after *Measure for Measure*, which is about the saving powers of a governor, and *Pericles* with its miraculous deliveries from the sea.

A more specific occasion for the play's rendering of the storm as a feat of providential magic is offered by Strachey's description of the St Elmo's fire that danced like Ariel about the rigging:

> Onely upon the thursday night Sir George Summers being upon the watch, had an apparition of a little round light, like a faint Starre, trembling, and streaming along with a sparkeling blaze, halfe the height upon the Maine Mast, and shooting sometimes from Shroud to Shroud, tempting to settle as it were upon any of the foure Shrouds: and for three or foure houres together, or rather more, halfe the night it kept with us; running sometimes along the Maine-yard to the very end, and then returning. At which, Sir George Summers called divers about him, and shewed them the same, who observed it with much wonder, and carefulnesse: but upon a sodaine, towards the morning watch, they lost the sight of it, and knew not what way it made. (p. 11)

The elusive, mockingly playful fire and light in the encompassing total darkness, observed with wonder and carefulness by the crew, is poignantly ironic. Strachey leaves the natural phenomenon very ripe for transmutation into stage symbol. 'The superstitious Sea-men', he says, 'make many constructions of this Sea-fire, which neverthelesse is usual in stormes.' The Ancients took it for Castor and Pollux, perhaps, and 'an evill signe of great tempest'. The Italians call it 'Corpo sancto'. The Spaniards call it 'Saint Elmo, and have an authentic and miraculous Legend for it'. The irony is that it could do nothing to help the seamen, but rather quickened their torment:

> Be it what it will, we laid other foundations of safety or ruine, then in the rising or falling of it, could it have served us now miraculously to have taken our height by, it might have strucken amazement, and a reverence in our devotions, according to the due of a miracle. But it did not light us any whit the more to our knowne way, who ran now (as doe hoodwinked men) at all adventures. (p. 11)

It is one of the play's discoveries that this mocking hell is providentially (and indeed playfully) contrived. While allowing Ariel's tale to mimic the lightning, Shakespeare recalls the sonorous miseries described in an earlier passage:

> our clamours dround in the windes, and the windes in thunder. Prayers might well be in the heart and lips, but drowned in the outcries of the Officers: nothing heard that could give comfort, nothing seene that might incourage hope. It is impossible for me, had I the voice of Stentor, and expression of as many tongues, as his throate of voyces, to express the outcries and miseries, not languishing, but wasting his spirits, and art constant to his owne principles, but not prevailing. (p. 7)

By personalizing, in Prospero, the *natural* process of the storm and its happy outcome, Shakespeare displays theatrically the exacting cruelties of a providence that works to saving purpose:

Prospero   My brave spirit!
  Who was so firm, so constant, that this coil
  Would not infect his reason?
Ariel   Not a soul
  But felt a fever of the mad, and play'd
  Some tricks of desperation.

(i. ii. 206–10)

Human reason is 'infected' and human skill disarmed in order that all might be brought to shore safely:

                          Not a hair perish'd
  On their sustaining garments not a blemish,
  But fresher than before.

(i. ii. 217–19)

This allusion to the shipwreck of St Paul at Malta (Acts 27: 34–44) reminds us that catastrophic voyages and the ways of Providence are readily considered together. God uses shipwrecks. But the play is more insistent than the New Testament upon the waywardness and apparent arbitrariness of Providence (men hoodwinked, in a maze, amazed) and it has taken its signals from the prose of the voyagers.

At the utmost point of their despair, when skill and energy can do no more, the sailors are ready to surrender passively to the sea. As Jourdan puts it:

> All our men, being utterly spent, tyred, and disabled for longer labour, were even resolved, without any hope of their lives, to shut up the hatches, and to have committed themselves to the mercy of

the sea, (which is said to be mercilesse) or rather to the mercy of
their mighty God and redeemer. (p. 195)

That drift from commonplace 'mercy of the sea' through 'said to be
mercilesse' to 'their mighty God and redeemer', is not inertly conventional.
It testifies to the quite palpable presence in both stories (but particularly
in the opening paragraphs of Jourdan's) of the sequence – storm, fear,
death, miraculous renewal of life. While Shakespeare follows Strachey in
his treatment of Ariel's description of the last moments of the wreck, he
follows Jourdan where he hints at a ceremonious leave-taking on the stricken
ship ('Let's all sink wi' th' King . . . Let's take leave of him'):

> So that some of them having some good and comfortable waters
> in the ship, fetcht them, and drunke the one to the other, taking
> their last leave one of the other, untill their more ioyfull and happy
> meeting, in a more blessed world. (p. 195)

The play does not allow too intrusive a ceremonious piety, but rather a
wry nostalgia for 'an Acre of barren ground' tempering Gonzalo's patient
acquiescence: 'The wills above be done! but I would faine dye a dry death.'
The 'more blessed world' is offered nevertheless when all hope is dead, for,
as Strachey reports 'Sir George Summers, when no man dreamed of such
happinesse, had discovered, and cried Land.'

After the ordeal by sea, the island inheritance. Both Jourdan and Strachey
are moved by the paradox that made 'The Devils Ilands' (the name
commonly given to the Bermudas) 'both the place of our safetie, and meanes
of our deliverance'. Jourdan is particularly eloquent in confronting general,
superstitious expectations of the islands with his own ecstatic experience of
them. 'But our delivery,' he says, 'was not more strange in falling so
opportunely and happily upon the land, as our feeding and preservation,
was beyond our hopes, and all mens expectations most admirable.' It has
the quality of Gonzalo's marvellings. Jourdan tells us that the islands were
never inhabited by Christian or heathen but were ever esteemed 'a most
prodigious and inchanted place affording nothing but gusts, stormes, and
foule weather'. 'No man was ever heard, to make for this place, but as
against their wils, they have by stormes and dangerousnesse of the rocks,
lying seaven leagues into the sea, suffered shipwrack.'

Jourdan's phrases seem to license the play's magical, paradisial and
mysterious atmosphere, and some may be the germ of the rival versions of
Shakespeare's island voiced on the one hand by Gonzalo and Adrian, and
on the other by Sebastian and Antonio:

> Yet did we find there the ayre so temperate and the country so
> abundantly fruitful of all fit necessaries for the sustenation and
> preservation of man's life . . . Wherefore my opinion sincerely of

this Island is, that whereas it hath beene, and is still accounted, the most dangerous, infortunate, and forlorne place of the world, it is in truth the richest, heathfullest, and pleasing land (the quantity and bignesse thereof considered) and merely natural, as ever man set foot upon. (p. 197)

Shakespeare intervenes to associate the auspicious vision of the island ('The air breathes upon us here most sweetly') with the innocent courtiers, and the inauspicious ('As if it had lungs, and rotten ones') with the culpably sophisticated. But Strachey and Jourdan are equally clear that 'the foule and generall errour' of the world distorts the truths about the islands which are in time revealed to those who experience it.

In the sources, as in the play, the island deliverance is a beginning and not an end. Once saved from the wreck, the survivors have still to be saved from each other. Strachey tells how Sir Thomas Gates dispatched a longboat (duly modified) to Virginia, moved by 'the care which he took for the estate of the Colony in this his inforced absence' and 'by a long practised experience, foreseeing and fearing what innovation and tumult might happily arise, amongst the younger and ambitious spirits of the new companies'. The Governor's authority, however, proves equally essential to the prosperity of both the communities, of the Bermudas and of Virginia. Strachey writes of the onset of the island mutinies:

And sure it was happy for us, who had now runne this fortune, and were fallen into the bottome of this misery, that we both had our Governour with us, and one so solicitous and carefull, whose both example (as I said) and authority, could lay shame and command upon our people: else, I am perswaded, we had most of us finished our dayes there, so willing were the major part of the common sort (especially when they found such a plenty of victuals) to settle a foundation of ever inhabiting there . . . some dangerous and secret discontents nourished amongst us, had like to have been the parents of bloudy issues and mischiefs. (p. 28)

And the *True Declaration* discloses the analogous issues and mischiefs in Virginia:

The ground of all those miseries, was the permissive Providence of God, who, in the fore-mentioned violent storme, seperated the head from the bodie, all the vitall powers of Regiment being exiled with Sir Thomas Gates in those infortunate (yet fortunate) Ilands. The broken remainder of those supplyes made a greater shipwracke in the

Continent of Virginia, by the tempest of Dissention: every man over-valuing his owne worth, would be a Commander: every man underprizing anothers value, denied to be commanded. (p. 67)

The play's second act does most to explore the mutinous disaffections that attend upon and threaten 'the vitall powers of Regiment'. Its Neapolitan courtiers fittingly convey the temper of Virginia's 'younger and ambitious spirits':

> There be that can rule Naples
> As well as he that sleeps; lords that can prate
> As amply and unnecessarily
> As this Gonzalo; I myself could make
> A chough of as deep chat.
>
> (II. i. 262–6)

'Every man underprizing anothers value, denied to be commanded.' And the drunken, anarchistic landsmen represent the discontents of the 'common sort' on the Island. By extending the powers of Ariel and Prospero over both groups of conspirators, moreover, Shakespeare allows a fuller expression to the moral ideas that issue in the *True Declaration*'s reflection on 'the permissive Providence of God'. The conspiracies are at once permitted and constrained.

It is altogether appropriate that the Governor's authority should be represented as a care for 'the state of the Colony' and not as a bent for empire and sovereignty. The *True Declaration* finds for the word 'colony' its richest meaning and fullest resonance: 'A Colony is therefore denominated, because they should be Coloni, the Tillers of the Earth, and Stewards of fertilitie,' 'Should be'; but are not, for:

> our mutinous Loyterers would not sow with providence, and therefore they reaped the fruits of too deere bought Repentance. An incredible example of their idlenesse, is the report of Sir Thomas Gates, who affirmeth, that after his first comming thither, he hath seen some of them eat their fish raw, rather then they would go a stones cast to fetch wood and dresse it. (p. 68)

The tillers of the earth and the fetchers of wood, runs the argument, are the heirs to God's plenty: 'Dei laboribus omnia vendunt, God sels us all things for our labour, when Adam himselfe might not live in Paradise without dressing the Garden.' It is this thought that seems to hover mockingly behind the log-bearing labours of Ferdinand. Prospero, imposing the task, does not do as Sir Thomas Gates and set his own hand 'to every meane labour', dispensing 'with no travaile of his body'. He rather exercises over the Prince (himself a potential governor) the rule of Providence's dominant law; he sells Miranda (the richest of the island's bounties) only in return for work.

Once the recalcitrant passions of the Virginian colonizers have been tamed, once they have ceased to 'shark for present booty' out of idleness and lawlessness, they may hope to enjoy the bounty of nature. This idea is in itself almost enough to suggest the invention of Caliban. Strachey speaks of the 'liberty and fulness of sensuality' that drew the 'idle, untoward and wretched' to murmuring discontent, and 'disunion of hearts and hands' from labour (p. 28). The grotesque, spectacular figure of Caliban, and his conspiracy with the butler and the jester, enable Shakespeare to make Strachey's point within the conventions of masque and comedy.

Caliban, however, seems like Prospero to be doubly fashioned from the travel literature. Not only is he a theatrical epitome of the animal, anarchic qualities of the colonizers, he is also the epitome of the primitive and uncivilized condition of the native American. Strachey tells how the Virginian Indians severely tested the magnanimity of the Governor 'who since his first landing in the Countrey (how justly soever provoked) would not by any meanes be wrought to a violent proceeding against them'. But, like Caliban, they have natures on which nurture cannot stick; pains humanely taken are quite lost. One of the Governor's men – alas for tractable courses – is carried off into the woods and sacrificed; and the Governor 'well perceived, how little a faire and noble intreatie workes upon a barbarous disposition, and therefore in some measure purpose to be revenged' (p. 62).

But when Caliban consorts with Trinculo and Stephano the play expresses, with joyous irony, both the common appetites and the distinctive attributes of man primitive and man degenerate. Caliban's scorn of Trinculo's tipsy acquisitiveness, 'Let it alone, thou fool; it is but trash', measures the distance between them. Fittingly, the strictures of the *True Declaration* fall most heavily upon those delinquent colonizers who 'for their private lucre partly imbezeled the provisions', spoiling the market by leaving the Virginians 'glutted with our Trifles' (p. 70).

As witnesses both to the fine energies of Caliban and to his truculence, the first audiences of *The Tempest* might well have asked for themselves the questions that Purchas sets in the margin of *The True Repertory*:

> Can a Savage remayning a Savage be civill? Were not wee our selves made and not borne civill in our Progenitors dayes? and were not Caesar's Britaines as brutish as Virginians? (p. 62)

To this last question *Cymbeline* had already supplied something resembling Purchas's own answer, 'The Romane swords were best teachers of civilitie to this & other Countries neere us.' *The Tempest* leaves us to wonder at a range of possible answers to the first. For Shakespeare's understanding of Caliban is not co-extensive with Prospero's. 'Liberty' and 'fulness of sensuality' (to recall Strachey's terms) are auspicious when opposed, not to temperance, but to constraint and frigidity. Hence Caliban's virtue and dignity, and the quickness of his senses accords with his love of music – an Indian and a Carib characteristic remarked by the voyagers.

As his name may be meant to remind us,[2] Caliban is conceived as much out of the reports of the Caribana as of those of the Bermudas and Virginia. *Purchas His Pilgrimes* tells of the *Caraibes*, the priests of the Cannibal territory in the north of Brazil, to whom 'sometimes (but seldome) the Divell appears', and of their witches 'called *Carayba*, or holiness'.[3] There is here just enough pretext for associating Caliban with the blacker kind of sorcery that Shakespeare allows to Sycorax.

Sycorax represents a natural malignancy ('with age and envy . . . grown into a hoop') consonant with her negative and confining skills. Unlike the *Carayba* of Purchas's account, however, she does not embody a native devilry and priestcraft, but is a disreputable exile from Argier with only a casual claim to dominion over the island. Thus the play qualified the righteousness of Caliban's resentment and complicates the relationships between native and colonial endowments. We are left to wonder about the ultimate sources of the moral virus that has infected what might have been a golden world, and Prospero's account of Caliban's genesis ('got by the devil himself / Upon thy wicked dam') may be taken either as imprecation or as a fragment of bizarre biography.

When Shakespeare confronts Prospero with Caliban he does not restrict the range of his implications in the theatre to the command that a colonial governor might seek by kindness and by torment to secure over a native. That relationship itself is only one expression of what Montaigne, in a passage familiar to Shakespeare from the 'Essay on Cannibals', called the bastardizing of the original naturality by human wit. Shakespeare's scepticism, like Montaigne's, recoils upon authority itself. Prospero's malice ('tonight thou shalt have cramps') is a comic instance of the barbarism of civilization that Montaigne finds more shocking than cannibalism; we mangle, torture and mammock our living neighbours not from natural

---

[2] Gustav H. Blanke, *Amerika im Englischen Schrifttum des 16. und 17. Jahrhunderts* (1962), points out that one Bodley atlas has the version 'Caliban' for 'Cariban'. The genesis of names is always elusive. It is noticeable that Strachey (p. 14) names the historian of the West Indies, Gonzalus Ferdinandus Oviedus, which might have supplied Gonzalo and Ferdinand.
[3] 3rd edn (1617), bk 9, ch. 5, p. 1039.

perversity but 'under pretence of piety and religion'.

The secret dialogue that, metaphorically speaking, Shakespeare conducts with Florio's Montaigne is an intricate one. Gonzalo's Utopian vision is at its centre. Much of Florio's prose is assimilated into the routine of the verse, but the quiet climax of Gonzalo's musings – to do with the fecundity of the anarchic paradise – is intensely in the mode of the last plays:

> Nature should bring forth,
> Of its own kind, all foison, all abundance,
> To feed my innocent people.
>
> (II. i. 163–5)

Florio says that his admirable savages have no need to gain new lands, 'for to this day they yet enjoy that naturall ubertie and fruitfulnesse, which without labouring toyle, doth in such plenteous abundance furnish them with all necessary things, that they need not enlarge their limits.' Gonzalo is mocked by the sophisticated conspirators for, as it were, his reading of Florio. Shakespeare contrives to vindicate Montaigne's contempt for the 'unnatural opinion' that excuses the 'ordinary faults' of 'treason, treacherie, disloyaltie, tyrannie, crueltie, and such-like'; for however apt and amusing the taunts of Antonio and Sebastian, their persistent malice is seen for what it is, and Gonzalo's words are never quite out of key with the mood that the island scenes have created in the theatre. At the same time, Montaigne's sanguine vision of uncultivated innocence is exquisitely, and critically, related to the dreams that a benign but vulnerable ageing courtier might have of sovereignty. Where Montaigne believes (or pretends to believe) that the wild nations in reality 'exceed all the pictures wherewith licentious Poesie hath proudly imbellished the golden age', Shakespeare leaves the notion to an old man's fantasy. But a significant fantasy, properly entertained by 'Holy Gonzalo, honourable man'.

When 'foison and abundance' are again at the centre of attention we are contemplating the betrothal masque. The masque has several kinds of appropriateness in a play about colonization. It accords with Strachey's concern with bounty and the proper regulation of passion, and it reminds us of the indivisible integrity of the laws of nature and government. Miranda's presence on the island has some occasion, perhaps, in the story of Virgina Dare, granddaughter of Captain John White, born in 1587 in the first English colony of Virginia and left there in a small party.[4] But it matters more that Purchas comments in his marginal note to Strachey's

---

[4] See Wright, *The Elizabethans' America* (1965), p. 133.

account of the marriage of one of Sir George Summers's men: *The most holy civill and most naturall possession taken of the Bermudas by exercise of Sacraments Marriage, Childbirth, &c.* (p. 38). The sacrament of marriage is looked upon as the perfection of the island's sovereignty. Prospero's admonition that Ferdinand should not break Miranda's 'virgin-knot before / All sanctimonious ceremonies may / With full and holy rite be minister'd,' is not only in character (the officiously solicitous father), it is also a full recognition that heaven rains down blessings only upon those who honour the sanctities of its order:

No sweet aspersion shall the heavens let fall
To make this contract grow; but barren hate,
Sour-ey'd disdain and discord shall bestrew
The union of your bed with weeds so loathly
That you shall hate it both.

(IV. i. 18–22)

The metaphors take life from the island truths about 'the tillers of the earth and the stewards of fertility'; life flourishes best by cultivation and restraint.

The masque decoratively, but with a quick pulse, endorses the sustaining idea; the 'sweet aspersion' that the heavens let fall is recalled by Ceres' 'upon my flowers / Diffusest honey-drops, refreshing showers'. There is much to remind us of the continuity of the play with pastoral comedy – with *As You Like It* and *The Winter's Tale*. 'So rare a wondered father and a wise,' says Miranda, 'Makes this place Paradise.'

Purchas almost immediately follows his note on the marriage sacrament with another on a camp atrocity – '*Saylers misorder*'. The effect in the narrative is a paler version of that in the play when Prospero suddenly remembers 'that foul conspiracy / Of the beast Caliban and his confederates'. Strachey tells how a sailor murdered one of his fellows with a shovel, and how others conspired to rescue him from the gallows 'in despight and disdaine that Justice should be shewed upon a Sayler'. The 'mischiefs of mariners' reported by Strachey are intensified by the activities of 'savage spies' from among the disaffected Indians (p. 50). The Governor's nerves and moral resolution are, like Prospero's, severely tested.

The Tempest does not, however, return to the moral antinomies of pastoral comedy – opposing the seasonal, fecund processes of nature to human sophistication. Its most memorable nature has little to do with that which fills the garners and brings shepherds and sheep-shearing into *The Winter's Tale*. It is not the 'great creating nature' that Perdita honours in her festive ceremonies. It is an elemental nature, made of the air, earth and water that meet on a tempestuous coast, and in listening to the play's many mysterious and subtle evocations of the ways of the elements we may be aware still of the poet's transfigurations of the sailors' experience.

Shakespeare is sensitive to the narrative sequence (already noticed) of storm, fear, death and the miraculous renewal of life in the island's 'temperate air'. Shakespeare's tact sustains the sequence without surrender to superstition (*pace* Gonzalo's marvellings) and without inviting moral exegesis. In Ariel's opening songs and in Ferdinand's exquisitely mannered reception of them, the truth of the sequence becomes lyrical and musical:

> Sitting on a bank,
> Weeping again the King my father's wreck,
> This music crept by me upon the waters,
> Allaying both their fury and my passion
> With its sweet air.
>
> (i. ii. 390–4)

The quieting of storm and sorrow have in the theatre become the same process. Grief is transposed into melody. The word 'air', like Ariel's song itself, hovers elusively between atmosphere and melody:

> This is no mortal business, nor no sound
> That the earth owes. I hear it now above me.
>
> (i. ii. 407–8)

The island's airs are themselves melodious, and when Ferdinand finds Miranda 'the goddess / On whom these airs attend' the suggestions of etherial harmony are perfected.

Ariel's second song offers what is perhaps the play's most eloquent and characteristic symbol:

> Those are pearls that were his eyes:
>   Nothing of him that doth fade,
> But doth suffer a sea-change
>   Into something rich and strange.
>
> (i. ii. 399–402)

The sea-change metaphors are a more searching expression of moral change as *The Tempest* presents it than the overtly pastoral convention could supply, and can touch more closely the mysteries of death.

Its beginnings in Shakespeare are familiar in Clarence's dream in *Richard III* – significantly a *dream*, and a reaching-forward to the mood and tenor of the last plays:

> O Lord, methought what pain it was to drown,
> What dreadful noise of waters in my ears.
>
> (i. iv. 21–2)

The pain and noise of drowning were still 'beating' in Shakespeare's mind when he wrote *The Tempest*, and the consolatory transformations are remembered too:

> and in the holes
> Where eyes did once inhabit there were crept,
> As 'twere in scorn of eyes, reflecting gems,
> That woo'd the slimy bottom of the deep
> And mock'd the dead bones that lay scatter'd by.
>   (I. iv. 29–33)

It is (as A. P. Rossiter once said) 'submarine Seneca'; but it is ready to become 'Those are pearls that were his eyes'. The marine fantasy seems to owe nothing to seaman's lore (Hakluyt and Purchas collect mostly matter-of-fact accounts of the genesis of pearls) although the travel books have much to say about the 'great store of pearl' to be found in Bermuda seas. It suffices that Shakespeare's early experience in the mode enabled him to refine and to amplify his distinctly surrealist vision of death by water. But Clarence expresses too the continuing physical ordeal:

> but still the envious flood
> Stopp'd in my soul and would not let it forth
> To find the empty, vast, and wand'ring air;
> But smother'd it within my panting bulk,
> Who almost burst to belch it in the sea.
>   (I. iv. 37–41)

The sentiments and images are soon quite subdued to the English Senecal conventions – the 'melancholy flood / With that sour ferryman which poets write of'; but not before Shakespeare had written:

> O, then began the tempest to my soul.
>   (I. iv. 44)

The sequence, storm, fear, death, is in Clarence's experience unconsummated by the liberation that the strange word 'belch' seems to promise.

It is otherwise in *Pericles*, another play in which marine nature is more poignantly mysterious, more eternal and more consolatory than pastoral nature:

> Th' unfriendly elements
> Forgot thee utterly; nor have I time
> To give thee hallow'd to thy grave, but straight
> Must cast thee, scarcely coffin'd, in the ooze;
> Where, for a monument upon thy bones,
> The aye-remaining lamps, the belching whale

> And humming water must o'erwhelm thy corpse,
> Lying with simple shells.
>
> (III. i. 57–64)

In *Timon of Athens* too, the sea retains its cleansing sanctity when the pasture that lards the rother's sides and the sun that breeds roots in the corrupt earth are forgotten:

> Timon hath made his everlasting mansion
> Upon the beached verge of the salt flood,
> Who once a day with his embossed froth
> The turbulent surge shall cover.
>
> (v. i. 215–18)

The sea 'whose liquid surge resolves / The moon into salt tears' is symbol too of a perpetual compassion:

> rich conceit
> Taught thee to make vast Neptune weep for aye
> On thy low grave, on faults forgiven.
>
> (v. iv. 77–9)

The prose accounts behind *The Tempest* offer Shakespeare new opportunities for this morally expressive sea-eloquence.[5] Ariel admonishes the courtiers as if their survival from the wreck were owed to their destined unfitness for the sea's digestion:

> You are three men of sin, whom Destiny, –
> That hath to instrument this lower world
> And what is in't – the never-surfeited sea
> Hath caus'd to belch you up.
>
> (III. iii. 53–6)

But the sea-swell of the rhythm subdues the joke to the solemnity of the occasion. Prospero, in a slow movement of the play (the still figures and the leisured speech) that makes it remarkably fitting, uses the figure of the cleansing, clarifying sea:

---

[5] See for example *Purchas His Pilgrimes*, p. 654.

> Their understanding
> Begins to swell, and the approaching tide
> Will shortly fill the reasonable shore
> That now lies foul and muddy.
>
> (v. i. 79–82)

The sea is an almost constant presence in the play's verbal music; both the dancing kind:

> And ye that on the sands with printless foot
> Do chase the ebbing Neptune.
>
> (v. i. 34–5)

and the more sombre:

> Methought the billows spoke, and told me of it;
> The winds did sing it to me; and the thunder
> That deep and dreadful organ pipe, pronounc'd
> The name of Prosper; it did bass my trespass.
> Therefore my son i' th' ooze is bedded; and
> I'll seek him deeper than e'er plummet sounded,
> And with him there lie mudded.
>
> (iii. iii. 96–102)

The moral sonorities are the sonorities of the sea. The apprehension of final judgement is expressed by way of sea, wind, and thunder; but 'deep and dreadful' and 'bass' are as apt for the sea as they are for the thunder; while the thunder lingers upon the next lines stirring the words 'deeper' and 'sounded' as they are used of the plumb-line, and coming to rest in 'mudded'.

Elsewhere, language used about music and about haunting noises is not directly about the sea, but might well have been:

> Even now we heard a hollow burst of bellowing.
>
> (ii. i. 311)

It might be a breaking wave. Recalling the 'humming water' of *Pericles*, it is apt that Caliban should speak of instruments that 'hum' about his ears. Humming is a common spell of the play's language:

> The noontide sun, called forth the mutinous winds.
>
> (v. i. 42)

What is manifest in the detail of the play's accomplishment is manifest still in its large design – which owes more to the literature of sea-survival. The suggestion that the action of *The Tempest* takes place under the sea is witty and illuminating. The first scene is about men drowning, and its conventions are decisively naturalistic – there at least the storm is not merely symbolic. But the second scene changes the mood and the convention; the perspectives shift; time and place lose meaning, and characters and events shed a measure of their routine actuality. The play becomes a masque; and not improbably a masque resembling a masque of Neptune, with Ariel and Caliban seen as mutations of triton and sea-nymph. If contemporary productions, however, had looked for hints for figures and décor in the literature of Virginian colonization, they would have found them in John White's 'True Pictures and Fashions'.[6]

To dwell upon the 'sea-sorrow' and 'sea-change' processes of the play is to recognize the difference from the more usual changes associated with pastoral in other comedies and late plays. Only *Pericles* resembles *The Tempest*. In *The Winter's Tale* moral growth is presented as a seasonal process, enabling Leontes to greet Perdita, when innocence returns to Sicilia in the last act, with the words: 'Welcome hither as is the spring to earth', and 'the blessed gods / Purge all infection from our air / Whilst you do climate here.' But conversion and repentance are not in *The Tempest*, simple processes of growth. They are elusive mysteries, requiring strange mutations and interventions; occurring within dream states, under spells, conditionally ruled by laws that Shakespeare is content to offer as 'magical'. But it is the sea, as the Elizabethan imagination dwelt upon it, that supplied the language of moral discovery.

Shakespeare's gift, it might be said of this and other plays, was to allegorize the actual; to conjoin his responsiveness to the moral order with his sense of turbulent, intractable realities. In lesser degree that was Strachey's gift too, and Jourdan's. But to the reconciliations accomplished in this play, Shakespeare's theatrical art brings a severe qualification – one that might be expected at this mature and resourceful phase of English drama. It is brought home to us that harmony is achieved in the human world only by allowing to Prospero and to Providence the powers of a playwright; particularly of a playwright skilled in masque – for the cloud-capped towers and all the things that vanish when the magician forfeits his power are recognizably the paraphernalia of masque. In this sense Prospero is indeed Shakespeare, but not Shakespeare the private man (whether retired or exhausted) but Shakespeare the professional playwright and masque-maker, perceiving that the order he seems to reveal in the world that the voyagers disclose to us is a feat of theatrical illusion. The magic

---

[6] *The True Pictures and Fashions of the People in ... Virginia ... draowne by Iohn White*, appended to *A briefe and true report of the new found land of Virginia* (Frankfurt, 1590). See particularly the figure of *The Coniuerer* or *The Flyer*.

does not work everywhere and for ever. From the poetic world there is the return to Milan where Sebastian and Antonio will keep their hard identities. Prospero returns himself and the audience to vulnerable humanity.

The end of the play, however, does not wholly determine its final impression. The climax of the moral magic discovers Ferdinand and Miranda playing at chess. We may take it that the game is a proper symbol of comedy – of conflict transposed into play. As T. E. Hulme once said – 'Many necessary conditions must be fulfilled before the chess-board can be poised elegantly on the cinders.' Life is only provisionally, for the span of a play which obeys all the unities, a perfectly coherent moral order; and where there is no art – no play – we have leave to doubt that there can be order. Unless it is to be found among Montaigne's savages.

17 The Island of *The Tempest*

[THE SCENE, an uninhabited island]

'They say miracles are past,' observes Lafeu, 'and we have our philosophic persons to make modern and familiar, things supernatural and causeless.' Some eight or nine seasons later Shakespeare's art again suspends us between that modern and familiar scepticism which makes us dubious of miracles and that fideist scepticism, in the tradition of Erasmus and Montaigne, which makes us dubious of human understanding: 'La peste de l'homme, c'est l'opinion de savoir.' Alonso, trying to make sense of his island experience, finds it 'as strange a maze as e'er men trod' but, responding to his appeal, there have been oracles enough offering to rectify our knowledge. It is possible to propose a choice of what Keats might have called 'palpable designs upon us'. It can be represented as an insight into the responsibilities of the monarch in a colonizing phase of its history, for example, or as an allegory of the atonement. But an authentic oracle has a way of playing back at us truths that we are already in a position to perceive. It insinuates more than it insists.

The Tempest was performed, perhaps for the first time, at Hallowmas in the presence of the King at Whitehall in 1611; and perhaps for the second time, again at court, in the following season, to assist in the celebrations of the betrothal of Princess Elizabeth of England to Frederick the 'Prince Pallatyne Elector'. The occasion was of high political as well as intimate

A shorter version of this paper was given to the Royal Shakespeare Theatre Summer School in 1978, and at the University of Tunis in 1981. While it was intended to change the perceptual perspective and look towards Africa rather than America, there are topic-overlaps with the previous chapter and some echoes of phrase and observation. For a later in the poetry of the islands of Bermuda see J. P. Brockbank, 'The Politics of Paradise', in *Approaches to Andrew Marvell*, ed. C. A. Patrides, 1978.

consequence, for as things turned out, the marriage was to keep England uncomfortably close to involvement in the Thirty Years War, particularly in the reign of Elizabeth's brother, Charles I.[1] Yet it was meant, of course, not to promote conflict but to resolve it. The celebrations made the marriage auspicious of a harmony and unity of kingdoms, and the playing of both *The Tempest* and *The Winter's Tale* at the festival has been thought of as a way of bringing bridal innocence and expectation into the centre of Europe's political aspirations. Young lovers, it was hoped, would re-create what old haters had all but destroyed. This spacious reflection, however, would be easier to entertain were it not that other plays performed at the same time have a very different tenor.[2]

The aptness of *The Tempest* for the occasion has led some to believe that it was specifically adapted for it. Since the play is about those hopes and fresh prospects that attend the betrothal of the young, it is entirely fitting that it should become, like the masque within it, a 'donation freely to estate / On the bless'd lovers'. But the forthcoming marriage is not the only occasion to call out the play. There is another, a now familiar event in the history of colonization. In 1610, there appeared a number of accounts of the wreck and the deliverance of the party under Sir Thomas Gates and Sir George Summers in the *Sea Venture*, on the coast of the Bermudas, in the summer of 1609. The ship was apparently lodged between rocks on a reef, and the crew found itself able to take to its boats and 'with extreme joy, even almost to amazednesse, arrive in safetie, though more than a league from the shore'. Making modern what is supernatural and causeless, it might be said that what amazed them was the sudden transition from the fury and weight of the Atlantic to the calm of one of Bermuda's many lagoons and sheltered bays. After some 'rare and remarkable experiences' they built a new boat and a pinnace, the *Deliverance* and *Patience*, and set sail in May 1610, to join the rest of the expedition in Virginia. I have tried already to track in some detail the art, partly accomplished in the prose of William Strachey and Sylvester Jourdan, but perfected in the play, which allegorized an actual event or (to put it another way) actualized a complex of metaphors.[3] The opening up of the new world was a matter of both economic exploitation and imaginative pilgrimage. The relationship between the Golden World of mercantile capital, risk, enterprise, courage and ruthlessness, and the Golden World of pastoral idyll, primordial

---

[1] See Frances A. Yates, *Shakespeare's Last Plays: A New Approach* (1975), and *The Tempest,* ed. Stephen Orgel, pp. 30–1.

[2] The fourteen plays are listed by E. K. Chambers, *William Shakespeare* (1930), p. 343.

[3] See ch. 16 above, and Charles Frey, '*The Tempest* and the New World', *Shakespeare Quarterly*, 30: 1, (1979), pp. 29–41.

nostalgia and the City of God is intricate and perplexing.[4]

The perspectives of *The Tempest* have many vanishing points, the lines of sight converging on a choice of remote horizons. The scenes 'dissolve' and we are 'justled' from our senses, left uncertain, wondering, 'amazed', and yet held by the consistent, even rigorous, spell of the playwright's art. Henry James said of *The Tempest* that it put before him 'the very act of the momentous conjunction taking place for the poet, at a given hour, between his charged inspiration and his clarified experience'.[5] For 'the given hour' we may reflect upon the marriage-occasion and the voyage-occasion on which we have already alighted. The 'clarified experience' has many dimensions both in the playmaker's art and in what Keats calls his life of allegory. 'A writer,' says Jonson in *The Masque of Queens*, 'should always trust somewhat to the capacity of the spectator, especially at these spectacles, where men, besides inquiring eyes, are understood to bring quick ears'.[6]

The 'charged inspiration' of the poet calls for quick ears, but for the clarification of our own perceptions we do well, I think, to ask ourselves what a contemporary with enquiring eyes and quick ears might have made of the play. Among those attending the first court performances it is not an extravagant speculation to imagine the distinguished statesman and poet Fulke Greville, Lord Brooke, described on his tomb as 'Counsellor to King James, Friend to Sir Philip Sidney'. As an Atlantic voyager, a sometime acquaintance of Giordano Bruno, as a playwright and the creator of a sequence of love poems, Fulke Greville may be thought of as the ideal spectator to *The Tempest*, capable of responding to its full range of subtleties and audacities. It is not a matter of defining intentions and effects, but of tuning in to evocations, to the play's many voices upon an unlocatable island.

'The Scene, an uninhabited Island', says the Folio, in what may be Shakespeare's own opening (and misleading) Folio words, but are more likely to be Ralph Crane's; (there is only one other prefatory location, also probably Crane's, in *Measure for Measure* – 'The Scene, Vienna'). Where is it? In what corner of the earth or territory of the imagination? However active the literature of Atlantic voyaging in the language and structure of the play, the 'still-vexed Bermoothes' are only at the periphery of Ariel's world (his source for morning dew) and therefore, in a sense of Shakespeare's. Yet to members of the Virginia Company who saw it, including quite possibly William Strachey himself, who was a Sharer in the Revels Company at Blackfriars, the Bermudan experience must itself have been among those

---

[4] D. G. James, *The Dream of Prospero* (Oxford, 1967).

[5] Henry James, '*The Tempest*', in *Selected Literary Criticism*, ed. Morris Shapira, ch. 22, p. 301.

[6] *Works*, ed. Herford and Simpson (1941), VII, p. 287.

clarified by *The Tempest*. Since the play is so profoundly made out of the voyage literature, why does Shakespeare displace it from the Atlantic to the Mediterranean? I would not wish to answer this, or any other question about *The Tempest* too directly.

Many plays about English colonial enterprise in this period appear to have been lost. The evidence reaches us in a celebrated passage from a sermon (discussed by D. G. James) that Shakespeare could easily have heard, given as 'a newe yeres Gifte to Virginia' by William Crashaw (father of the poet Richard) just before Lord De la Warr set out in the wake of the Gates expedition.[7] The Company, in Crashaw's eloquent account, is engaged in a divine mission through which 'we may rise up from the death of our sins to newness and holiness of life'. 'We being converted must labour for their conversion,' he says of 'the savages of Virginia', for 'the same God made them as well as us, gave them as perfect and good souls and bodies, as to us, and the same Messiah is sent to them.' 'If a Virginian,' he asks, 'having our language had learned our religion . . . would God deny him salvation?' The moral intentions are exalted: 'We will take nothing from the savages by power nor pillage, by craft nor violence', and will offer 'Civilitie for their bodies, Christianity for their souls'. But the history of Empire is economic and political still: 'We will make them much richer even for matter of this life, then now they are'; but also, 'As the present state of England stands, we want room, and are likely enough to want more.' Crashaw recognizes that among those sent to Virginia are 'the very excrement of a full and swelling state', but 'transplanted to a more bare and barren soil' and, required by strict government to conform to the rule of law in an exacting environment, they too will prove convertible. There are good prospects even for 'the sows that still wallow in the mire of their profit and pleasure'.

We may tune in here to a range of significances (*signi*ficances) for Caliban, Stephano and Trinculo. Missionary endeavours must undertake the salvation alike of the 'savage' and the 'drunken layabouts' of the home community. 'This isle is mine,' says Caliban, 'by Sycorax my mother.' It is the natural state of uncultivated man, at once (so the play says) brutal and sensitive.

Crashaw is sanguine about most obstacles to the Virginian enterprise: 'How fair, safe and easy, the passage to Virginia is . . . no rocks, shelves, sands, nor unknown Islands lie in our way', and he even takes in his stride the recent Bermuda disaster:

[7] William Crashaw, *A Sermon Preached in London before the Lord Lawarre, lord governour of Virginia at his departure for Virginia February 21 1609* (1610) (*STC*, 6029). It is discussed by D. G. James in *The Dream of Prospero* (1967).

> And let no man object that our last flet was dispersed and sore shaken by a storm; for he cannot but know that such as sail by sea must as wel expect tempests of wind as travellers on land showers of rain.

Their comfort must be that, 'at God's word the stormy wind ariseth, and lifteth up the waves of the ocean.' The play is consonant with contemporary ways of thinking about sea-voyages in spiritual spaces. But among the alleged enemies of the Virginian adventurers, Crashaw sets aside the Spanish and the French (rivals playing the same game) and fastens upon three others – the Devil, the Papists and the Players. 'Players do mock at religion and abuse the holy scriptures':

> they play with Princes and Potentates, Magistrates and Ministers, nay with God, religion, and all holy things: nothing that is good, excelent or holy can escape them: how then can this action? But this may suffice, that they are but Players: they abuse Virginea, but they are but Players; they disgrace it: true, but they are but players, and they have played with better things, and such as for which, if they spedily repent not, I dare say Vengeance waites for them.

Why are the players enemies to this plantation? Crashaw asks. And answers, 'First that they are so multiplied here, that one cannot live by another, and they see that we send all trades to Virginia but no players', and second 'Because we resolve to suffer no idle persons in Virginia.'

Unfortunately, none of the anti-Virginian plays has survived.[8] *The Tempest*, in which Shakespeare plays 'with Princes and Potentates' and even with 'all holy things', is generously and almost religiously conceived from the Virginia Company's own propaganda, and might have redressed the balance. But it does not quite do that. Virginia, like the Bermudas, is an invisible presence in the play; Caliban is not a Virginian savage, or even a Caribbean one. Trinculo and Stephano are as often connected with the *commedia dell'arte* as with the drunken subordinates of Gate's Virginian party.

Before returning to the New World we may look towards the play's Mediterranean vanishing point. Had Shakespeare chosen to write more directly about colonization, had England and Virginia instead of Italy and Tunis spanned its geography, *The Tempest* would have forfeited some of

---

[8] Henslowe in 1601 has references to at least one play by Rowley on the 'Conquest of the West Indies'. In the Stationers' Register of 1623 there is an entry for a tragedy called *The Plantation of Virginia*, 'For the company at the Curtain', 'the profaness to be left out, otherwise not tolerated'. It is just possible that an early version of this play provoked Crashaw in 1609.

its most characteristic and valued effects. Mediterranean Italy for Shakespeare, as for other English writers, is the centre of much that is creative and destructive in the culture and courtly civilization of the Renaissance – creative, for example, in Portia's Belmont, and destructive in Iachimo's Rome or Tybalt's Verona. In *The Tempest* we are made more than usually aware of the high reach of Italian speculative thought – Prospero is 'in liberal arts without a parallel', but also of the self-destructive energies of Italian ducal politics: 'as thou got'st Milan, / I'll come by Naples. Draw thy sword. One stroke / Shall free thee from the tribute which thou payest / And I the King shall love thee.' Prospero, as the maker of storms and calms, or as the play's counterpart of the solicitous 'Governour with his authority' commended by Strachey, might have found appropriate mid-Atlantic asylum. But the deposed Duke and the magus whose name can be read as an Italian translation of 'Faustus' does not belong to Bermuda. His island is between the Old World and the New in quite another range of senses than those suggested by association with the Bermudan sources. Thinking of the Bosun and the navigator, the island may be somewhere in the Tyrrhenian Sea off the coast of Sicily, or somewhere in the Sicilian channel – Ustica, Egadi, Zembra. In the old atlases Shakespeare could have found such evocative names to chime with Illyria. But a strange and cryptic passage of Island dialogue invites us to place it somewhere between Tunis (said to be 'ten leagues beyond man's life) and Naples, the one auspicious but remote, the other closer to home but highly unstable. Taking a hint from Gonzalo's reverie, it lies between the ancient and lost civilization of Carthage and the modern, but in a different sense, still 'lost', civilization of Renaissance Italy.

Among the exiles and victims of that civilization was Giordano Bruno. Frances Yates sees Prospero as 'the immortal portrait of the benevolent Magus, establishing the ideal state' and asks, 'How much does Shakespeare's conception of the role of the Magus owe to Bruno's reformulation of that role in relation to the miseries of the times.'[9] Without hastening to answer, we can usefully remember that Bruno, having learned and taught others better hope for European civilization during his exile in Navarre (whose academy was also attended by Shakespeare's Berowne), returned to his native Italy only, in due course, to be burned at the stake. It would be tantalizingly unprofitable to try to set up specific analogues between Bruno's modes of thought and Prospero's. But the island is apt setting for the isolation of the magus and scholar in his study, and among the books that Prospero brought with him to the island, one might readily think of the poetic work of Bruno. The island is not only asylum for the Italian magus,

[9] Frances A. Yates, *Giordano Bruno and the Hermetic Tradition* (1964), p. 357.

it is also the only territory in which his magic or theurgy is effective. Back
home Prospero may again be easy to depose as Bruno was easy to burn.

The omniscience, omnipresence and omnipotence of Prospero, the scholar
and magus, diminish upon his island the importance and urgency of human
freedom, action and conflict. Much is made of 'purpose', and the conspirators,
high and low, are found 'bending towards their project', but for the span
of the play the only satisfied purpose is Prospero's. We are largely denied
the experience of watching and listening to 'character in action', because,
freshly to apply Lafeu's words, those who make trifles of terrors and
ensconce themselves into seeming knowledge are required to submit
themselves to an unknown fear. Frances Yates speaks of Shakespeare's
'profound preoccupation with significant language', language, she says,
culling the phrase from Bruno, 'which captures the voice of the gods'. The
voice of the gods, however, may be a remote voice, and there are many
human voices heard elsewhere in the plays, and many significances of
language that are not to be heard on the island. *Measure for Measure*, for
example, a play in some respects comparable, gives a more searching account
of moral experience, and a more dynamic one of human frailty. But what
The Tempest loses in this respect it gains in others. Both its language and
its spectacle of event are the more consistently addressed to the reflective
intelligence.

If we feel sceptical about the possibilities of 'magic' and distrust modes
of thought that aspire to it, we can remind ourselves that Hotspur and
Glendower in *1 Henry IV* were also acted at the betrothal festival:

> Where is he living . . .
> Can trace me in the tedious ways of art,
> And hold me pace in deep experiments?
> *Hotspur* I think there's no man speaks better Welsh.
> I'll to dinner.
> *Glendower* I can call spirits from the vasty deep.
> *Hotspur* Why, so can I, or so can any man,
> But will they come when you do call for them?
>
> (*1 Henry IV*, III. i. 43, 47–54)

It is possible, indeed essential, to give an account of Prospero's magic which
sets it at a distance from Glendower's. Prospero as magus has power to
command the energies of the natural world in the service of the moral and
contemplative virtues. His art, as Kermode puts it, quoting Cornelius
Agrippa, manifests 'an intellect pure and conjoined with the powers of the
gods without which we shall never happily ascend to the scrutiny of secret

things and to the power of wonderful workings'.[10] There indeed is a remote
vanishing point.

Correspondences between our experience of the natural world and our
moral experience have always been a source of understanding and imaginative
satisfaction. In the visual art as well as the poetry of the Renaissance, the
voyage, with its catastrophes, discoveries, conflicts and arrivals was an
important metaphor for the process of human life; not least, because for
many in seagoing countries it is often the process itself. As Gonzalo puts
it:

> Our hint of woe
> Is common: every day some sailor's wife,
> The masters of some merchant, and the merchant
> Have just our theme of woe; but for the miracle
> (I mean our preservation), few in millions
> Can speak like us.
>
> (ii. i. 3–8)

Among the miraculously preserved in earlier literature, classical and biblical,
were St Paul and Aeneas. The victims of Shakespeare's wreck, like that in
Acts 27: 34–44, are untouched:

> Not a hair perish'd;
> On their sustaining garments not a blemish,
> But fresher than before.
>
> (i. ii. 217–19)

Gonzalo on the island remembers, or misremembers, the story of Dido and
Aeneas when he thinks of Carthage and Tunis. Shakespeare glances distantly
at a Virgilian analogy and at other versions of the story when he allows us
another way of locating the island. Aeneas's voyage from Naples to Carthage
is a tale of shipwreck often allegorized in the Renaissance. Rubens, Elsheimer
and other masters working in the opening decades of the seventeenth
century treated these great catastrophes as divinely ordained, opening up
new visionary possibilities. In Hans Eworth's celebrated allegoric portrait
of Sir John Luttrell, of much earlier date, and possibly known to
Shakespeare, a splendid naked figure, waist-deep in angry seas where the
ship splits and the drowned and drowning lie in the water, strides towards
a suspended prospect of paradise, where there waits a voluptuous woman,
said to represent 'Peace', and we are left to wonder where she is and in
what mortal or immortal condition.[11] It is said of Ferdinand that: 'He trod

---

[10] *The Tempest*, ed. Frank Kermode (1954), pp. xlvii–xlviii.
[11] See Roy Strong, *The English Icon: Elizabethan and Jacobean Portraiture* (1969),
p. 86; and F. A. Yates, 'The Allegorical Portraits of Sir John Luttrell', in *Essays*

the water, / Whose enmity he flung aside, and breasted / The surge most swoll'n that met him.' He alone appears to owe his survival to his own noble and heroic endeavour, while Miranda, 'The Goddess / On whom these airs attend', unknowingly waits for him on the island shore. The others in contrast are all washed up.

The island waits for us after the wreck, at the other side of the 'sea-swallowing'. In the play's past it waited for Prospero and Miranda after their exposure to 'sea-sorrow' in a 'rotten carcass' that the 'very rats had quit'. In the play's present we reach the peace of the desolate island after the cries 'We split, we split', 'Let's all sink wi' th' King', and after Gonzalo's closing word 'death'.

Shakespeare's last plays are not obsessed with death, but they are attentive to it in comprehensively metaphoric or allegoric ways. All have to do with the *loss of life*. Years are lost, kingdoms are lost, wives, children, friends are lost, and in some transfigured condition of life they are found again. Shakespeare was well aware that the living can know nothing about death but can know much about the loss of life – its actualities and its potentials. In *The Tempest* the Italian courtiers are taken out of life and exposed to critical inspection. And we make the discovery that Dante invites us to make in the figure of Capaneus in the *Inferno*: 'What I was living, that I am dead.'[12] The 'unearthly' tenor of the play ('There is in this business more than nature was ever conduct of') lends theatrical reality to the hints of the Bermuda pamphlets; the *True Repertory* tells of the 'troubled and overmastered sences' of those exposed to the wreck, as they bid goodbye to each other and hope to meet in 'a more blessed world'. That world is not, in the play, the 'after-life' of pious expectation. No one dies in *The Tempest*; but to say that none dies on the island may be to make a different point: life and death are there within the magus's power; and there is no death after death.

The island is not the same experience for all the sea-swallowed. The Bermudan sources offer us a double image, finding it 'still accounted, the most dangerous, infortunate and forlorne place of the world', yet proclaiming it 'the richest, healthfullest and pleasing land . . . as ever man set foot upon'. 'Here is everything advantageous to life,' says Gonzalo, meeting Antonio's retort, 'True, save means to live.' This is one of several devices in the play which encourage us to look inwardly rather than outwardly for Prospero's island, making it an unlocatable state of our understanding and sensibility; as Blake said, 'The Fool sees not the same trees as the Wise Man sees.' But the story of the play requires a place, not a state of mind,

---

in the History of Art presented to Rudolph Wittkower (1967), pp. 149–60. The picture is at the Courtauld Institute of Art.

[12] *Inferno*, XIV, 51.

and with the help of Gonzalo Shakespeare supplies Prospero with all he needs, including the grand ducal robes he calls for in the last scene: 'Rich garments, linens, stuffs and necessaries, / Which since have steaded much'. Shakespeare does require him to conjure hallucinatory garb from the circumambient air – the sort, presumably, that furnish the clothes line that diverts Trinculo's party. Again, Prospero's rich garments make the island's proximity to civilized, courtly Italy clear in the spectacle.

Yet no elaboration or refinement of its Mediterranean setting will quite locate the island outside ourselves; we are not in Pantellaria or Lampedusa, any more than in the Bermudas. Not only is the play addressed to our reflective intelligence, its poetry of 'sea-sorrow' and 'sea-change' is distinctively in touch with the strange but familiar transience of the natural and the human world, moving often in ways that narrow the spaces between waking and sleeping, seeing and dreaming, living and dying:

> Where should this music be? I' th' air, or th' earth?
> It sounds no more; and sure it waits upon
> Some god o' th' island. Sitting on a bank,
> Weeping again the King my father's wrack,
> This music crept by me upon the waters,
> Allaying both their fury and my passion
> With its sweet air; thence I have followed it,
> Or it hath drawn me rather. But 'tis gone.
>   (I. ii. 388–95)

The exquisitely hovering 'air', to be breathed and to be heard, expresses the stilling of the tempest and the quietening of grief. The solace is in the elusiveness of Ariel's magical songs:

> The ditty does remember my drown'd father.
> This is no mortal business, nor no sound
> That the earth owes. I hear it now above me.
>   (I. ii. 406–8)

Ferdinand, when we look upon the play as marriage comedy, is its hero and its Aeneas. He is made to undergo an island ordeal before he is found fit for Miranda in Prospero's dispensation. With some help from our ideal spectator, Fulke Greville, we may see how this element in the play's structure chimes with the story of the Bermuda wreck. One of his poems, although not directly related to the play, is in touch with some of its central metaphors. It may have been written some years before the wreck of the *Sea Venture*, for the uncertain location of Bermuda and its hidden rocks had long been a hazard for those making the crossing to Virginia. Greville sees the mariner's journey as a figurative shadow of the lovers's:[13]

> Whoever sails near to *Bermuda* coast,
> Goes hard aboard the Monarch of Fear,
> Where all desires (but Life's desire) are lost,
> For wealth and fame put off their glories there.
>
> Yet this Isle poison-like, by mischief known,
> Weans not desire from her sweet nurse, the Sea;
> But unseen shows us where our hopes be sown,
> With woeful signs declaring joyful way.
>   *For who will seek the wealth of Western Sun,*
>   *Oft by* Bermuda's *miseries must run.*
>
> Who seeks the God of *Love*, in Beauty's sky,
> Must pass the Empire of confused Passion
> Where our desires to all but Horrors die,
> Before that joy and peace can take their fashion.
>
> Yet this fair Heaven that yields this Soul-despair,
> Weans not the heart from his sweet God, *Affection*;
> But rather shows us what sweet joys there are,
> Where constancy is servant to perfection.
>   Who *Caelica's* chaste heart then seeks to move,
>   Must joy to suffer all the woes of *Love*.

The lovers, as well as the voyagers, are required to undergo an Island ordeal; they must 'pass the Empire of confused Passion' and discover that 'constancy is servant to perfection'. Prospero, as father and as governor, presides over both territories, the newly awakened affections and the shipwrecked ambitions.

From another point of view, Shakespeare in Prospero has resolved into one figure the 'Governour with his authority' and the miraculous deliverer from the calamities of the sea described by Strachey and Jourdain. From yet another, however, he was persisting in traditions created by his own art of comedy. In *Measure for Measure*, it might be said, the Duke has to salvage a moral wreck that ordinary human resources would have found irretrievable.

Prospero too is a surrogate playwright, and the powers we see him exercise are, after all, the playwright's powers: the storm, the calm, the elusive music, arrested swords, apparitions of harpies, vanishing banquets, and the spirits in shape of dogs and hounds, are all within the proper

---

[13] Fulke Greville, 'Caelica, Sonnet LIX, *Poems and Dramas of Fulke Greville*, ed. Geoffrey Bullough (2 vols., Edinburgh, 1938), I, p. 109. The spelling has been modernized.

domaine of the theatre. The play frequently teases us about the nature of illusion, and we are made to feel the consonance of Shakespeare's art with Prospero's; both may offer to 'bring forth a wonder to content' us, or speak of 'some vanity of mine art' or 'some enchanted trifle'. Even his power to call back the sleepers from the graves (v. i. 49) may remind us that Shakespeare was commended by Nashe for bringing back Talbot 'fresh bleeding' for the tears of ten thousand spectators. The playwright's role is not indivisible, however, and *The Tempest* comes to us in many forms – romance, comedy, tragicomedy, pastoral, masque, *commedia dell'arte*, *commedia erudita*, morality, allegoric history and pageant; each requires its own kind of 'magic', and asks that the playwright cast a spell to its own end. Like the courtiers in Prospero's power we are 'justled from our senses'. The hospitalities of the art take in allusions to Montaigne and a gaberdine monster with four legs. Shakespeare is expert in the magic of theatre, offering for example in the chorus of *Henry V* to convey us to France in our seats and bring us back, 'charming the narrow seas' to give us 'gentle pass'. In the theatre it is with 'magic' as it is with 'ghosts', we cannot question the illusions of art when they are so tantalizingly related to life.

Prospero at the end of the play discards the paraphernalia of the magus, calls for his hat and rapier, and re-presents himself as the 'wronged Duke of Milan'. He reasserts an authority that he had once, 'by neglecting worldly ends', virtually abdicated. In committing himself to the contemplative life, it is sometimes censoriously said, he neglected the active one. But it is a part of the play's structure that his islanded engagement in the contemplative arts enables him to exercise the active arts of government more decisively and more comprehensively in the domains of both intimate and political life, leaving Gonzalo to marvel:

> Was Milan thrust from Milan, that his issue
> Should become king of Naples? O, rejoice
> Beyond a common joy, and set it down
> With gold on lasting pillars: in one voyage
> Did Claribel her husband find at Tunis,
> And Ferdinand, her brother, found a wife
> Where he himself was lost; Prospero, his dukedom
> In a poor isle; and all of us, ourselves,
> When no man was his own.
>
> (v. i. 205–13)

The magician-playwright-duke-governor-father, performing in the court of King James, appears to be wonderfully vindicated. But that vindication is at this point inseparable from the sympathetic response of 'Holy Gonzalo, honourable man'; and Gonzalo, warmly commended though he is in the play, is not exempted from its persistent and searching scepticism.

Gonzalo carries into the play Montaigne's bewilderments about the nature and topography of innocent island states. 'It is very likelie this extreme ruine of waters,' says Montaigne, speculating on the Deluge and the vanished island of Atlantis, 'wrought strange alterations in the habitations of the earth.' He sets aside the idea that Atlantis could be 'the new world we have lately discovered', and he recalls a time when the Lords of Carthage banished citizens who had colonized 'a great fertill island' they had discovered in the Atlantic, for fear 'they should one day supplant them and overthrow their own estate.' From the reports of a 'simple rough hewen fellow' and others, Montaigne confronts Plato with 'a nation':

> that hath no kinde of traffike, no knowledge of Letters, no intelligence of numbers, no name of magistrate, nor or politike superiority; no use of service, of riches or of povertie; no contracts, no successions, no partitions, no ocupation but idle; no respect of kindred, but common, no apparell but naturall, no manuring of lands, no use of wine, corne, or mettle. The very words that import lying, falshod, treason, dissimulations, covetousness, envie, detraction, and pardon, were never heard of amongst them.
>
> ('Of the Caniballes', I. 50, 259)

Our ideal witness, Fulke Greville, would be well-placed to notice the skill with which Shakespeare almost casually nods and nudges the prose into the poetic dialect of The Tempest, and to look upon the episode (II. i. 141–306) under the cool, bright shadow of Montaigne's irony. The hostile courtiers' mockeries stick ('The latter end of his commonwealth forgets the beginning'), but we are made keenly aware of the 'dissonance' of ideal and actual. 'King' Gonzalo knows better than the sleeping king and his would-be usurper that the authenticaly free commonwealth is without prerogatives of property, inheritance, rank and power. The watchful, usurping magus, however, recognizes that the commonwealth over which he presides must be built on a slave base.

Through what I have called its choice of vanishing points, the island is suspended between life and death, action and contemplation, sleeping and waking. In the play's second scene the storm reaches us through the compassion of Miranda:

> O! I have suffered
> With those that I saw suffer. A brave vessel
> (Who had, no doubt, some noble creature in her)
> Dash'd all to pieces! O, the cry did knock
> Against my very heart. Poor souls, they perish'd.
> (I. ii. 5–9)

Her innocent concern for humankind is of a piece with her love-awakened and love-awakening response to Ferdinand, and it is a condition for the prosperous growth of human community. Prospero is confronted, as God and the gods of human devising have often been, by protesting innocence:

> Had I been any god of power, I would
> Have sunk the sea within the earth or ere
> It should the good ship so have swallow'd and
> The fraughting souls within her.
> (I. ii. 10–14)

The scene that follows is not merely expository device, although it is that; it is actively attentive to the isolation of innocence and experience, story and memory, daughter and father. For Prospero the old tale is a fresh re-enactment of events; for him an ordeal prompting a bitterness that bewilders and dismays Miranda:

> O, my heart bleeds
> To think o' th' teen that I have turn'd you to,
> Which is from my remembrance!
> (I. ii. 63–5)

Prospero is importunate ('I pray thee mark me') but Miranda has only a child's recollection of what her little world afforded:

> 'Tis far off;
> And rather like a dream than an assurance
> That my remembrance warrants. Had I not
> Four, or five, women once that tended me?
> (I. ii. 44–7)

He is exasperated that her memory cannot find occasion for the response he looks for:

> Thou had'st; and more, Miranda. But how is it
> That this lives in thy mind? What sees thou else
> In the dark backward and abysm of time?
> (I. ii. 48–50)

Prospero's conjuring-up of the past and the intensity of his demands upon Miranda's sensibility are part of the play's human and domestic comedy, its everyday magic – the father initiating his daughter, putting his experience and understanding of the past before her, casting a spell of words upon her, demanding that she 'Obey, and be attentive.' Miranda is unable to give him the kind of attention he demands; she grieves for his grief but not for his story; she does not share his memories, which reach her only as an old tale.

The islanded conditions of Miranda and Prospero are distinguished in other ways too. She sleeps through the next phase of the exposition, while Prospero's mind is still actively upon the past. Miranda's innocence remains unspoiled by her father's story and by her encounters with the untameable Caliban. The tense distance between father and daughter is caught in Prospero's celebrated irony, meeting Miranda's delight: 'How beauteous mankind is! O brave new world / That has such people in it!' – ' 'tis new to thee.' Although the distance is perfectly consistent with admiration, sympathy and affection, the new life must nevertheless disengage itself from the old. Miranda disobeys her father when she gives Ferdinand her name and Ferdinand himself draws his sword on Prospero. At certain points of the play, disobedience is a condition of freedom. Prospero's probings of Ariel's past set up different relationships between the past and the present, freedom and constraint, 'age and envy', and the 'brave spirit'.

Prospero's name, we have said, may be translated as 'Fortune' or 'Faustus'. Fortune, in a twelfth-century poem, the *Anticlaudianus*, by Alanus de Insulis,[14] lives upon an island which undergoes continual transformations and has a double nature; one stream upon it is a very sweet liquid – 'with its honey it seduces many', and another is 'dark and sulphurous'; on it 'the laurel wanes, the myrtle gives fruit'; 'it suffers all the tempests of the winds', yet sometimes 'it is covered with flowers and Zephyr breathes upon it.' The ambiguities of Prospero's island also have analogues in the voyage material, but that is perhaps to be expected at a time when Spanish navigators were instructed to search for the fabulous fortunate islands of other stories, and for the several magical and symbolic islands of St Brendan's vision. The Island of *The Tempest* is not consistently and continuously an inheritance from the *Anticlaudianus*, but Shakespeare's presentation of it spans a similar range of menacing and auspicious conditions. The island conditions too are expressed in different theatrical conventions and dramatic forms. The tempestuous and dangerous island of the first scene is made live to us through the naturalistic conventions of Jacobean drama; the bounty of the island, is figured forth – to use Sidney's phrase – in the ceremonious styles of the marriage masque, which is itself a kind of island in the play. So the artifice and tradition of the masque provide yet another vanishing point in the play's intricate perspectives.

Jonson's masque of *Hymenaei* has often been suggested as a possible source for *The Tempest*, and it is true that there are certain striking likenesses as well as unlikenesses between Shakespeare's play and the court masque.[15] For the likenesses, we could listen to certain etherial effects

---

[14] Alanus de Insulis, *Anticlaudianus*, VII, viii–ix and VIII, i (Migne, vol. 210, cols. 557–60); see Howard R. Patch, *The Goddess Fortune in Medieval Literature* (1967), pp. 126–9.

[15] See *Tempest*, ed. Stephen Orgel, pp. 43–50.

persisting from the poetry of Jonson's masques, through *The Tempest* to
Milton's *Comus*. They would remind us of the proximity of poetry to music,
spectacle and dance, leaving it doubtful, to quote Jonson speaking of the
masquers, 'whether the *Formes* flow'd more perfectly from the author's
braine, or their feete'.[16] In the play, as in the masques, we can admire (to
stay with Jonson's phrases) the 'delicacy of dances', the 'strangeness of the
habits', 'magnificence of the scene' and the 'divine rapture of music':

> Come unto these yellow sands,
> And then take hands:
> Curtsied when you have, and kissed,
> The wild waves whist:
> Foot it featly here and there,
> And, sweet sprites, the burthen bear.
>   (I. ii. 375–80)

Fragile devices and effects are made to carry, on tip-toe, moral claims of
great weight and urgency, 'Those are pearls that were his eyes' (I, ii. 399).
When we listen closely to the verse, however, and look attentively at its
spectacle, we find that while the play appropriately contains a masque, it
refuses to be one. In its wedding masque it expresses pleasure in the
fecundity and plenitude of the earth, but it carries no lasting assurance that
we can depend upon a transcendent order or upon that 'great creating
nature' which Perdita honours at her festival in *The Winter's Tale*. The
dissolution of the masque is attended by an apocalyptic vision of cosmic
dissolution, itself collapsing at its climax into age and ill-temper: 'Sir, I am
vexed; / Bear with my weakness, my old brain is troubled.' The magus
confesses the human vulnerabilities – he too is part of the human comedy,
and must pass 'the Empire of confused Passion'. Yet the play as a whole
continues to resemble the masque in its recognition of the transience of art
addressed to the senses, and the lastingness of what Jonson called 'the
things subjected to understanding'.

The understanding is given a lot of material to work upon. Round and
about the masque itself, the play's dominant metaphor remains the storm
at sea, and aerial and marine nature are more active in its language than
the fruitful earth. The wrath of the sea, the wrath of Prospero and the
wrath of God are poignantly interrelated, making the human and divine
comedies consonant and interdependent:

> But remember
> (For that's my business to you) that you three
> From Milan did supplant good Prospero,

[16] Ben Jonson, *Works*, ed. Herford and Simpson, VII. pp. 203–41.

> Expos'd unto the sea (which hath requit it)
> Him and his innocent child; for which foul deed
> The pow'rs, delaying (not forgetting), have
> Incensed the seas and shores – yea, all the creatures
> Against your peace.
>
> (III. iii. 68–75)

The sonorities of air and sea sound the play's intimately heard moral music:

> Methought the billows spoke, and told me of it;
> The winds did sing it to me; and the thunder
> That deep and dreadful organ pipe, pronounc'd
> The name of Prosper; it did bass my trespass.
>
> (III. iii. 96–9)

But alongside the more formidable daemonic presences assisting Prospero in his mastery of the elemental world, are children at play, 'with printless foot', chasing 'the ebbing Neptune'; and even the Divine voice has its wit:

> You are three men of sin, whom Destiny, –
> That hath to instrument this lower world
> And what is in't, – the never-surfeited sea
> Hath caused to belch up you.
>
> (III. iii. 53–6)

Men are only allowed to drown if they don't make the sea sick.

Prospero presides over the play's final movement with the figure of the cleansing, clarifying sea:

> Their understanding
> Begins to swell, and the approaching tide
> Will shortly fill the reasonable shore
> That now lies foul and muddy.
>
> (v. i. 79–82)

It is as if the magic depended upon the sea's invincible and continuous flooding of the beaches. The wrath of the sea, its judgements, mercy and compassion, and above all, its capacity to erase the past and 'faults forgiven', all find a place in the poet's and magician's spell. Only those who can hear the moral music of the poet's re-created sea are fit to enjoy the bounty offered by the masque on the fortunate and paradisal island. And among the initiates with ears to hear, it is to be hoped, were on one occasion Princess Elizabeth, Frederick Prince Palatine and King James.

Whether or not the King shared Prospero's fatherly anxiety about his daughter's pre-marital chastity, while Elizabeth watched, with Frederick's head in her lap, we cannot know. But if the King himself had ears to hear he would have learned much about the nature of sovereignty. Shakespeare's plays rarely leave us wholly content with kings and governments, but *The Tempest* remains in the old phrase a 'mirror for magistrates', telling the king that 'He who hath not order within him / Cannot have order about him.' Prospero's ideal monarchy, on its base of servile labour, does not survive the play. Our delinquent sympathies may be only a little stirred by the invitation to join the Stephano and Trinculo demo, crying 'ban ban Cac-caliban, Freedom, high-day! High-day, freedom!' and with joyous but bloody thoughts march to kill the King. But the play takes delight in its drunken butler and jester, and invites sympathy for the primitive sensitivities of our Caliban-selves, while it alienates us from the untamed recalcitrance of Antonio, who serves to remind us of the 'horrible wickedness' and 'wretched devices' by which, according to *Nennio*, men obtain 'the privileges of nobility'. It does, in Fulke Greville's words about his own tragedies, 'trace out the high ways of ambitious governors' to show 'that the more audacity, advantage, and good success such sovereignties have, the more they hasten to their own desolation and ruin.' Kings and dukes are called to account, by 'powers delaying, not forgetting', and James himself, as spectator to the wreck, would have visited 'the monarch of fear'.

As a parable of sea-deliverance the play offered, in a contemporary form, the solace of Psalm 107:

> They reel to and fro and stagger like a drunken man, and are at their wits' end. Then they cry unto the Lord in their trouble and he bringeth them out of their distresses. He maketh the storm a calm, so that the waves thereof are still.

The young and innocent may take their cue from Miranda and delight in the play's affirmation and solace. Age and experience may, like Gonzalo, bravely persist in innocence; or it may, like Antonio, stay aloof and let the mind canker; finally, like Prospero, it may assiduously practise the 'liberal arts' and cultivate the kind of scepticism that diminishes despair, even if it is not proof against fits of bad temper.

As a marriage celebration *The Tempest* renews our confidence in generations to come. The serenities of Ferdinand's and Miranda's game at chess are undamaged by her cry 'sweet lord, you play me false', for conflict has been transmuted into inconsequential, affectionate play. But the literary sophisticates in the audience might have known that Fortune in some of the old Romances played at chess with her human challengers, and might have seen in the episode a gloss on Prospero and his Neapolitan antagonists.

Some bring the play to rest in the Epilogue, and would have us follow Shakespeare and Prospero out of the theatre into the church. I am one of those most ready to believe that piece of gossip which says that the part of Prospero was played by Shakespeare himself, not because he was about to retire to Stratford to hoard malt and engage in lawsuits, or because Elysium was beckoning to him from Illyria, but because there is a profound and necessary relationship between Prospero's magic and Shakespeare's art. They are efficacious only in the Island and in the Theatre, where life is held in suspense and momentarily put into order. Where is the island of *The Tempest*? The final answer to this question must be, 'in the theatre'. It is (remembering Crashaw) the players after all who have called the voyagers to account. Every Shakesperian play is 'islanded' from the flux of life to which the epilogue returns us at the end of *The Tempest*, and having left the island-theatre we know that the fuller significance of our lost lives was there brought home to us.

Index

Osborne, John (*A Place Calling itself Rome*) 141
Overbury, Sir Thomas 34, 45, 52, 55
Ovid, Publius Ovidius Naso 129, 168

Palmer, Kenneth 31n., 40, 54n
parables 3–7, 11, 27, 49
Pasco, Richard 29
Peck, Bob 157
Perkins, William 29, 224–5, 226
Phelps, Samuel 65
Pliny the Elder (Gaius Plinius Secundus) 212
Plutarch 20, 128, 131, 132, 133, 135–6, 142, 143, 144, 146, 149, 150, 227
Pope, Alexander 248
private and public selves 53–4, 90, 116, 128, 129, 170, 175, 182
processes of history 80, 147, 155, 173
Purchas his Pilgrimes 312–13, 314–15, 317
Puttenham, George 109, 112, 117

Ralegh, Sir Walter 30
Rare Triumphs of Love and Fortune 275, 281
Rome; imperial and republican spirit, 124, 128, 129, 130, 131, 135, 142, 143, 145
Rose, Mark 109–10, 116
Rossiter, A. P. 317

Salter, Elizabeth 105, 121
Schopenhauer, Arthur 29, 66
Scott, Sir Walter 65
screen memories 145, 218
sea imagery 211–12, 284–5, 292–4, 300, 308, 316–20, 325, 328, 330–2, 337–9
The Second Maid's Tragedy 282
Seneca, Lucius Annaeus 70, 129, 133, 168, 175, 231, 301; *Hercules Furens* 228–9, 301, *Hercules Oetaeus* 70, 90; *Oedipus* 222; *Thysetes* 92; *Troades* 92, 228
Seward, Thomas 62
Shakespeare, William: *Antony and Cleopatra* 20, 61–6, 119, 124, 142, 151, 190, 196–7, 199, 221, 250, 294; *see also* New Variorum Shakespeare;

All's Well that Ends Well 47, 247, 250–6, 322; *As You Like It* 19, 30, 41, 56, 351; *The Comedy of Errors* 27, 247; *Coriolanus* 20, 124, 141–2, 147–51, 160, 206, 217; *Cymbeline* 254, 272–82, 284, 326; *Hamlet* 20, 22, 24, 53, 70–1, 128, 159, 167–84, 262; *1 Henry IV* 33, 53, 55, 62, 81, 161, 168, 195, 208, 213, 328; *2 Henry IV* 122, 137–8, 195, 197; *Henry V* 31, 36, 59n., 94, 142, 261, 333; *1 Henry VI* 25, 41, 80–7, 90, 101, 124, 280; *2 Henry VI* 41, 82, 87–95, 96, 97, 98, 152, 153, 154, 155, 163, 194, 201, 242, 280; *3 Henry VI* 95–103, 152, 154, 201, 228, 280; *Henry VIII* 123, 273; *King John* 42, 138, 162–3, 223, 280; *Julius Caesar* 87, 95, 122–39, 142, 143–7, 156, 190, 195, 197, 227; *King Lear* 19, 20, 35, 70, 71, 100, 122, 135, 162, 190, 191–3, 201, 220–43, 280, 299; *Love's Labour's Lost* 32, 111, 280; *Macbeth* 22, 56, 70, 99, 134, 144, 155–6, 280; *Measure for Measure* 22, 189, 225, 247, 248, 252, 256, 258–71, 307, 324, 328, 332; *The Merchant of Venice* 13–19, 30, 71–4, 106, 202, 258, 326; *The Merry Wives of Windsor* 57, 199, 213, 214, 215, 232; *A Midsummer Night's Dream* 107, 221, 250, 280; *Much Ado About Nothing* 37, 213, 251, 265; *Othello* 24, 70, 190, 198–219, 227, 250, 255, 280, 305; *Pericles* 199, 223, 254, 283–302, 305, 307, 319, 320; *The Rape of Lucrece* 116, 150; *Richard II* 89, 104–21; *Richard III* 88, 97, 102, 105, 131, 132, 162, 201, 249, 284–5, 294, 316, 317; *Romeo and Juliet* 107, 111, 190, 251, 263, 326; *Sir Thomas More* 94; *The Taming of the Shrew* 251; *The Tempest* 25, 199, 223, 225, 247, 249, 273, 284, 285, 294, 303–21, 322–40; *Timon of Athens* 3–29, 32, 185, 197, 318; *Titus Andronicus* 71, 92, 127, 129, 133, 146, 167, 168, 190, 227; *Troilus and Cressida* 25, 30–59; *Twelfth Night* 216; *The Two Noble